Building the Ultimate Dam

DEVELOPMENT OF WESTERN RESOURCES

The Development of Western Resources is an interdisciplinary series focusing on the use and misuse of resources in the American West. Written for a broad readership of humanists, social scientists, and resource specialists, the books in this series emphasize both historical and contemporary perspectives as they explore the interplay between resource exploitation and economic, social, and political experiences.

John G. Clark, University of Kansas, Founding Editor
Hal K. Rothman, University of Nevada, Las Vegas, Series Editor

BUILDING the ULTIMATE DAM

JOHN S. EASTWOOD AND THE CONTROL OF WATER IN THE WEST

Donald C. Jackson

 University Press of Kansas

Published by the University Press of Kansas (Lawrence, Kansas 66049), which
was organized by the Kansas Board of Regents and is operated and funded by
Emporia State University, Fort Hays State University, Kansas State University,
Pittsburg State University, the University of Kansas, and Wichita State
University

Library of Congress Cataloging-in-Publication Data

Jackson, Donald C. (Donald Conrad), 1953–
    Building the ultimate dam : John S. Eastwood and the control of
water in the West / Donald C. Jackson.
        p.   cm. — (Development of western resources)
    Includes bibliographical references and index.
    ISBN 0-7006-0716-1
    1. Arch dams — West (U.S.) — Design and construction — History — 20th
century.   2. Eastwood, John S.   3. Water resources development — West
(U.S.) — History — 20th century.   I. Title.   II. Series.
    TC547.J33   1995
    627 '.82 '0978 — dc20   95-2355

British Library Cataloguing in Publication data is available.

Printed in the United States of America

10 9 8 7 6 5 4 3 2 1

The paper used in this publication meets the minimum requirements of the
American National Standard for Permanence of Paper for Printed Library
Materials Z39.48-1984.

Einstein is Right! All lines are curved and all things mundane are relative.

John S. Eastwood, 1922

To the staff of the Water Resources Center Archives,
University of California, Berkeley,
and especially to Gerald J. Giefer, librarian (1959–1991),
who created one of the best dam archives in the world.

Contents

Preface

In simplest terms, this book is concerned with water storage (a truly ancient technology) and examines some of its manifestations in the early twentieth-century American West. But at a deeper level it seeks to document how *choices* are made when a society confronts possibilities proffered by the technical/engineering community. These choices do not emanate from the machinations of an objective, neutral process. Rather, they reflect the complexity, confusion, and self-serving subjectivity of humanity itself, because that is what they are — the products of human culture.

The author's experiences as an undergraduate in civil engineering and his subsequent graduate study in American history have heightened his appreciation of the importance of bringing technical issues into the realm of historical discourse. This can only be accomplished by discussing topics that might, on first impression, lie beyond the capacity of a general audience to comprehend. Recognizing that some readers might be hesitant to confront technical and mathematical issues related to hydraulic engineering, *Building the Ultimate Dam* strives to present in clear, simple terms the most important practical and theoretical concerns associated with dam building. Only in this way can the subject be taken out of its technological

"black box" and considered on equal terms with social, political, and economic factors that affect historical development. To help achieve this, Chapter 2 provides a general discussion of dam design in terms accessible to a lay audience; Chapter 8 offers a more detailed examination of how practical and theoretical considerations affected dam design in the early twentieth century; and a glossary is included to provide definitions for technical terms. In addition, numerous photographs and drawings visually complement many of the technical issues discussed in the text. These illustrations are intended as more than mere pictorial window-dressing; they are a primary feature of the book's effort to explicate dam design technology and its relation to the physical environment.

Aside from its treatment of technical issues involved in water resources development, this book largely consists of a narrative that traces the professional career of a hydraulic engineer who was active in the West during the late nineteenth and early twentieth centuries. Through the experiences of John S. Eastwood, the character of western economic development is investigated in a manner that emphasizes the importance of private corporate financing and capital-intensive investment in defining the region's economic landscape during the modern era. A study of Eastwood's work in designing and building dams yields more than generalities and abstractions about how water has been (and continues to be) controlled in the West. The specific events and circumstances described illustrate the complicated relationships that exist between competing engineers and between engineers and businessmen. In addition, readers are made aware of the tensions that can arise between engineering creativity and government-sponsored regulations instituted to protect the unwary public from "unsafe" technology.

Of course, any work that closely examines the activities of a particular person runs the risk of becoming either adulatory or too critical. Perhaps human nature itself inclines a researcher to adopt either a protective or a derogatory posture toward a biographical subject. In regard to Eastwood, the author has not necessarily escaped this dilemma. More significant to themes explored in *Building the Ultimate Dam,* however, are arguments that the hydraulic technology championed by Eastwood truly constituted a viable and practical alternative, and that, despite many technical and economic advantages, his dam designs failed to find acceptance primarily for nontechnical reasons. In pursuing such arguments, the author has not hesitated to offer an affirmative (yet always realistic) assessment of Eastwood's ideas and accomplishments.

Perhaps above all, Eastwood's professional experiences illuminate the difficulties of separating the notions of "public works" and "private interest" as they relate to western water use and to technological development as a whole. Within the context of American economic growth, these phrases are often used with great assurance that they represent distinct and dissimilar concepts. But the story of Eastwood's efforts to bring to American society what he considered to be the benefits of increased access to water storage demonstrates how easily the line between "public works" and "private interest" can be blurred. Technological progress may be easy to conceptualize abstractly, but when manifest in (literally) concrete artifacts affecting the real world, the concept assumes a complexity that challenges facile explanations about how human culture evolves. And that challenge is central to what *Building the Ultimate Dam* is all about.

Acknowledgments

While working on this book, I received support from a predoctoral fellowship at the National Museum of American History, Smithsonian Institution (1985–1986), and from a Fletcher Jones Research Fellowship at the Henry E. Huntington Library (winter/spring 1993). Research and writing spanned more than a decade. At the risk of inadvertently omitting someone or some organization, I gratefully acknowledge the help and contributions of:

Mrs. Hobart Bosworth, former president of the Littlerock Creek Irrigation District; Glenn Enke, professor emeritus, Brigham Young University; Horace Hinckley, former manager of the Bear Valley Mutual Water Company; Charles Allan Whitney, formerly of the Southern California Edison Company; Richard K. Anderson Jr. for his superb maps and drawings; and William Myers for his valuable insights into the history of hydroelectric power in California.

Gerald Giefer, Linda Vida, Donald Smith, Susan Munkres, and Mary Deane, Water Resources Center Archives, Berkeley; Sharon Hiigle and Bob Ellis, Fresno City and County Historical Society; Karen Kerns, Peter Blodgett, and the staff of the Huntington Library; Ron Mahoney, Special Collections, California State University at Fresno; Mary Patton, Michigan State University Archives and Historical Collections; Liz Andrews, Archives and Special Collections, Massachusetts Institute of Technology; and staff members of the University of California at San Diego, the San Diego Historical Society, the Prints and Photographs Division of the Library of Congress, and the National Archives.

Colleagues in western history, including Donald J. Pisani, James E. Sherow, Gene Gressley, John Snyder, David Introcaso, Richard Lynch, William Willingham, Fred Quivik, Craig Fuller, and Robert Walls. Colleagues in the history of technology, including Terry Reynolds, David Billington, Bruce Sinclair, Robert Post, Carroll Pursell, Patrick Malone, Martin Reuss, Robert Gordon, Thomas Hughes, Nicholas Schnitter, Bruce Seely, Jeffrey Stine, William Worthington, Robert Vogel, Judy McGaw, and Charles K. Hyde. And colleagues associated with the Historic American Engineering Record and the National Park Service, including T. Allan Comp, Arnold Jones, Douglas Griffin, Beverly Baynes, Marjorie Baer, Larry Lankton, Eric Delony, Robert Kapsch, Gray Fitzsimmons, Jean Yearby, Judy Bullock, Greg Kendrick, and Ann Huston.

Others who assisted in myriad ways, including Murray Murphey, Mel Hammerberg,

Robert Siedenglanz, Ned Nelson, Donald Bones, June Hume Browning, John Dayton, Steve Fosberg, Steve Mikesell, Clay Fraser, Nick Saloman, and my colleagues in the History Department at Lafayette College, along with B. Vincent Viscomi, Jim Lennertz, and Tom Bruggink.

Cynthia Miller, Melinda Wirkus, Steven Gray, and the staff of the University Press of Kansas.

Friends and loved ones, including Kate De-Fuccio, Jamie Bischoff, Joan Mentzer, Jessie Tufts Jackson, and last but not least, Carol Dubie.

CHAPTER 1

Dams, Water, and the West

We must find more water, settlers would say to themselves; we must use every possible technology to extract as much as we can out of this place. We must not rest until we have achieved control over every molecule of moisture. Each river we come to must be turned into a commodity and consumed entirely. The West must be redeemed everywhere by hard work and unflagging dedication until it has lost all semblance of naturalness.

Donald Worster, 1987

The California slogan e're should be, that 'tis a crime to let our rivers reach the sea.

John S. Eastwood, 1914

In his 1931 book, *The Great Plains,* Walter Prescott Webb surveyed the expanse of America lying west of the 98th meridian and attributed much of the region's historical character to the paucity of precipitation.[1] Since Webb, a growing number of historians, including Donald Worster, Donald Pisani, Norris Hundley, Lawrence Lee, Stanley Davison, and James Sherow, have perceived water resources development as a key factor in regional growth and have nourished the concept of water history as constituting a distinctive historiographic field.[2] While much has been written about the social, legal, and economic dimensions of western water use, especially in relation to the federal Bureau of Reclamation (and its predecessor. the U.S. Reclamation Service) and landmark projects such as Los Angeles's Owens Valley Aqueduct, relatively little work specifically examines either the technology of water storage or the history of western dam building.[3]

This lack of attention to dam technology per se is somewhat surprising, especially since dams offer an important means of maximizing use of the region's limited water resources. Precipitation in the West is not evenly distributed over the landscape in either density or seasonality; and although torrential downpours may dump billions of gallons of water on the desert in the period of a few weeks, heavy storms can be spaced years apart. In addition, many rivers depend on water from melting mountain snowpack to sustain their flow through the summer. But while historians may be reticent to confront water control technology, westerners have long recognized the importance of capturing floods. Thus, in 1923, the California Department of Public Works pontificated: "[The] erratic behavior of the state's streams, whereby their courses are intermittently deluged by rising floods or emptied by vanishing waters, necessitates that their regimen be rectified if man is to utilize their powers in accelerating his advancement."[4]

Beyond conditions bound to natural hydrology, western dams are also significant in the context of water rights and water law. In the humid regions of Eastern America, "riparian" water rights are granted to landowners simply because their holdings encompass portions of a river bank. Their riparian rights permit landowners to draw water from a stream so long as the overall flow is not noticeably diminished. In contrast, the "doctrine of appropriation" recognizes rights based on the diversion and use of water from a stream, rather than on simple ownership of property bordering a river. Under the appropriation doctrine, which forms the basis of water use in much of Western America, rights to floodwaters can be obtained only if the waters are captured in reservoirs and put to beneficial use. Thus, dam builders invoking this doctrine can accrue powerful—and essentially permanent—economic privileges once they begin impounding floodwaters. Appropriated rights are not the only approved system in the arid region (for example, California operates under a dual system of both riparian and appropriated rights), but they possess legal standing in all states west of the Great Plains.[5]

The value of storage reservoirs in controlling water was first widely publicized in John Wesley Powell's 1878 *Report on the Lands of the Arid Region*.[6] Since that time, practically all major plans to develop western water resources have, in some capacity, involved dam construction. Nonetheless, historians often act as though dam design in and of itself lies outside the bounds of what is appropriate for historical study. After all, engineers presumably formulate efficient, scientific answers; and although some parties may view these as politically or socially undesirable, they represent rational solutions that respond to the technical parameters of a problem. As a corollary, this perspective fosters the notion that all engineers would discern a similar "objective" design if only they devoted sufficient time and effort to studying an issue. Of course, this is not true. Regardless, however, historians (and society as a whole) are reluctant to abandon the notion that engineering is an exact science capable of developing ideal responses to technological quandaries. Thus, dams are considered historically meaningful for what they do, but the designs themselves are rarely evaluated as part of a more general process of historical analysis.

Although observers might question the utility or environmental desirability of a particular dam, western reservoirs are usually viewed as being built in response to significant (or at least putatively significant) economic needs. The import of economic issues in the history of dam development is undeniable; but when simply considered, such concerns provide an incomplete explanation of dam development and the exploitation of the region's water resources. Myriad technical, social, and political factors also come into play when engineers, financiers, and public works administrators select a design for a particular site at a particular time. One objective of this book is to investigate how specific dam designs are chosen and to assess these choices in a broader historical context.

Rather than generally examining a profusion of dam technologies, this book concentrates on the work of one early twentieth-century hydraulic engineer and his efforts to promote an innovative and inexpensive method of water storage. John S. Eastwood built the world's first reinforced concrete multiple arch dam at Hume Lake, California, in 1908-1909; and for the next fifteen years, he specialized in developing designs that minimized the cost of impounding water. Never bashful in trumpeting the significance of his engineering accomplishments, he soon characterized his designs as representing "The Ultimate Dam" (Fig. 1.1). The rationale for this

The Eastwood Multiple-Arched Dam
—— IS ——
THE ULTIMATE DAM

Safety, Service and Economy

Each One a Monument, a Monolith, and a Unit of the Terrain.

1.1 *Excerpts from the "Eastwood Bulletin," a promotional brochure distributed with the March 1915 issue of* Western Engineering.

lofty claim related with equal force to both the structural characteristics of his designs and the ability of his designs to reduce dam construction costs by 30 to 40 percent (or more) over competing technologies. Eastwood's designs sought to minimize the amount of concrete required to hold back a given height of water, decreasing the material quantities necessary to build a dam and reducing the capital needed to fund construction. In turn, this invited development of water projects that otherwise would have remained economically marginal or even prohibitively expensive. In simplest terms, Eastwood is worth studying because he developed a substantially less expensive means of storing water, and water storage has proven absolutely vital in fostering the West's economic growth.

More than sixty different dam design projects occupied Eastwood's attention from 1906 through 1924. These served numerous and varied primary purposes in western locations (Fig. 1.2): redwood logging in the Sierra Nevada; hydroelectric power development for Fresno, Los Angeles, San Francisco, and British Columbia; municipal water supply for Salt Lake City and San Diego; irrigation projects in California, Utah, Idaho, New Mexico, and Sinaloa, Mexico; flood control in Phoenix; and gold mining in Amador County, California.

In their recent book *Thirst for Growth: Water Agencies as Hidden Government in California,* Robert Gottlieb and Margaret Fitzsimmons argue that:

Local agencies rise out of local initiatives, rather than from a general logic of water development in arid environments. . . . [W]ater issues are local issues that have become embedded in, and given rise to, an increasingly elaborate articulation of local, state, and federal powers and organizations.[7]

Working from a similar perspective, this study of Eastwood expands the concept of "water agencies" to encompass logging companies, electric power utilities, mutual water companies, flood control districts, and mining firms, as well as such entities as the state engineers' office, the California Railroad Commission, municipal departments of engineering, and, perhaps most importantly, consulting engineers and engineering firms. Local activities and initiatives—be they the posting of water rights claims on a mountain stream, deliberations by the board of directors of an electric power company, the surveying of an irrigation canal, the construction of a flume, or an engineer's mathematical analysis of a dam design—constitute the basic building blocks of western water history. In

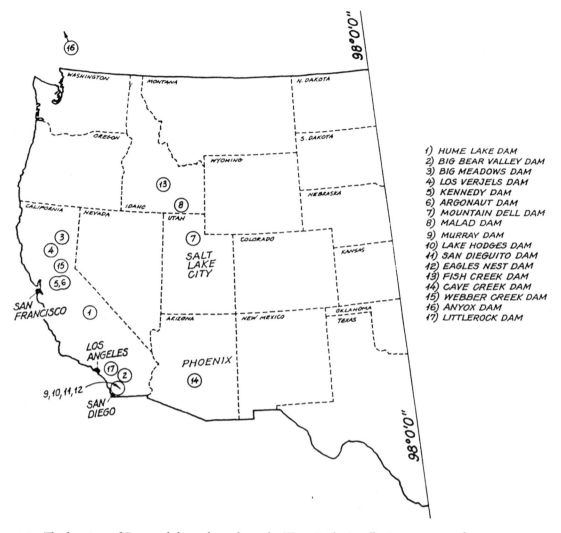

1) HUME LAKE DAM
2) BIG BEAR VALLEY DAM
3) BIG MEADOWS DAM
4) LOS VERJELS DAM
5) KENNEDY DAM
6) ARGONAUT DAM
7) MOUNTAIN DELL DAM
8) MALAD DAM
9) MURRAY DAM
10) LAKE HODGES DAM
11) SAN DIEGUITO DAM
12) EAGLES NEST DAM
13) FISH CREEK DAM
14) CAVE CREEK DAM
15) WEBBER CREEK DAM
16) ANYOX DAM
17) LITTLEROCK DAM

1.2   The locations of Eastwood dams throughout the West. (Author's collection, courtesy of Richard K. Anderson)

detailing Eastwood's interactions in the arena of water resources development, *Building the Ultimate Dam* illuminates the importance of local history in bringing the story of western dam building to life. At the same time, the book shows that the tentacles of seemingly "local" water development projects often extend beyond the bounds of where the water is actually used and into far-flung regional and national networks of engineers, businessmen, financiers and bureaucrats.

CAPITALISM AND THE "PSYCHOLOGY" OF DAM DESIGN

In recent years, historians such as Donald Worster, James Sherow, William Cronon, and William G. Robbins have pointedly linked the exploitation of the West's natural resources to the capitalistic system that has controlled America's economic life during the past two centuries.[8] These authors have sought to demonstrate how an economic system that rewards growth and resource utilization has wrought dramatic environmental changes in the West. In Worster's words: "The highest economic rewards go to those who have done the most to extract from nature all it can yield."[9]

Eastwood fits well into a paradigm depicting capitalism as a principal factor in western resource exploitation. Practically his entire career revolved around projects financed by private capital; and from his early work on lumber flumes and hydroelectric power systems in the Sierra Nevada to his extensive activities as a dam designer, profitability and "return on investment" represented profound imperatives. Of his seventeen dam designs that reached the construction stage, all except the Mountain Dell Dam (built as part of Salt Lake City's municipal water supply system) and the Cave Creek Dam (built by a consortium of public and private organizations to protect Phoenix from floods) were financed by private capital. Certainly, Eastwood's personal motivations extended beyond a simple desire to maximize the money he could make. In the course of his career, his enthusiasm for building dams and power projects became intertwined with an ambition to serve what he perceived as the greater public good. And toward the end of his life, the thrill of building seemed to offer him even more satisfaction than the rewards of material success. Beneath all his efforts, however, lay the capitalist mandate that a particular development was feasible only if project costs could be recouped on terms acceptable to the investment market.

While working for the San Joaquin Electric Company, Eastwood experienced firsthand how dam construction costs can influence the operation of a hydraulic engineering project. In 1896, the fledgling utility began operating a hydroelectric power system to serve Fresno, but it could not afford a large storage dam that might mitigate the effect of drought. When an extended dry spell enveloped central California in the late 1890s, power production faltered, revenues plummeted, and the firm succumbed to bankruptcy. Unquestionably, this experience fueled Eastwood's desire to develop a water storage technology requiring minimum capital expenditure. But contrary to what might be expected in a regional economy plagued by shortages of capital, Eastwood's designs did not win easy acceptance.[10]

Dam technology has two salient characteristics: a relatively few large-scale structures are built, and the consequences of failure are great. As a result, there exists a natural tendency toward conservatism in design. Taking into account the high cost of miscalculation, and coupling it with limited opportunities for experimentation, a businessman might reasonably favor tradition over innovation when financing a dam. Nonetheless, to characterize opposition to Eastwood's ideas strictly within such a framework would be misleading.

Many of Eastwood's difficulties in promoting the multiple arch dam are traceable to the opposition of John R. Freeman of Providence, Rhode Island, an influential engineer with strong ties to America's eastern business elite. Most significantly, Freeman did not challenge Eastwood's designs on technical grounds so much as he criticized how they might be regarded by "the more or less ignorant public." Asserting that multiple arch dams would be judged "not from a technical standpoint, but by comparison with the familiar type of solid gravity dam of masonry or earth," he censured the technology because "the psychology of these airy arches . . . is not well suited to inspire public confidence."[11] Taking advantage of his stature within America's engineering and financial communities, Freeman promoted a visual criterion for dam design that played upon perceived public fears as well as the anxieties of technically unsophisticated businessmen.

The Eastwood/Freeman confrontation over the "psychology" of multiple arch dam design highlights the fact that the development of modern technologies involves more than a rational exercise in applied mathematics or a simple unfolding of events under the economic guidance of "market forces."

5

Technical issues are molded and defined by individuals such as Freeman, Eastwood, and the businessmen who financed their work; these people, interacting with consumers and society as a whole, influence the form of designs and determine which ones will (and which ones will not) be deemed acceptable for construction. At its core, dam engineering is an act of human creativity in which results are not predetermined by abstract and objective criteria.

"SECOND NATURE": TECHNOLOGY AND THE TRANSFORMATION OF THE PHYSICAL WORLD

In recent years, dams have often been criticized because of their impact on the environment, and many books have energized public interest in the ecological changes wrought by large-scale reservoirs.[12] Although such criticism has its place, the treatment of dams in environmental history should not be confined simply to lamentations of ecological ruin. In *Nature's Metropolis: Chicago and the Great West,* William Cronon postulates the existence of a pervasive "second nature" created by human action. In the context of environmental history, he stresses the importance of analyzing how technology has effected this massive transformation of the physical world.[13] Adopting a similar perspective, Donald Worster advocates studying "the technological environment, the cluster of things that people have made, which can be so pervasive as to constitute a kind of 'second nature.'" And, in relating technology to the more general concept of "modes of production," Worster entreats researchers to focus on "productive technology as it interacts with the environment . . . [with] one of the most interesting questions [being] who has gained and who has lost as the modes of production have changed."[14] Nothing represents "second nature" in Worster's terms better than the

multitude of storage reservoirs that inundate the streambeds of the arid region and create what the average citizen perceives as "natural" lakes. Consider for a moment a description of Huntington Lake, the reservoir that Eastwood envisaged as the key component of his Big Creek hydroelectric power system. Written in the mid-1920s as part of a promotional brochure intended to entice people to vacation in the Sierra Nevada, this description strikingly conveys how the environment created by dams can meld into a vision of what is natural and good:

Nature must have designed this spot to cradle a lake. As she made the sheltered valleys and wide alluvial plains, and invited man to make them fruitful by his labors, so she hollowed out these great spaces in the granite hills and waited patiently for the men of wide vision and vast resources to wall up the narrow outlets with their titanic buttresses of steel and concrete. . . . And the beautiful lake, following the contour of the mountains, not only serves the useful purposes of industry but has added to this wonderland a new jewel glowing in its pine-fringed setting.[15]

Operating within parameters consistent with Worster's view of environmental history, this book's analysis of Eastwood and the multiple arch dam is not intended to be either "pro-dam" or "anti-dam." Instead, it highlights a critical aspect of the West's "second nature" in order to further understanding of the forces that define the form of water storage projects. Certainly, environmental activists would be unlikely to herald Eastwood as an enlightened advocate of limited water resources development. For example, he publicly advocated that all flow in California's rivers be impounded in reservoirs ("The California slogan e're should be, that 'tis a crime to let our rivers reach the sea."), and he enthusiastically developed preliminary plans for a dam that would flood the lower Grand Canyon.[16] Nonetheless, Eastwood's work offers an opportunity to reflect on provocative ecological and political issues inherent in a technology developed to minimize dam construction costs. Although in physical terms the environmental impact of a multiple arch dam might be identical with that of a massive gravity dam, the relatively low cost of multiple arch designs offered more "local agencies" the chance to build storage reservoirs. And under the doctrine of appropriation, a more widely dispersed system of dam ownership would necessarily facilitate more localized control of the West's water resources.

In assessing the social and economic efficacy of irrigation projects in the upper Arkansas River Valley, James Sherow's *Watering the Valley* lauds the small-scale Rocky Ford Ditch Company as it contrasts with the larger Fort Lyon Canal Company and the Bessemer Irrigating Ditch Company. Specifically, Sherow gauges the environmental and economic efficacy of water projects largely on their ability to avoid "costly technological improvements [designed to] . . . solve the problem of supporting market-culture values in a region of limited water supplies."[17] In a twist on Sherow's perspective, this study of multiple arch dams looks at a technology that offered even relatively impoverished groups of water users the chance to implement long-term water storage. Although Eastwood would gladly have extended his services to any potential client (he first conceived the multiple arch dam as part of a project controlled by Henry Huntington, perhaps the ultimate "market-culture" maven of the early twentieth-century West), his fervent promotion of inexpensive dams inherently supported more widely diffused authority over water control systems. And by reducing the amount of capital required to implement water storage projects, the multiple arch dam undercut the ability of large aggregations of capital to hold sway over regional development as a whole.

In the final analysis, of course, dams do not create water, they only store what nature provides in the form of rain and snow. The technology of water impoundment represents no panacea for problems involved in "conquering" the arid region, and there is good reason to be concerned about the long-term environmental consequences of the West's dam-based hydraulic infrastructure. Without ignoring these problems, *Building the Ulti-*

mate Dam attempts to direct more historical attention to the ideas, motivations, and actions of the engineers responsible for actually creating the region's "second nature."

PROGRESSIVISM AND CONSERVATION

For American historians, the late nineteenth and early twentieth centuries represent a time of fervent public debate over the need to "reform" society and thus create a better nation for all citizens.[18] Although Eastwood has not been treated as a member of the Progressive movement in previous studies, his work as an engineer adheres to many progressive ideals, especially with regard to the efficiency and scientific rationality that he claimed lay at the core of his designs.[19] For example, he promoted his services with slogans such as: "Why Build Any Other Types of Dam When You Can Get the Best for Less Money?" and "[The multiple arch dam possesses] greater economy of cost for safety than any other type, because it is designed on TRUE SCIENTIFIC PRINCIPLES." More substantively, in 1913 he sounded the themes of "antimonopolism" and "social efficiency" when counseling the California Railroad Commission that:

The storage of water has become of vital interest to the people of California [and] . . . any advance in the economy of storage by new and better methods than have been used in the past should be encouraged. Therefore, the possibility of reducing the cost of storing water is of special interest to the people of this state . . . there are many projects that would become profitable by the use of my type of dam that would otherwise remain undeveloped owing to the prohibitive cost of construction. When safety is provided in excess of that in other dams, at a less cost, it is a conservative step in advance [of] the art, and the public should be permitted to benefit thereby.[20]

A variety of western engineers, businessmen, and boosters advocated the conservation of water resources as a key element of the progressive agenda. In turn, this helped prompt formation of what is termed the "conservation movement" to aid in husbanding America's natural resources. In his influential book *Conservation and the Gospel of Efficiency: The Progressive Conservation Movement, 1890–1920,* Samuel Hays stresses the importance of the U.S. Reclamation Service (renamed the Bureau of Reclamation in 1923) in furthering western water resources development, and many recent books echo his view.[21]

In contrast, western historians might be surprised to learn that in 1920 only 6.5 percent of the West's irrigated land bore any relation to the Reclamation Service, while 80 percent of irrigation was financed completely with private funds.[22] Similarly, a 1934 survey of western hydroelectric plants with capacities exceeding 20,000 horsepower included only one facility built by the Reclamation Service; this survey also documented more than sixty operating hydroelectric plants, with a combined capacity exceeding 3.6 million horsepower, built by private utilities or municipalities.[23] In focusing on an engineer such as Eastwood, who espoused progressive ideals of resource utilization within the context of privately financed initiatives, this book helps clarify how water development and the operation of investor-owned utilities relate to the broad theme of Progressivism. It also becomes possible to extend historical analysis of the West's hydraulic infrastructure beyond the realm of the Reclamation Service and gain fresh insight into economic and political forces that affected the region in the pre–New Deal era.

HYDROELECTRICITY

The importance of electric power in shaping the modern world is reflected in many sources, ranging from Lenin's famous 1920 pronouncement that "Communism is Soviet power plus the electrification of the whole country," to historian Marc Bloch's admonition that "the conquest of the earth by electricity . . . [has] more meaning and greater possibilities of shaping our immediate future than all the political events combined."[24] More recently, technological historian Thomas Hughes has provided the first comprehensive analysis of early electric power history. In his book *Networks of Power,* Hughes notes:

A great network of power lines which will forever order the way in which we live is now superimposed on the industrial world. Inventors, engineers, managers, and entrepreneurs have ordered the man-made world with this energy network. The half-century from 1880 through 1930 constituted the formative years of the history of electric supply systems and from a study of these years one can perceive the ordering, integrating, coordinating and systemizing of modern human societies.[25]

Eastwood participated as an important figure in the growth of California's hydroelectric power industry during the late nineteenth and early twentieth centuries. To understand the impetus underlying his development of the multiple arch dam, it becomes necessary to appreciate how the development of alternating-current power systems relates to the topography and environment of America's Pacific Slope.[26]

The theoretical basis of electric power generation is simple: electrical current is induced in a conductor (for example. a copper wire) by moving the conductor through a magnetic field. Thus, a steady current can be produced by simply rotating a conductor around a magnet. There are many ways to power this rotation, including coal-fired steam engines or windmills, but one of the most efficient is a water turbine that converts the energy of falling water into the circular motion of a drive shaft. By connecting a generator to a water turbine's rotating drive shaft, it is possible to produce *hydro*electric power.

In 1882, Thomas Edison's Pearl Street Station in New York City demonstrated the commercial viability of general-purpose electric power distribution using coal-fired steam engines to turn the generators. However, Edison's direct-current (DC) system proved incapable of transmitting power efficiently for more than 10 miles. Experimental work in the late 1880s demonstrated that alternating currents (AC) could efficiently transmit electricity over great distances, and a commercial "battle between the systems" soon ensued as electrical entrepreneurs sought to exploit the potential of AC.[27] In the early 1890s engineers working for George Westinghouse built AC systems at Telluride, Colorado, and Portland, Oregon; but because a single circuit (or single phase) of alternating current could not easily power motors or other mechanical devices, the ability of such installations to compete with DC systems proved limited. Researchers soon discerned, however, that AC technology could support power transmission if two or more (that is, polyphase) AC circuits were energized at the same time. Without getting into technical issues, it is clear that polyphase AC systems are historically important because, for the first time, they allowed transmission of electricity over great distances for use in lighting and in powering machines.[28]

Prior to the end of the nineteenth century, the use of hydropower was confined to the particular site where water wheels or turbines would convert the energy of falling water directly into mechanical power that (for example) could turn millstones, rotate textile spindles, or operate bellows.[29] The potential relationship between water power and long distance electric transmission systems was of particular interest to entrepreneurs in California, where the most significant hydropower sites were usually located in remote mountain settings. In 1887, the journal *Mining and Scientific Press* observed:

If the expectations of the electricians shall come to be realized, as is altogether probable, there is no calculating the effect it [long-distance power transmission] will have on the industries of the state. The horsepower that could be generated [in the Sierra Nevada] may be estimated by the hundreds of thousands. It would be ample to drive all the machinery in the New England states and if utilized only in part would make California a great manufacturing country.[30]

When the viability of polyphase AC technology first became apparent, California fostered commercial development of high voltage power systems on a scale unequaled anywhere in the world. Eastwood played a prominent role in the industry: his involvement in building and designing hydroelectric power systems in the Sierra Nevada undoubtedly constitutes the defining episode in his professional career. In particular, the operation of hydroelectric plants places great value on the storage of floodwaters high in the mountains, because this maximizes the amount of power that can be generated downstream. Eastwood viewed electricity as providing a central support for an expanding modern world. To best promote the benefits that he believed hydroelectric power offered to all people, he eventually concentrated his engineering skills on developing "The Ultimate Dam."

STRUCTURAL ART

Eastwood's multiple arch designs are significant because of their role in larger economic and technological systems, but they were promoted as a superior water storage technology because of their physical form and shape (Figs. 1.3 and 1.4). Consequently, understanding this aspect of his work depends on considering it within the context of structural engineering and, more specifically, the technology of reinforced concrete. Important insight into the technological character of Eastwood's designs can be gained by relating them to the concept of "structural art" formulated by David Billington of Princeton University. An engineer by training and a leader in the development of thin-shell design theory, Billington has devoted much of his career to the study of technological history. In his book *The Tower and the Bridge: The New Art of Structural Engineering*, he describes how the proliferation of wrought iron, steel, and reinforced concrete during the nineteenth and early twentieth centuries allowed engineers to develop new structural

1.3   *The upstream side of Big Bear Valley Dam, illustrating the characteristic shape of a multiple arch design; the portrait is of Eastwood, circa 1912. (John S. Eastwood Papers, Water Resources Center Archives)*

forms of bridges, roofs, and towers distinct from those suited for traditional stone masonry.[31] Denoting these forms as "structural art," he relates their design to three ideals:

> *Efficiency:* the use of small amounts of material
> *Economy:* minimizing construction and maintenance costs
> *Elegance:* the creation of graceful designs

In equating structural art with design that does not rely simply on bulk for stability, Billington differentiates the concept from the aesthetic of mass often associated with masonry construction. Characterizing massive design as a feature of the "preindustrial imperial era," he rejects the aesthetic forms of traditional masonry structures because they represent, in his view, "autocratic" systems of government. In contrast, Billington sees structural art as exhibiting "a lightness, even a fragility, which closely parallels the essence

of a free and open society"; and ironically, he notes that the United States—one of history's most prominent democracies—suffers from a "relative lack of structural artists," which he attributes to American engineers' considering themselves as "servants of business."[32]

Although the analogy should not be stretched too far, Billington's characterization of structural art as serving the ideals of democracy in the face of autocratic rule finds resonance in opportunities extended by the multiple arch dam to less affluent western water users. In addition, Billington's insight in bringing the issue of elegance into the discussion of large-scale structural design is more relevant to the history of dam construction than might be initially presumed. Visual appearance, especially as it related to massive physical form, became a significant criterion by which engineers assessed the validity of dam technologies in the early twentieth century.

1.4   *Detail view of buttresses on the downstream side of Eastwood's Mountain Dell Dam. These buttresses support the upstream arches and lend the design a distinctive visual character. (Historic American Engineering Record, Library of Congress)*

Eastwood's work exemplifies how the ideals of efficiency, economy, and elegance relate to dam design practice, and his slogan "Bulk Does Not Mean Strength" could be taken as a basic creed of all structural artists. Perhaps even more importantly, Billington's observations on the relationship of abstract mathematical theory to structural art—and the way many engineers embraced mathematics in order to demonstrate the scientific validity of their work—help explain professional reactions to Eastwood's design methodology.[33]

SUCCESS AND FAILURE

In general, dam engineering attracts only minimal interest from nonspecialists until a calamitous failure occurs. Then death and destruction galvanize public attention, and the engineering profession is implored to ensure that such horror will never visit humankind again. During the nineteenth century, several major disasters, including the collapse of the 164-foot-high Puentes Dam in Spain in 1802 (approximately 600 dead) and the 95-foot-high Dale Dyke Dam in England in 1864 (approximately 250 dead), gained international notoriety.[34] For Americans, the most horrible dam failure of the era produced the infamous Johnstown Flood that swept through the Little Conemaugh River Valley in southwestern Pennsylvania, killing more than 2,200 people.[35] Originally built to supply water for the Pennsylvania Main Line Canal, the reservoir created by the South Fork Dam was by the 1880s used only for recreational purposes. On May 31, 1889, the structure's spillway proved inadequate to discharge runoff from an intense spring storm, and the dam overtopped. The earthen structure quickly eroded, unleashing a huge mass of water upon the unsuspecting citizenry of Johnstown. The disaster became a permanent part of American folklore and has forever influenced the general public's understanding that failures in dam technology can have horrendous consequences.

Eastwood realized the carnage that could result from a failure; and as his designs grew larger, so did the professional risk he took in advocating their construction.[36] This risk was even greater because he actively promoted his dams as being less expensive and as using less concrete than other types of designs. To a public that often equated structural safety with greater cost and increased size, his claim of having developed a technologically superior method of water storage represented a counterintuitive approach to the science of dam design. Although Eastwood's dams have required maintenance during the last 80 years and some have been "repaired" or altered—supposedly in order to make them safer—none has ever failed or caused loss of life or property. Consequently, in terms of performance, they can be considered a success worthy of his claims. In another sense, however, multiple arch dams represent a profound failure, since they never achieved great influence in the development of America's water resources. Although approximately fifty multiple arch dams were built in the United States in the first part of the twentieth century, this number pales in comparison to the hundreds of earthen and concrete gravity dams built during the same period; by 1945 the technology had almost completely disappeared from the design lexicon of American dam engineers.

Thus, the history of Eastwood and the multiple arch dam encompasses both success and failure, depending on the context of analysis. For historians, this dichotomy is significant because it offers insight into important aspects of western water development that might be overlooked in analyses of more traditionally "successful" or prominent technologies. Eastwood's hopes of deploying "The Ultimate Dam" throughout the arid region proved chimerical, but his accomplishments and frustrations survive as touchstones for those seeking to comprehend the modern West's hydraulic infrastructure.

CHAPTER 2

Dams: A Technical and Historical Review

In dam building . . . there is nothing quite so satisfying as a big solid mass of concrete.

John R. Freeman to Guy C. Earl, 1911

Ultra conservative [dam engineers] pile up masses of materials to greater and greater volumes, and a few of the bolder ones build daring structures that appear to defy all theories of stability.

James Dix Schuyler, 1909

Thousands of years ago, beaver-built brush dams or the accidental lodging of trees and debris across a creek or desert arroyo acquainted humans with the possibility of artificial water control. As evidenced by a small water impounding structure at Jawa in Jordan's Black Desert dating to the fourth millennium B.C., the first man-made dams were simple constructs of earth and stone. By 2800 B.C., Egyptian builders had expanded on this basic earth-and-rockfill technology to erect the 62-foot-high Sadd el-Kafara Dam, featuring a maximum thickness of 300 feet. After that time, many ancient cultures in Mesopotamia, Yemen, China, Palestine, and elsewhere practiced the art of building dams; thus, a wide range of water control techniques was available by the time Europeans began to colonize the Western Hemisphere.[1]

Dams can be defined in functional terms as either storing or diverting water. Diversion dams (also known as *weirs*) raise the elevation of a river and divert water into a canal or flume for transport to a mill, power plant, irrigated field, or other destination. Not necessarily designed to block off a water course fully, these dams may channel only a portion of the flow, allowing the rest to escape over the top of the structure. Storage dams, whose primary intent is to impound water in a reservoir for relatively long periods of time, are usually designed to block river flow completely, preventing the release of water except through specially built gates or valves. To ensure that unexpected floods do not produce uncontrollable overflow, storage dams are usually equipped with spillways to carry away inflowing water that exceeds the reservoir's

13

storage capacity. Some large structures, known as flood-control dams, are built primarily to hold back floodwaters temporarily in order to protect downstream areas from washouts. Their reservoir areas are usually left dry in anticipation of impounding as much sudden flood flow as possible; they represent a special type of storage structure that was not widely built until the modern era.[2]

An insightful engineering axiom from the early twentieth century directs dam builders to "construct one water-tight surface and build the remainder of the structure to support that surface."[3] Known as *Dillman's Hydraulic Principle* (the American engineer George Dillman actively publicized it), this postulate provides a means of characterizing all types of dam design. No matter how it is shaped, or what materials it contains, every successful dam consists of a surface that directly blocks the passage of water and an adjoining structure that supports this surface. With some structures, such as a concrete gravity dam, the upstream face and the supporting structure are visually and physically contiguous. But with others, such as a rockfill dam with wooden upstream face, the two constitute separate and distinct features. A corollary to Dillman's Hydraulic Principle is the notion that a dam is only as strong as its foundation. Many seemingly solid structures have washed away because they were built on weak or porous foundations incapable of bearing the hydrostatic pressure exerted by a reservoir. Even for sites that do not present dramatically dangerous conditions, foundation analysis constitutes a critical aspect of dam design and construction; in other words, a strong dam on a weak foundation may soon be no dam at all.

In its most elementary form, a dam consists of a mass of material (rock, earth, wood, concrete, or any combination thereof) that by its weight holds back a volume of water. Structures that are too heavy for the impounded water to move, tip over, or otherwise dislodge are usually referred to as *gravity dams*. The simplest type of gravity structure is an *embankment dam*, which consists of a

large pile of earth or rock (or perhaps an amalgamation of the two) that is massive enough to resist the hydrostatic pressure exerted by a reservoir (Fig. 2.1). Earthfill and rockfill embankment dams may incorporate a wooden lattice (often called a *timber crib*) into their interior to help provide structural cohesion; at times, structures of the latter type are often referred to as *timber crib dams* (Fig. 2.2).[4]

Embankment dams are highly susceptible to erosion and to washouts, especially when floods surging into a reservoir cannot be handled by the spillway and water "overtops" the structure. As water rushes across the downstream face of the embankment, the structure usually erodes and then quickly collapses. Failure by overtopping can affect all types of dams; but whereas masonry and concrete designs can often withstand overtopping (in fact, many are specifically built as "overflow" dams), earthfill and rockfill designs that do not contain substantial timber cribbing almost invariably fail when overtopped; some of the world's most famous dam failures, including the collapse that precipitated the Johnstown Flood in 1889, were caused by the overtopping of an embankment dam.[5]

While earth, rock, and stone have long been considered excellent materials to use for a permanent water impoundment structure, a loose matrix of rockfill or a porous mound of soil requires the deployment of a special impervious barrier (provided by a layer of dense earthen clay, timber planks, steel sheets, or a concrete slab) to block off water flow. In grappling with problems related to percolation and seepage, early dam builders developed techniques for placing masonry blocks that were similar to methods used for building solid walls (Fig. 2.3). By filling in the cracks and interstices between stones with mortar, cement, or concrete, a builder can create a waterproof barrier that acts as a good upstream face—hence, the masonry gravity dam. By the early twentieth century the basic form of this technology had been adapted for applications involving structures built completely out of concrete.

2.1   *The ill-fated rockfill Lower Otay Dam near San Diego, a gravity dam completed in the 1890s. Its upstream and downstream faces were built with steeper slopes than could have been used for an embankment dam built exclusively of earthfill. See Figure 9.1 for evidence of this structure's demise. (Walter L. Huber Papers, Water Resources Center Archives)*

A dam need not rely solely on the force of gravity for stability. If the dam site is in a narrow canyon with hard rock foundations, masonry/concrete *arch dams* can resist the water pressure (or hydrostatic load) by pressing against the canyon walls of the dam site. As the name implies, an arch dam does not extend straight across a valley but instead is built along an arc that curves upstream into the reservoir. The water pressure exerted on the dam is then carried by "arch action" into the canyon walls (Fig. 2.4). Of course, many dam sites are too wide or have foundations too weak to allow construction of arch dams, so the technology does not always represent a viable alternative to gravity designs.

Although gravity dams and arch dams utilize different design principles, visually distin-guishing between the two can be difficult. Confusion arises when a structure contains enough material to function as a gravity dam but is built along a curved axis so that it appears to be an arch dam. In a curved gravity dam the dimensions of the profile (or of the vertical cross section) are so great that negligible arch action develops and the design functions simply as a gravity structure (Fig. 2.5). In an arch dam, the structure's profile is insufficient to resist the water loading through "gravity action." Therefore, it *must* function as an arch in resisting hydrostatic loads. In other words, if a curved gravity dam could somehow be straightened out, it would still impound water without tipping over. But if an arch dam were straightened out, the structure would collapse backward under full

15

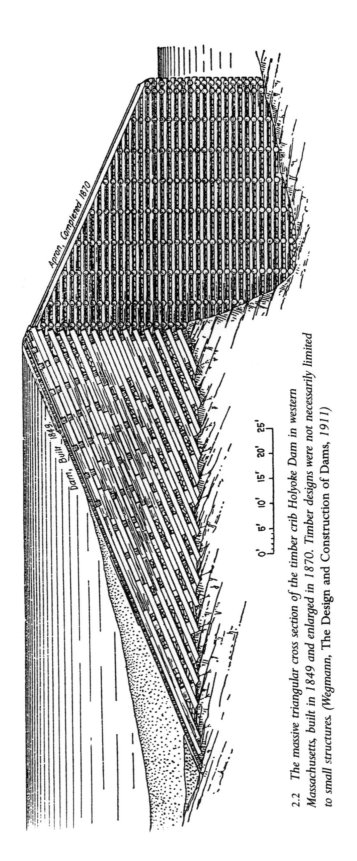

2.2 *The massive triangular cross section of the timber crib Holyoke Dam in western Massachusetts, built in 1849 and enlarged in 1870. Timber designs were not necessarily limited to small structures. (Wegmann, The Design and Construction of Dams, 1911)*

2.3   *The 297-foot-high Croton Dam north of New York City, a masonry gravity dam completed in 1907. (Historic American Engineering Record, Library of Congress)*

water loading. Given that the cross-sectional dimensions of a curved gravity dam are capable of stability even if the structure's arch shape is eliminated, the value of arcing the design remains problematic. Using a curved plan does seem to reduce the likelihood that shrinkage cracks (created as the temperature of the dam fluctuates or as concrete gradually cools during the hardening process) will develop across the face of a dam. But perhaps more importantly, the psychological impact of a large, curving mass extending across a canyon and visually "holding back" a reservoir of water is significant, commanding popular awe and respect.

A third type of dam shares characteristics with gravity and arch structures but is significant in its own right. Known collectively as *buttress dams,* this type of design relies primarily on the force of gravity for stability, but in a manner requiring less material than is necessary for a standard gravity structure. Early Roman and Spanish dams of this type featured buttresses built perpendicular to the downstream side of a relatively thin masonry wall. Just as flying buttresses were designed to stabilize the high walls of Gothic cathedrals, early buttress dams utilized a type of "bracing" to help resist hydrostatic loads. By the nineteenth century, designs in which buttresses simply supplemented a gravity structure were superseded by ones in which buttresses constituted the entire structure behind the upstream face (Fig. 2.6). These types of dams (which can be built of wood, masonry, concrete, steel, or some combination thereof) consist of two basic parts: the upstream face, which provides a barrier against the water;

17

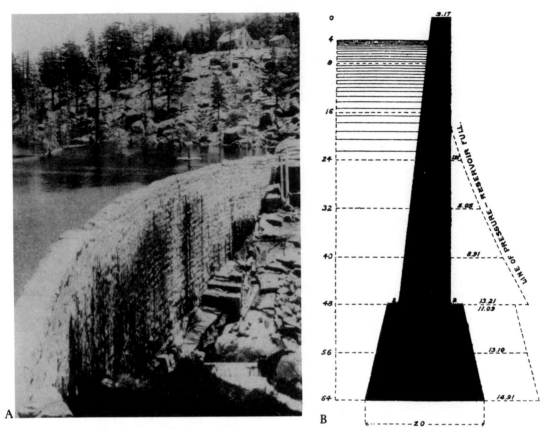

2.4 *(A) Bear Valley Dam, completed in 1884, an arch dam built with stone masonry blocks. (B) Cross section (or profile). The masonry arch is so thin that it could not stand as a gravity dam. (Wegmann,* The Design and Construction of Dams, *1911)*

and the buttresses, which carry the hydrostatic loading down to the foundations.

Known generically as *hollow dams*, buttress structures that utilize a flat surface for the upstream face are called *flat-slab dams*, while those using a series of arches are known as *multiple arch dams*. Because flat-slab and multiple arch buttress dams are not monoliths, they do not feature a solid cross section along the entire length of the structure, and thus they need less material than gravity dams of comparable height. In particular, Figure 2.7 shows how buttress dams that feature an inclined water face (as opposed to a vertical face) can be built with relatively small quantities of material; they take advantage of the fact that water in the reservoir

pushes *down* on the structure, thus helping prevent the dam from overturning or sliding downstream.

TRADITIONS: MASSIVE AND STRUCTURAL

The world's earliest dams depended on massive bulk to hold back water, and their builders did not utilize mathematical formulas to calculate the best theoretical shapes to serve this purpose. Instead, basing their structures on known precedents, or perhaps relying entirely on intuition, the builders would pile up earth, rock, timber, and so on until the struc-

2.5 *(A) Hoover Dam (also known as Boulder Dam), extending across the Colorado River near Las Vegas, Nevada; a good example of a curved gravity dam. (B) Although constructed with a prominent upstream curve, Hoover Dam features a cross section that would be stable without arching; this construction view, taken in 1934, documents the massive dimensions of the design. (Author's collection)*

ture's weight (or mass) could resist the force exerted by a reservoir without sliding or tipping over. Gradually, a massive tradition of dam design developed around this process, fostering construction of structures that resist hydrostatic pressures merely because of their size. Although designs exemplifying the massive tradition can be based on sophisticated engineering analysis, the basic principle underlying the tradition is simple: accumulate as much material as possible, thus increasing the likelihood that the structure will achieve long-term stability. Largely due to this conceptual simplicity, massive dam technology was employed for the earliest known dams (such as those at Jawa and Sadd-el Kafara); at

2.6 *Reinforced concrete buttress dam at Juniata, Pennsylvania, under construction in 1906.*
The flat upstream face is supported on a series of slender buttresses extending downward into
the foundations. This view shows why buttress designs were sometimes termed "hollow dams."
(*Wegmann,* The Design and Construction of Dams, *1911*)

the turn of the twenty-first century, most of the world's water storage structures remain gravity dams in the massive tradition.

In contrast, the structural tradition relies less on bulk than on a dam's shape to resist hydrostatic pressure. Consequently, adding bulk to a structural dam does not necessarily increase its strength. While dams built in the structural tradition (namely, thin arch dams and buttress dams) require less material than comparable massive structures, the principles underlying their operation are not immediately obvious and they have not been built in large numbers. Nonetheless, the structural tradition can be traced back to the days of the Roman Empire, when Roman engineers built the first known arch dam and several buttress dams. After the fall of Rome, the tradition (and large-scale dam building in general) waned, but it did not disappear completely. For example, during the thirteenth and fourteenth centuries, Ilkhanid Mongols in Persia built some of the most noteworthy arch dams of the premodern era, including the 190-foot-high Kurit Dam, which stood as the world's tallest dam for over 500 years. By the beginning of the twentieth century, a resurgence of interest in the structural tradition was under way; John Eastwood's efforts to promote the multiple arch dam constitute a part of this movement.

While massive dams are simple to conceptualize, they make profligate use of construction materials. In contrast, structural dams require relatively small amounts of material, but can present more sophisticated problems in design and construction. Structural dams are typically less expensive than comparable

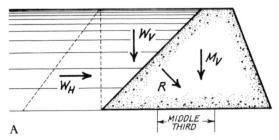

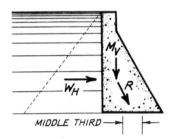

A

NOTE: W_H AND W_V REPRESENT COMPONENTS OF HYDROSTATIC PRESSURE EXERTED ON DAM BETWEEN BUTTRESSES.

B

W_H = HORIZONTAL WATER PRESSURE VECTOR
W_V = VERTICAL WATER PRESSURE VECTOR
M_V = VERTICAL DAM MASS VECTOR
R = RESULTANT VECTOR = $W_H \times W_V \times M_V$

2.7 *Contrast between an inclined-faced buttress design (A) and a vertically faced gravity design (B). The first drawing shows how an inclined face allows a buttress dam to replace part of its mass with a weight of water that pushes down on the foundation. (Author's collection, courtesy of Richard K. Anderson)*

massive dams because they require smaller quantities of material (be it rock or concrete); as a result, transportation costs for construction material, equipment, and fuel are reduced. Offsetting these savings is the need to rely on more skilled (and potentially more expensive) workers to erect a design requiring an intricate system of construction. Consequently, in choosing a design from either the massive or the structural tradition, engineers (and the financial organizations that sponsor them) are confronted with a range of competing technical factors that influence the selection process.

Historically, most dam builders have not consciously considered themselves proponents of either the structural or the massive tradition. They merely designed dams similar to those built by their mentors or in accord with the technology most prevalent in their culture. But faced with unfamiliar alternatives, they could exhibit strong preferences for one tradition over the other. Historians must appreciate the conflict between the massive and structural traditions in order to come to grips with many of the controversies that attended dam building during the early twentieth century.

THEORY AND MATHEMATICS

Achievements in sixteenth-century Spain mark the beginning of modern dam building in Western civilization. Operating within an arid environment plagued by limited water supplies, Spanish engineers were responsible for several major structures including the curved gravity dam at Almansa (50 feet high, in operation by 1586), the gravity dam at Alicante (140 feet high, 1594), the arch dam at Elche (76 feet high, ca. 1650), and the arch dam at Rellue (105 feet high, ca. 1650). During this time, principles to guide construction were written down, and portions of the Codex of Juanelo Turriano represent the first known manuscript that describes dam building. By 1736, a book written by the Basque nobleman Don Pedro Bernardo Villa de Berry outlined geometrical rules to follow when dimensioning a dam and pointed the way toward a more rationalized, less intuitive approach to design.[6]

For centuries, dam builders had not relied upon mathematics to help determine the structural dimensions required for stability. This gradually began to change as engineers started adopting techniques of physical logic pioneered by Isaac Newton and Robert Hooke.[7] In the late eighteenth and early nineteenth centuries, several French and English engineers, including Bernard Belidor, Charles Bossut, Charles Augustin Coulomb,

John Smeaton, and Henry Moseley, published treatises on how the theory of statics could be related to construction of gravity dams.[8] Their publications did not immediately and dramatically transform the dam design process; in fact, for embankment dams, the rules governing design have remained relatively empirical even into modern times. Nonetheless, these treatises established important precedents for adapting mathematical theory to the practice of dam design.

EMBANKMENT DAMS: EARTHFILL AND ROCKFILL

The erection of embankment dams using huge quantities of earth or rockfill has been common since ancient times, largely because these materials are often readily available near dam sites. Building embankment dams relies on three engineering steps: proportioning structural dimensions in accord with years of empirical observation; placing good-quality materials on a solid foundation; and building some kind of spillway to make sure that the structure is not overtopped by floods. For stability, earthfill and rockfill dams require massive amounts of material, and their basic form is determined by the physical characteristics of the two materials. Both earth and loose rocks take on a sloped, moundlike shape when formed into a large structure. If the side slopes are too steep, the mound will tend to realign itself into a more natural (that is, flatter) profile. While basic theories of engineering statics developed in the eighteenth and nineteenth centuries (such as those used to calculate where the "resultant force" of water pressure and the weight of the dam act on the foundation) provided a way to conceptualize how much material was required to build a safe embankment dam, their utility was limited and engineers did not rely upon them for dramatic innovations in design. In fact, in 1900 Edward Wegmann reported: "the profiles of earthen dams are determined entirely by practical considerations. The general dimensions of the profile depend upon the materials used and the height of the bank, additional strength [that is, more material] being given to high dams."[9]

Providing strictures reminiscent of Don Pedro's eighteenth-century design guidelines, Wegmann recommended the construction of designs in which the inner (upstream) slope has a height-to-width ratio of between 1:2 and 1:3 and the outer (downstream slope) has a height-to-width ratio of between 2:3 and 2:5. He further advised that the top of the dam should be at least 10 to 30 feet wide and that the water level in the reservoir should never be allowed to rise within 5 feet of the dam's crest. Wegmann's design methodology for earthfill dams was reiterated decades later in the 1945 book *Engineering for Dams*, which advised:

Precise and highly mathematical methods of design or analysis of the various features of earth dams are seldom justified because we know in advance that the assumptions which must be made are sufficiently wide so that no precision is justifiable. Consequently, the engineer whose function it is to investigate, design and construct will, in most cases, do well to confine himself to the simple, less precise methods of design and analysis.[10]

Rockfill dam design is analogous to that used for earthfill structures; both focus primarily on the development of massive triangular cross sections. However, some factors differ between the two technologies. For example, because of its density and other physical properties, rockfill can be placed on steeper slopes than earthfill can; similarly, for a rockfill dam the design of an impervious upstream face can be of more immediate concern because loose rockfill is extremely susceptible to having water seep through the spaces between individual stones.

MASONRY GRAVITY DAMS

While masonry gravity dams can be built without resort to mathematical formulas, nineteenth-century engineers came to appreciate that structures of this type were amenable to a rationalized, quantifiable design method. The most significant theoretical development affecting the technology occurred in France in the early 1850s with a paper published by J. Augustine DeSazilly.[11] Knowing the hydrostatic force exerted by a given height of water and the approximate weight of masonry used in dam construction (usually about 150 pounds per cubic foot), DeSazilly postulated what came to be known as the "profile of equal resistance." Using basic formulas of statics, he developed a vertical cross-section for masonry gravity dams in which the stresses at the upstream face when the reservoir is empty equal the stresses at the downstream face when the reservoir is filled. By considering these two extreme conditions (the reservoir filled and the reservoir empty) and making sure that the stresses on the masonry were equalized across every horizontal cross section, DeSazilly hypothesized a design that should, at least in cross section, minimize the amount of material required for a stable gravity dam (Fig. 2.8(A)).

Although DeSazilly himself never built a dam based on his "profile of equal resistance," in 1858 the French engineer F. Emile Delocre employed the theory for the 183-foot-high Furens Dam across the Loire River. Working with Auguste Graeff, Delocre utilized data derived from analyses of two French and six Spanish dams (including Almansa and Alicante) to determine empirically that 86 pounds per square inch (psi) would constitute a safe maximum compressive stress for masonry.[12] Completed in 1866, the massive curved gravity Furens Dam towered above all other European dams and contained over 52,000 cubic yards of masonry; within a few years, it was being characterized in engineering textbooks as the first masonry dam "built in accordance with correct scientific principles."[13]

In the early 1870s, British interests wishing to build a large dam in Madras, India, approached the famous mathematician/engineer W. J. M. Rankine for advice on a gravity dam design. Rankine confirmed the validity of DeSazilly's and Delocre's work and noted that a stable gravity dam must have sufficient cross section so that the combined vector force (or "resultant force") of the horizontal hydrostatic pressure and the vertical weight of masonry falls within the middle third of the structure's base.[14] If the profile is too thin and the resultant falls outside the "center third," a gravity dam will develop tension (instead of compression) along the downstream edge and thus become susceptible to dangerous cracking; if the "resultant force" falls completely beyond the downstream edge, the structure will tip over backward. While the precept of having the "resultant force" fall within the "middle third" of a gravity dam had been met empirically by the DeSazilly/Delocre profiles, Rankine is credited with having overtly established it as a principle of design.[15]

The ideas of DeSazilly, Delocre, and Rankine served as models for major structures such as the Gileppe Dam in Belgium (1875), the Vyrnwy Dam (completed in 1890, the first large masonry storage dam in Great Britain), and the Remscheid Dam in Germany (1892).[16] They also formed the basis for the first edition (1888) of Edward Wegmann's landmark *The Design and Construction of Dams.* Using the methodology presented in this book, Wegmann developed a cross section for New York City's New Croton Dam (it was intended to replace a much smaller structure built in the 1840s) that became widely known as the "Croton Profile" (Fig.2.8(B)). Within a few years the "Croton Profile" had achieved international recognition and served as a basic standard for gravity dam design.[17] In addition, Wegmann developed a series of gravity profiles (known as Wegmann Profiles No. 1, No. 2, No. 3, and so on) that varied slightly in shape depending on the density (the weight per cubic foot) of masonry available for use in a particular structure (Fig. 2.8(C)). Not always content to adopt Wegmann's profiles, engineers frequently developed their own particular gravity designs; however, these represented only minimal vari-

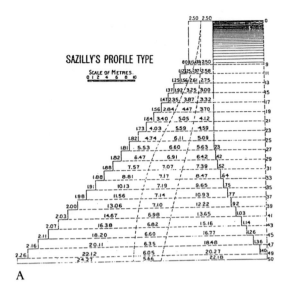

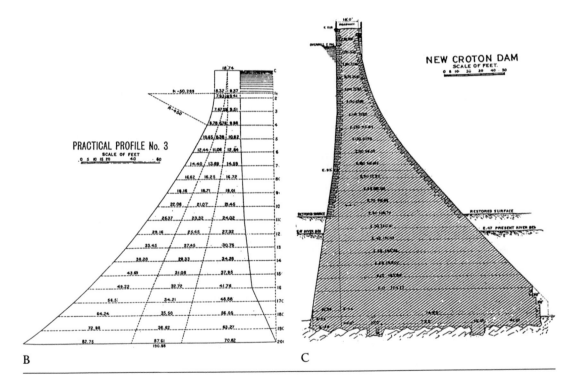

2.8 *(A) DeSazilly's "Profile of Equal Resistance" for masonry gravity dams. (B) Edward Wegmann's "Practical Profile No. 3." (C) The cross section of Croton Dam, showing the "Croton Profile." (Wegmann,* The Design and Construction of Dams, *1911)*

ations on the basic "profile of equal resistance" proposed by DeSazilly.

Beginning in the 1890s, concern began to grow about the effect of "uplift" on the structural stability of gravity dams. In simple terms, "uplift" is caused by water that seeps under a dam's foundation and then pushes up, thereby increasing the tendency of the structure to slide horizontally. The "uplift" issue (and a concurrent concern about the distribution of internal stresses) attracted the attention of twentieth-century hydraulic engineers, but it did little to affect the basic design of gravity dams except to encourage the use of thicker, more massive, profiles.[18]

The obdurate character of gravity dam design was succinctly summarized by George Holmes Moore in a 1913 *Engineering News* article in which he noted that practically all masonry gravity dams feature a profile with a height-to-thickness ratio of at least 3:2 (hence, for example, a gravity dam 100 feet tall will feature a base thickness of at least 66 feet). Thus, despite the use of seemingly sophisticated mathematical analysis, gravity dam technology had reached a point in the early twentieth century where empirical methods of design (based on a 3:2 height-to-thickness ratio) could produce results almost identical to those derived from theoretical calculations.[19]

In an economic context, the most significant drawback to the "Croton Profile" and similar designs involved the enormous material and capital outlay they required. The "profile of equal resistance" may have offered a mathematically rational basis of design, but this did not mean that structures adhering to this precept would be inexpensive to build. For major cities (such as New York with regard to the Croton Dam, or Boston with regard to the Wachusett Dam), the high cost of masonry gravity structures did not present an insuperable problem; the economic benefits of increased water storage more than compensated for the expense of such designs. In turn, municipal authorities (and the engineers who advised them) frequently came to view costly masonry gravity structures as representing the most conservative—and hence the most appropriate—method of dam building. As a result, conservative designs in the massive tradition found favor because their thicker, heavier profiles were perceived to provide greater safety and security for the citizens who funded their construction. This tendency to equate greater mass with greater safety persists among many engineers and constitutes an enduring legacy of early gravity dam design.

ARCH DAMS

Although the seventeenth-century Spanish dam at Elche and the Italian Ponte Alto Dam featured profiles insufficient to stand as gravity structures, masonry arch dam construction remained relatively dormant until the nineteenth century. At that time, the technology was reintroduced by two engineers an ocean apart: Lieutenant Colonel John By of the British Army in Canada and Francois Zola in France. By's arch dam was erected in the wilderness at Jones Falls in 1828–1831, as part of the Rideau Canal connecting Lake Ontario with the Ottawa River.[20] The slender profile of the Jones Falls Dam (58 feet high, maximum thickness 19 feet) was apparently adopted to accelerate the speed of construction. Any theoretical calculations that By may have used remain unknown, and the dam fostered little interest among contemporary engineers. The case of Francois Zola and the Zola Dam is quite different.

In the 1830s, Zola developed a plan to increase the water supply of Marseilles, France, that included construction of a 130-foot-high arch dam.[21] The dimensions for this dam were to be determined by means of a simple but useful mathematical equation known as the "cylinder formula" (Fig. 2.9). First derived by the French mathematician Louis Navier in 1826, this formula states that for cylindrical shapes placed under hydrostatic pressure, the arch thickness T can be calculated according to the equation:

$$T = (P \times R) / Q$$

where

P = Hydrostatic pressure (based on the density of water and on the height of water being stored)
R = Radius of the cylinder or arch
Q = Maximum allowable stress (for instance, $Q = 100$ pounds per square inch)

The cylinder formula is highly idealized and, for absolute accuracy, requires an arch to be infinitely thin and supported on completely

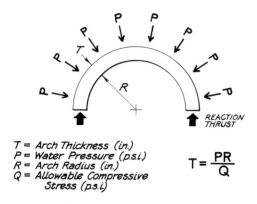

T = Arch Thickness (in.)
P = Water Pressure (p.s.i.)
R = Arch Radius (in.)
Q = Allowable Compressive
Stress (p.s.i.)

$$T = \frac{PR}{Q}$$

EXAMPLE:

P @ 100 ft. depth
= 62.5 lbs./ft.³ x 100 ft.
= 43.4 p.s.i.

R = 20 ft. or 240 in.

Q = 300 p.s.i.

For T @ 100 ft. depth:

$$T = \frac{PR}{Q} = \frac{43.4 \times 240}{300}$$

= 34.7 in.

2.9 *The Cylinder Formula. (Author's collection, courtesy of Richard K. Anderson)*

rigid foundations. But despite being based on such unattainable assumptions the formula provides a useful means of estimating stresses in many arch dams. In designing his dam, Zola conceived the structure as consisting of a stack of horizontal arches. At the dam's crest, where water pressure is at a minimum, the stack is thinnest. As the water pressure increases in lower parts of the dam, the thickness of Zola's design also increases; the rate at which the arch becomes thicker is calculated from the cylinder formula.[22]

Construction of the Zola Dam began in 1847 and the project attracted attention among engineers through the next decade. Nonetheless, the work of DeSazilly and Delocre in designing gravity dams overshadowed interest in arch dams during the mid-nineteenth century; and aside from one small structure in Australia, no other major arch dams were built until the 1880s. Then, in 1884, the Yale-educated American engineer Frank E. Brown completed construction of a daring masonry arch dam in Southern Cali-

fornia in which the "resultant force" did not simply fall outside of the "middle third," but fell well beyond the downstream edge of the foundation.[23] Brown's 64-foot-high Bear Valley Dam featured a maximum thickness of only 20 feet and, by operating successfully for several years, demonstrated that the cylinder formula could foster designs that radically reduced the amount of material necessary for a solid masonry dam. In 1886, Brown began building another arch structure (50 feet tall, base width 10 feet) on the Sweetwater River near San Diego. He erected only a portion of the dam before the San Diego Land and Town Company (a real estate enterprise financed by the Atchison, Topeka & Santa Fe Railway) placed James Schuyler in charge of construction. Schuyler revamped the design so that it featured a thicker profile than Brown had proposed; nonetheless, the 90-foot-high, 46-foot-thick Sweetwater Dam, completed in 1888, further confirmed the value of the cylinder formula in dam design (Fig. 2.10). In 1895, Schuyler's design provided especially dramatic proof of the potential strength of arch dam technology when it withstood a prolonged overtopping in the midst of a heavy storm.[24]

Brown's and Schuyler's accomplishments in the 1880s served as an important catalyst for investigating how the arch principle could be adapted to design more efficient, less costly, water storage projects. Eventually, this growing interest in the cylinder formula yielded a significant design variation that, although not actually implemented until 1913, represented the final important innovation derived from the theory. A few years before construction of the Bear Valley Dam, Albert Pelletreau had published a theoretical study in France based on the insight that the same horizontal radius need not be used for all parts of the arch.[25] Because the cylinder formula stipulates that the arch thickness T is directly proportional to the radius R, it follows that the thickness of any particular arch slice can be reduced by making the radius smaller. Because most canyons are narrower

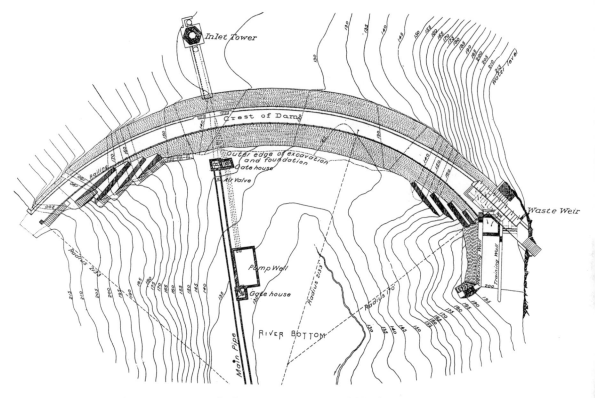

2.10 *Plan drawing of Sweetwater Dam, built near San Diego in 1888, showing its prominent upstream curve. (*Transactions of the American Society of Civil Engineers, *1888)*

at the bottom than at the top, it is easy to conceptualize the construction of arch dams consisting of a stack of arches with progressively smaller radii. Usually referred to as *constant-angle arch dams* (because the angle remains relatively constant while the radius gets smaller), structures of this type visually resemble cones that are pointed downward. Following Pelletreau's initial conception of this type of dam in 1879, the idea was discussed further by Gardiner Williams in 1904 and by John Eastwood in 1910.[26] Although actual construction of a constant-angle arch dam did not occur until 1913—when Lars Jorgensen designed the Salmon Creek Dam for a hydroelectric plant near Juneau, Alaska (Fig. 2.11)—the theoretical basis for this structural form was developed in the late nineteenth century.[27]

BUTTRESS DAMS

While the Zola, Bear Valley, and Sweetwater dams demonstrated that thin arch dams constituted a viable technology, skepticism about a dam design theory that did not follow the precepts of DeSazilly prevailed among many engineers. For the civil engineering profession, arch dams represented a significant challenge (and opportunity) because of their prospective economy. A similar challenge was eventually presented by buttress dams, the other basic design type within the structural tradition.

Masonry dams supplemented by downstream buttresses had been built by both the Romans and post-Renaissance Spanish engineers. Although the upstream faces of these early buttress dams were not thick enough to

A

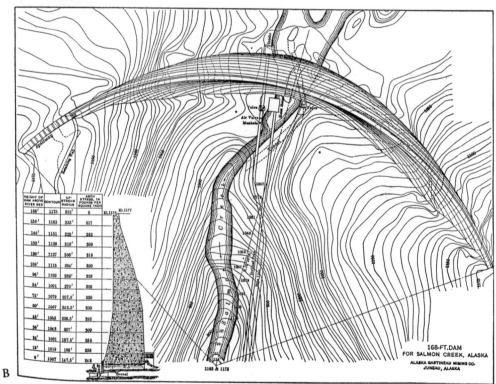

B

2.11   *The concrete Salmon Creek Dam near Juneau, Alaska, completed in 1913. (A) View along the top of the dam, showing the arch. Although the idea of varying the radius of an arch dam in order to reduce the amount of construction material required had been proposed at least 30 years earlier, Salmon Creek was the world's first "constant-angle" (or variable-radius) dam actually built. (Author's collection) (B) Plan drawing showing the "conic" shape of the constant-angle design. This type of structure demonstrates how creative use of the cylinder formula can foster innovative forms of design.* (Transactions of the American Society of Civil Engineers, *1915*)

A

B

2.12   *Two mid-nineteenth-century timber designs featuring inclined upstream faces supported on wooden posts. (A) Pile and frame dam. (B) Hollow frame dam. Buttress dam technology was not unknown to American builders prior to the twentieth century; it was simply confined to small-scale structures. (James Leffel,* Construction of Mill Dams, *1881)*

stand alone as gravity dams, they were generally quite ample.[28] By the mid nineteenth century, small-scale wooden buttress dams featuring inclined upstream faces began to be built in America and were common enough to warrant illustration in James Leffel's book *Construction of Mill Dams* (Fig. 2.12).[29] These latter structures differed substantially from earlier, bulkier designs and served as precursors for the modern form of buttress dam.

At the close of the nineteenth century, buttress dam design theory bore greater similarity to earthfill dam theory than it did to gravity or arch dam design. During the eighteenth and nineteenth centuries numerous buttress dams were built but their designs were derived either empirically or by simple application of the laws of statics. There was no development of widely discussed theories of "rational" design for buttress dams, as

2.13   *Redridge Dam in northern Michigan, 1980. This photograph shows the dam as it looked more than 75 years after it first impounded water. (Historic American Engineering Record, Library of Congress)*

there was for massive gravity dams. For buttress dams with flat upstream faces, of course, engineers had no reason to consider the issues related to arch analysis. For multiple arch dams, the value of analyzing arch stresses was more relevant; but because of the paucity of multiple arch dam designs prior to 1908, interest in pursuing such theoretical investigations was slight.

The first major nonwooden, nonmasonry buttress dam was the 42-foot-high all-steel Ash Fork Dam built in northern Arizona by the Atchison, Topeka & Santa Fe Railway in 1898.[30] Designed with an inclined upstream face consisting of plates that rested on compression struts spaced 8 feet apart, the Ash Fork Dam adopted the form of the timber

buttress dam but replaced the wooden members with steel. Designer F. H. Bainbridge's theoretical considerations largely focused on placing the resultant of the dam's weight and the vertical and horizontal components of the water load through the center third of the foundation. The success of the Ash Fork Dam prompted construction of a second steel dam (70 feet high) at Redridge, Michigan, in 1902, and the technology of steel buttress dams appeared to be on its way toward widespread acceptance (Fig. 2.13).[31] The third steel dam, however—a 75-foot-high structure built in 1907 at Hauser Lake, Montana—collapsed the following year because its foundations were not firmly keyed into bedrock. This failure, in conjunction with rising steel prices and concern that metallic superstructures would corrode, ended development of steel buttress dams. An unsuccessful effort to revive the technology briefly surfaced in the 1930s; but after 1910, steel designs no longer played a significant role in dam engineering.[32] Instead, initiative in the field was assumed by builders relying on reinforced concrete.

In 1903, Nils F. Ambursen designed and built the first reinforced concrete flat-slab buttress dam, at Theresa Falls in upstate New York.[33] Although only 10 feet high, this structure established a precedent for scores of other designs promulgated by the New England–based Ambursen Hydraulic Construction Company during the next several decades. As described in the company's early promotional literature, the design was predicated on placing the resultant force of water pressure and dam weight through the middle third of the foundation. The Ambursen Company took out many patents to protect its position as a reinforced concrete dam builder and made major efforts to promote the utility of buttress dams.[34] In 1908–1909, the company built the 125-foot-high La Prele (or Douglas) Dam in eastern Wyoming, confirming that reinforced concrete buttress dams need not be limited to small-scale structures.[35] Although Ambursen dams required substantially more material than their multiple arch brethren, flat-slab structures led the way in establishing reinforced concrete as a viable material for dam construction.

The sixteenth-century Codex of Juanelo Turriano provides the first description of multiple arch dams with inclined upstream faces; and in the eighteenth century, small multiple arch dams first appeared in the Spanish landscape.[36] With one major exception, the hydraulic technology received little further attention from engineers until the late nineteenth century; but this exception was quite remarkable and constituted what dam historian Nicholas Schnitter has termed "one of the rare, true strokes of genius."[37] Constructed in 1803–1804 by the British engineer Henry Russle, the Meer Allum (Mir Alum)

Dam in southern India incorporates twenty-one masonry arches (with spans varying from 70 to 155 feet) into a structure more than 2,000 feet long (Fig. 2.14). The arches extend to a maximum height of 40 feet and feature vertical upstream faces; consequently, the structure does not utilize any vertical water load to help resist horizontal water pressure. Despite its great size and successful operation (it remains in use after almost 200 years of service), the Meer Allum Dam apparently prompted no further development of the multiple arch concept in India, Europe, or elsewhere. Instead, the gradual increase of small-scale buttress dams over the course of the nineteenth century eventually led to the modern form of the multiple arch dam.

A key event in buttress dam development came in 1897, when Henry Goldmark proposed a large (105-foot-high) concrete multiple arch dam for construction by the Pioneer Electric Company near Ogden, Utah (Fig. 2.15).[38] Although Goldmark's dam was never built, his design featured seven inclined upstream arches supported on buttresses placed 32 feet apart. Setting forth basic design principles for multiple arch structures, Goldmark described the structure as one in which the "arch rings act simply to transfer the water pressure to adjacent piers, which must be of sufficient size and strength to withstand the entire hydrostatic pressure that comes on both the piers and the arches." He further averred that, because the arches (built on 25-foot radii) were "circular segments" and their central lines coincided with "the line of pressure for water pressures acting normally to the extrados," then "the compressive [stresses] are uniform in the arch-ring at any given elevation and are readily found by the formula $T = PR$."

Goldmark's arch-rings did not gradually vary in thickness according to the cylinder formula, but instead featured a "stepped" design in which the top 60 feet of the arch rings were to be 6 feet thick, the next 25 feet were to be 7 feet thick, and the lowest 20 feet were to be 8 feet thick. The rest of his design was predicated on conventional standards of grav-

VIEW·OF·MEER·ALLUM·LAKE·AND·DAM

·PLAN·OF·DAM·

MEER ALLUM LAKE

0   100 200 300 400

SCALE OF FEET

"THE SANITARY ENGINEER AND CONSTRUCTION RECORD"

2.14   *Sketch and plan drawing of Meer Allum Dam, a masonry multiple arch dam built near Hyderabad, India, in 1804. This remarkable structure was more than 2,000 feet long and featured 21 individual arches with vertical upstream faces.* (The Sanitary Engineer and Construction Record, *1888)*

ity dam design, whereby he determined that the resultant of the water and masonry loads would fall within the center third of the buttresses.[39] Goldmark devised the first major multiple arch design that incorporated an inclined upstream face and utilized the cylinder formula to calculate arch thickness; nonetheless, when he presented his ideas to the engineering community in the *Transactions of the American Society of Civil Engineers,* the proposed structure elicited little notice, comment, or discussion.

Almost contemporaneously with Goldmark's proposal, in 1896–1897, the Australian engineer Oscar Schulze built a buttress dam on the Belubula River west of Sydney. Known as the Belubula Dam, this structure is 60 feet tall, 431 feet long, and built out of

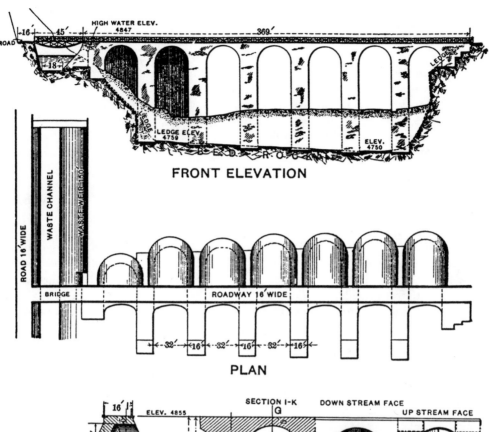

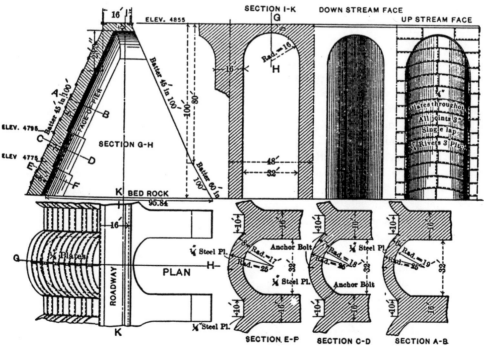

2.15 *Drawings of Henry Goldmark's 1897 multiple arch design. Although never built, this design offered the first illustration of a multiple arch dam featuring an inclined upstream face and having arches proportioned in accordance with the cylinder formula. (*Transactions of the American Society of Civil Engineers, *1897)*

33

bricks and concrete. In the center of the dam, six buttresses spaced 28 feet apart support an upstream face inclined at an angle of 60 degrees. On the dam's downstream side, the facing appears to be formed by five elliptical brick arches; but on the upstream side the spandrels between the arches are filled with concrete so that the water face consists of a smooth, flat surface. With this flat concrete face, Schulze eliminated radial hydrostatic loading on the arches and, in essence, created a hybrid design that falls somewhere between a flat-slab and a multiple arch dam. The Belubula Dam's "filled spandrel" design exerted little influence on subsequent designs. But unlike Goldmark's proposal, Schulze's creation constituted a functioning structure that could not be dismissed as fanciful theorizing.[40]

In 1902, a brief paper by George Dillman in the *Transactions of the American Society of Civil Engineers* described a 100-foot-tall buttressed dam with a flat, vertical upstream face. Dillman proposed building his dam with parabolic arches to connect the buttresses along the downstream side of the vertical face, thus creating a design akin to that of the Belubula Dam. Although in many ways the Dillman design appeared less practical than Goldmark's 1897 proposal, it engendered substantially more discussion among ASCE members. Some engineers expressed doubt that Dillman's design would actually achieve any financial savings over comparable gravity dams, while other engineers were concerned that the relatively thin upstream face would prove too difficult to make watertight. In the most lengthy comment accompanying the article, Edward Wegmann related Dillman's proposal to the Goldmark design and acknowledged that, if it proved possible to make "a thin wall of masonry practically watertight under considerable pressure [then] dams consisting of piers joined by vertical arches would be likely to be constructed in the future, with a view of saving expense."[41]

During the next six years, nothing of substance appeared in the technical press to contradict, confirm, or expand on Wegmann's informal predictions. Compared with gravity, arch, and flat-slab buttress dams, the multiple arch concept occupied a minor—almost nonexistent—place in the world of hydraulic engineering at the start of the twentieth century.

EARLY DAMS IN THE WEST

When John Eastwood began construction of the Hume Lake Dam in 1908, his design represented an innovative technological form, but it by no means constituted the first water storage structure in the American West. His interest in water storage had been preceded by several decades of dam building in the region.

Although precontact Native American cultures such as the Hohokam and Hopi Indians developed major irrigation systems utilizing diversion dams, they did not seek to increase water supplies by building large-scale water storage structures.[42] When the Spanish began settling the Southwest, they brought with them techniques for controlling water; and in the eighteenth century, they built small masonry dams for missions in San Antonio [Texas] and San Diego [California] (Fig. 2.16).[43] The significance of these structures was relatively limited, however, because they did not provide for long-term storage. Members of the Church of Jesus Christ of Latter-day Saints (Mormons) who migrated to the Salt Lake Valley in the late 1840s were the first group of Anglo-Americans to attempt large-scale settlement in the arid West. Although early Mormon pioneers built many small rock-and-timber diversion dams as part of their numerous irrigation systems, most streams in the eastern Great Basin carry relatively little flow and there is evidence of only one large storage dam built by the Mormons before the end of the century.[44]

In the late 1870s, John Wesley Powell drew on his knowledge of Mormon settlements in

2.16   *In the late eighteenth century, Spanish colonists built this simple masonry diversion dam to supply water to the San Diego Mission; its design differed little from structures built in Mesopotamia more than 3,000 years earlier. (Huber Papers, WRCA)*

preparing the federal government's *Report on the Lands of the Arid Region of the United States* and helped initiate the so-called "Irrigation Movement."[45] Enthusiasts involved in this movement faced uncertainty over available water supplies; as a result, in 1888 Congress authorized Powell to direct a special irrigation survey that would measure the streamflow of western rivers, locate potential reservoir sites, and assess what land was best suited for agricultural development.[46] In fulfilling this task, Powell helped publicize the relationship between artificial reservoirs and increased agricultural production. The true origins of storage dam construction in the American West, however, lie not in irrigation work but in mining endeavors that evolved out of the California Gold Rush.

Within a few years after gold was discovered at Sutter's Mill in 1848, the industry became dependent on hydraulic mining methods that required water storage for continuous, long-term operation. From the 1850s through the 1870s, rockfill structures such as the English Dam (100 feet high) and the Bowman Dam (96 feet high) were built in the northern Sierra Nevada to supply water for hydraulic mining operations (Fig. 2.17).[47] Utilizing locally quarried rock as the main structural material, these embankment dams could also employ wood planking for the upstream faces or utilize timber cribbing within the structure's interior. Rockfill provided a cheap, durable, and widely available material that was suitable for many sites; as a result, logging and irrigation interests eventually adopted the technology for several structures. These included the 1892 Shaver Lake Dam

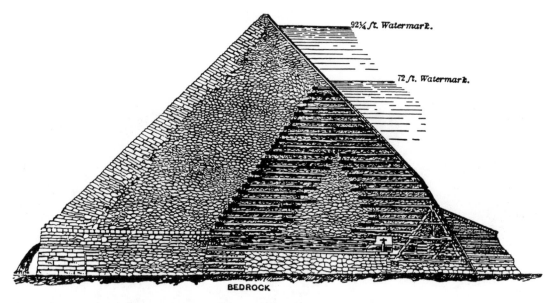

92¼ ft. Watermark.

72 ft. Watermark.

BEDROCK

2.17   *Cross section of Bowman Dam, a timber crib/rockfill structure built to support mining operations in Northern California. Rockfill dams became popular in many parts of the West during the late nineteenth and early twentieth centuries because they utilized locally available materials and could be constructed by relatively unskilled laborers. (Bowie,* A Practical Treatise on Hydraulic Mining in California, *1905)*

(approximately 50 feet high) built by a logging company east of Fresno and the 1897 Escondido Dam (76 feet high) erected north of San Diego to support agricultural development.[48] Rockfill technology was not a panacea for western dam builders, however, since (like all embankment dams) rockfill structures are susceptible to failure by overtopping; the most catastrophic dam collapse in the nineteenth-century American West occurred in February 1890 when floods poured over the 110-foot-high Walnut Grove Dam near Prescott, Arizona, killing more than 120 people in the local mining district.[49]

Earthfill embankment dams are similar to rockfill structures in their use of large amounts of relatively inexpensive material. However, designs of this type were not generally suited for use in early mining systems, because of a lack of readily available, easy-to-transport soil within the rocky terrain of the Sierra Nevada. During the 1860s and 1870s, however, several earthfill dams were built to supply municipal needs in Oakland and San

Francisco. These included the Temescal Dam (105 feet high), the San Leandro Dam (115 feet high), and the San Andreas Dam (77 feet high), which were built with central cores of dense clay to reduce water seepage.

In the late nineteenth century, innovation in earthfill construction did not come so much in design as in devising a new method of moving earth that was cheaper than using horse-pulled carts and scrapers. The key development in the field involved the adaptation of placer mining techniques to earth dam construction. Large-scale hydraulic mining operations would hose down hillsides with pressurized water and then transport the resultant muck by pipe or flume for processing downstream (Fig. 2.18).[50] When this method is used to deliver earth for placement in an embankment dam, it forms what is called a *hydraulic fill dam*.

While construction of the Temescal and San Leandro dams utilized some hydraulic sluicing, the greater portion of these earthen structures was accumulated and placed by

A

B

2.18   *California's nineteenth-century mining industry developed "hydraulicking" as a technique for
processing large quantities of gold-bearing earth. (A) In hydraulic mining, a stream of water under high
pressure is used to create a slurry of wet muck; the muck is then processed to separate gold flakes from
the worthless rock and mud. The technology was subsequently adapted for building "hydraulic fill" earth
dams. (Author's collection) (B) In constructing a hydraulic fill dam, builders arrange for earthen muck
to be transported by flumes to a dam site and then allow it to settle into a large mound. If the structure
is designed properly, the water will drain away, leaving the soil to form an embankment capable of
impounding water. This circa 1905 photograph shows Tenango River Dam No. 1 near Mexico City,
built under the direction of James D. Schuyler.* (Transactions of the American Society of Civil
Engineers, *1907*)

2.19 *San Mateo (Crystal Springs) Dam, a concrete curved gravity structure built to provide San Francisco with water. As shown in this 1895 photograph, the San Mateo Dam featured a massive design similar to major municipal dams in the eastern United States and Europe. (Division of Engineering and Industry, National Museum of American History)*

means of carts and scrapers.[51] In the 1890s, Julius Howells built a 32-foot-high hydraulic fill earth dam as part of a municipal water supply system for Tyler, Texas; he followed this up with a 60-foot-high irrigation dam at La Mesa near San Diego in 1892 and a 70-foot-high dam for the San Joaquin Electric Company at Crane Valley near Fresno in 1902. During this time, Howells introduced James Schuyler to the possibilities of hydraulic fill construction and eventually served as the senior engineer's colleague/assistant on several projects. In 1907, Schuyler published a prominent article on the technology in the *Transactions of the American Society of Civil Engineers,* and the construction technique became widely known.[52] Although some large non-hydraulic fill earth dams continued to

be built in the early twentieth century, in Western America they were largely superseded by hydraulic fill structures, at least until the development of motorized earth-moving equipment in the 1920s and 1930s.[53]

Because the massive gravity designs developed by DeSazilly and his followers required large amounts of material and labor, they were not suited to a region deficient in capital and manpower. Consequently, in the nineteenth-century West, the massive tradition was most closely associated with embankment dam technology. By the 1880s, however, masonry gravity designs proved feasible for some western projects. The most prominent of these was the 1888 San Mateo Dam (Fig. 2.19) (original height, 146 feet) built by the Spring Valley Water Company as part of San

Francisco's water supply system. Constructed out of plain concrete, the San Mateo Dam (also called the Crystal Springs Dam) is a massive curved gravity design featuring an incredibly thick cross-section in which the maximum width (170 feet) actually exceeded the maximum height (146 feet) of the original structure. The use of concrete proved practical because cement could be easily (and inexpensively) transported to the site from barges on nearby San Francisco Bay.

Other masonry gravity dams, such as the Folsom Dam near Sacramento (50 feet high, built using convict labor), Hemet Dam (110 feet high) in Southern California, and the La Grange Dam (125 feet high) in the central part of the state, were built in the 1890s for hydroelectric power production or for irrigation. Nonetheless, the technology did not find great use away from municipal centers.[54] In the early twentieth century, Denver erected the Lake Cheeseman Dam (220 feet high) for municipal water supply; and until completion of New York City's Croton Dam in 1907, this was the tallest water impounding structure in the world.[55] Masonry gravity dams were always expensive to build in the West (as elsewhere), and this limited their construction within the region. However, if a company or city chose to invest sufficient financial resources in a project, the technology could represent a viable option.

2.20 *After the success of the Bear Valley and Sweetwater dams, the structural tradition continued to attract interest among some western dam builders. The 1902 Upper Otay Dam south of San Diego featured a thin arch concrete design, with a height of 84 feet and a maximum thickness of only 14 feet; it was built under the direction of E. S. Babcock, president of the Southern California Mountain Water Company, and constitutes his only known dam design. (Huber Papers, WRCA)*

Despite their economic attributes, structural dams were not widely built in Western America prior to 1900. Nonetheless, a few western structures, such as the 1902 Upper Otay Dam (84 feet high, 14-foot base width) near San Diego (Fig. 2.20) continued the traditions of construction pioneered by Brown at Bear Valley and Schuyler at Sweetwater.[56] Large-scale buttress dams did not constitute a numerically significant portion of western water storage structures, but the few that did exist at the turn of the century helped open the door for future development. The all-wood Faucherie Dam in Northern California, built by mining interests in the 1870s, was a prominent (albeit physically remote) early buttress dam.[57] In 1898 the all-steel Ash Fork Dam in northern Arizona further demonstrated the technology's potential, although the collapse of the Hauser Lake Dam in Montana in 1908 brought interest in this particular form of the technology to an abrupt halt. In contrast, the Ambursen Company's 135-foot-high reinforced concrete La Prele Dam in Wyoming, completed in 1908, offered the promise of a more permanent form of flat-slab buttress structure. By the time the La Prele Dam became operational, the reinforced concrete multiple arch dam had already found expression within the work of John Eastwood, and the West was poised to enter a new era of dam building within the structural tradition.

CHAPTER 3

Early Years in Fresno: Rise and Fall of the San Joaquin Electric Company

*Come to Fresno, the land of sunshine, fruits and flowers! No snow! No ice!
No blizzards! No cyclones! No tempests! No thunder! No lightning! But
health, wealth and happiness for all.*

Description of Fresno County, 1886

*[John S. Eastwoood's] experience in the construction and operation of the
San Joaquin Electric Company's plant at Fresno, Cal., has given him
invaluable information concerning the longest distance high potential
transmission plant in the world, [he] is a very progressive young man.*

Journal of Electricity, April 1897

Born on a farm near Minneapolis, Minnesota, in 1857, John Samuel Eastwood grew up within a first-generation Dutch immigrant family.[1] After spending his adolescence in a rural environment, he matriculated to the University of Minnesota in the late 1870s for training in the technical arts and mathematics. He never formally graduated; but when later queried about his educational background, he spoke proudly of his affiliation with the university.[2] In 1880 Eastwood traveled west to build railroads in the Pacific Northwest, working for three years as a surveyor and construction engineer. In late 1883,

he headed south to Fresno and, aside from short business trips, resided in the Golden State for the remainder of his life.[3]

When Eastwood arrived on the Pacific Coast, mining no longer constituted the only major economic activity in California. After the Civil War, much of the state's economy began to center on agriculture, especially in the several thousand square miles of flat, arable land forming the expansive Central Valley. Drained by the Sacramento River to the north and the San Joaquin River to the south, the ecology of the Central Valley is nourished by numerous streams flowing westward out of

1884.

3.1 *Soon after moving to Fresno, Eastwood (on left) was drawn to the forests of the Sierra Nevada. This photograph records an 1884 visit to a sawmill in the Pine Ridge logging district about 40 miles east of Fresno. (Fresno Historical Society Archives)*

about 20 miles farther south), established a train yard at a site designated as Fresno. In 1874, the settlement became the county seat and soon developed into a regional commercial center; by 1886, 21 irrigation colonies were in active operation, covering an aggregate of 45,000 acres and supporting 7,500 residents. Drawing water from the Kings River or (less frequently) from the San Joaquin River, colonies in Fresno County were promoted by real estate speculators and large landholding syndicates. These entrepreneurs built diversion dams and canals to supply their holdings with water. Small plots (with water rights) were then marketed to prospective farmers lured by flyers advertising "The Most Promising Investment Ever Offered in the Country."[5] In 1875, the Central California Colony offered 20-acre homesteads for $1,000 ("at $100 down and $12.50 per month for six years with no interest") and sold hundreds of lots within three years; similarly, the Washington Colony purchased 7,000 acres of land about 8 miles south of Fresno in 1878 and quickly sold over 380 small tracts.[6]

Presumably attracted by leaflets, posters, or "word-of-mouth" within the world of railroad employees, Eastwood arrived in Fresno in 1883, seeking an outlet for his technical skills. With the division of land for real estate development, the laying out of roads, and the construction of irrigation systems, Fresno and its hinterlands presented a fertile venue for a young "civil engineer–surveyor." Undoubtedly, other parts of California and the West in the early 1880s offered comparable engineering opportunities, but Fresno is where Eastwood chose to put down roots and seek his fortune.[7] Within a few years he had married his wife Ella (a traveling Sunday school teacher from San Francisco), and they became respectable members of the city's nascent professional class.[8] On his arrival, he opened a small office near the courthouse and soon began laying out roads as a "Deputy County Engineer." He also started exploring the mountains east of the city to learn about the Sierra Nevada's voluminous timber resources (Fig. 3.1).[9]

Fresno's agricultural development provided the young engineer with income, but survey-

the Sierra Nevada, the highest mountain range in the continental United States. In the late 1860s and early 1870s, large irrigated ranches were established in the southern half of the Central Valley (usually called the San Joaquin Valley in reference to its largest river).[4] Within a few years irrigation "colonies" were also established, offering the promise of prosperity to small-scale farmers who migrated to the region.

In the early 1870s, the Southern Pacific Railroad extended its tracks southward from the Bay area and, on the table lands between the San Joaquin River and the Kings River (located

ing on a broad, flat terrain is not particularly difficult, and Eastwood sought additional outlets for his skills. Joining with other civic boosters, he began advocating Fresno's formal incorporation as a way to improve municipal services and enhance the community's image. In the fall of 1885, voters approved the incorporation initiative; and in recognition of his support for the measure, Eastwood was appointed Fresno's first city engineer and secretary of the city's health board.[10] Although service as city engineer carried some status, the job entailed minimal pay (mostly derived from fees paid by landowners requiring his services in dividing lots) and involved bureaucratic work that apparently gave him little satisfaction.[11] After a year he left these posi-

tions and never again held a government job. While his interest in fostering the "progressive" development of Fresno and the West as a whole continued throughout his life, Eastwood subsequently concentrated on endeavors supported by private capital.

During the next few years he displayed great entrepreneurial zeal in exploring professional ventures that encompassed the fields of logging, mining, petroleum development, irrigation, and eventually electric power generation (Fig. 3.2). The California State Mining Bureau's *Tenth Annual Report of the State Mineralogist* (1890) credits him as a source "for much information" on the resources of Fresno County, and filings in the county recorder's office chronicle several min-

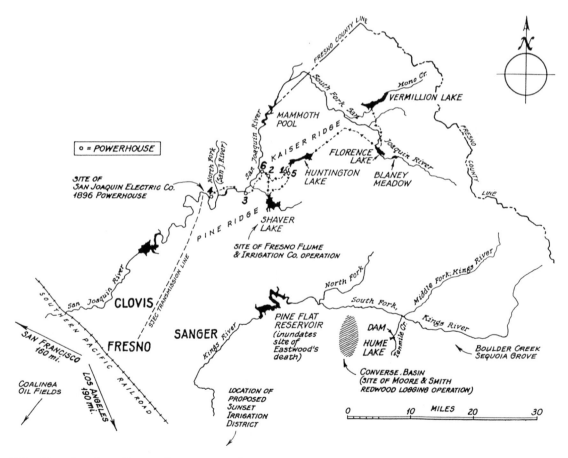

3.2 *Map identifying Eastwood's activities in the Fresno region, including elements of the Big Creek hydroelectric system. (Author's collection, courtesy of Richard K. Anderson)*

ing claims in his name (for both placer mines in the Sierra Nevada and oil tracts in the Coalinga district) and land purchases that document his far-ranging search to exploit the region's natural resources. In addition, during 1888 he surveyed the Mountain View Cemetery (where he is now buried), and a few years later he laid out the 8-mile-long Kearney Boulevard leading out of Fresno to the estate of Theodore Kearney.[12] But after he relinquished the post of city engineer, Eastwood's most important work occurred in the Sierra Nevada, where an expanding lumber industry offered challenges in the cutting, processing, and transporting of timber.[13]

Because of their remote location and mas-

sive size, the region's giant sequoia (which, aside from some fungi, are considered the world's largest living organisms) and big sugar pine presented special problems to logging entrepreneurs. In particular, loggers were hard pressed to transport cut timber out of the mountains at costs low enough to permit commercial marketing. In the 1870s and early 1880s, giant sequoia began to be harvested as a source of commercial lumber (Fig. 3.3); the earliest trees to be felled grew at relatively low elevations (the species only flourishes between 4,000 and 7,000 feet above sea level), and the cut logs were simply hauled down to the valley by teams of oxen. Hauling proved inefficient for logging operations at

3.3 *The felling of the "Mark Twain" giant sequoia in the upper Kings River Basin, 1891. Although Eastwood is not known to have participated in the actual cutting of redwood and big pine, he estimated timber quantities in various groves and surveyed rights-of-way for logging roads and lumber flumes during the 1880s and early 1890s. (Fresno Historical Society Archives)*

higher elevations, however, and it would have been too expensive to build a railroad through the steep and rough terrain of the upper Kings River watershed. Instead, the preferred means of conveyance became a flume in which timber was floated down from a mountain sawmill to a site accessible to railroads in the lower valley. Lumber flumes were usually built with a gradient (or drop) of about 30 feet per mile and could extend for more than 50 miles. As water flowed down the flume, it could carry a sizable continuous "cargo" of timber downstream, Surveying a flume line is not appreciably different from laying out a railroad right-of-way. The key is to ensure that the flume maintains a steady decline in elevation without steep drops or flat stretches.[14]

In 1886, Eastwood joined the Smith and Moore outfit (later known as both the Kings River Lumber Company and the Sanger Lumber Company) to lay out the right-of-way for the company's 54-mile-long flume from the Millwood sawmill to lumber yards in Sanger. He also compiled section-by-section estimates of the quantities of redwood timber available in the famous "Converse Basin" and in the Boulder Creek district; eventually, he purchased in his own name a 160-acre tract in the Boulder Creek sequoia grove about 30 miles east of Millwood.[15]

In competing with firms from the Pacific Northwest (who could market timber relatively easily), loggers in the Sierra Nevada operated at an economic disadvantage. This prompted detailed surveys of terrain and the construction of extraordinary lumber flumes. By modern standards, however, the techniques employed by loggers to harvest huge, ancient trees deep in the mountains caused a great waste of timber; and concerns about the wanton destruction of America's timber resources during the period energized conservation efforts by Gifford Pinchot and others in promoting the federal Forest Service.[16] In locating timber tracts and in surveying locations for flumes and roads, Eastwood exhibited no hesitancy or regret at facilitating the felling and removal of some of the most remarkable trees in the world. Thus, whereas naturalist John Muir explored the virgin Kings River sequoia groves with a feeling of religious awe, Eastwood could view them simply as a resource to be utilized in the natural course of furthering California's economic growth.[17]

While remaining intermittently involved in the Kings River sequoia logging industry through the early 1890s, Eastwood also became engaged with the Fresno Flume and Irrigation Company's operations in the San Joaquin River watershed about 40 miles further north. This company was primarily devoted to logging sugar pines, but it appreciated that the water carried through its flume (Fig. 3.4) subsequently could be used for irrigation. Besides laying out a railroad in the mountains to deliver cut trees to the logging pond/sawmill, Eastwood devoted much of his time to planning the company's irrigation system surrounding Clovis.[18] During his tenure, the company also built a large rockfill dam to impound the Shaver Lake logging pond, at an elevation of more than 5,000 feet above sea level. Although he is not known to have participated in this project, he was undoubtedly familiar with the work, which would have acquainted him first-hand with problems involved in building storage dams.[19]

As he gradually shifted his attention away from the logging industry, Eastwood began to pay special heed to irrigation development in the San Joaquin Valley—an area of endeavor that constituted a significant part of his work for the Fresno Flume and Irrigation Company. By the early 1890s, the "colony" system of irrigation (popularized in the 1870s) had largely run its course, and farmers and irrigation proponents were seeking new ways to finance projects. The limitations of the colony system, along with recent legal rulings involving water rights in California, prompted passage of the 1887 Wright Act. Named for C. C. Wright, a legislator from Modesto, this state law authorized the creation of irrigation districts to be funded through publicly sanctioned bond sales. During the late 1880s and early 1890s, this statute fostered many proj-

3.4 *Part of the 46-mile-long Fresno Lumber and Irrigation Company lumber flume connecting Shaver Lake to the town of Clovis in the lower San Joaquin Valley. Eastwood worked for the company during construction of the flume in the early 1890s. (Fresno Historical Society Archives)*

ects, including the Sunset Irrigation District south of Fresno along the banks of the lower Kings River.[20]

Following the district's initial promotional stage, Eastwood succeeded Hermann Schussler (a prominent consultant who also served as chief engineer for San Francisco's Spring Valley Water Company) in planning the water distribution system. Developed around a plan to utilize water rights held by the Rancho Laguna de Teche (a large land grant dating to the Mexican era), the Sunset District seemed an ambitious but viable irrigation project. It became mired in controversy, however, when promoters tried to manipulate financing arrangements and use bonds to pay off debts on lands that lay outside the district's jurisdiction. Once this fraud came to light, investors grew wary and funding collapsed. Eastwood was not personally associated with any of the irregularities that

sullied the Sunset District, and he perhaps took solace in the fact that many other early Wright Act districts experienced financial distress.[21]

Despite the Sunset failure, Eastwood did not lose interest in furthering Fresno's economic growth. Instead, he soon initiated plans for the San Joaquin Electric Company, one of the West's most noteworthy early hydroelectric power projects. In becoming the company's chief engineer, he ended the apprenticeship phase of his career and moved into the high-powered world of finance capital and sophisticated technological systems centered on the West's water resources. On the surface, little in Eastwood's early career distinguishes him as an engineer of uncommon experience; his education at the University of Minnesota was not particularly eminent, and his involvement in railroad construction fit a pattern common among nineteenth-century civil engineers. In migrating to Fresno, he abandoned the nomadic life of a railroad engineer; but once settled in the city, he was drawn to the Sierra Nevada, where he demonstrated skill as a surveyor in a harsh, mountainous terrain. His tenure as city engineer as well as his work with the Sunset Irrigation District certainly provide evidence of a desire to improve the material quality of community life, but his vision of technological progress found its most important expression when combined with experience he gained in the mountains. In the 1890s, working from his knowledge of mountain streams, he became a pioneer proponent of hydroelectric power technologies that soon transformed the character of California's culture and economy.

ELECTRIC POWER DEVELOPMENT IN CALIFORNIA

The San Joaquin Electric Company (SJEC) was not Fresno's first utility. A few small gas companies supplied heating and lighting service to parts of the city in the 1880s; and by the early 1890s, the Fresno Gas and Electric Company was providing small amounts of electricity, using a coal-powered direct-current generator. This plant did not offer any possibility of extended growth or expansion, however, because it depended on expensive fossil fuels as a power source. By August 1894, the situation had grown critical: a newspaper article under the headline "Doused the Glim: The Electric Light Turned Off for a Time, the Company Replaces it with Gas" reported that "the company [has been] running the works at a loss since the city lights were cut off . . . rumors abroad that the [Fresno Gas and Electric Company will] lose its franchise."[22] It was clear by the mid-1890s that, if Fresno was to support a substantial electric power system, that system could not be based on fossil fuels.

For many years, California engineers had recognized the power potential inherent in the swift mountain streams of the Sierra Nevada; prior to the 1890s, however, they were prevented from utilizing most of this power by the fact that it was situated far from any commercial or municipal market. Electricity offered a means of surmounting this obstacle, but only if a way could be found to transmit current efficiently over long distances for both lighting and power. Direct current (DC) and single-phase alternating (AC) systems could not manage this feat, but then it was discovered in the late 1880s that systems employing more than one circuit of alternating current (that is, polyphase AC) could. In the summer of 1891, German engineers attracted international attention by building a 112-mile, 30,000-volt, three-phase transmission line between Lauffen and Frankfurt, Germany. This line was not put to practical use, but it did demonstrate the viability of polyphase AC technology. And within a year, its success spawned construction of the world's first commercial polyphase AC system, serving Heilbronn, Germany.[23] In 1893, the world's second (and America's first) commercial three-phase AC system came on-line in Redlands, California. Designed by Almerian W. Decker, the Redlands plant established California as a key center for polyphase power development.

Born in 1852, Almerian Decker spent his early career in Cleveland as an electroplater before tuberculosis prompted him to move to Southern California in 1891. In the fall of that year, the San Antonio Light and Power Company in Pomona designated Decker as its electrical engineer, and the development of hydroelectric power in California entered a new era.[24] Under Decker's guidance, the company accepted Westinghouse's plans for a 10,000-volt, single-phase system that would serve Pomona over a 15-mile-long line and San Bernardino over a separate 28-mile-long circuit. Although limited to providing power for lighting, the Pomona plant featured the highest voltage ever employed for commercial service in the United States at the time it came on-line in 1892.[25]

After completion of the Pomona plant, Decker joined the Redlands Electric Light and Power Company to help plan another hydroelectric power system for Southern California. Led by president H. H. Sinclair, an electrical engineering graduate from Cornell University who would later become a major advocate of Eastwood's multiple arch dams, this company sought to generate polyphase AC power in a hydropower plant on Mill Creek (a tributary of the Santa Ana River) and distribute it throughout the San Bernardino/Redlands region.[26] Aware of the Frankfurt–Lauffen success, Decker set out to convince electrical manufacturers of the superiority of polyphase technology.[27] Almost contemporaneously with Decker's call for bids in February 1893, General Electric had begun searching for ways to compete with Westinghouse in manufacturing AC systems.[28] Decker understood the economic advantages of three-phase technology—especially in regions where power sites are located far from population centers—and so, with Sinclair's backing, he rejected Westinghouse's two-phase proposal in favor of a General Electric three-phase system.[29] Although General Electric limited the facility to 2,500 volts (instead of the 5,000 volts Decker had requested) and did not use high-voltage transformers, Redlands became America's first commercial polyphase system.[30]

Shortly before "start-up" of the Redlands plant in fall 1893, Decker succumbed to tuberculosis. The success of his work at Redlands, however, helped General Electric establish a regional office in San Francisco, and the company soon began promoting its three-phase system as a technology ideally suited to conditions in the West. In recognition of Decker's pioneering role in this effort, the *Journal of Electricity Power and Gas* described him in 1903 as the "first to define presently accepted practices in transmission engineering."[31]

In 1894, General Electric's Pacific coast office initiated work on a system to supply Sacramento with hydroelectric power. Formed as an adjunct to the Folsom Water Power Company, the Sacramento Electric Power and Light Company built a 22-mile-long, 11,000-volt, three-phase transmission line from a power station on the American River at Folsom to downtown Sacramento.[32] Put on-line in July 1895, the system incorporated transformers that allowed significantly higher voltages than those used at Redlands; as such, it represented a significant advance in the field of electrical technology. But in terms of hydraulic technology, it bore little resemblance to the western hydroelectric power systems that would follow. The Folsom plant operated under a head of 55 feet and relied on a huge overflow masonry dam to create its power drop. The project was only feasible because convict laborers (supplied from nearby Folsom Prison) built what otherwise would have been a prohibitively expensive gravity dam.[33]

THE SAN JOAQUIN ELECTRIC COMPANY

Three months before the Sacramento system came on-line in the summer of 1895, Eastwood began construction of the first electric power plant to incorporate every element of what technological historian Thomas Hughes terms the "California Style" of hydroelectric power system.[34] This style features three key components: high-voltage, three-phase AC technology; high head penstocks; and long-distance transmission lines from remote sites in the mountains to load centers in the lowlands. Decker's Redland's plant was an important prototype of the style, but it operated under a relatively modest pressure of 2,500 volts, utilized a hydraulic head of less than 400 feet, and transmitted power less than 10 miles. The Folsom–Sacramento system transmitted power 22 miles under a pressure of 11,000 volts (and used transformers), but its turbines operated under a head of less than 60 feet. At Fresno, Eastwood combined for the first time all of the style's elements—high head (1,410 feet), long distance (35 miles), and high voltage (11,000 volts)—in a three-phase system. At the time of the plant's construction, no power system in the world operated under a higher head or transmitted power over a greater distance, and no other commercial system utilized a higher voltage.[35]

For its electrical technology the SJEC system depended on equipment supplied by General Electric; fabrication of the penstock was handled by the Risdon Iron and Locomotive Works of San Francisco and the National Tube Works of McKeesport, Pennsylvania.[36] But in devising the system's overall physical layout and hydraulic design, Eastwood relied on his knowledge of the San Joaquin watershed and on engineering skills acquired during his early career. He had frequently journeyed through the territory drained by the San Joaquin River, and he understood how various streams, tributaries, and ridges related to one another; this practical knowledge of topographic conditions underlay formulation of the Fresno plant as an engineering system.[37] A lack of documentary records makes it difficult to explain exactly how Eastwood was introduced to the idea of building an electric power facility at such an early stage in the development of polyphase AC technology. Clearly, he kept abreast of engineering advances in the technical press; and at some point in 1894, he must have commenced communications with General Electric's Pacific Coast office. However, he acted independently in adapting polyphase technology to the physical conditions and commercial needs of a city that, theretofore, had been undistinguished in any national context.

In November 1893, Eastwood filed his first claim to use water from the North Fork of the San Joaquin River; two months later, he joined with J. J. Seymour, president of the Fresno Water Company, to promote a hydroelectric power system based on these filings.[38] In April 1895, the SJEC was formally incorporated, with Seymour as president and Eastwood as vice president and chief engineer.[39] The substantial capital required to build the proposed power system forced the company to

look for support beyond the Fresno business community. Through the influence of Seymour's brother-in-law Julius Howells, the SJEC obtained financing from the Municipal Investment Company of Chicago.[40] The exact cost of construction is unknown, but in 1895 the *Fresno Daily Evening Expositor* reported that "around $200,000" would be expended initially to bring the system on-line.[41] Although huge by the standards of nineteenth-century Fresno, this level of financing allowed the company to erect little more than the most basic facilities necessary to operate the system. In retrospect, the most significant effect of the firm's limited capitalization was the rather small retaining basin (90 acre-feet capacity) constructed to store water above the penstocks. Formed by a 20-foot-high earth embankment, this basin (later called Corinne Lake) served as a meager substitute for a large storage reservoir that could impound the North Fork's spring floodwaters for use later in the year.[42]

In overseeing building activities that stretched out over more than 40 miles of sparsely settled territory, Eastwood could obtain only minimal guidance from other hydroelectric projects and from published sources.[43] Starting in the spring of 1895, he led a survey team that laid out the flume/ditch system, the alignment of the penstock, and the right-of-way for the transmission line. Although some lumber mills and the remains of a few mining operations fell within the area encompassed by the hydroelectric plant, Eastwood made no use of any preexisting flumes or ditches.[44] To provide access to the powerhouse, a new 4-mile-long road was built from the small community of Auberry; all electrical equipment and steel pipe came in over this road. Because the plant was located on the north side of the San Joaquin River, Eastwood built a large wooden truss bridge to carry equipment over the river. Wood for the flumes came from sawmills in the area; granite for the powerhouse came from local quarries. Aside from the work done by a General Electric crew responsible for stringing the power line and installing the

3.5   *Eastwood sitting atop a section of the newly completed San Joaquin Electric Company ditch/flume system, 1895. (A. W. Peters Collection, Fresno Historical Society Archives)*

3.6   *The aqueduct spanning the North Fork of the San Joaquin River, bringing the flow of Willow Creek into the SJEC's main diversion ditch, 1895. The graceful curve of the structure presages Eastwood's later use of the arch in dam design. (A. W. Peters Collection, Fresno Historical Society Archives)*

3.7   *Clearing the shallow retaining basin (Corinne Lake) used to regulate waterflow into the SJEC penstock, 1895. Because the company did not have enough funds to build a major storage dam, this small reservoir served as the system's only means of mitigating the effect of drought. (A. W. Peters Collection, Fresno Historical Society Archives)*

electrical equipment, all construction was carried out by scores of workers drawn from local agricultural, mining, and logging operations.[45]

Water for the SJEC's plant was diverted from two branches of the North Fork of the San Joaquin River (today known as Willow Creek and Chilkoot Creek) and transported through 7 miles of flumes and ditches (Figs. 3.5 and 3.6).[46] The terrain of the region is so steep that, within these 7 miles, the riverbed drops vertically more than 1,400 feet. From the retaining basin built at the end of the diversion ditch, water entered a 4,020-foot-long steel penstock connected to the granite powerhouse (Figs. 3.7. 3.8, and 3.9). At the powerhouse, the water reached a pressure of 609 pounds per square inch. Under this extreme pressure, a small stream of water was released from the penstock and directed toward the Pelton water wheels. A drive shaft extending through the wall of the powerhouse connected the spinning Pelton wheels to three

350-kilowatt, 700-volt, three-phase generators (Fig. 3.10). Air-cooled transformers raised the current's potential to 11,000 volts before transmission over the 35-mile-long line to Fresno (Fig. 3.11).

By the beginning of 1896 the powerhouse and water delivery system were almost complete, and the company began stringing the transmission line.[47] Full-scale testing of the generating system occurred on April 3, 1896, and the *Evening Expositor* reported that "for the first time water was turned on and the country in the vicinity of the powerhouse was transformed into a scene of brilliant splendor . . . the power was turned on about 7 o'clock in the evening, the test continuing for about two hours."[48] Eleven days later, Ella Eastwood pushed a button at the Fresno substation alerting her husband to open a valve on the penstock. This caused the three-phase generators to spin, current to flow through the transmission line, and illumination to flood the Fresno County courthouse.[49] During the

3.8 *Workers take a break while hauling sections of the SJEC penstock, 1895. This 4,000-foot-long pipeline delivered water from Corinne Lake down to the powerhouse on the banks of the San Joaquin River. The penstock dropped a vertical distance of 1,410 feet, providing the highest "head" of any hydroelectric plant in the world in 1896. (A. W. Peters Collection, Fresno Historical Society Archives)*

3.9 *Exterior of the completed SJEC powerhouse, 1896. The penstock is buried in the foreground and connects into the receiving tube on the building's left side. The power lines leave the building through the opening at the end of the roof. (A. W. Peters Collection, Fresno Historical Society Archives)*

3.10   *A 700-horsepower, three-phase AC generator inside the SJEC powerhouse, directly connected to a Pelton water wheel via a drive shaft extending through the exterior wall. The device on the left was used to regulate the rotational speed of the generator. (A. W. Peters Collection, Fresno Historical Society Archives)*

spring, the new system experienced a few initial glitches with the electrical equipment; but by early summer, the company was supplying power for irrigation pumps, for the Fresno Water Company, and for the Sperry Flour Mill in downtown Fresno.[50] On June 25, the *Evening Expositor* noted that "at noon yesterday the Fresno Agricultural Works company abandoned steam power in favor of electrical, and today the ponderous machinery of that big establishment is being moved by 'the mysterious agent.'" Soon thereafter, to the dismay of the competing Fresno Gas and Electric Company, the SJEC's system began delivering electric power for residential use and for the city's municipal street lights.[51]

Eastwood proved adept at operating the SJEC, and the San Francisco–based *Journal of Electricity* soon featured the system in two major articles; periodicals such as *Electrical World* (published in New York) and the London-based *Electrical Review* also described it in laudatory tones.[52] Only a few years earlier,

Eastwood was at most a minor engineer of regional significance; now he had achieved a measure of national recognition. The April 1897 *Journal of Electricity* commented that his "excellent knowledge of electrical transmissions and his extended practical experience ha[ve] given him a vast fund of most interesting and valuable experience in the art [of hydroelectric power]."[53]

Following the successes at Redlands, Sacramento, and Fresno, polyphase power projects began to spring up throughout California and the West, and a professional community of engineers and financiers interested in electric power systems arose on the Pacific coast. The region gained further notice and visibility in 1895 when George P. Low began publishing the *Journal of Electricity* in San Francisco. Later known as the *Journal of Electricity Power and Gas*, this monthly publication provided information on western power systems, new technologies and inventions, books, people, and professional

3.11 *A work crew from General Electric stringing the transmission line connecting Fresno with the SJEC powerhouse 35 miles away. In the spring of 1896, this constituted the world's longest commercial electric power transmission line. (A. W. Peters Collection, Fresno Historical Society Archives)*

activities.[54] In 1897, Low's journal fostered establishment of Pacific Coast Electric Transmission Association (PCETA), a professional association dedicated to improving the electrical arts in Western America.[55] Although the PCETA flourished for little more than five years, during this time it attracted the attention of almost all key participants in the development of the region's commercial electric power systems.

The first PCETA convention took place in Santa Cruz, California, on August 17, 1897. The SJEC was well represented at the meeting. Seymour was appointed to the Board of Directors, and Eastwood presented a paper describing the company's 35-mile-long transmission line. Published under the title "The Construction of Transmission Lines," this paper represented Eastwood's first foray into the larger professional engineering world. In his PCETA presentation, Eastwood discussed particular issues associated with pole line construction (such as the advantages of straight transmission lines versus the expense of obtaining right-of-way); however, the paper is perhaps most significant in documenting his espousal of engineering efficiency. He asserted:

Good engineering consists of good judgment, mingled with technical knowledge . . . [and occurs when] all the factors bearing on the case are given their proper value in the resulting equation. . . . [This leads to] work costing the least money for construction consistent with the most economical maintenance.[56]

Clearly, Eastwood did not view engineering problems as existing in isolation from the marketplace; with the construction of the SJEC project, he had his first opportunity to grapple with the economic ramifications of building and operating a large-scale technological system. Unfortunately for him and for the SJEC as a whole, the company soon experienced the bitter reality of failure within a capitalist economy.

FAILURE OF THE SJEC

In the late 1890s, hydroelectric power development in California and other parts of the West continued to accelerate. By 1898, transmission lines were operating at potentials of 16,000 volts and stretching for more than 60 miles.[57] Eastwood was on the cutting edge of these technological advances. In the summer of 1898, he upgraded the SJEC's main transmission line to 16,000 volts and lengthened it to 68 miles in order to reach the H. G. Lacey Company's electric distribution system in Hanford, 30 miles south of Fresno.[58] On the surface, the future appeared bright, but two major problems plagued the SJEC: one due to competitive maneuvering by the gas company, and one that resulted from the vagaries of California's unpredictable climate.

The SJEC's early operation reportedly was impeded by sawdust released into the river above its diversion flume. Although the company denied the existence of such problems, rumors of this type highlighted difficulties in protecting waterflow in the upper North Fork watershed.[59] The Fresno Gas and Electric Company exploited this vulnerability by convincing the owners of the Goode Ranch (located upstream from the SJEC's flume) to divert water out of the North Fork and thus prevent its use in electric power production.[60] In addition, the SJEC and the gas company squared off over Fresno's municipal lighting franchise. To obtain this contract, Eastwood and Seymour offered the city low rates, an action that reduced their company's cash flow but ensured support from city trustees. Subsequently, the political influence of the gas company seems to have been behind delays in payments to the SJEC that were supposedly occasioned by shortages in the city treasury. In addition, while the SJEC wanted to provide continuous dusk-to-dawn street lighting, the gas company lobbied to minimize the city's electrical bill by limiting full service to "moonless" nights. On other nights, the lights were to be operational for only five hours.[61]

During times of normal precipitation, the gas company's actions might have hindered the SJEC's operation, but probably would not have threatened its corporate existence. The late 1890s, however, constituted one of the driest periods in California history.[62] As the hydraulic engineer J. B. Lippincott later acknowledged: "From seventy-five years of rainfall records in Southern California we have found that the seven year period extending from 1897–98 to 1903–04 is the critical or driest group of years."[63] Similarly, historian Donald Pisani recently reported that "overall, 1898 was California's driest year in two decades."[64] Approximately 80 percent of precipitation in the San Joaquin River watershed accumulates as rain and snowfall in the mountains between December and March; but 80 percent of the river flow occurs between April and July.[65] Consequently, even during the wettest years, water becomes scarce between August and November; in times of drought, this period of dryness becomes more extensive and debilitating.

Of course, the best way to mitigate drought conditions is by building a storage dam to retain spring floods for distribution later in the year. Early on, Eastwood had appreciated the importance of water storage, but he had been limited to building only a small retaining basin (Corinne Lake) above the penstock. Based on hydrological conditions in the 1880s and early 1890s, the normal flow of the San Joaquin's North Fork appeared capable of meeting the company's initial power production needs. Consequently, in 1895 the SJEC did not seem to be acting imprudently when it focused on getting the system on-line and generating revenue instead of on building a more substantial storage dam. Three years later, in April 1898, Eastwood and Seymour sought to expand the reservoir capacity of the SJEC system, filing a "notice of reservoir location" for a dam across the North Fork of the San Joaquin.[66] But dams do not create water; they only store what nature provides. The prolonged drought thus rendered this initiative inconsequential in the short term.

The combined effect of the drought and the actions of the gas company proved devastating for the SJEC. During 1898–1899, the company experienced extreme difficulty in keeping its penstock full of water; the generators could only operate intermittently, and

revenues rapidly declined. Finally, in August 1899, the SJEC could not make its bond payments, and the firm went into receivership.[67] The bankruptcy action reflected the company's poor financial condition, but the bondholders understood that the drought was primarily responsible for the failure. In recognition of this, they appointed Seymour the receiver in charge of business activities, while Eastwood continued overseeing technical operations. However, both men were now displaced from any long-term financial interest in the firm.

During the three years following its financial failure, the SJEC remained operational. Although the company was technically bankrupt, its bondholders wished to protect their investment, so they raised funds to finance construction of a storage dam along the North Fork of the San Joaquin River. Eastwood surveyed the site for this dam, but he was not put in charge of constructing it. This responsibility fell to Julius Howells, Seymour's brother-in-law and an engineer who was gaining a reputation as a builder of hydraulic fill dams.[68] Known as the Crane Valley Dam (Fig. 3.12), Howells's structure formed the reservoir now called Bass Lake. The earthen dam was erected in 1901 but installation of a defective outlet pipe almost triggered its collapse during construction. Water from the moisture-laden earthfill began to seep into the damaged pipe and cause internal erosion. Howells halted this erosion before complete loss of stability, but prudence dictated that the dam be limited to 70 feet in height rather than the 100 feet originally planned. Although he was not responsible for this project, Eastwood learned during the construction process of both the possibilities and the limitations inherent in hydraulic fill technology.[69]

With the drought's gradual alleviation, the SJEC became more attractive as an investment property. The company's bondholders wished to liquidate their holdings and apparently offered to sell an option on their interests for $35,000. However, even this modest price remained beyond the financial means

3.12   *Crane Valley Dam shortly after construction in 1902. Eastwood did not build this earthen structure, but he surveyed both the site and the right-of-way for the ditch that transported the hydraulic fill. (A. W. Peters Collection, Fresno Historical Society Archives)*

of any Fresno investors.[70] Into the breach stepped two southern California businessmen who figured prominently in Eastwood's subsequent work (discussed in Chapter 4). In August 1902, William Kerckhoff and Allan C. Balch bought the option to purchase the SJEC's outstanding bonds; and the next year, they reorganized the firm as the San Joaquin Power Company (which eventually evolved into the San Joaquin Light and Power Corporation).[71] They placed A. G. Wishon, former manager of the nearby Mount Whitney Power Company, in charge and arranged a truce with the gas company whereby each agreed not to interfere in the other's operation.[72] With their access to financial capital,

Kerckhoff and Balch successfully expanded the former SJEC system, and the enterprise became very profitable—eventually merging with the Pacific Gas and Electric Company in 1931.

Eastwood's Fresno plant represented a major technological advance in the development of high-head, long-distance, high-voltage AC transmission systems, and the bankruptcy of the SJEC should not be ascribed to mismanagement or malfeasance. Instead, the economic failings of the company reflect the perils that beset any undercapitalized enterprise struggling to create a market within a competitive environment. The drought of 1898–1899 devastated the SJEC, diminishing revenues while the company's financial obligations to bondholders remained constant. If initially the company had been able to build a storage reservoir, it is less likely that the drought would have precipitated bankruptcy in 1899. But lacking such capital, Eastwood and Seymour had only one "safe" alternative: to abandon their plans and await some unspecified time when success could somehow be assured. Rather than demur in the face of risk, they forged ahead. Although Eastwood received little monetary reward for conceiving and building the SJEC system, he was evidently gratified that the system ultimately proved to be both a technological and a financial success. By the time the San Joaquin Power Company took over the SJEC, he was already promoting plans for a hydroelectric power system that dwarfed his original foray into the field. And for this new project, he was to devote special attention to the problem of water storage.

CHAPTER 4

Big Creek, Henry Huntington, and the Origins of the Multiple Arch Dam (1900–1907)

No stream can be assumed to have been developed to its true value as a power source unless some portion of the water used is stored to fill the gap caused by an occasional dry year or drought period.

John S. Eastwood, 1902

Having had occasion to design dams for a large proposed hydroelectric development on Big Creek, a tributary of the San Joaquin River, where the reservoir site called for three dams of considerable size, the subject of dams was gone into with a view of reaching the ultimate type, having in mind the characteristics of permanence and stability, coupled with economic capital cost and upkeep.

John S. Eastwood, 1909

The bankruptcy of the San Joaquin Electric Company forced Eastwood to realize that adequate upstream water storage was mandatory for any major hydroelectric power system in California. He also appreciated that prospective financiers would require assurance that the whims of Nature could not render their investment worthless. With this in mind, Eastwood began exploring the upper San Joaquin River watershed for potential reservoir sites and, by 1900, began planning a system to harness the hydraulic power of the river's main stem. The

SJEC's plant utilized the relatively small flow of the San Joaquin's North Fork, a stream with a watershed extending to an elevation of less than 8,000 feet. In contrast, the remainder of the San Joaquin watershed rises to elevations exceeding 13,000 feet, encompassing almost thirty times the drainage area of the North Fork. And where the original SJEC system provided a capacity of less than 2,000 HP, development of power plants on the upper San Joaquin offered to provide more than 100 times this amount.

59

4.1   *The flow of the San Joaquin River at Mammoth Pool, summer 1901. Eastwood initially proposed building a rockfill diversion dam at the site by blasting granite into the riverbed. (Henry E. Huntington Library)*

By 1901, the drought afflicting central California began to subside, and interest in hydroelectric power development gained momentum. The viability of long-distance power transmission had received a significant boost from completion of an 83-mile-long, 33,000-volt Santa Ana-to-Los Angeles transmission line in 1899 that soon merged into the Edison Electric Company of Los Angeles to create a regional network for Southern California.[1] Northern California also fostered the growth of long-distance systems, as engineers and businessmen realized that hydroelectric plants built for mining operations northeast of Sacramento could serve the San Francisco environs. Most notably, the possi-

bility of transmitting power out of the Sierra Nevada culminated in the Bay Counties Power Company's 1900–1901 construction of a 142-mile-long, 40,000-volt line from the Colgate Powerhouse to Oakland.[2] Eastwood was not involved with the Bay Counties system, but its success encouraged him to promote his own power plan for the San Francisco market.

Joining with H. G. Lacey and other local investors who had helped sponsor the SJEC's Hanford extension, Eastwood formed the Mammoth Power Company in October 1900 to develop a hydroelectric power plant along the upper San Joaquin. After months of reconnaissance in the mountains, at times accompanied by Lacey's son Robert and by photographer A. W. Peters, who assisted him in surveying and filing water rights claims, Eastwood proposed building a new 120,000-HP generating plant based on diverting water from the San Joaquin River at Mammoth Pool, a site about 30 miles upstream from the 1896 SJEC plant (Figs. 4.1 and 4.2).[3] Water from Mammoth Pool was to flow through a 20-mile-long tunnel (designed to ensure year-round, ice-free operation), and feed into pressurized (1,700-foot head) penstocks connected to a large powerhouse on the banks of the lower San Joaquin. High-voltage, three-phase AC current would then reach consumers in San Francisco via a 200-mile-long transmission line. First distributed in September 1901, Eastwood's Mammoth Power Company proposal stressed the importance of ensuring a "permanent water supply" and described the location of six storage reservoirs high in the headwaters of the San Joaquin. To allow the retention of spring snowmelt, he envisaged enlarging several natural lakes by erecting dams 25 to 40 feet high (mostly of rockfill or earthfill design) across their outlet streams. Eastwood proposed enlarging the natural storage capacity of Mammoth Pool it-

4.2 *August 1901 photograph of Garnet Lake, taken by A. W. Peters as part of efforts to promote the Mammoth Power Company. As with several other natural lakes in the upper San Joaquin watershed, Eastwood proposed to build a small dam across Garnet Lake's outlet and create a storage reservoir that would ensure a steady water supply for the Mammoth power plant. In the background, Banner Peak extends to a height of more than 12,000 feet above sea level. (Henry E. Huntington Library)*

4.3   *Big Creek Falls, circa 1902, showing streamflow as it drops toward the main stem of the San Joaquin River. (Fresno Historical Society Archives)*

self by blasting apart a massive outcropping of granite to create a rockfill diversion dam extending about 40 feet above normal river level.[4]

Eastwood intended his Mammoth Pool prospectus to illuminate the project's feasibility, and he actively promoted the scheme to the engineering/financial community. In early November, for example, hydroelectric power entrepreneur H. H. Sinclair (the vice president and general manager of power development for the Edison Electric Company) came north from Los Angeles to meet with him in Fresno.[5] Nonetheless, fears of not find-

ing a reliable market for this prodigious amount of power, along with concerns over the 20-mile-long tunnel, curtailed interest among financiers and businessmen.[6] By the end of 1901, Lacey and his associates' interest in the proposal flagged, and the Mammoth Power Company ceased to be promoted actively as an investment opportunity. Despite the lack of support, however, Eastwood held fast to his hopes for a new hydroelectric power project, and during early 1902 he dramatically transformed and enlarged plans for the proposed upper San Joaquin system.

Flowing north and west out of the upper

reaches of the Sierra Nevada, the San Joaquin River follows a pronounced curve or hook. In the middle of this hook lies Kaiser Ridge, a tall outcropping that rises to an altitude of more than 10,000 feet and separates the upper San Joaquin from the watershed of Big Creek. Big Creek is an important tributary of the San Joaquin River, but (because of Kaiser Ridge) does not enter the main stream until it has dropped to an elevation of about 2,300 feet (Fig. 4.3). In his earlier scheme, Eastwood simply proposed adding the flow of Big Creek into the Mammoth Pool diversion tunnel. By early 1902, he realized that the geographical relationship of the Big Creek basin and the upper San Joaquin offered an opportunity to de-

velop an even greater proportion of the region's hydraulic power potential.

Rather than concentrating the water power into a single generating facility, Eastwood now envisaged a series of power plants operating under a cumulative head of almost 6,000 feet. Water from the upper San Joaquin River ultimately would be diverted through a tunnel drilled under Kaiser Ridge (known today as Ward Tunnel) and stored in a reservoir built at the headwaters of Big Creek. This artificial lake would be formed by three dams positioned to close topographical "gaps" at the periphery of a natural depression called the Big Creek Basin (Fig. 4.4); the reservoir would hold more than 100,000

4.4 *View looking out over the Big Creek Basin, at an elevation almost 7,000 feet above sea level. In 1902, Eastwood proposed transforming the basin into a storage reservoir. The top of the hill in the center now forms a small island in the middle of Huntington Lake. (Author's collection, courtesy of Charles Allan Whitney)*

acre-feet of water at an elevation 6,900 feet above sea level. His revised scheme did not abandon the idea of building a dam/tunnel facility to exploit the power potential of the Mammoth Pool site, it merely subordinated the earlier plan to a more productive project focusing on Big Creek. He had projected that the Mammoth Pool system would supply 120,000 HP, but his new scheme promised to develop at least triple this amount. Because the proposed Big Creek project required a heavily capitalized water storage, power generation, and electrical distribution system, Eastwood was again forced to seek extensive financial support from outside investors. And in searching for a wealthy patron to underwrite development of Big Creek, he became involved in the business empire of Henry E. Huntington.[7]

HENRY HUNTINGTON AND THE PACIFIC LIGHT AND POWER COMPANY

In 1901, Henry Huntington moved his base of operations from San Francisco to Los Angeles. There, at the age of 51, he commenced building what recent biographer William Friedricks describes as:

A triad of interrelated businesses critical for regional development [consisting] of a vast trolley network, electric power generation and distribution, and real estate development. Because Huntington operated this group of companies in an era when city and county planning commissions held little regulatory power, he became, in effect, the region's metropolitan planner.[8]

A nephew of Collis P. Huntington, Henry Huntington inherited much of the fortune his uncle had accumulated as one of the "Big Four" founders of the Central Pacific Railroad and as president of the Southern Pacific Railroad. During the latter part of the nineteenth century, Henry loyally served his uncle and ultimately worked his way up to the vice presidency of the Southern Pa-

cific; on Collis P.'s death in 1900, Henry received an inheritance of over $10 million. Through corporate maneuvering by E. H. Harriman, however, he was denied the presidency of the Southern Pacific. Frustrated in his efforts to follow in his uncle's footsteps, he began divesting his Southern Pacific holdings and concentrating on development opportunities in the "Southland" of greater Los Angeles.

Soon Huntington established a network of enterprises, including the Los Angeles Railway (originally incorporated in 1895 and taken over by Huntington in 1898), the Pacific Electric Railway, the Huntington Land and Improvement Company, and the Pacific Light and Power Company. He "usually set up [these enterprises] as small syndicates that Huntington dominated by holding a controlling share of stock . . . it was only on rare occasions that he allied himself with other members of the business community."[9] Perhaps the most important of these "rare occasions" involved the formation of the Pacific Light and Power Company in association with William G. Kerckhoff and Allan C. Balch.

Kerckhoff and Balch were electric power entrepreneurs who, in 1896, formed the San Gabriel Electric Company to provide power for Los Angeles. Kerckhoff, the older of the two and the more traditional businessman, arrived in Southern California in the late 1870s and quickly became a leader in the regional lumber trade. Seeking to increase the scope of his business, Kerckhoff undertook to build an ice manufacturing plant in the early 1890s, and this venture led him to develop plans for operating hydroelectric power plants. Kerckhoff possessed no training as an engineer and relied on others for technological guidance in planning and operating electric power systems. In this capacity, Balch became his trusted junior partner in charge of technical matters. After graduating from Cornell University in 1889 with degrees in electrical and mechanical engineering, Balch moved west to Portland, Oregon. In 1896, Balch moved south to Los Angeles and began a lifelong career as Kerckhoff's technological alter ego.

In the summer of 1898, the San Gabriel Electric Company began operating its first hydropower plant—a 1,400-HP facility on the San Gabriel River near Azusa, about 20 miles east of Pasadena. Gradually, Kerckhoff expanded his firm's operations in competition with the hydroelectric power system developed by H. H. Sinclair, which had been controlled since 1899 by the Edison Electric Company of Los Angeles.[10] When Henry Huntington arrived in Southern California in 1901, Kerckhoff and Balch recognized in him a potentially significant new partner and source of financial support for their business ventures. In turn, Huntington appreciated the value of electricity in powering his rapidly expanding transportation network. In this context, he agreed to meld his interests into the San Gabriel Electric Company to form the Pacific Light and Power Company (PL&P). As agreed on at the time of incorporation in March 1902, Huntington controlled 51 percent of the PL&P's stock; in addition, his Pacific Electric Railway constituted the major recipient of PL&P power.[11] Huntington controlled the PL&P financially, but Kerckhoff (as president) and Balch (as general manager) managed its day-to-day business and much of the long-range planning. Within a few months, this planning effort yielded financial support for Eastwood's Big Creek project.

The PL&P joined the Pacific Coast Electric Transmission Association at the June 1902 conference in San Francisco, and Balch may have attended as the company's official representative. Unquestionably, Eastwood was there (he delivered a paper on hydropower engineering), as was R. S. Masson, an electrical engineer previously associated with Huntington's streetcar company in San Francisco; Masson had also helped Eastwood with electrical designs for the Mammoth Power Company.[12] Exactly when and how Eastwood and Balch first met is unclear, but Masson played a role in bringing the two men together.[13] On July 15, 1902, Eastwood signed

an agreement with Balch stipulating that he was to receive logistical support for filing all water rights claims and obtaining all water conveyance permits necessary for building and operating Big Creek. The Fresno-based engineer was also to prepare complete plans for the project, including surveying for dams, tunnels, penstocks, powerhouses, transmission lines, and access roads. For Eastwood's primary compensation, the agreement stated that:

> If said party of the second part [Balch et al.] shall after the completion of said surveys and examinations elect to do so he shall organize a corporation [ultimately named the PL&P Corporation] to own said properties, and the stock therein shall be divided as follows, the party of the first part [Eastwood] shall convey to said corporation all of his interests in said properties, locations, reservoir sites, etc. on said Big Creek branch of said San Joaquin River, and shall receive therefor one tenth (1/10) of all the stock of said corporation, to be organized, in full payment therefor, which stock shall be free and clear at the time of said issuance from all debts, obligations or claims of any nature.[14]

As a commission (or "finder's fee"), Eastwood also agreed to transfer 10 percent of his holdings in the new corporation to Masson. The remaining 90 percent of stock representing the Big Creek development was to remain in the hands of Huntington, Kerckhoff, Balch, and any other investors brought into the deal. The Huntington interests were to be responsible for raising all capital required to construct the system; hence, Eastwood's 10 percent share seems quite reasonable. In the meantime, he was to receive a modest stipend of approximately $12 to $15 per day while in the field and working on plans.[15]

In the July 15 agreement, Balch made no commitment compelling him, Huntington, or anyone else associated with the PL&P to build the Big Creek system. Instead, Balch simply engaged Eastwood as his personal agent and assigned him to explore the possibility of building a hydroelectric power system on the upper San Joaquin. Exactly how feasible Balch and Kerckhoff initially considered Eastwood's proposal to be is unclear; they did not inform Huntington about it until

December 1902. The two may have deemed Big Creek to be worth exploring only because it required what Kerckhoff characterized as "small investments in engineering." In fact, by the time the PL&P Corporation was formally organized in 1910, preliminary costs for the Big Creek project had only reached about $63,000 — a minute portion of Huntington's net worth.[16] But for Eastwood, this "small investment" represented an invaluable opportunity to imprint a "second nature" of reservoirs, tunnels, penstocks, and power plants of unparalleled scale across the landscape of the southern Sierra Nevada.

GENESIS OF
THE MULTIPLE ARCH DAM

Within weeks after signing his agreement with Balch, Eastwood was deep in the San Joaquin/Big Creek watershed developing detailed maps and plans. By the late summer of 1902, he could report to Kerckhoff: "I have completed the surveys for a tunnel line to the junction of Pitman and Big Creeks and I can place before you the most remarkable power project yet presented."[17] During 1902–1903, Eastwood refined these plans and spent much of his time traversing the back country of the upper San Joaquin, making waterflow measurements, posting water claims, surveying prospective reservoir sites, and laying out power plant locations (Figs. 4.5 and 4.6). For 1903, he reported making:

A total of over 2,000 miles of horse back and over 1,150 miles of stage travel . . . [and] these reconnaissances, surveys and water appropriations have broadened the scope of the scheme to such an extent that it now includes the whole of the commercially available waters of the San Joaquin River, all of which can be condensed in one system in the Big Creek Basin.[18]

Under state law, claiming water rights involved a two-part procedure: posting a written notice at the proposed diversion site, including specification of the amount of flow claimed and the purpose of the appropriation; and formally registering the claim in the recorder's office at the county courthouse (for Big Creek, most filings were in Fresno County, but a few occurred in Madera County). Water rights filings in California are given priority depending on their registration date; thus, Eastwood kept his activities in the upper San Joaquin unpublicized until the most important filings had been registered (in the late summer of 1903) and hence became a matter of public record.[19]

After legally establishing a right under state law to appropriate water in the San Joaquin/Big Creek watershed, Eastwood needed to comply with federal laws governing the use of public lands in the Sierra National Forest. Some of the land that fell within the area of the Big Creek project was privately owned, but most of it remained under the direct control of the federal government. Under the Act of February 15, 1901, "Relating to rights of way through certain parks, reservations, and other public lands," authorization to use of federal land for power projects could be obtained after filing applications with the General Land Office based on detailed survey data and then receiving formal permits from the Secretary of the Interior.[20] Between 1903 and 1905, Eastwood received several such permits authorizing the use of federal land for purposes such as impounding the Big Creek reservoir, constructing tunnels and powerhouses, and building transmission lines (Fig 4.7). Eastwood's initial receipt of these permits occurred without fanfare or difficulty.[21] However, the 1901 law permitted the revocation of such permits at the discretion of the Secretary of the Interior. Later, after control over the national forests was transferred to the Department of Agriculture in 1905, the threat of revocation developed into an issue affecting the PL&P's financing of Big Creek.

To keep Kerckhoff, Balch, and Huntington officially informed of his progress, Eastwood submitted a preliminary report in early 1903; in March 1904, his activities were summarized in a 56-page report that contained the first complete description of all features in the Big Creek system.[22] The project revolved around three powerhouses descending in a "stairstep" configuration along Big Creek and the lower San Joaquin. Water for these power plants (designated Big Creek No. 1, No. 2, and No. 3) was to be stored in the reservoir filling Big Creek Basin. When built a decade later, this reservoir became known as Huntington Lake; and although it is now supplemented by several other reservoirs (including one at Mammoth Pool), it still serves as a primary facility for regulating the system's power production.

In his presentation at the June 1902 PCETA conference, Eastwood had counseled that "no stream can be assumed to have been developed to its true value as a power source unless some portion of the water used is stored to fill the gap caused by an occasional dry year or drought period," and, in an overt reference to earthfill and rockfill structures, he characterized dam design as "largely a matter of natural selection, as dams usually can be built of the materials found near the site."[23] In line with this, his 1904 report discussed building three hydraulic fill dams for the Big Creek reservoir, using "materials to be obtained from the hillside to the eastward of [Dam No. 1], the water for sluicing the material to be pumped up from Big Creek." Mindful of the recent near collapse of the SJEC's Crane Valley Dam, Eastwood proposed that the earthfill for Big Creek Dam No. 1 be

4.5 *Survey party crossing Big Creek, circa 1903. Eastwood is straddling the upstream rope. In the wilds of the high Sierra, even simple matters of transportation could pose significant risks. (Author's collection, courtesy of Charles Allan Whitney)*

4.6   *Eastwood and his survey party along Stephenson Creek below Big Creek. This dramatic view illustrates the steep, difficult terrain encompassing much of the Big Creek Basin area. (Henry E. Huntington Library)*

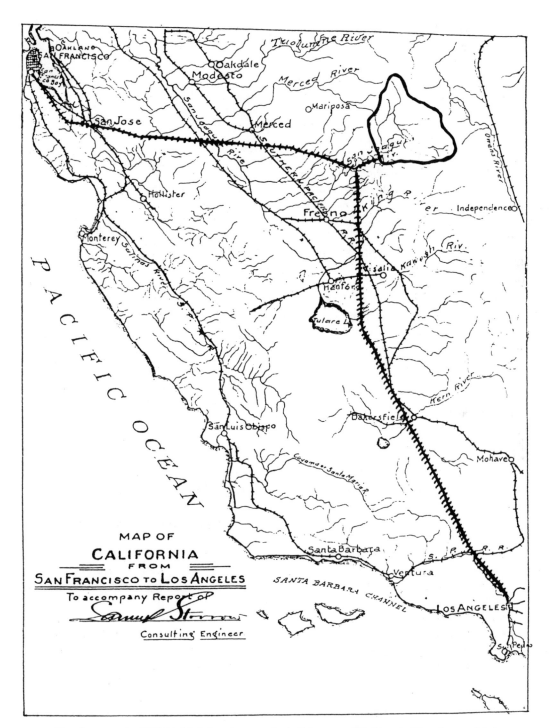

4.7   *Map drawn up in 1903 highlighting the watershed of the upper San Joaquin River (upper right) and showing two proposed transmission lines to carry power from the Big Creek plants to San Francisco and Los Angeles. This map was part of a report submitted to Kerckhoff verifying the feasibility of Eastwood's Big Creek project. (Southern California Edison Company, courtesy of William Myers)*

strengthened by a reinforced concrete core-wall. Extending along the centerline axis from the bedrock foundations to the dam's crest, this corewall was intended to make the structure "absolutely safe from all chances of a leak."[24]

By 1905, all work associated with Big Creek's water rights, location surveys, and the like had been completed. Eastwood then began designing the system's engineering facilities, including the main storage reservoir; all penstocks, turbines, and electrical apparatus associated with powerhouses #1 and #2; and the main transmission line.[25] Much of this effort involved an extension of work he had already undertaken in designing, building, expanding, and maintaining the landmark SJEC system. But he had not previously considered the issue of large-scale dam design in detail; and now, as planning for Big Creek began to culminate, this critically important (and expensive) technology became a central concern.

Although his preliminary proposals called for the construction of hydraulic fill dams, Eastwood refused to endorse the technology in his final report without considering other options. Study of how best to support the corewall of an earthen dam led him to conceptualize an all-concrete, buttressed structure. In later life he remarked that "it is a curious circumstance that this study of a hollow corewall [for earth dams] led to the perfection of the multiple-arched type of dam," but he declined to explain further the creative nature of his thought process.[26] Although Henry Goldmark's 1897 article in the ASCE *Transactions* might have served as an inspiration, Eastwood never acknowledged it as a source for his new design. Regardless of what sparked his engineering imagination, in 1906 (at the age of 49) Eastwood finally hit on the idea of a multiple arch dam.

The Eastwood Papers at Berkeley include a 19-page, handwritten commentary simply entitled "Dams" that documents some of Eastwood's earliest thoughts on why multiple arch dams were the best choice for Big Creek.[27] In a more polished form this draft

probably constituted part of his final Big Creek report; and it provides a synopsis of arguments he undoubtedly presented to Kerckhoff and Balch regarding his new design. Claiming that his analysis was based on "careful and exhaustive study," Eastwood explained:

In the investigation of the study of dams for closing the openings in Big Creek Basin, the subject was taken up on the basis of arriving at the best and cheapest type, and with that end in view three types were taken up . . . [including] the solid masonry gravity dam of the section of the world famous Croton Dam, and designated the "Croton Type," a dam of solid faced or unfaced rubble masonry designed on the theory of the weight of the various blocks resisting overturning and sliding . . . an earthfill dam with drained concrete corewall, a new idea in corewall and earth dam construction, with rock paved slopes of 2 to 1 on both upstream and downstream faces . . . and the arched buttressed concrete type which is fully described herein . . . the foundations at all the sites [are] granite rock, either exposed or near the surface in which a shallow excavation will terminate in sound unseamed granite, and hence the foundation is suitable to any type of dam [Fig. 4.8].[28]

Within this passage, Eastwood uses the phrase "arched buttressed concrete type" to refer to what he later called simply a multiple arch dam. His original design of this type (to be used for Big Creek dams Nos. 1, 2, and 3 as illustrated in Fig. 4.9) defined a structure consisting primarily of a series of arches 40 feet wide (at the end sections, some arches were to have 20-foot spans) supported on buttresses sloped upstream at an angle of about 53 degrees (yielding a length-to-height ratio of 3/4).[29]

To highlight the positive structural attributes of his new multiple arch "buttress type" design, Eastwood emphasized the value of the inclined upstream face in resisting "sliding and overturning" and in allowing "the weight of the water to put all parts of the dam in compression." He also considered the "arch as the form to use" for the upstream face, "as by its use the materials used are all put in direct compression, and hence the highest service is obtained." Rejecting the use of flat slabs instead of arches as "impractical," he observed

4.8   *The granite foundations of Big Creek Dam No. 1, circa 1903. Eastwood considered this an ideal dam site because the bedrock was not covered by any loose soil ("overburden") that would have to be excavated. (Henry E. Huntington Library)*

that tensile stresses on the slabs' downstream side would necessitate closer spacing between buttresses and "render them wasteful of material [and make them more] expensive."[30] Eastwood urged adoption of multiple arch dams because they represented "the ultimate scientific use of the materials." They did not rely on bulk for stability, but instead "resist[ed] the waterthrust by the compression of the materials" that formed the structure's arches and buttresses. In other words, the shape of the multiple arch design was more important than the volumetric magnitude of its dimensions. In contrast, he decried the "absolute waste of material and low safety factor" in earthfill and masonry gravity dams as being "due to the fact that [in these gravity designs] the mass performs its work by the imposition of its weight alone to counteract the water

thrust."[31] In making this conceptual distinction between standard masonry/earthfill gravity designs and his buttressed arch proposal, Eastwood succinctly identified the key characteristic separating the massive and structural traditions of dam design.

Three 1906 drawings document the different designs Eastwood considered using for Big Creek and indicate the amount of material required to build each dam type.[32] In juxtaposing the estimated quantities of concrete necessary for the gravity profile and for the arched buttress design, he revealed a startling difference: the multiple arch designs for Big Creek dams nos. 1, 2, and 3 cumulatively required only 73,000 cubic yards of concrete; comparable "Croton" designs required 323,900 cubic yards. Although the earthfill designs were to consist primarily of soil

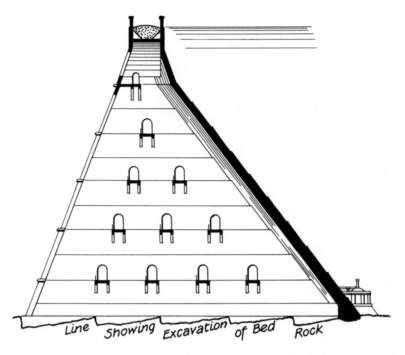

4.9   *Cross section of Eastwood's 1906 "arched buttress" design for Big Creek. The design prefigures his later projects in its reliance on a sloped upstream face and its use of the cylinder formula to determine the dimensions of the arches. (Original in the Henry E. Huntington Library, retraced by Richard K. Anderson)*

and rock excavated from Big Creek basin (an estimated 1.34 million cubic yards), their corewalls would still require more than 64,000 cubic yards of concrete—almost as much as would be needed for the multiple arch designs. Working from these calculations, Eastwood estimated that multiple arch dams would save more than $2 million over comparable "Croton" gravity dams and approximately $500,000 over earthfill structures.[33]

In submitting his new idea to Huntington, Kerckhoff, and Balch, he undoubtedly anticipated that they would appreciate the financial advantages of multiple arch designs and would work with him to implement their construction. No correspondence or communication from the period 1906–1909 survives to document the PL&P hierarchy's specific reaction to the new design, but Eastwood's overtures clearly met with stolid rejection.

A WAITING GAME

While Eastwood toiled in the Sierra Nevada backcountry, Huntington, Kerckhoff, and Balch positioned themselves to take comprehensive control of all power holdings on the San Joaquin River. The public may have perceived the "Huntington Interests" in the upper San Joaquin and Big Creek watersheds as being synonymous with Kerckhoff and Balch's San Joaquin Power Company (that is, the old SJEC system on the North Fork); but in truth, a more convoluted corporate structure evolved to assert control over Eastwood's Big Creek proposal. In 1905, Huntington and Kerckhoff acted to solidify their position by buying out the original investors of the dormant Mammoth Power Company, thus gaining control over all of Eastwood's pre-1902 water rights filings on the San Joaquin. Before September 1905, all of the Mammoth company's officers resided in either Fresno or Hanford; after this time, Kerckhoff served as president and all shareholders except Eastwood lived in the Los Angeles area. In 1907 the corporate offices were officially relocated to Los Angeles (and placed in the same building as the PL&P and the San Joaquin Light and Power Company)—a move symbolizing that future developments would hold few financial ties to Fresno or the surrounding Central Valley.[34]

During the summer of 1906, preparations were made in anticipation of an early start in building Big Creek. In August, the Huntington interests reached a compromise agreement with Miller & Lux, a powerful ranching/agricultural enterprise retaining riparian water rights on the lower San Joaquin, that permitted construction of storage reservoirs at Mammoth Pool and the Big Creek Basin in return for a guaranteed, regular streamflow through Miller & Lux's lands. The complex document (signed by Eastwood, Huntington, Kerckhoff, and Balch) stipulated that construction on the Big Creek dams was to start in the fall of 1906, reach the 100-foot level by November 1907, and be completed to the 160-foot level by November 1909; as part of this agreement, Eastwood also signed a "declaration of trust" indicating that his various filings and permits were all being held in his name for the benefit of the Huntington interests as a whole.[35] In March 1907, Huntington formed a new corporation, called the Sierra Nevada Electric Company, that assumed 93 percent ownership of the Mammoth Power Company—an action that appeared to presage the beginning of the Big Creek project.[36] Beginning in late 1906, however, the desires of President Teddy Roosevelt and U.S. Forest Service Forester Gifford Pinchot (a close friend of Roosevelt's) injected an element of turmoil and uncertainty into plans for implementing the Big Creek project.

Much of the land encompassed by the Big Creek project lay within the boundaries of the federally owned Sierra National Forest. Since 1905, the Forest Service (and not the General

Land Office under the Secretary of the Interior) had exercised control over how the national forests were to be developed, including jurisdiction over the licensing of hydroelectric power plants and right-of-ways for transmission lines. Pinchot thus possessed the authority to revoke power permits covering national forests at any time, and he sought to use this authority to exact concessions and long-term compensation from privately financed power companies. In particular, Pinchot wished to require substantial annual payments from utilities based on such things as the amount of power produced, the area of land inundated by reservoirs, and the distances traversed by transmission lines. He also wanted to ensure that franchises were not granted in perpetuity, to prevent monopolization of the nation's hydropower resources by private utilities.[37]

Pinchot and his staff realized that "They [Huntington, Eastwood, and their associates] have surveyed and estimated all the power in [the Sierra National] Forest and have filed on most of it. They expect to reservoir and use the whole watershed of the Sierra Nevada."[38] Pinchot was adamant about protecting what he perceived to be the national interest, and he saw no reason to grant any favors to businessmen who wished to "monopolize" water power for the financial benefit of a few privileged investors. The uncertainty that Pinchot's actions brought to the development of hydroelectric power projects fostered an attitude of "wait-and-see" on the part of the Huntington interests, delaying efforts to finance construction of Big Creek. In addition, the "Banker's Panic" of 1907 dried up available capital in the U.S. investment markets and did little to encourage the Huntington/ Kerckhoff/Balch triumvirate to accelerate the construction process. As a result, Eastwood's scheme entered financial limbo while Kerckhoff and other private power interests sparred with the Forest Service over what constituted reasonable payment for use of the public domain. In 1909, the Huntington interests finally reached an accord with the Forest Service that set forth a payment structure governing operation of the project for a period of 50 years.[39] But more than three years had passed between the date of signing of the earlier agreement with Miller & Lux and the date when Eastwood formally received a Forest Service permit authorizing the Big Creek project. And during this time, Eastwood's interactions with the PL&P hierarchy grew ever more distant and tenuous.

In the spring of 1907, Eastwood submitted his final report describing the Big Creek system and the facilities necessary to build it (Fig. 4.10).[40] But having completed this task, he was not content to sit idly by and await a decision to commence construction. Instead, he set out to prove the viability of his new dam design concepts. To this end, in 1908, he began erecting the world's first reinforced concrete multiple arch dam for a logging company in the Kings River watershed about 50 miles south of Big Creek. Although the Hume Lake Dam commission was intended to serve as a training ground for building the

Big Creek dams, it also distanced Eastwood from the corporate affairs of the PL&P. Once he had successfully completed the Hume Lake project in 1909, he discovered that the PL&P hierarchy held little interest in his accomplishment.

In 1910, undaunted by the indifference of his supposed partners, Eastwood forged ahead and accepted a commission to design and build his second multiple arch dam, in the San Bernardino Mountains of Southern California. These early efforts drew him into the larger world of western water development and promised to introduce him to a large market of private clients anxious to reduce the cost of water storage; nonetheless, until 1912, he considered Big Creek a primary forum for his dam design labors. But from 1908 onward, Kerckhoff, Balch, and Huntington sought no further interaction with the Fresno-based engineer beyond that legally required under the 1902 Balch/Eastwood contract. They may have been put off

4.10   *Corporate review of Eastwood's plans for Big Creek. Pacific Light and Power Company president William Kerckhoff is in the center with his hand on the table; A. G. Wishon is to his right, and Eastwood is to his left; A. C. Balch is to Eastwood's immediate left. Henry Huntington, who remained distant from actual planning for the Big Creek project, does not appear in this photograph. (Author's collection, courtesy of Charles Allan Whitney)*

by his advocacy of a new type of dam technology, or they may simply have viewed him as a mere technician who had performed his function at Big Creek and was no longer needed. Regardless of the reason, once Eastwood's water rights and reservoir filings became vested in a larger entity, he was to be treated as an expendable commodity.

EASTWOOD'S BANISHMENT

The first public signal of Eastwood's waning influence came in 1909, when the San Joaquin Light and Power Company (operated by Kerckhoff and Balch) decided to renovate Eastwood's original North Fork power system. This expansion involved building an enlarged concrete powerhouse to replace the 1896 structure, as well as raising the height of the hydraulic fill Crane Valley Dam from 70 feet to 150 feet. For the latter work, Kerckhoff and Balch bypassed Eastwood to hire J. G. White & Company, a New York–based contracting firm.[41] In 1909, Huntington and Kerckhoff also prepared a financial "prospectus of a proposed corporation to be formed for the purpose of consolidating certain gas, electric light and power companies in Southern California," that featured Big Creek as a key component; the prospectus concluded with an assurance that: "The New Company will be controlled by Mr. H. E. Huntington and Associates of Los Angeles . . . [and] the expenditures of the money for betterments will be under the supervision, in an advisory capacity, of Messrs. J. G. White & Company, engineers, of New York and London."[42] In 1903 Kerckhoff had described Eastwood as "our engineer" when corresponding with Huntington; by 1910, he referred to "our engineers, J. G. White & Company" during a discussion of Big Creek water supply issues.[43] A builder of electric utilities and electric railroads since the 1890s, J. G. White & Company had previously focused their dam building efforts on massive gravity designs; after

being brought into the San Joaquin projects, they exhibited no inclination to learn about Eastwood's recent design innovations.[44]

In January 1910 (shortly after Pinchot was dismissed as head of the Forest Service by President Taft), the long-anticipated organization of the PL&P *Corporation* occurred, with Kerckhoff serving as president and Huntington maintaining control of over 51 percent of the new company's stock.[45] A month later, arrangements were made for Eastwood to transfer all Big Creek water rights, permits, and other filings to the new corporation. Because the PL&P Corporation included several power plants unrelated to Big Creek, Eastwood agreed to accept $600,000 worth of PL&P common stock "in full and complete settlement" of the July 1902 contract. In return, Eastwood turned over "all the filings made by him on the Big Creek Branch of the San Joaquin River and all the filings made on the main branch of the San Joaquin together with the permits issued by the government to him, covering these filings," and he delayed taking control of his PL&P stock until all the transfers had been confirmed.[46] After this, Kerckhoff and Balch generally ignored Eastwood as they worked with J. G. White & Company and others during the spring and summer of 1910 to assemble data documenting Big Creek's waterflow.[47]

In November 1910, Huntington changed the focus of his acquisition strategy, transferring his interurban railway interests to the Southern Pacific Railroad. In return, Huntington received transportation concessions that consolidated his hold on the more urban Los Angeles Railway.[48] Huntington's desire to exploit the Big Creek project did not disappear, but plans were scaled down to an "initial development" (namely, the first stage of the Big Creek reservoir, powerhouses Nos. 1 and 2, and the transmission line to Los Angeles) in which power would be marketed through the existing PL&P distribution system. Gone were dreams of creating a huge power and transportation conglomerate that would dominate Southern California; in fact, the PL&P's Big Creek facilities would not even merge with the existing San Joaquin Light & Power Company system on the North Fork of the San Joaquin.

On November 28, 1910, Balch informed Eastwood that "we wish to discontinue your engagement in connection with the property [Big Creek] beginning December 1st 1910," and directed him to turn over "all the maps and plans and engineering data which you have developed in the last few years."[49] Two days later, the Fresno engineer formally acquiesced and, in return, accepted 5,400 shares of PL&P common stock (with a par value of $100 per share), as agreed the previous February; simultaneously, he transferred an additional 600 shares to R. S. Masson — the person responsible for introducing him to Balch almost ten years earlier.[50]

After formally dismissing Eastwood, the PL&P dropped the engineering services of J. G. White & Company in favor of the Stone & Webster Construction Company of Boston, as primary contractors for Big Creek.[51] Charles Stone and Edwin Webster had graduated from the Massachusetts Institute of Technology in the late 1880s and formed a partnership to exploit opportunities in the burgeoning field of electric power.[52] Well connected to the world of investment capital through Webster's father (a partner in the Boston banking firm of Kidder, Peabody & Company), the young duo rapidly gained a reputation for skill in evaluating the earning capacity of utility companies. They also designed electric power systems and assumed responsibility for financing and operating these systems commercially. Although Stone & Webster had never worked in California prior to their involvement with Big Creek, the firm had been managing electric power systems in the Pacific Northwest for several years. Construction of the Big Creek system involved financial backing from an array of eastern investors; and although the historical record is inconclusive on this point, Huntington, Kerckhoff, and Balch apparently wished to let the Big Creek contract to a firm familiar to the nation's financial establishment.[53]

Financing for Big Creek came slowly, and

Stone & Webster did not formally sign a contract with the PL&P until January 1912.[54] Beginning with construction of the 56-mile-long San Joaquin and Eastern Railroad, a narrow-gauge line that cost over $1.1 million and supplanted the wagon road laid out by Eastwood for transporting material to the project area, Stone & Webster undertook a two-year project to bring Big Creek's initial development on-line.[55]

Despite Eastwood's familiarity with the planning and design of Big Creek, Stone & Webster did not consult him, and none of the firm's later promotional material or articles in the *Stone & Webster Public Service Journal* refer to the Fresno engineer. In this regard, the completeness of Eastwood's fieldwork helped exclude him from the project, as his detailed engineering reports provided the Boston firm with sufficient information to begin construction.

At the start of 1912, Eastwood attempted to convince Stone & Webster's project manager, S. L. Shuffleton, that multiple arch dams were both financially desirable and technically feasible for the Big Creek sites. Drawing on his recent experience in building the Big Bear Valley Dam, he presented new designs and compared them with the concrete gravity structures that Stone & Webster planned to build. In calculating the amount of concrete necessary to impound the Big Creek reservoir to its full capacity, Eastwood determined that his multiple arch designs required only 73,498 cubic yards of concrete compared with 294,665 cubic yards for the massive gravity designs. Figuring that the concrete for the multiple arch dams would cost twice as much per cubic yard as for the gravity structures ($23.60 vs. $13.20), he calculated that his design would save the PL&P in excess of $2 million, or more than 15 percent of the estimated total project cost.[56] Enlisting the help of E. H. Rollins, a major financier and a key investor in the PL&P, Eastwood made a final attempt to obtain the dam design commissions for Big Creek. After meeting with Shuffleton that spring, Rollins wrote to Stone & Webster in Boston, arguing as follows:

4.11   *Stone & Webster's massive curved concrete gravity structure built as "Big Creek Dam No. 1" to impound Huntington Lake. The photograph was taken on June 7, 1913, during a visit by many corporate dignitaries. Eastwood was not invited. (Eastwood Papers, WRCA)*

I knew that you had this design [multiple arch] under consideration for the Big Creek development and your Mr. Shuffleton was kind enough to call on me and explain his objections to this design. His criticisms, however, were not particularly severe, and I summed up your position to be that you did not feel like taking the responsibility of deviating from the old and well established engineering paths. . . . [T]he immense saving of material, and to my mind, the increased strength of the Eastwood dam, is something to be carefully considered.[57]

In May, Eastwood offered to travel to Boston at his own expense to explain more fully the multiple arch design, but Stone & Webster rebuffed this overture.[58] Later that summer,

work commenced on three concrete gravity dams to impound Huntington Lake (Fig. 4.11), an action that symbolized Eastwood's final dissociation from Big Creek as a technological endeavor.

THE PL&P STOCK ASSESSMENT OF JULY 1912

Almost contemporaneously with the start of dam construction, Huntington initiated action that would precipitate Eastwood's permanent financial severance from the Big Creek project. On July 5, 1912, the PL&P Board of Directors (with Huntington as president of the company, chairman of the meeting, and majority shareholder) unanimously approved a $5 per share assessment on all of the firm's capital stock (including first preferred, second preferred, and common). This move was ostensibly to help fund construction of Big Creek.[59] Explicitly authorized by California corporation law and invocable by a majority vote of the shareholders, a stock assessment can be considered the reverse of a stock dividend: instead of receiving a payment, the stockholder must pay into the corporate treasury.[60] If a shareholder proved unable or unwilling to pay an assessment, the law authorized the forced sale of his/her stock at public auction. If no bids were sufficient to pay off the assessment then the stock was declared forfeit, canceled, and absorbed into the corporation without any compensation given to the delinquent shareholder. Stock can be explicitly defined as "nonassessable" and thus exempted from this type of action; however, none of the PL&P capital stock fell into this category. In his 1902 contract with Balch, Eastwood stipulated that his payment for Big Creek be "free and clear at the time of said issuance from all debts, obligations or claims of any nature"—a condition met when he received his PL&P stock in December 1910. But nothing precluded the company from invoking stock assessments at a later date.

The terms of the PL&P's assessment required Eastwood to raise $27,000 (5,400 shares × $5 dollars) by August 30 if he wished to keep his stock. For a person of his financial means, this represented an enormous sum to raise within a few weeks; such a payment was especially burdensome because it would do nothing beyond permitting Eastwood to retain stock that other investors were (quite understandably) hesitant to purchase. The next spring, the depressed value of PL&P common stock was reflected in Huntington's own "Balance Sheet" when his

60,630 shares were listed at a market value of $504,331, or only $8.32 per share.[61] The par value of Eastwood's stock may have been $100 per share, but in the wake of the 1912 assessment its true value effectively plummeted to zero.

Along with several other shareholders, Eastwood failed to meet the assessment deadline; and in late September, the delinquent stock was auctioned to the highest bidder. Had any bids for Eastwood's stock exceeded $5 per share, then he could have sold off some of his stock and used the proceeds to pay the assessment on the rest. It appears, however, that no bids were offered for delinquent common stock; thus, as the minutes of the PL&P Board of Directors meeting blandly noted, "the Secretary be and he is hereby authorized and directed to cancel the twenty (20) certificates covering the 15,945 shares of stock sold at public auction on the 27th day of September, 1912."[62] In "selling" these shares, the PL&P merely took ownership of (that is, canceled) them, in return for absorbing the cost of the assessment. Eastwood received nothing. As David Redinger phrased it in *The Story of Big Creek*: "[Eastwood] received only a small salary—just sufficient for living expenses—during the several years he was engaged on the preliminary work of the Big Creek Project, because the future seemed bright. At last he lost everything."[63]

At the time of the assessment, Eastwood was the third largest stockholder in the PL&P after Huntington and Kerckhoff, but he owned the least valuable type of stock (common) and stood almost no chance of receiving any significant dividends for the foreseeable future. In addition, he did not hold a position on the board of directors and could exert no meaningful influence on the corporation's business. Regardless, the assessment seems to have been intended specifically to exclude Eastwood from future involvement in the PL&P; at least no other motive makes sense under the circumstances. At that time, Huntington, Kerckhoff, and their close associates together controlled almost 95 percent of

PL&P's outstanding capital stock (Eastwood held about 2.5 percent and another 2.5 percent or so was scattered among a few dozen other investors); to raise revenue, the main investors could just as easily have contributed to their own corporate coffers by purchasing bonds.[64]

In 1912, fewer than 20,000 shares of stock (out of 233,960 total) were held outside the control of the PL&P's central hierarchy, meaning that the company could not have raised more than $75,000 from minority shareholders if all assessments on those shares had been paid. The cost of Big Creek's initial development through the end of 1913 came to more than $13 million—a figure that dwarfs any amount that possibly could have been generated by PL&P minority shareholders through the July 1912 assessment. More likely, Huntington desired to obtain complete control of the PL&P; by pressuring other shareholders he accomplished the first step in this takeover. The second step came in the spring of 1913, when Huntington and Kerckhoff formally dissolved their business relationship (Balch later indicated that they had "divorced"), with Kerckhoff and Balch assuming ownership of the PL&P's gas subsidiaries in return for turning over all their other PL&P holdings to Huntington. At the conclusion of this monumental deal, Huntington directly controlled 96.8 percent of PL&P capital stock.[65]

BIG CREEK'S LEGACY

Ironically, Stone & Webster's decision to erect concrete gravity dams came close to destroying Big Creek's fiscal viability. In seeking to reduce the cost of dam building by several hundred thousand dollars for the initial development (and upward of $2 million for the completed dams), Eastwood was not merely hoping to save a little bit of money at the margin of an otherwise amply funded project; he considered his cost savings initiative

an integral part of the complete proposal. A year after originally budgeting the project at a little less than $10 million, Stone & Webster submitted a "revised estimate" for the initial development equaling almost $11.2 million, including $1.4 million for the partially complete dams; the company estimated that raising the dams to their full height would cost an additional $2 million. During 1913, the cost of the initial development continued to escalate, ultimately reaching more than $13.8 million.[66] The PL&P experienced great difficulty in financing ongoing construction, and a work stoppage was avoided only when E. H. Rollins purchased an additional $4 million worth of bonds issued by the Huntington Land and Improvement Company for use in completing Big Creek.[67] To help offset these expenses, which in part resulted from a decision to upgrade the initial generating capacity from 40,000 kw to 60,000 kw, the PL&P sought to limit the permit fees they had previously negotiated with the U.S. Department of Agriculture for rights to operate within the Sierra National Forest. To help rationalize a fee reduction, the company claimed in the summer of 1913 that "an inspection of the contours of the reservoirs in the vicinity of the Big Creek Power Sites will make it clear why only massive and extremely expensive dams can be used."[68] In this way, the PL&P acknowledged the great burden that concrete gravity designs were placing on its financial structure; and by claiming that using such "massive and extremely expensive dams" was necessary, the company attempted to evade responsibility for this component of its budgetary problems in order to exact concessions from the Forest Service. The effort was not successful, but the incident highlights the great expense incurred by the decision to build gravity dams and, conversely, helps validate Eastwood's effort to develop a less expensive form of water storage technology.

In November 1913, Stone & Webster completed Big Creek's initial development (Fig. 4.12), and transmission of 60,000 kw (or about 80,000 HP) of energy began over a 220-mile-long, 150,000-volt, three-phase transmission line to Los Angeles.[69] The system pumped enormous amounts of power into Southern California, and the PL&P quickly took the place of the Huntington Land and Improvement Company as the financier's most important source of revenue. By 1915, Huntington began to seriously consider retiring from the business world in order to concentrate on his library and other philanthropic interests. Soon talks were opened with the Southern California Edison Company to explore the possibility of a merger, and in 1917 an agreement was reached whereby Huntington would turn all his PL&P holdings over to the Edison Company and receive in return stock with a market value of at least $16 million.

Kerckhoff and Balch liquidated their interest in the Big Creek project in 1913, but their separation from the Huntington empire bore scant resemblance to Eastwood's. Although Kerckhoff weathered the 1912 stock assessment with little overt hardship, by the next spring he and Huntington had agreed to dissolve the partnership they had formed in 1902. Huntington took all the electric power components of the PL&P, while Kerckhoff and Balch assumed control of the gas entities (including Southern California Gas Company and Midway Gas Company) and retained ownership of the San Joaquin Light and Power Corporation's North Fork system. The holdings of Kerckhoff and Balch proved to be solid investments, and by the time they jointly liquidated their assets in the mid-1920s, both men were millionaires. They made no arrangements to preserve their business or personal papers in any library or archive, although they became known as generous benefactors to institutions of higher learning in Southern California. Before his death in 1929, Kerckhoff funded prominent buildings at both the California Institute of Technology (Cal Tech) and the UCLA Westwood campus.

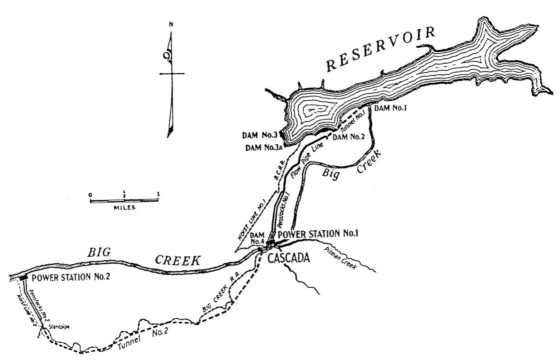

4.12   *Map of Big Creek's "Initial Development," showing the dams built to form Huntington Lake and the penstocks and tunnels connecting Power Stations No. 1 and No. 2. (Stone & Webster,* Water Powers, *1920)*

Along with sizable monetary bequests, Balch contributed his personal time to Cal Tech, becoming president of the board of trustees in 1933 and serving a ten-year term before his death in 1943.[70] Although their philanthropy never achieved the prominence of Huntington's, both Kerckhoff and Balch invested some of the monies generated from their work as utility entrepreneurs (and from their association with projects designed by Eastwood) in the cultural life of Southern California.

For his part, Eastwood was reticent to discuss Big Creek after 1912, except to take credit for his involvement in filing water rights and preparing all preliminary plans for the project. For example, in *The Story of Big Creek,* David Redinger quotes him as writing in 1914:

It is a pleasure to state that I did all of the preliminary work in what is now the largest plant on the Pacific Coast, the longest transmission in the world, and the highest head in the world, that which is used for the large plant, the Big Creek development of the Pacific Light and Power Corporation.[71]

In 1918, after the Southern California Edison Company took over Big Creek, Eastwood prepared a report for the company on how the Shaver Lake properties of the Fresno Flume and Lumber Company could be melded into the system.[72] Similarly, in 1923 Redinger accompanied Eastwood on a tour of the Big Creek system and — in describing him as "a quiet, unassuming man, keenly interested in everything he saw" — gave no indication that his visitor expressed any regrets over his earlier experiences with the PL&P. Eastwood certainly lamented losing control over the project; but after accepting the harsh financial toll exacted by the 1912 stock assessment, he relegated Big Creek to the past and focused on the future. And that future soon became inextricably intertwined with the promotion and development of the multiple arch dam.

Since 1917, Big Creek has been operated by the Southern California Edison Company, and under its stewardship the system has expanded in general accord with Eastwood's plans (Fig. 4.13). Before the start of World War II, Big Creek supplied almost 70 percent of the utility's annual electric power production; but since that time the increased construction of steam plants has reduced its share of the firm's generating capacity. Today, Big Creek's capacity is approaching 1 million HP and the system constitutes Southern California Edison Company's most profitable generating facility (compared with fossil fuel or nuclear plants, Big Creek's operating costs are practically nil). Company historian William Myers estimates that, depending on rainfall and snowpack accumulation, Big Creek currently generates about 3.5 billion kilowatt-hours of power — approximately 5 percent of the firm's total power production.[73] As legal inheritor and financial beneficiary of the water rights and hydropower system that Eastwood surveyed and planned almost 100 years ago, the Southern California Edison Company appreciates the value of his work and recently dedicated an underground power plant near Shaver Lake in his name. Meanwhile, Henry Huntington — who apparently made only one trip into the upper San Joaquin during his entire life — is forever associated with Huntington Lake, the reservoir Eastwood planned to impound with his first multiple arch dams.[74]

EASTWOOD AND CORPORATE CULTURE

Considered within the context of events such as Almerian Decker's planning for America's first polyphase AC system at Redlands and the formation of the Pacific Coast Electric Transmission Association, Eastwood's efforts in designing the SJEC's Fresno Plant and the PL&P's Big Creek system — and his concomitant work in conceiving the multiple arch dam — exemplify the efforts of an engineering community based in the West to assume the initiative in developing new technologies. The

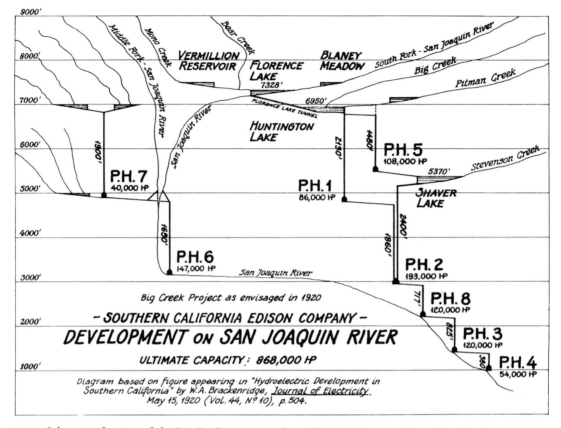

4.13 *Schematic drawing of the Big Creek system as planned in 1920; power plants No. 6 and No. 7 were never built. (Journal of Electricity, 1920, retraced by Richard K. Anderson)*

region's engineers did not build their hydroelectric power systems in isolation, but neither they did they passively accept technologies developed in the eastern United States or in Europe and merely adapt them to their own topographic, economic, and social conditions. Nonetheless, as became apparent in the resistance that Eastwood encountered in promoting a new dam type within the PL&P, efforts by western engineers to take the lead in implementing new technologies sometimes trespassed on the interests of engineers based outside the region; and such trespasses assumed greater significance because of the evolving capitalistic economic order that supported financing for America's large-scale electric power systems.

In his recent book *Colony and Empire: The Capitalist Transformation of the American West*, William G. Robbins examined the origins of the Montana Power Company (formally organized in 1913 as a subsidiary of the New York–based Anaconda Copper Mining Company) and called attention to:

the broader reorganization of property relations and investment policies in the United States between 1890 and World War I . . . [in which capitalism was transformed] from a "proprietary-competitive stage" to a "corporate-administered stage" . . . [This] transition marked the historic passage of the U.S. economy from competitive, free-market conditions to industrial oligopoly and the emergence of a new market ideology based on concentrated, heavily bureaucratized corporations.[75]

In the context of Robbins's observations, the introductions of J. G. White & Company and of Stone & Webster into the affairs of the PL&P can be seen as important manifesta-

PL&P can be seen as important manifestations of a new era in the West—an era in which eastern financiers and engineers asserted increasing influence over the growth of power systems and over water resources development in general. Consonant with this, Eastwood's involvement in and influence over the corporate bureaucracy that controlled the PL&P steadily waned during the first decade of the twentieth century. Thus, as the West's economy shifted from regionally focused "proprietary capitalism," to relatively centralized and bureaucratic "corporate capitalism," it is perhaps not surprising that the Fresno-based engineer was left behind with little more than an unpaid stock assessment bill, seemingly a victim of larger economic forces transforming American society.

Unfortunately, the dearth of material documenting any interactions between J. G. White & Company or Stone & Webster and the PL&P makes it impossible to document why Eastwood's new (and dramatically less expensive) dam designs should have proved so distasteful to the PL&P corporate hierarchy. On the surface, however, Eastwood's estrangement from Huntington, Kerckhoff, and Balch seems to be most easily explained with reference to the radical nature of his multiple arch dam proposal. In this scenario, the PL&P leadership acted reasonably and conservatively in implementing the massive gravity designs advocated by Stone & Webster to impound Huntington Lake. And given the PL&P's dependence on eastern investment markets, it is unrealistic to think that they could or should have acted in any other way. Considered in isolation, this point of view might offer a satisfactory rationale for why the PL&P eventually jettisoned Eastwood from the corporation.

But the multiple arch dam was not necessarily too avant garde to fit into the corporate culture of large-scale electric power utilities of the period. Supporting this view is the counterexample of Eastwood's treatment by the Great Western Power Company and its vice president H. H. Sinclair during development of their Big Meadows hydroelectric power dam in 1911–1913. In contrast to the events surrounding Big Creek, the history of Eastwood's efforts to design and build a multiple arch dam for the Great Western Power Company is well documented, and little mystery clouds the actions of the major participants in the project. Eastwood's association with Sinclair on this project constituted his last major involvement in the world of hydroelectric power, and it occurred contemporaneously with Stone & Webster's completion of Big Creek. However, informed analysis of the Big Meadows controversy requires an understanding of the multiple arch dams constructed at Hume Lake and Big Bear Valley beginning in 1908. These pioneering structures proved that Eastwood's ideas were more than fanciful dreams; they also helped show that dam design concepts originally conceived for the purpose of impounding the waters of Big Creek could hold relevance for western America as a whole.

CHAPTER 5

Success at Hume Lake and Big Bear Valley (1908–1911)

[The Hume-Bennett Lumber Company has] a fine improvement at a reasonable cost . . . [we] hope that the dam will prove a valuable advertisement for your skill.

George Hefferan to John S. Eastwood, August 1909

At the time of the quake I was sitting on the end of the [Big Bear Valley] Dam and all at once felt a tremble, looked across the dam, she was sure going some. She was vibrating from eight to ten inches and N & S, jumping up and down 2 feet thought sure she was gone, but she is here yet and is holding the water back in good shape. . . . Was looking over the dam a few days before the quake and looked over it the day after and there wasn't a crack in it.

B. T. Weed to John S. Eastwood, January 1921

Upon embarking on hydroelectric power initiatives in the early 1890s, Eastwood curtailed his involvement in the Sierra Nevada logging industry. The cutting of giant sequoia in the Converse Basin continued at a furious pace; but despite the large number of trees destroyed, the costs of processing and transporting cut timber proved too high to generate sustained profits within the Pacific coast lumber market. By the early twentieth century the Smith and Moore interests that had employed Eastwood as a surveyor in the 1880s were bankrupt. Soon, their expansive timber tracts in the upper Kings River watershed (including the Boulder Creek groves) became

available to anyone wishing to enter the risky game of Sierra Nevada logging.[1] Confident that profits could be attained through more efficient production, a major Michigan-based lumber firm began planning a move into the sequoia region. One result of this company's expansion was that Eastwood found a client willing to finance his first multiple arch dam.

Following the Civil War, Charles Hackley and his sons had established a successful business serving the Chicago lumber market.[2] Based in Muskegon, Michigan, the Hackley timber empire centered on the Great Lakes region but eventually encompassed holdings throughout

85

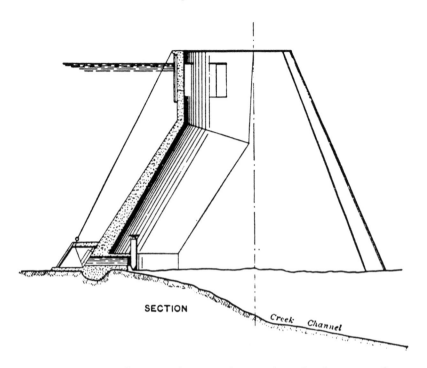

SECTION

Creek Channel

5.1   *Cross section of Hume Lake Dam, showing the inclined upstream face and "vertical head" of Eastwood's first multiple arch dam.* (Journal of Electricity Power and Gas, 1909)

the central and southeastern United States. In the 1870s, Thomas Hackley assumed control of his father's business and, working with junior partner Thomas Hume, maintained this position until his death in 1905. Shortly afterward, timber entrepreneur Ira Bennett presented Hume with a plan to buy the Smith and Moore holdings and restart logging operations in the Kings River watershed. Seeking to expand operations into the Pacific coast market (a move that the recently deceased Hackley had resisted), Hume accepted Bennett's proposal. In December 1905, the newly formed Hume-Bennett Lumber Company purchased the Smith and Moore tract, and sequoia logging entered a new era.

The elder Hume dispatched his son George to supervise work in California and refurbish the old Smith and Moore plant.[5] Within a year, the new company realized that too little uncut timber remained in the Converse Basin to justify continued operation of the sawmill on Mill Flat Creek. Other than writing off the investment as a

complete loss or seeking an unsuspecting buyer for their holdings, the company's only option was to push deeper into the mountains and build a new sawmill closer to previously unexploited groves. This move would require developing a logging complex along Ten-Mile Creek, the next tributary of the Kings River above the Converse Basin. The possibility of building a reservoir at Long Meadow on Ten-Mile Creek had long been recognized; in fact, a surviving field notebook reveals that Eastwood himself had surveyed the Long Meadow dam site in December 1886.[4] Prior to 1907, however, the future site of Hume Lake remained undeveloped.

With an eye to limiting capital expenditures whenever possible, the company began planning a facility at Long Meadow structured around a new storage reservoir. This artificial lake would hold logs prior to cutting and would supply water for the transportation flume. During the late summer of 1907, the company negotiated with at least two engineers involved in the logging industry for construction of the dam. These efforts proved fruitless, however, and in mid-September the situation remained unresolved. Eastwood then approached the company about building a new type of dam, which he promised would save money over a standard rockfill design.[5] Although he had maintained little formal contact with the logging industry during the previous fifteen years, Eastwood was well-informed about the region. In particular, he had surveyed hydroelectric power sites along the North Fork of the Kings River the previous summer and probably had learned about the proposed Hume-Bennett expansion during the course of this work.[6]

Eastwood's initial communications with the Michigan-based company are not well documented; but from his perspective, its need for a dam came at an opportune time. He had recently completed design work for Big Creek and was awaiting word to proceed with construction. During the previous year, he had developed plans for multiple arch buttressed dams and was eager to see them translated from drawing-board sketches to reality. Not interested in a long-term association with the logging industry, Eastwood regarded the Hume Lake project as a stepping stone for further work in hydroelectric power and dam construction in general.

Writing to the Hume-Bennett Lumber Company in early October, Eastwood stressed the economic advantages of a multiple arch design over rockfill dams previously built in the region.[7] As with the original Big Creek design, his initial Hume Lake proposal entailed using arches that varied in width depending on their height: for the shallow sections at either end of the dam, he proposed building twenty arches with 20-foot spans; in the center section of the dam (where the reservoir was to be deepest) he intended to build two 30-foot-wide arches and one 40-foot-wide arch. Within a few months, Eastwood abandoned this multiwidth arch design in favor of using 50-foot-span arches for the entire Hume Lake Dam. A decade later, he returned to the idea of using arches of varying span in a single design; but after the fall of 1907, all of Eastwood's early projects featured constant-width arches.[8]

That autumn, the Hume-Bennett Lumber Company sent Eastwood's proposal to a Michigan engineer for appraisal. After receiving what must have been a negative assessment, Thomas Hume expressed opposition to "the building of this high, expensive and dangerous dam."[9] Unfortunately, records of corporate deliberations during the first half of 1908 and of subsequent negotiations with Eastwood have not survived. Thus, it is somewhat mysterious why the previously skeptical Hume soon opted to bankroll construction of the world's first reinforced concrete multiple arch dam.[10] Evidently, Eastwood's salesmanship, combined with a strong desire to reduce expenditures at Long Meadow, prompted Hume to adopt the new design. In truth, the dam constituted a minuscule fraction of the more than $1 million the company needed to invest in moving to the Ten-Mile Creek watershed (for improvements that included housing, logging railroads, a sawmill, and a lengthy addition to the Sanger flume).[11] The decision to build a multiple arch dam was thus not essential to the project's economic viability. But perhaps because financial risk-taking constituted an integral part of the entrepreneurial culture surrounding the logging industry, Hume was willing to experiment with a new technology that promised to reduce the cost of water storage. The firm's biggest gamble, of course, involved buying the Smith and Moore holdings in the first place. In comparison, the risks associated with the particular form of dam chosen for construction may have seemed relatively minor. Whatever the cause, in the spring of 1908, Hume-Bennett Lumber Company authorized Eastwood to prepare a multiple arch design and to supervise its construction. The company paid for all labor and materials, while he worked for a fixed fee of $1,770. In the end, the dam cost approximately $46,000, including Eastwood's salary.[12] Given that a comparable rockfill design was estimated to cost more than $70,000, the company did not suffer financial embarrassment in choosing to build a multiple arch dam.

As built, the dam is 61 feet tall and features a series of twelve 50-foot-wide arches supported on thirteen buttresses that rest on granite bedrock (Fig. 5.1).[13] Including short "end walls," the structure's total length is 667 feet. Interestingly, the height of the dam was determined by non-

5.2   *Detail view of excavation work, showing the character of the Hume Lake Dam's granite foundations. (Michigan State University Archives and Historical Collections)*

technological factors: a tract of land on the southern edge of Long Meadow did not belong to the Hume-Bennett Lumber Company; and because the owners of this land did not wish to sell or be flooded out, their property line dictated the limit of the reservoir and hence the maximum height of the dam.[14] Spillways (later filled in with concrete) were provided by 5-foot by 8-foot openings built in the four central arches. Water for the lumber flume was released through two 12-inch-diameter pipes.

Each of the arches in the Hume Lake Dam encompasses an arc of 118 degrees, as measured along the extrados (the outside surface). The arc of the intrados (the arch's inside surface) varies as each arch gradually becomes thicker in order to resist increased

hydrostatic pressures. The upper arch has a minimum thickness of 18 inches; at a depth 36 feet below the top of the dam, it begins to increase in thickness at a rate of 1 inch for every 2-foot vertical drop. The buttresses are 32 inches wide at the top, and they also increase in width at a rate of 1 inch for every 2-foot vertical drop. Because an inclined upstream face at the top of the dam was not necessary to ensure structural stability, Eastwood designed the arches with a 16-foot-high "vertical head." Below 16 feet, the buttresses are inclined at a 32-degree angle to ensure that the dam will not slide or tip over. In employing a design in which various dimensions increase in relation to increased hydrostatic pressure, the Hume Lake Dam embodied key principles lying at the root of all subsequent Eastwood dams.

As planner of the construction plant, Eastwood could not rely upon any previous experience as a reinforced concrete contractor. By 1908, however, reinforced concrete represented a well-established construction technology in California, and he need not have undertaken any dramatic experimentation to build with it. In San Francisco in 1889, Ernest Ransome had built America's first reinforced concrete bridge; during the next decade, several engineers began actively promoting use of the material for bridges and buildings.[15] In the early twentieth century, the technology was still new, but it had long since passed from the experimental stage. For information on general construction techniques, Eastwood could have consulted several major books on the subject, including Reid's *Concrete and Reinforced Concrete*

Construction (1907), Taylor and Thompson's *Concrete Plain and Reinforced* (1905), and Buel and Hill's *Reinforced Concrete* (1906). Thus, he did not need to "invent" the technology of reinforced concrete construction as he adapted existing techniques for his own special needs at Hume Lake.[16]

Eastwood began "final location surveys" at Long Meadow on June 20, 1908. Blasting and other foundation work followed within a few weeks.[17] Although the site's hard granite foundation is close to the surface, he directed that foundation trenches be dug out along the entire length of the dam to ensure a tight "keying" of the structure into granite (Fig. 5.2). At the start of construction, a wooden trestle was built across the valley at an elevation slightly greater than the maximum height of the dam (Fig. 5.3). A tramway ran along the trestle's top, permitting delivery of construction materials to any part of the structure.

5.3 *General view looking downstream in midsummer 1908. A wooden trestle extends along the axis of the dam, to be used subsequently to deliver material to various parts of the structure. The concrete mixing plant and hoisting derrick are in front of the trestle on the left. The flume in the left/center foreground was built to carry the flow of Ten-Mile Creek so that it would not disrupt the building process. (Michigan State University Archives and Historical Collections)*

5.4   *The derrick hoisting a bucket of wet concrete up to the trestle. The concrete was mixed, transported, and placed in batches of ½ cubic yard each. (Michigan State University Archives and Historical Collections)*

5.5   *Makeshift shed built to keep cement dry. The rock crusher for the concrete aggregate is being hauled by a team of mules. (Michigan State University Archives and Historical Collections)*

5.6 *A "skeleton" of the buttress formwork. The trestle extends directly across the top of the buttress. The diversion flume for Ten-Mile Creek is in the foreground. (Michigan State University Archives and Historical Collections)*

Eastwood erected a hoist in the middle of the construction site to carry buckets of wet concrete from the concrete mixer and deliver them to tramcars located on the trestle (Fig. 5.4). Like other crushing, mixing, and lifting equipment, this hoist was powered by "much-used logging donkeys."[18] In addition to the main trestle, a smaller trestle was used to carry stone from a quarry to a storage area adjacent to the rock crusher. The stone aggregate produced by the crusher was then mixed with sand and cement to produce con-

crete. Only the cement was imported to the site (Fig. 5.5) from the Hume-Bennett Lumber Company's railhead at Sanger; all other components of the concrete were obtained in and around Long Meadow.

Before the process of pouring concrete began, carpenters constructed wooden forms in the shape of the buttresses and arches (Figs. 5.6 and 5.7). These forms consisted of $1/2$-inch by 6-inch boards supported by 2-inch by 4-inch studs. To ensure that the arch forms held the correct circular shape, they were re-

5.7   *Arch (closest to the camera) showing the formwork for the inside (or intrados) of the arch. Relatively smooth planks are being laid across the skeletal frame; the arches in the background show the completed formwork for the outside (or extrados) of the arches. (Michigan State University Archives and Historical Collections)*

strained by "segments of a circle, cut to the template of a pattern and assembled in place in sections."[19] For the most part, construction of the thirteen buttresses preceded erection of the arches; Eastwood wanted the buttresses to have sufficient time to harden before bearing the weight of the arches. When concrete placement started in mid-August, however, initial work focused on completing four buttresses and three shallow arches located at the west end of the structure. Presumably, Eastwood wished to confirm that his method for joining the buttresses and the arches into a monolithic unit was satisfactory before he committed himself to the technique for the entire structure. His scheme proved practical, and all the other buttresses were completed before any work started on the remaining arches (Figs. 5.8 and 5.9).

Eastwood recognized that temperature changes within the structure could create tensile stresses (that is, stresses acting to pull the concrete apart and create cracks), so he placed steel reinforcement in the arches to resist these stresses. Rather than paying to haul steel reinforcing bars from Sanger, he reused wire cable that had previously been employed to hoist logs. Some 7 1/2 miles of 1 1/4-inch-diameter cable went into the arches with "these cables running horizontally and extending from end to end of the arch ring and into the next [arch] or into the buttress wall." In addition, Eastwood used "railroad scrap iron" for reinforcement around the spillway openings.[20]

Work on the dam continued steadily from July through November 1908, with a construction crew of roughly forty local logging men (Fig. 5.10). Common laborers earned $2.25 to $2.50 per day; skilled laborers, $3.00 per day; and carpenters, $3.50 per day. Because they had to build the formwork to the exact configuration of Eastwood's design, the carpenters merited a higher wage than the rest of the work crew. In total, 114 working days were expended in constructing the dam.[21] To ensure that minor floods in the Ten-Mile Creek watershed did not disrupt construction, a flume was built to carry the

creek's flow through the dam site. A special opening was left in the deepest arch to provide passage of water in the flume prior to completion of the dam. Rather than immediately closing the flume opening in November 1908, Eastwood allowed the structure to stand empty until the next June, to test its ability to withstand tensile stresses induced by temperature extremes. Following successful completion of this test, he ordered the opening for the flume to be closed, and the reservoir began to fill. When finished, the structure contained 2,207 cubic feet of concrete and impounded a reservoir with a surface area of 87 acres and a capacity of 1,411 acre-feet (Fig. 5.11).

During the summer of 1909, work continued on the Hume Lake facility; and in September 1909, water first flowed into the flume extension that would carry lumber to Sanger. Once cut down, sequoia and sugar pine were hauled to the lake by small trains and dumped into the water. There they floated in the lake until towed into the sawmill for processing; the cut timber was dried in kilns before being bundled into small packets and placed in the flume to float downstream. For eight years the dam operated as part of an extremely active—though not always profitable—timber-cutting operation. In November 1917, a fire destroyed the main sawmill, and logging in the Hume Lake region began a rapid decline.[22] The U.S. Forest Service bought the dam (along with many other holdings) from the Hume family in 1935 and incorporated it into the Sierra National Forest. Recreational uses soon gained prominence, as tourists took advantage of swimming and boating opportunities that sharply contrasted with the dam's original industrial function. Under the stewardship of the Forest Service, the Hume Lake Dam has continued to impound the waters of Ten-Mile Creek (Fig. 5.12); and bolstered by a resurfacing of the upstream face, Eastwood's original structure remains intact as it approaches ninety years of service.[23]

5.8 *The downstream side of the dam after all the buttresses were poured. As Eastwood stated in a caption accompanying this view, "the true shape of the structure begins to manifest itself." (Michigan State University Archives and Historical Collections)*

5.9 *Arch construction under way after completion of buttresses. The two arches at center/left show the flat wooden "chutes" used to deliver concrete from the trestle into the formwork. (Michigan State University Archives and Historical Collections)*

5.10 *A workman dumping concrete onto a "chute" leading into one of the arches; the concrete then slides down to the bottom of the formwork and becomes integrated into the structure. (Michigan State University Archives and Historical Collections)*

5.11 *Hume Lake Dam in operation in 1909. The sawmill is in the background, and the ramp for hauling logs out of the reservoir is on the left. The rectangular spillway openings in the center arches are also visible.* (Journal of Electricity Power and Gas, *1910*)

5.12 *The Hume Lake Dam's buttresses after more than seventy years of service. By this time (1982) the original spillways had been filled in with the concrete. As is apparent, excess water in the reservoir is released simply by letting it flow over the top of the arches. (Historic American Engineering Record, Library of Congress)*

PUBLICITY AND REACTION

In July 1909, Eastwood completed his work at Hume Lake, and the Hume-Bennett Lumber Company soon thanked him for "a fine improvement at a reasonable cost" that they hoped would "prove a valuable advertisement for your skill" (Fig. 5.13).[24] Anxious to explore other markets for the technology, Eastwood recognized the importance of having actually built a multiple arch dam. In October 1909, an article in the *Journal of Electricity Power and Gas* provided his first public description of a multiple arch dam.[25] East-wood realized that general acceptance of his ideas had to be preceded by their diffusion throughout the engineering community— something that could only be accomplished by means of publication. In the same issue of the journal that contained his article, he placed a small ad billing himself as "Designer of Dams of the Eastwood Multiple Arch Type" that were "suitable for any height or site," and projected the Hume Lake Dam as the first of many structures to be built using his ideas.

The "Hume Lake Dam" article revealed his intention to devise "the ultimate [dam] type, having in mind the characteristics of permanence and stability, coupled with economic capital cost and upkeep." He described the structure's purpose, dimensions, and method of construction, with the last subject receiving the greatest attention. Eastwood did not explicitly describe the structural theory or calculations he used to dimension the arches and buttresses. Instead, he simply indicated that the arch ring thickness increased at a rate of "one foot to each 24 feet vertical," while the size of the buttresses was defined in terms of the slope of their four

sides (for instance, "the batter of the downstream edge is 5 inches to one foot").[26]

Beyond describing construction techniques used at Hume Lake, the article offered some hyperbolic statements about the structural merits of the design. Asserting that the Hume Lake Dam was "as permanent as the cliffs of the great Kings Canyon upon which it faces," Eastwood proclaimed that the multiple arch dam "cannot be touched by any other type of dam of a permanent nature, in cost, in permanence, in freedom from upkeep charges or

5.13 *A 1909 photograph of Eastwood from the album he gave to the Hume-Bennett Lumber Company documenting construction of the Hume Lake Dam. (Michigan State University Archives and Historical Collections)*

in the safety against destruction from any cause." To his mind, "when its merits are fully understood, [it will become] the standard structure for dams at all places" where concrete can be obtained at reasonable cost. To skeptics such statements might have the ring of arrogant self-promotion, but Eastwood believed them and eventually risked his reputation in their defense.

The first published response to Eastwood's article came from C. E. Grunsky, a prominent West Coast engineer who had previously served as San Francisco's city engineer and as a member of the Isthmus Canal Commission. Grunsky acknowledged the success of Eastwood's accomplishment, but asserted that "it is not for a moment to be assumed that the multiple arch dam lends itself to use under all conditions." Nonetheless, in locations where solid foundations were accessible, Grunsky believed that a multiple arch design might "possess advantages over other types of structures making it worthy of consideration." Referring to the recent failures of the Hauser Lake Dam (a steel buttress design) and an Ambursen flat-slab buttress dam in Pittsfield, Massachusetts, in which the upstream faces did not extend deep enough to prevent water from undermining the structure, Grunsky particularly stressed the importance of securing "an impervious foundation" when building any type of dam.[27] The journal also published a letter from Edward Wegmann, the renowned author of *The Design and Construction of Dams*, which confirmed that the Hume Lake Dam was the "first dam" of its type in the United States. While noting the existence of both the Meer Allum Dam in India and the Belubula Dam in Australia (and also drawing attention to Goldmark's 1897 design), Wegmann's acknowledgment enhanced Eastwood's standing as a technological pioneer.[28]

If nothing else, Wegmann's and Grunsky's letters provided Eastwood with an opportunity to reiterate and reformulate his thoughts on the advantages of the multiple arch dam. Commenting upon the failure of the Hauser Lake and Pittsfield dams, he noted that both structures were built on "water-bearing gravel stratum" and that use of any other dam type would have led to "as great or worse a failure if set on the same insecure foundation." Eastwood reacted skeptically to comments questioning the economic attributes of multiple arch designs, making a spirited (if brief) attempt to demonstrate how the designer must relate various factors, such as the arch span and arc and the slope of the buttresses, to one another in developing the most material-conserving design for a site. In conclusion, he claimed that the existence of earlier multiple arch dam designs noted by Wegmann showed "how old the first conception of merit in the arch really is, [and] . . . the problematic value of a patent on such a device." To his mind, "these earlier attempts at the use of the arch . . . [represented] gropings for the structural idea in dam construction" as well as "rays of light on his patch." Beyond this, he considered the Hume Lake Dam to stand as a piece of innovative engineering and believed that other civil engineers should acknowledge it as a significant contribution to the art of dam-building.[29]

BIG BEAR VALLEY DAM

Eastwood's February 1910 response to comments on his Hume Lake Dam article included a drawing for a tall multiple arch design that featured braces between the buttresses. Usually termed strut-tie beams, braces of this kind were included in his designs for Big Creek (but not for Hume Lake), and their illustration here confirms that Eastwood anticipated building larger multiple arch dams. Although Kerckhoff and Balch remained unimpressed by his exploits, he reported to *Engineering News* in April 1910 that he had been "getting so many inquiries for statements on this type of dam that it has been almost impossible for me to keep up with my work."[30] Unquestionably, the most important of these inquiries involved replacing the famous single arch Bear Valley Dam with a structure that would increase the capacity of Big Bear Lake and boost agricultural growth in the San Bernardino region. A year earlier, many legal problems encumbering expansion had been resolved; by the fall of 1909, the Bear Valley Mutual Water Company was actively exploring ways to build an enlarged dam.

The greater community of San Bernardino/Redlands is located about 80 miles east of Los Angeles, near where the Santa Ana River flows southeast out of the San Bernardino Mountains. Irrigation in the region started in the 1820s with the construction of a *zanja* (irrigation ditch) to serve the needs of local Spanish/Mexican farmers. Shortly after the United States' takeover of California following the Mexican War, Mormon pioneers established a large irrigation-based settlement on the former Rancho del San Bernardino. Although the Mormon colonists abandoned their expansive ranch by the mid-1850s in order to concentrate on settling the Great Basin, an important precedent had been set. Soon other Anglo-American settlers in the San Bernardino area began developing their own irrigation systems to supplement those built during the period of Mexican rule. During the latter half of the nineteenth century, the greater Santa Ana River Valley established a strong agricultural tradition in what later residents called the "Inland Empire."[31]

In 1880 the California State Engineer's office undertook a survey of potential reservoir sites in the San Bernardino Mountains. At about 6,700 feet above sea level, the agency discovered a broad valley along Bear Creek (a tributary of the Santa Ana River) that it considered "one of the best locations for [water storage] in Southern California."[32] The state government had neither the desire nor the means to build a storage dam at this site; but within a few years irrigation promoters from the new settlement of Redlands — a privately financed irrigation colony located a few miles south of San Bernardino — initiated plans to store floodwaters in Bear Valley. The leader

of this reservoir construction project was Frank E. Brown, a young engineering graduate from Yale and a co-founder of Redlands in 1881. Brown had confidence that he could design and build a masonry arch dam requiring substantially less material (and financial capital) than would a more traditional gravity dam.[33] Under the auspices of the Bear Valley Land and Water Company, he began building a 64-foot-tall arch dam in the summer of 1883, using large masonry blocks quarried near the dam site. The remoteness of the site and the skimpiness of financing prompted Brown to adopt a design with arch dimensions that featured a thickness of only 8 feet at a depth 40 feet below the crest.

Brown's arch dam was completed in the summer of 1884 and immediately began storing water for irrigators in the valley. From a technical point of view, the dam functioned flawlessly, holding back spring floods and providing a storage capacity of more than 22,500 acre-feet. However, Brown encountered legal challenges from farmers who held water rights antedating the claims of his company. In response, he had new canals built to ensure that water from the Bear Valley Water and Canal Company system could be delivered to preexisting irrigation interests.[34] After meeting the demands of these prior appropriators, Brown formed the Bear Valley Irrigation Company in the early 1890s to absorb the original Redlands system and to provide water for newly settled districts to the south and east; water for the enlarged project was to be stored behind a new earthfill dam at Bear Valley.[35]

Unfortunately for farmers and investors, the distribution plan proved too adventuresome. By 1894, the Bear Valley Irrigation Company entered bankruptcy — a condition that precluded building a new dam for several years. Although Brown never regained control over the system's operation, by 1908 the locally run Bear Valley Mutual Water Company had emerged from the legal morass with renewed hopes of enlarging the reservoir in Bear Valley. As Horace Hinckley, a former manager of the mutual water company, later reported: "Big Bear Lake was completely dry in the summers of 1898, 1899, 1900 and 1904 and it was clearly evident that a higher dam providing more holdover storage was necessary at Big Bear."[36] With the impending construction of a larger dam, the expanded reservoir became known as "Big Bear Lake," and this name eventually became attached to the dam itself.

Initial plans for the new Big Bear Dam were developed in the fall of 1909 when, at the invitation of the water company, James D. Schuyler examined the site and offered a series of cost estimates for building a concrete gravity, a hydraulic fill, or a rockfill dam to replace Brown's arch dam. In "strongly recommend[ing] . . . a rockfill dam with a facing of reinforced concrete," he judged that a design with a spillway approximately 12 feet above the crest of the 1884 structure would cost $140,000.[37] The water company balked at financing Schuyler's design and during the following winter learned about Eastwood's work for the Hume-Bennett Lumber Company. Impressed by the economy of the Hume Lake Dam, the company engaged Eastwood on April 7, 1910, to design and build a multiple arch dam that would provide storage at least 13 feet above the crest of Brown's arch dam (that is, to the same height as Schuyler's rockfill proposal). The terms of the contract stipulated:

That $80,000 be considered the base estimate; that I [Eastwood] will accept $6,000 as my fee, being a fixed sum for taking entire charge of the construction of the dam, as well as furnishing plans and specifications, turning it over complete to your company . . . that should I exceed the estimated cost of $80,000, which will include my fee and all other costs of the dam, that the company should rebate such fee by the amount of 10% of all cost of such dam over $80,000.[38]

To highlight his faith in the economic advantages of the multiple arch design (and to increase the likelihood that the company would engage his services), Eastwood risked a significant portion of his payment by guaranteeing a price for the completed structure. At some point during the initial stages of construction, Eastwood and the company agreed to raise the structure's height by an additional $7^1/_2$ feet and to expand the reservoir's storage capacity to more than 70,000 acre-feet. Costs for building the enlarged multiple arch dam came to approximately $137,000, while Eastwood's fee remained $6,000.[39]

The design and construction of the Big Bear Valley Dam followed the same basic principles and methods used for Hume Lake. Because the Big Bear Valley Dam was taller, however, Eastwood specified different dimensions for the arches and called for "strut-tie beams" to connect adjacent buttresses (Figs. 5.14 and 5.15). While his basic approach to multiple arch design remained substantially unchanged throughout his career, Eastwood continually sought to improve his designs and erection methods. Thus, in executing the Big Bear Valley Dam commission, he did not merely repeat what he had done at Hume Lake; rather, he developed a design especially suited to the new site.

The Big Bear Valley site lay 55 miles southeast of the railroad depot at Victorville in the Mojave Valley (from which most cement and other supplies had to be hauled) and 30 miles northeast of Redlands (site of the water company's offices). To reduce transportation costs, Eastwood attempted to take as much construction material as possible from the local environment. Stone aggregate for the concrete came from a quarry opened up above the south end of the dam, and sand "was gathered from the washes of streams entering the lake . . . [and conveyed to the dam site] by means of scows towed by motor boats." Wood for the forms was cut at a sawmill about 6 miles away, and fuel for the steam boilers came from nearby forests. The key difference between the Hume Lake and Big Bear Valley construction plants was the employment of a wire cableway—rather than a trestle—at Big Bear Valley to carry material and equipment around the site (Fig. 5.16). Described as "consist[ing] of two standing cables strung across the canyon without towers from anchorages, on which was operated a universal hoisting and conveying system that

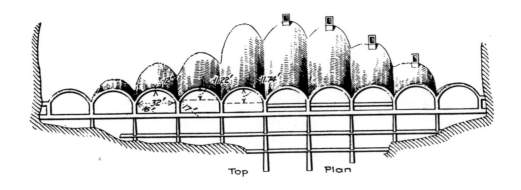

Top   Plan

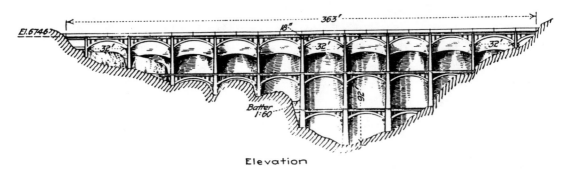

Elevation

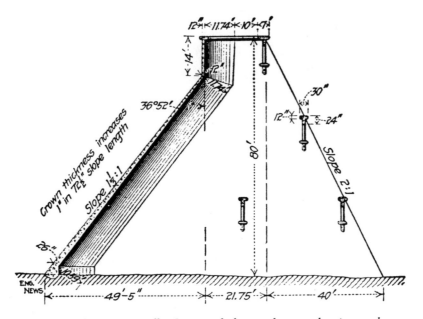

5.14 *Drawings of Eastwood's Big Bear Valley Dam, including a plan, an elevation, and a cross section of a buttress.* (Engineering News, *1913*)

5.15 *Downstream side of Big Bear Valley Dam during construction in 1911. The strut-tie beams run perpendicular to the buttresses. (Eastwood Papers, WRCA)*

covered the entire base of the dam," the cableway was strong enough to carry a 2-cubic-foot "controllable bottom-dump" bucket. Concrete was mixed at a location slightly upstream from the dam and then hauled to the formwork via the steam-powered cableway. As Eastwood later noted, "the interest of the watching public often became greater in the hoisting plant than in the structure itself." In fact, the Bison Moving Picture Company visited the dam during construction and used the cableway as a featured part of a short movie titled "Lucky Bob."[40]

As built, the Big Bear Valley Dam features ten 32-foot-span arches that, in conjunction

with two "wing walls," form a structure 363 feet long. The top of the dam consists of a 14-foot-high "vertical head" while the lower sections are inclined upstream at an angle slightly greater than 53 degrees (yielding a length-to-height ratio of 3:4). The arches range in thickness from 12 inches at the top of the structure to almost 29 inches at a depth 92 feet below the crest. The buttresses are 18 inches thick at the top and reach a maximum thickness of more than 5 feet at the bottom. Four series of strut-tie beams extend through the buttresses, with each segment supported by a reinforced concrete arch. Eastwood took pride in the visual character of the strut-tie beams and reported that "to add to the architectural effect of the structure, the arches of the strut members terminate in imposts, built as part of the buttresses."[41]

At first, Eastwood envisioned using wooden forms for the buttresses and for both the inner (intrados) and outer (extrados) faces of the arches. Although he adhered to this technique for the intrados and buttress forms, by the time construction actually began, he chose to use corrugated steel plates for the arches' outer forms. Known as the *ferro-inclave* method of concrete construction, this system did not require removing the steel forms after the concrete had hardened.[42] Instead, they were left in place as reinforcement for the arch and then covered with a thick coating of "cement plaster." The 10-foot by 20-inch ferro-inclave sheets were supported on (and fastened to) iron angles curved to match the dimensions of the extrados. The corrugated sheets were intended to serve as

"reinforcement, an impervious film and as a keying foundation to hold the plaster coat."[43]

The strut-tie beams were erected in accordance with an innovative method that could be characterized as a type of "prefabricated" technology. Eastwood described the technique:

All parts of the arch parts were cast in moulds as yard members, the reinforcing rods to join them to the beam being left protruding. When sufficiently hard, and when needed, they were lifted from the forms by means of the cableway, a chain being [hooked onto] hoops of steel placed in them for this purpose, then carried to the place of use by the cableway . . . The placing of the strut arches was one of the most spectacular features of the erection [process] as they weighed over four tons each . . . this being also an illustration of the efficiency of this type of cableway for erection work where heavy loads are handled.[44]

The strut-tie beams were integrated into the freshly poured buttress walls by being attached to the protruding bars. Steel reinforc-

5.16 *The upstream side of Big Bear Valley Dam shortly after completion in summer 1911. The cableway platform carrying two men looms above the site; rectangular spillway openings similar to those used at Hume Lake are visible on the far left.* (Journal of Electricity Power and Gas, *1911*)

ing bars extended through the entire length of the strut-tie beams; and where they intersected the buttresses, short sections of reinforcement tied them into the buttress walls. Eastwood explicitly described the purpose of the strut-tie beams as being to absorb "lateral thrusts that might be set up by seismic disturbances or vibrations of any kind"—a comment revealing Eastwood's mindfulness of the threats posed by earthquakes.[45]

Because of the site's high elevation, work on the dam could only take place during the summer and fall seasons of 1910 and 1911; no substantive construction occurred during the intervening winter. The first summer's work concentrated on excavating the foundations and erecting the buttresses; the second summer's activity involved constructing the arches and completing all finishing work, such as placing the spillway gates. The size and the origin of the work force are uncertain, but the water company probably recruited about forty to fifty men from Victorville and the Redlands/San Bernardino area to work on the project. Construction proceeded without major incident, and by the fall of 1911 the dam was ready to store water for the next irrigation season.

FLOODS AND EARTHQUAKES

During the Big Bear Valley Dam's first decade of operation, the structure experienced two dramatic events that testified to the strength of Eastwood's design. The first came in January 1916 when, in the midst of heavy storms that buffeted all of Southern California, water spilled over the dam's crest, demonstrating the structure's ability to withstand an "overtopping" undamaged (Fig. 5.17). The incident received coverage in the nationally distributed *Engineering News* and offered convincing proof that, in contrast to earthfill and rockfill designs, a multiple arch buttress dam would not quickly erode and collapse if water from the reservoir passed

over the structure and onto the foundations.[46] The second major test came on April 21, 1918, when a major earthquake shook the San Bernardino region. Centered near the town of San Jacinto in Riverside County (only about 30 miles due south of the Big Bear Valley Dam), the San Jacinto earthquake registered 6.8 on the Richter Scale and affected an area estimated at 150,000 square miles; the temblor was later rated at 9 on the Modified Mercali Intensity Scale, meaning that "damage [was] considerable in specially designed structures, well-designed frame structures thrown out of plumb, great in substantial buildings with partial collapse. Buildings shifted off foundations."[47] The Bear Valley Mutual Water Company's newly hired dam keeper, B. T. Weed, was perched on Eastwood's dam when the shock wave hit; and he reported that "she was vibrating from eight to ten inches and N & S, jumping up and down 2 feet thought sure she was gone, but she is here yet and is holding the water back in good shape."[48] Weed also informed Eastwood that the dam had not sustained any cracks from the quake. The Big Bear Valley Dam's successful weathering of the San Jacinto earthquake added to the luster of Eastwood's accomplishments as a dam builder and, at least among his supporters, fostered increased confidence in the strength of his designs during the early 1920s.

Throughout the final fourteen years of his life, Eastwood remained on good terms with the Bear Valley Mutual Water Company and its president/general manager, H. H. Garstin. When the company offered to let the state build a road across the dam crest in the early 1920s, they retained Eastwood as a consulting engineer to review the proposed highway design. After some delay, his safety concerns were addressed by the highway engineers; and acting as a representative of the dam owners, he approved the bridge design in March 1924.[49] Construction began the next July and was completed in November 1924. Since then, the dam has become known to millions of visitors to the Big Bear Lake resort community (Fig. 5.18).

5.17 *Floods overtopping Big Bear Valley Dam during January 1916. Notice of the dam's ability to withstand overtopping appeared in* Engineering News *along with a print of this photograph. (Eastwood Papers, WRCA)*

THE FIRST DAMS IN RETROSPECT

In contrast to the indifference manifested by Balch and Kerckhoff, both the Hume-Bennett Lumber Company and the Bear Valley Mutual Water Company embraced the new technology of multiple arch dams as a way to further ongoing initiatives. Both organizations were in the midst of capital improvement projects focused on creating new or enlarged reservoirs, and both found that Eastwood's ideas offered significant economic advantages. Eastwood was not active in either of his client's internal business affairs, and he played no role in the initial decision to build a new dam. Rather, plans were under way to build gravity structures before Eastwood proposed less expensive alternatives. Neither Hume-Bennett nor the Bear Valley Mutual Water

5.18 *Postcard published in 1938 showing the highway bridge atop Big Bear Valley Dam. Upon completion of the "Rim o' the World" Highway, Big Bear Lake became one of Southern California's most famous tourist resorts. (Author's collection)*

Company held a vested interest in Eastwood's work; they engaged his services simply as a way to save money. In this context, his initial success as a dam builder related solely to the economic attributes of his designs and not to any preexisting relationship binding him to his clients.

Although the Long Meadow expansion and the enlargement of Big Bear Lake were small projects in comparison to the PL&P's Big Creek development, both involved financial organizations operating within the parameters of a larger capitalist system. As longtime participants in America's highly competitive logging industry, the Hume interests understood how a company could easily falter under the weight of excessive debt. Similarly, the Big Bear Valley interests had witnessed the bankruptcy of their predecessor firms and they appreciated the importance of limiting expenditures. In financing the construction of a new type of reinforced concrete dam that promised significant cost savings, both organizations also acted within traditions of risk-taking that included (in the first case) the purchase of Smith and Moore's timber holdings and (in the second) Frank E. Brown's bold experimentation in arch dam

design. Characterizing the two organizations as risk takers does not explain exactly *why* they financed construction of multiple arch dams, but it does suggest how Eastwood managed to garner initial corporate support for his dam design efforts.

In the final analysis, the Hume Lake and Big Bear Valley projects constituted a critical phase of Eastwood's professional development, marking the transformation of his theoretical ideas into concrete structures. Conceivably, Eastwood's peers might have viewed the Hume Lake Dam as an interesting, yet relatively minor project; but the Big Bear Valley commission involved one of California's best-known reservoirs and associated Eastwood's name with one of the world's most famous thin-arch dams. In supplanting F. E. Brown's dam, Eastwood perceived himself to be part of a continuing tradition of innovative dam building:

[The original Bear Valley Arch Dam] has been the subject of much adverse criticism, and it has been said by many engineers that by all the rules it should have fallen down and failed, but to this day it has proven that the dam was right and the engineers were wrong. . . . [It] is a worthy monument to that pioneer engineer Mr. F. E. Brown, to whom all honor is due as the designer and builder of the first of a type that in due time will be recognized as the only proper design, a structure using the arch principle, rather than a mere mass of material placed in the path of the water."[50]

Characterizing Brown's design a "long step in the right direction" of proper dam construction, Eastwood viewed his own efforts as constituting further strides toward the goal of "The Ultimate Dam." Unlike Brown, however, he had no wish to abandon his dam-building career after one or two successful ventures. Through his work on the Hume Lake and Big Bear Valley projects, he learned the hands-on process of building dams, and he came to perceive his work as constituting part of a larger crusade to transform how hydraulic engineers conceptualized their craft. And long before pouring the final bucket of concrete at Big Bear Valley, Eastwood had drafted plans for a major hydroelectric dam in the mountains of Northern California—one that would rival the scale of his Big Creek proposal.

CHAPTER 6

Confrontation at Big Meadows: John R. Freeman and the "Psychology" of Dam Design (1911–1913)

The psychology of these airy arches and the lace curtain effect of
[Eastwood's] stiffening props is not well suited to inspire public confidence.
John R. Freeman to A. P. Davis, September 1912

The [Great Western Power] Company will be called upon to expend a large
amount of money for changes and alterations, if the recommendations of
Mr. Freeman are followed out, that will not only fail to satisfy the public but
will be a source of annoyance and regret on the part of the company....
Many of [the proposed changes] instead of being psychological are idiotic.
John S. Eastwood to A. W. Burchard, October 1912

In November 1910, the Pacific Light & Power Corporation officially severed Eastwood's ties to the Big Creek project. While still harboring hope that the PL&P might utilize his multiple arch designs, Eastwood was not precluded from participating in other water storage projects. His first interaction with the Great Western Power Company (GWPC) remains undocumented; but during the 1910–1911 winter lull between construction seasons at Big Bear Valley, he began planning the Big Meadows Dam for the company's Feather River power system in Northern California.

Eastwood's work on the Big Meadows Dam

derived directly from the support of H. H. Sinclair, a pioneer in California's hydroelectric power industry, who became vice president of the GWPC in 1909.[1] As president of the Redlands Electric Light and Power Company in 1892, Sinclair worked directly with Almerian Decker in building America's first three-phase AC power system. A few years later he supervised operations of the Southern California Power Company during construction of the 33,000-volt, 83-mile-long Santa Ana–Los Angeles transmission line. When the Edison Electric Company absorbed the Southern California Power Company (the re-

109

sulting combination became the Southern California Edison Company in 1909), Sinclair became vice president and general manager in charge of power development. In 1909 he could report: "I have personally located, acquired and built during the past sixteen years all of [the Edison Electric] Company's seven operating water powers and a number under construction."[2] Health problems forced his retirement from the Edison Company in 1907, so a few years later, when his strength returned, he was free to explore other employment opportunities. By coincidence, during the spring of 1909, the GWPC experienced problems in operating its Feather River power system—a circumstance that prompted the firm to appoint Sinclair vice president in charge of California operations. Acting in this capacity, he eventually advocated construction of an Eastwood dam.

As vice president of the Pacific Coast Electric Transmission Association in 1897–1898 and later as a member of the association's executive committee, Sinclair knew about the San Joaquin Electric Company and about Eastwood's efforts to promote power development in the Sierra Nevada. During November 1901, the two met in Fresno, presumably to discuss the proposed Mammoth/Big Creek project.[3] After Eastwood joined the Huntington/Kerckhoff/Balch syndicate in 1902, he and Sinclair seem not to have crossed paths for several years, until work started on the enlarged Big Bear Valley Dam in 1910. Sinclair knew Frank E. Brown; he was also familiar with Brown's 1884 Bear Valley arch dam, because the Southern California Power Company's Santa Ana power plant depended on Bear Lake as a source of water.[4] Given Sinclair's knowledge of regional water supply issues, his interest in the erection of a multiple arch dam in the headwaters of the Santa Ana River is not surprising. Indeed, a new dam technology would have been doubly intriguing to him in light of the GWPC's efforts to build a diversion dam across the Feather River at Big Bend and its plan to build a storage reservoir at Big Meadows.

THE GWPC AND JOHN R. FREEMAN'S BIG BEND DAM

The Feather River flows out of the southern slopes of Mt. Lassen and enters the Sacramento River about 50 miles upstream from the state capital. At an elevation of slightly more than 4,000 feet above sea level the stream's North Fork passes through an expansive, flat area called Big Meadows. This locale had been known to Anglo-American settlers since the days of the Gold Rush when "49ers" on the Lassens Cutoff used it as a temporary campsite.[5] The origins of the Great Western Power Company date to 1902, when Julius Howells, acting at the behest of a syndicate led by Guy Earl, filed water rights claims to develop hydroelectric power along the Feather River.[6] Howells envisaged building a storage dam to inundate Big Meadows, thus creating a reservoir to serve a series of power plants downstream.

The scheme's basic concept was simple, and it did not require a particularly deep understanding of the region's hydrographic terrain. In fact, almost contemporaneously with Howells' work, a competing syndicate also filed water rights claims to the Big Meadows site, forcing the GWPC to validate the priority of its claims in a protracted, yet ultimately successful legal battle.[7] Following his initial water rights filings, Howells retreated into the background as the Earl syndicate engaged James D. Schuyler to assess the project's technological soundness and to promote its financial feasibility.[8] Because construction would require substantial amounts of money, a few East Coast capitalists such as railroad entrepreneur Edwin Hawley were drawn into the project. Concurrently, the project attracted the attention of East Coast engineers connected to the New York investment community.

The most important of these Eastern engineers was John R. Freeman (Fig. 6.1), a prominent consultant from Providence, Rhode Island, who had graduated from the Massachusetts Institute of Technology in

1876. First employed by the Essex Company—the owner of water power rights in the industrial city of Lawrence, Massachusetts—he was quickly appointed an "Engineer and Special Inspector" for the Associated Factory Mutual Fire Insurance Companies of Boston. In the 1890s Freeman became president of the Manufacturers Mutual Fire Insurance Company, a position he held for the rest of his life and in which he served (and cultivated) America's manufacturing elite. By the turn of the century, he also had established a practice as a consulting engineer specializing in water power and municipal water supply. In the latter capacity he provided guidance regarding Boston's expanding water supply system (which included the masonry gravity Wachusett Dam); and by the turn of the century, he was also serving as a key adviser for New York City's proposed Catskill Aqueduct. Freeman further solidified his national reputation by securing both the presidency of the American Society of Mechanical Engineers and the vice presidency of the American Society of Civil Engineers before turning 50 years old.[9]

In 1905–1906 Freeman's work expanded westward to California, where, together with Schuyler, he served as a consulting engineer to help select the right-of-way for the Owens Valley/Los Angeles Aqueduct.[10] Contemporaneously, he also helped plan the initial development of the Feather River power system. Beyond providing traditional engineering services to the GWPC, Freeman sought a deeper, more enduring association with the firm by investing in the financial syndicate formed to underwrite construction of the initial power system. Never reluctant to remind businessmen that they were ill-equipped to comprehend the complexity of technological systems, he took advantage of both his background as an engineer and his standing as an investor to exercise influence within the corporate hierarchy of the GWPC and its parent firm, the Western Power Company.[11]

Before it attempted to build a storage dam at Big Meadows, the GWPC wanted to put a power house "on line," to generate revenue

6.1   *John R. Freeman in 1905. (Division of Engineering and Industry, National Museum of American History)*

and help finance subsequent capital improvements. Planning for this initial development focused on a site about 15 miles upstream from the town of Oroville (and 65 miles downstream from Big Meadows) where the Feather River forms an oxbow. In the late 1880s the Big Bend Tunnel and Mining Company had driven a 3-mile tunnel to bypass this bend and deliver water to a direct-current (DC) hydroelectric plant. Known as Big Bend, this station ultimately proved unprofitable when local gold mining operations yielded only small quantities of the precious metal. In the early twentieth century, the Big Bend tunnel and power plant were purchased by the GWPC, and Freeman helped design a 40,000-kw AC power plant to supplant the antiquated DC facility. Construction of the new $4 million system started in late 1906 and proceeded unabated through the financial panic of 1907. In early 1909, the renovated Big Bend plant began transmitting power to Oakland over a 154-mile transmission line; because initial operation of this system was plagued by frequent interruptions in service, the GWPC hired Sinclair as vice president to set things in order and ensure a steady stream of revenue.[12]

After the Big Bend plant became operational, the company authorized Freeman to plan a dam that would provide a storage "mill pond" and increase the hydrostatic head from 425 feet to more than 500 feet.[13] Big Bend is not the site where Eastwood planned his Big Meadows Dam. In the context of later events, however, the Big Bend project is important because it documents Freeman's orientation to dam design and illuminates his acrimonious relationship with Sinclair. In September 1909, Freeman lobbied the company to fund travel for two "members of contracting firms" to visit the site and help make estimates. Significantly, the engineers selected for this task had spent most of the previous twenty years helping build large gravity dams for the New York City and Boston water supply systems. In addition, Freeman indicated that, "outside of office hours," engineers on New York's Board of Water Supply had already begun to "proceed with the preparation of diagrams and details of design." Without considering any alternatives, Freeman regarded the construction of a gravity dam as a given; in September, he sketched a profile of a masonry gravity structure and referred to building "spillways of the Croton type."[14]

To validate his design proposal, Freeman also received permission to lead a three-man commission to investigate the site. The other members of the commission, Arthur P. Davis, chief engineer of the U.S. Reclamation Service, and William Mulholland, chief engineer for the Los Angeles Aqueduct, accompanied him to Big Bend in mid-October 1909. Later that month, the three engineers submitted a report to the GWPC calling for an amply proportioned curved gravity structure that would be "abundantly safe [even if] it were not arched."[15] The design was quickly endorsed by Alfred Noble, a former president of the American Society of Civil Engineers; and

in December 1909, the executive committee of the GWPC approved the proposed gravity dam for Big Bend. Although it gave Freeman authority over the design and requested him to submit "detailed plans, working drawings and specifications . . . within the very near future," the committee also indicated that the work was to be "done under the direction of Mr. Sinclair."[16]

Sinclair had become vice president of the GWPC in May 1909, but he did not meet Freeman until the next autumn. Their relationship proved rocky from the start. Writing to company president Edwin Hawley at the time Freeman, Davis, and Mulholland were en route to Big Bend, Sinclair complained that the handling "of detail work in New York which properly belongs here . . . has caused me uneasiness." He also protested that the company could not be managed successfully "unless all details of construction and operation are left to your California representative."[17] Soon after Freeman obtained approval for his Big Bend design, Sinclair began raising questions about practical matters of construction and about Freeman's relationship with the company. In March 1910, he noted that the foundation at the dam site was "in a poorer condition than was at first supposed" and recommended that the crest be much lower than Freeman advised. After a meeting of company officials at the dam site in April, Freeman acknowledged that the structure "would require somewhere in the neighborhood of at least a third more concrete" than he had initially estimated.[18] In May the GWPC's executive committee met in Hawley's office in New York to review cost problems at Big Bend; as a result, the committee rebuked Freeman and embraced Sinclair's counsel that the Big Bend Dam be terminated at an elevation 90 feet lower than called for in Freeman's design. By the end of the year, a small curved gravity structure (later called Las Plumas Dam) was completed at Big Bend (Fig. 6.2). Within a few weeks after the May meeting with Hawley, Freeman dropped all professional association with the company's construction work; but as later became clear, he

6.2   *The curved gravity Big Bend Dam (later called Las Plumas Dam), built by the Great Western Power Company in 1910. The construction of this dam first brought John Freeman and H. H. Sinclair into conflict with one another; as shown in this 1929 photograph, the height of the structure has been raised by temporary wooden "flashboards." (Huber Papers, WRCA)*

retained an interest in the company's financial affairs and in the proposed dam at Big Meadows.[19]

Sinclair's victory at Big Bend derived directly from the support of GWPC president Edwin Hawley and reflects the important role played by patronage in the administration of the company's affairs. Hawley was an experienced financier who had participated with Henry Huntington as a colleague/investor in lucrative railroad syndicates; by 1909, he had masterminded the merger of over 8,500 miles of railway lines into a vast national "system" that included the Chesapeake & Ohio, the Chicago & Alton, and the Missouri, Kansas & Texas railroads. As one of the earliest and most important investors in the "Feather River Power Project Syndicate" that spawned

the GWPC, Hawley's control of the presidency did not rest on mere ceremony. And in granting Sinclair full reign over the GWPC's California affairs, Hawley gave his vice president enormous influence in planning the Big Meadows Dam.[20]

EASTWOOD'S BIG MEADOWS DAM

After winning corporate support for a smaller dam at Big Bend, Sinclair began to focus on building a reservoir at Big Meadows. In late 1910, the GWPC began conducting surveys to locate a suitable dam site and to facilitate estimates for a concrete gravity dam.[21] Sinclair

113

was not necessarily opposed to building a gravity structure, but his experience with Freeman at Big Bend encouraged him to seek out alternative designs. During suspension of work on the Big Bear Valley Dam in the winter of 1910–1911, Eastwood and Sinclair started planning a multiple arch dam for the Big Meadows site; while the economic advantages of the proposed plan intrigued Sinclair, he desired independent validation of Eastwood's concept before moving ahead.

In February 1911, Sinclair sent James Schuyler plans for a multiple arch dam and a concrete gravity dam based on Wegmann's "Practical Profile No. 3," requesting a report on the adequacy of each for the Big Meadows site. This was the first time that Schuyler and Eastwood directly interacted on a proposed project (although a year earlier the Bear Valley Mutual Water Company had considered both of their proposals for the Big Bear Valley Dam). As has been mentioned previously, Schuyler was for decades the most widely known and respected hydraulic engineering consultant on the Pacific Coast. Born in 1849 in New York State, Schuyler had come west to work on railroad construction in the 1870s and soon settled permanently in California. He worked as chief assistant state engineer between 1877 and 1882 and subsequently established an active consulting practice in Los Angeles. After building the Sweetwater Dam near San Diego in 1888 (see Chapter 2) and other structures such as the Hemet Dam in Southern California, he became the West's primary authority on dam construction issues. His reputation continued to grow following publication of his book *Reservoirs for Irrigation, Water Power and Domestic Water Supply* in 1901, and through the next decade he counseled scores of clients in California, Colorado, Mexico, Hawaii, Japan, and elsewhere.[22] Even aside from Schuyler's involvement with the GWPC (which dated back to 1902), it was reasonable of Sinclair to retain someone of his background to assess Eastwood's proposal.

In reacting to the multiple arch design, Schuyler raised some questions about the structure's overall stability if one of the arches suddenly (and inexplicably) disappeared; he recommended that "in the upper part of the structure" the buttresses be tied together "with rods sufficiently heavy to take up" stresses that might result from such an event. In a related context, he indicated a preference for "massive gravity construction" because it would be "more likely to resist . . . earthquakes." But aside from a few such caveats, Schuyler approved Eastwood's proposal and recommended that "the choice between [the multiple arch and gravity designs] must be governed largely by the matter of difference in cost." In comparing the two designs he acknowledged that the multiple arch dam would be almost 50 percent cheaper (an estimated $596,000 versus $1,188,000) and that both were " 'safe and suitable' for the purpose desired."[23] Given that Eastwood had bested Schuyler for the Big Bear Valley Dam commission only a year before, the latter engineer's equanimity in endorsing the multiple arch design is rather striking.

With support from one eminent engineer in hand, Sinclair and the GWPC sought an additional review before committing to Eastwood's design. The company turned to Alfred Noble, the New York City–based engineer who previously had approved Freeman's Big Bend design, and asked him to report on the "safety and suitability of a multiple arch dam designed by Mr. J. S. Eastwood, as compared with a dam of gravity section." Eastwood recognized the importance of Noble's review; and at the end of April 1911, he traveled to New York City to meet with him. Beginning on May 3, they discussed the Big Meadows Dam during "several conferences." Noble subsequently prepared a 15-page report on Eastwood's design that differed in tone and style from Schuyler's assessment, but reached a similar conclusion.[24]

Noble raised questions about the possibility of arch stresses caused by "changes in temperature" and by "change in form produced by water pressure" (a phenomenon usually referred to as "rib-shortening"). But after drawing attention to these matters, he quickly con-

6.3   *Drawing of the downstream side of Eastwood's proposed Big Meadows Dam, 1912.*
(Institute Archives and Special Collections, Massachusetts Institute of Technology)

cluded that it did "not seem probable . . . that the structure would fail if built as designed." Reflecting a conservative bent, he recommended that more steel be placed in the buttresses, that the thickness of the arches be increased and that the number of strut-tie beams between the buttresses also be increased. Foreshadowing later events, Noble acknowledged these changes were "a matter for the exercise of judgement rather than for the application of mathematics." Even after increasing the steel in the dam and thickening the arches, Noble estimated the savings of the multiple arch design over the gravity design at approximately $500,000. Consequently, he advised the company that "Mr. Eastwood's design, carefully built and subsequently kept in order, would be safe, and that in view of the large saving in cost you are warranted in adopting it."[25]

While finishing work at Big Bear Valley, Eastwood incorporated Schuyler's and Noble's recommended changes into a revised design for Big Meadows that featured twenty-two arches with 30-foot spans. In September 1911, the company publicly announced — via a front page article in the *Journal of Electric-*

ity Power and Gas[26] — its intention to build a 720-foot-long, 150-foot-high dam "of the Eastwood multiple-arch type." During that autumn, the GWPC discovered that the dam site tested in 1910 lay outside the boundaries of its land, so a new site was selected several hundred feet upstream. Eastwood did not alter the basic form of his design to accommodate this change, but the dimensions did change, and the deepest parts were now to extend 180 feet below the crest. The new site was also slightly wider, causing Eastwood to increase the number of arches from twenty-two to twenty-six. Although some site preparation was done in late 1911, major construction work was held in abeyance until the following spring (Fig. 6.3).[27]

CHANGES IN
CORPORATE MANAGEMENT:
FREEMAN'S RETURN

During the year following Schuyler's and Noble's review, the GWPC experienced significant changes in management. First, in the summer of 1911, Sinclair temporarily resigned his vice presidency for health reasons.[28] He rejoined the company by the spring of 1912, but his absence deprived Eastwood of a strong, internal advocate for several months. This absence took on greater significance when Edwin Hawley, the company's 63-year-old president, fell ill in the fall of 1911 and died of a heart attack on February 1, 1912.[29] Hawley, of course, had been responsible for hiring Sinclair and for assigning authority over the Big Bend Dam project to him in the face of Freeman's objections. And Hawley had served as chief executive when the GWPC announced its intentions to build Eastwood's design at Big Meadows.

The presidency passed to Mortimer Fleishhacker, a banker who had become a vice president of the GWPC when it merged with San Francisco's City Electric Company in 1911.[30] The scion of a prominent merchant family that had settled in San Francisco in the 1860s, Fleishhacker (with his brother Herbert) held control of the city's Anglo-California Bank and the Anglo-London & Paris Bank.[31] But more importantly for the GWPC, Fleishhacker's City Electric Company controlled a valuable market in California's largest city. On its own, the GWPC could produce great quantities of electricity; but without a network to distribute this energy to consumers, it could not generate revenue. By bringing the City Electric Company's franchise to the GWPC, Fleishhacker dramatically enhanced the firm's potential profitability. His power and importance were manifested when the board of directors appointed him president. Fleishhacker had been uninvolved in the Big Bend controversy and apparently harbored no particular feelings of goodwill or animosity toward Sinclair, Freeman, or Eastwood when he became chief executive. But with Hawley gone, issues related to the Big Meadows Dam that had seemingly been settled reassumed a more fluid status.

Within days after Hawley's death, GWPC board member A. W. Bullard requested that Freeman make himself available as a consultant to "endeavor to determine with the least possibility of error, the location of and the type of dam to be constructed" at Big Meadows.[32] During the previous year, Freeman had remained involved in western water projects: he advised San Francisco on the city's plans to tap Hetch Hetchy Valley as a source of water, and he also worked as consultant for dams under construction in Montana and British Columbia.[33] He retained his investment in the GWPC and kept informed of the company's activities, including the decision to build an Eastwood dam at Big Meadows.

When Hawley became sick in the fall of 1911 and changes in management began to look more probable, Freeman expressed displeasure with Eastwood's design and advised board member Guy Earl that he "was sorry also not to have a chance to talk a little with Mr. Fleishhacker about his proposed dam at the outlet of Big Meadows. As [a] stockholder I am interested and have many doubts about the best type having been selected. It does not pay to carry economy to excess in dam building and there is nothing quite so satisfying as a big solid mass of concrete." Responding to Bullard a few months later, Freeman elaborated on these comments and offered assistance to the GWPC because of his "former association" with and "large financial interest" in the firm's business. Specifically, he made sure company officers realized that "in addition to my bonds, I have tucked away in my tin box about 600 shares each of the [company's] common and preferred stocks."[34]

Professing that he "fully believe[d] in the multiple arch principle for many sites," Freeman nonetheless averred to Bullard in February 1912 that, for "four or five of the [world's] largest storage reservoir dams" he had helped design, he would not have recommended a multiple arch design. After noting the destruction caused by the failure of the Austin Dam in Pennsylvania the previous fall, he urged that Big Meadows was "not the place to try out experiments on new types of dam." Without acknowledging that the Austin Dam was a concrete gravity structure,[35] he decried the use of concrete in the upstream face of multiple arch dams because of "imperfect theories of stresses" and because it was "a material whose shrinkage may be irregular." Beyond denigrating it in such vague terms, Freeman made no attempt to demonstrate any deficiency in multiple arch dam technology. Simultaneously, he failed to mention that concrete gravity designs (such as the ill-fated Austin Dam) might suffer from their own limitations.

In the absence of other evidence, Freeman's disparaging remarks concerning reinforced concrete could be taken simply as a very conservative assessment of a new structural technology. But in a separate context, he strongly endorsed reinforced concrete as an ideal choice for modern construction. Bruce Sinclair recently documented in his research on the history of the Massachusetts Institute of Technology that, in the period 1911–1913, Freeman (a former president of the school's alumni association) interjected himself into planning for erection of the new campus on the banks of the Charles River. During this effort, according to Sinclair, "most of all, Freeman argued for the use of reinforced concrete, [terming it] 'pre-eminently the building material of today.'"[36] Thus, depending on context, Freeman considered reinforced concrete to be either "the building material of today" or a material in which the possibility of "irregular shrinkage" or "imperfect theories of stresses" lurked. At Big Meadows, he vociferously opposed the technology.

Freeman's reentry into the affairs of the GWPC did not immediately affect planning for Big Meadows Dam. By April 1912, Sinclair was once again vice president, drafting a description of Eastwood's design that made prominent mention of the endorsements extended by Noble and Schuyler.[37] Almost simultaneously, Bullard informed Freeman that "we are proceeding with the excavations for the Big Meadows Dam and should have the work pretty well along within the next three months . . . I have put in a lot of time in studying the Eastwood type and in going

over the conditions at the Meadows and feel satisfied that we have selected a good type of dam."[38] Although Freeman was still to assist the GWPC as a consultant and, in Eastwood words, "[pass]on the sufficiency of the foundations for the Big Meadow Dam," Hawley's death appeared to have little impact on Eastwood's and Sinclair's plans in the short term.[39]

CONSTRUCTION BEGINS

Erection of the Big Meadows Dam utilized a cableway construction plant similar to the one used at Big Bear Valley. Approximately 300 men worked at the site, and during the summer of 1912 they expended most of their energy on buttress excavation. In mid-May Eastwood reported that "good headway is being made [on the] . . . uncovering of our bedrock," and within a month the first concrete was poured. The overburden of soil at the site proved deeper than anticipated, however, and more time was required for excavation than had initially been planned (Fig. 6.4).[40] Although it was possible to reach solid bedrock for most of the foundations, this rock remained moist because of a small, yet steady, subsurface flow of water (Fig. 6.5). As a result, Eastwood took special care to make the surface of the buttresses' foundations rough and jagged, to ensure a solid bond with the concrete. In addition, the bedrock on the east side of the site was of poor quality; Sinclair later expressed the magnitude of this problem:

We have developed a very large mass of disintegrated material on the east side of the flume, reaching up to finished buttresses on the east side, all of which material must be removed and replaced with concrete to give us a stable foundation . . . [this will] require the excavation of about 37,000 yards of material and its replacement with 20,000 yards of concrete, both of which amounts are in excess of the original estimate for the entire dam [Fig. 6.6].[41]

Although large quantities of concrete were placed in the deepest parts of the dam before

6.4 *Looking down into buttress pit "No. 10" on August 18, 1912. The wooden frame on top helped keep the pit from losing its narrow rectangular shape. Note the depth of the workers as they dig toward bedrock. (Eastwood Papers, WRCA)*

the end of the construction season, by August only five buttress/arch units were complete (Fig. 6.7). And because initial cost projections and construction schedules had been negated by unanticipated site conditions, Freeman's impending site evaluation assumed greater significance.

THE "PSYCHOLOGY" OF THE MULTIPLE ARCH DAM

When Freeman arrived in California in early June, he devoted his attention for the first several weeks to San Francisco's Hetch Hetchy project.[42] He did not visit Big Meadows until August 5 and even then stayed for only a single

6.5 *Detail view of the bedrock foundations for the Big Meadows buttresses. The rough, angular texture of the granite surface is apparent; the shiny, moist appearance of the rock gives evidence of the subsurface flow of water through the dam site. (Eastwood Papers, WRCA)*

day. In the company of Eastwood, Sinclair, and Bullard, Freeman examined the existing structure and many of the buttress foundations. Several weeks passed before Freeman put his thoughts on the visit into writing for the company's directors, but while at the site he evidently made some disparaging comments about the subsurface water flow and recommended that the upstream foundations of the dam be pressure-grouted with cement to help reduce seepage through the site.[45] Later in the month, Freeman denigrated the multiple arch design in discussions with company officials and with other engineers outside the firm. Word of this "unofficial" criticism quickly reached Eastwood and raised his ire.

Writing to Sinclair in early September, Eastwood characterized "Mr. Freeman's attitude" toward the multiple arch dam as "the most disturbing element that has arisen in some time to bring trouble on the Great Western Power Company." Eastwood surmised that Freeman's intention was "to take it out on me, in order to get even for having been dismissed from the Company's employ" in the wake of the Big Bend controversy. Perhaps most significantly, Freeman's "remarks of disparagement" became known outside the company, and Eastwood complained that "Mr. Fleishhacker told me that these things have been coming back to him from all directions" and that Freeman had brought "this matter up to the State Railroad Commission."[44]

As authorized by the Public Utilities Act of 1911, the Railroad Commission was charged with regulating the business activities of the GWPC as well as all other private utilities in

6.6   *Excavation into the east canyon foundations to remove disintegrated bedrock. The completed arch/buttress units are visible on the upper right. (Eastwood Papers, WRCA)*

California. The commission had previously taken little interest in the Big Meadows Dam, but after Freeman's visit they sought much more information about the design.[45] In particular, agency engineers became concerned about the spillway and the design of the gates to regulate water releases.[46] At Hume Lake and Big Bear Valley, the spillway gates were placed directly within the top of a few arches; at Big Meadows, however, Eastwood pushed for adoption of siphon spillways — a new type of hydraulic technology that would allow reservoir levels to be more carefully controlled. In September, Eastwood came under increasing pressure from the Railroad Commission engineers to verify their utility and reliability.[47] Because of its competitive relationship to the Pacific Gas and Electric Company, the GWPC did not relish any added scrutiny from the commission that might fuel rumors

120

6.7 *Overall view of the Big Meadows dam site in September 1912. Four completed arches are visible on the upper left. The concrete mixing plant is in the center/right background, and the buttress pits (with steel reinforcing bars extending upward) are in the foreground. (Eastwood Papers, WRCA)*

concerning the Big Meadows Dam. Consequently, the opinion of the Railroad Commission began to assume greater importance in the collective mind of the GWPC's leadership, and plans to use siphon spillways were soon dropped.

In his private communications with the Railroad Commission and with board members, Freeman apparently argued that a solid masonry dam was better suited to Big Meadows than a buttress dam. Eastwood took umbrage at this suggestion. Believing that subsurface water flow actually posed greater danger to a solid dam than to a multiple arch structure, because "uplift" could reduce the former's ability to resist sliding, Eastwood directed Sinclair's attention to recent comments made by Freeman in *Engineering News*.[48] In an article discussing the September 1911 fail-

ure of the Austin Dam (the same concrete gravity structure in Pennsylvania that he mentioned to Bullard in February), Freeman had explicitly acknowledged the susceptibility of solid gravity dams to the detrimental effects of "uplift" (Fig. 6.8). Thus, as Eastwood pointed out, Freeman's own statements directly contradicted the notion that a gravity dam would be well suited to the Big Meadows site. As the dispute between the two engineers progressed, Freeman never specifically acknowledged the inconsistencies inherent in his views of the Austin failure and the conditions at Big Meadows.[49] Indeed, the idea of replacing the multiple arch design with a gravity structure soon became a key part of his strategy to gain control over the Big Meadows project.

To help counter problems arising in the

6.8   *Remains of the Austin Dam in Pennsylvania after its failure by sliding in September 1911. Water seeping under the foundations and pushing upward (that is, "uplift") is believed to have caused the collapse. The triangular gravity profile of the solid concrete structure is clearly evident. (Author's collection)*

wake of Freeman's visit, Sinclair requested that the Hume-Bennett Lumber Company and the Bear Valley Mutual Water Company confirm the safety of their Eastwood dams; both quickly complied, and Sinclair was told that the Hume Lake Dam "is giving perfect satisfaction and has absolutely no leak, and shows no inclination toward seepage at any point whatever."[50] Contemporaneously, Eastwood prepared two discourses oriented toward a nontechnical audience (namely, Fleishhacker and the board of directors), defending the use of a multiple arch dam at Big Meadows.

In the first of these, Eastwood directly attacked the notion that the Big Meadows site might be better suited for a gravity dam. Referring to a "solid masonry dam at this site" as a "positive menace," he quoted at length from Freeman's *Engineering News* article on the Austin Dam failure, concentrating on the sections that emphasized the threat posed to gravity dams by "uplift pressures." Because of their widely spaced buttresses, he contended, his multiple arch designs obviated problems with uplift pressures and consequently were

better equipped to resist sliding. He also argued that the inclined upstream face of his design was superior to a vertical upstream face because it allowed loads to be "distributed evenly over the entire base of the dam." With a vertically faced gravity dam such balanced loading cannot be ensured. Eastwood also noted that his design allowed for a "lighter base loading than can be obtained in any other type," because of the great length of the buttresses (almost 150 feet in the deepest parts of the dam). In conclusion, Eastwood asserted that his design was "not a freak, or an accidental discovery, but the result of very much hard work," and he incautiously suggested that the "solid dam" would soon be placed "with other relics of the dark ages, where it belongs, in the junk heap, and no engineer will think of using it."[51]

In a second discourse on the "methods and purposes" of the Big Meadows Dam design, Eastwood stated his intent "to produce the perfect dam."[52] In support of this rather immodest claim, he reiterated several technical advantages inherent in multiple arch dams, including the elimination of threats posed by uplift, and the light, balanced loading on the foundation. He also advised readers that the steel reinforcement would "take care of all temperature change stresses," while strut-tie beams would absorb "vibratory stresses resulting from earthquake shocks." Although written without reference to mathematical formulas, this description of his design method was not always appropriate for a nontechnical audience. For example, when discussing the arches he observed that: "perfect arch action can only be obtained by the infinitely thin arch and the arch action will diminish from the infinitely thin arch to no arch action whatever when the arch becomes infinitely thick." Although the validity of this claim is unassailable, Fleishhacker and other members of the company's leadership probably did not find it particularly meaningful.

By late September, Freeman was back in New England preparing a formal statement relating to his visit to Big Meadows. But before sending this report to the GWPC, he confided to A. P. Davis—in a "personal and confidential" letter—his concern about Eastwood's design.[53] The exact purpose of this letter is unclear, since Davis, who was chief engineer of the U.S. Reclamation Service, played no official role in the affairs of the power company (although he had served on the advisory committee that approved Freeman's Big Bend gravity design). Most likely Freeman wanted to cover his flank with a respected member of the engineering community before criticizing the multiple arch dam. The letter also offers insight into the kind of comments Freeman probably was making in private about the design.

Freeman told Davis that he had "repeatedly informally urged" the company "to build a big massive lump of a dam," but he complained that the firm's executive officers were after him "so strong for an expression of opinion on the dam itself that I have to go write out something against my will." The latter comment strains the bounds of credibility, especially in light of the views Freeman expressed to Bullard the previous February. Still, Freeman understood the importance of

appearing to be a reluctant dissenter rather than an eager and vindictive competitor. In this vein, he referred to Eastwood as "an honest, intelligent, conscientious, hardworking engineer of good inventive capacity" but tempered his praise by adding that Eastwood "has become so impressed with the beauties of the multiple arch [dam] that I presume he will build his house shingled with semi-cylindrical tiles and ultimately have his hair trimmed in scallops." Eastwood's enthusiasm for his self-proclaimed "perfect dam" left him vulnerable to imputations of being obsessed with a single design, and Freeman did not let the opportunity pass unexploited.

Freeman offered little scientific or technical objection to multiple arch dams; instead he dwelt on nonengineering aspects of Eastwood's designs. Claiming that "the psychology of these airy arches and the lace curtain effect of [Eastwood's] stiffening props is not well suited to inspire public confidence," he confided to Davis that the GWPC would soon have troubles with "popular apprehensions and misapprehensions." While the *Sacramento Bee* (Northern California's most influential newspaper) and the *Marysville Appeal* (a newspaper published in a city located along the lower Feather River) reported some local interest in construction work at Big Meadows between August and November 1912, there is nothing to indicate that people residing in the Sacramento Valley regarded the dam with mass anxiety. In fact, nothing related to Big Meadow appears at all in the *Marysville Appeal* for this period, while the *Sacramento Bee* makes only brief reference (in an October news story) to potential safety concerns.[54] It is thus possible—and perhaps even probable—that most of the "popular apprehension and misapprehension" that Freeman predicted was a product of his own campaign to discredit the design by (in Eastwood's words) "innuendo and faint praise."[55]

In concluding his letter to Davis, Freeman pleaded rhetorically: "But have we a right to build these thin structures, under heavy unit loads, where failure would have such a terrible effect?" In fact, however, the multiple arch dam's supposed "heavy unit loads" on the concrete were almost certainly less than those within a comparable gravity dam. Thus, Freeman's emotional approach to such a technical issue is startlingly unscientific. Nonetheless, it deftly catered to the technological naïveté and fears of businessmen who felt ill-equipped to challenge the professional opinion of a highly respected engineer. In subsequent arguments, Freeman continued to castigate the dam's "thin" appearance and "psychological" attributes — ostensibly on behalf of the public — and the tactic soon became central to his strategy to force abandonment of Eastwood's structure.

On September 30, more than seven weeks after his one-day visit to the site, Freeman formally submitted his recommendations about the Big Meadows Dam.[56] Written as an official statement to company officers, the report's tone and style differ significantly from those adopted in his letter to Davis. In place of tendentious personal criticism, he gave a dispassionate and ambivalent assessment of the site and of Eastwood's design. Freeman described the foundation of the dam as a "heavy, hard columnar basalt" that "beyond all doubt or question . . . present[s] a bearing power abundantly ample for any weight that can possibly be imposed by any type of dam"; he also commented that the deepest portion of the excavations was "the wettest most leaky shaft that I was ever in." After reassuring the company that the "bedrock revealed by this shaft everywhere appeared abundantly hard," he quickly backtracked to say that "in a few places I saw evidence of thin clay seams into which a knife blade could easily be entered." Thus, while endorsing the ability of the bedrock foundations to support a dam (at least after they had been pressure-grouted with cement), he raised the ominous prospect of excessive leakage flowing through "thin clay seams."

With regard to the dam itself, Freeman recommended abandoning the siphon spillway (something he said Sinclair had already agreed to verbally) and urged the placement of "a very thick blanket of fine earth" about a thousand feet long that would form "an impervious earth dam with a very flat slope immediately upstream from the multiple arch concrete dam." Eastwood had previously expressed his intention to cover the dam's upstream foundation with a "backfill of mud or slickens" and was probably not surprised by Freeman's suggestion in this regard.[57] Then, however, Freeman remarked that, "in view of agitation of the public by unsubstantial reports, it might also be expedient to lessen the apparent height of the slender buttresses" by placing a "fill of loose fragments of rock and gravel" along the downstream side of the dam — a concept that was entirely foreign to Eastwood's plans. Arguing that the alteration was "desirable for diplomatic or psychological reasons," Freeman envisioned the multiple arch dam becoming "practically a core-wall in a great earth dam." He did not characterize this downstream fill as necessary from an engineering perspective (just as he did not formally suggest abandoning the multiple arch design in favor of a gravity structure); but in raising the issue, he knew that he was increasing the likelihood that the company would scrap the multiple arch design altogether.

Freeman's report struck a responsive chord within the GWPC, and a few days later he was directed "to work out a programme which will constitute an amplification and improvement of the [Eastwood] plan on which we have been proceeding and which will satisfy every reasonable requirement, both with respect to the stability of the structure and the psychology of the situation."[58] As part of this process, the company asked Alfred Noble to review Freeman's suggested changes. Noble responded in his own memo on October 10 and in a joint report with Freeman dated October 17. Ordinarily, the GWPC might also have requested advice from Schuyler at this time, but the Los Angeles-based engineer had died in September 1912 after a prolonged illness. The impact Schuyler would have had on the unfolding Big Meadows controversy cannot be predicted; but just one year earlier, he and Freeman had clashed over construction of the Coquitlam Dam in British Columbia, with Schuyler complaining about "the impossible location originally selected and stubbornly adhered to by Mr. Freeman."[59]

In his first memo to the GWPC, Noble agreed with essentially all of the recommendations included in Freeman's September 30 report, except the placement of fill on the downstream side of the dam. To Noble's mind, if the cost of transforming "the multiple arch [dam] to a hydraulic fill [dam]" equaled the cost of a regular concrete gravity dam, it would be more prudent simply to build a structure of the latter type. He also raised the issue of earthquakes (never mentioned by Freeman) and asserted that gravity dams were better than buttress dams in resisting seismic forces. Noble concluded by observing that "the question of [dam] types . . . is no longer purely one of engineering." Under the circumstance, he believed "much weight should be given by a public service corporation to public opinion, and if it cannot be instructed and objection overcome, some concession is wise."[60]

The joint Freeman/Noble report, issued a week later, reprised the emphasis on nontechnical factors. To be sure, the joint report reaffirmed technical recommendations offered in the September 30 report (including replacing the siphon spillway with an overflow design), but the most compelling sections did not deal with engineering issues. Freeman succeeded in changing Noble's mind about the practicality of placing hydraulic fill on the downstream side of the dam, and the two engineers now advocated this action "for the purpose of lessening the apparent height of the dam and the slender appearance which its thin buttresses here present to the popular view, *irrespective of their strength*" (emphasis added). Although the report claimed that the fill would help protect the dam "from frost" and "afford some measure of support" to the buttresses in case they cracked, they admitted that "the extent of the precaution proper rests on judgment rather than mathematical com-

putation." In conclusion, Noble and Freeman explained to the company that "plainly, it is worthy of some considerable expenditure beyond that necessary to satisfy engineers . . . in order to satisfy the more or less ignorant public . . . [which will] regard the dam not from a technical standpoint, but by comparison with the familiar type of solid gravity dam of masonry or earth." By this line of argument, technical analysis of Eastwood's design was superseded by issues of psychology, appearance, and public opinion.[61]

Eastwood attempted to defend himself, but he proved to be less effective than Freeman at boardroom diplomacy. When answering technical questions raised by the Railroad Commission, he had provided intelligent and persuasive explanations, especially when discussing the effect of temperature stresses on the design.[62] But when addressing the "psychological" issue raised by Freeman, he responded irritably and incautiously. This is especially evident in an October 29 letter Eastwood sent to GWPC board member A. W. Burchard. Acknowledging that he had seen both the Freeman and the Noble/Freeman reports, he asserted that they recommended "a lot of unnecessary things . . . that will not only fail to satisfy the public, but that will be a source of annoyance and regret." Referring to Sinclair, Eastwood expressed "grave doubts of [about] the ability of Mr. Freeman to overcome his prejudices against certain members of the [company's] management." And taking particular aim at Freeman, he chastised "engineers who have made a reputation and lots of money [brushing aside designs] without consideration . . . simply because they are not the methods that have been followed by the engineers themselves in their former practice." Eastwood clearly believed that Noble was being manipulated by Freeman, and he urged Burchard to have Noble personally visit the dam site in order to see that the proposal made "in order to meet the psychological conditions (as they are called by Mr. Freeman)" was in fact "idiotic" rather than "psychological."[63]

Presumably at Sinclair's behest, Eastwood

6.9 *State of construction on October 13, 1912. The ferro-inclave sheeting for the arches is visible in the foreground. Concrete in the deep central buttresses has reached the ground surface level. Within two weeks' time, construction of Eastwood's design came to a halt, never to resume. (Huber Papers, WRCA)*

soon prepared a more dispassionate "Description and General Specifications of the Big Meadows Dam" that incorporated many of the Freeman/Noble recommendations, especially with regard to thickening the arches and buttresses and increasing the steel in the structure.[64] While it demonstrated a willingness to accommodate changes to his design, Eastwood's new description made no mention of any downstream hydraulic fill. Instead, it referred to the large apron of an overflow spillway (replacing the siphons) that would cover the downstream side of the dam at its tallest part and thus reduce the apparent height of the buttresses. Evidently, Eastwood and Sinclair still thought they could regain

control of the Big Meadows Dam project; as such, without accepting the most extreme suggestions offered by Freeman and Noble, they attempted to respond to their adversaries' criticisms in a manner respecting the integrity of the multiple arch design.

Through most of October 1912, construction of the multiple arch dam continued at a fast pace, with more concrete (6,534.5 cubic yards) being placed during that period than during any previous month (Fig. 6.9). At the same time the "crushing plant" was processing unprecedented amounts of aggregate for concrete.[65] On October 22, ostensibly in preparation for a "winter shutdown," Fleishhacker ordered a halt to construction. Work on Eastwood's dam could have continued, at most, for only a few more weeks, but this stoppage evidently reflected the impact of the Free-man/Noble reports on the company's leader-ship.[66] Soon thereafter, the GWPC calculated the money already expended on the Big Meadows Dam and found (not surprisingly, since the new site required a taller and longer structure) that this sum exceeded the esti-mates made in 1911 for the original dam site. The company determined that, during 1911–1912, it had spent over $885,000 building the dam and related facilities, including a hydro-electric power station, roads, camp buildings, and a sawmill, separate from the dam proper. The cost of concrete actually placed in the dam was almost $188,500 (20,560 cubic yards at $9.16 per cubic yard), and excavation ex-penses exceeded $146,000.[67]

THE CONTROVERSY CONCLUDES

In late November, Bullard publicly reported that "the work generally has made such prog-ress that no difficulty should be experienced in completing the [multiple arch] dam in the summer of 1913"; and at least officially, the company held fast to Eastwood's design for Big Meadows.[68] Nonetheless, a serious reeval-uation of this commitment was under way. In January, Alfred Noble wrote a brief letter ex-pressing pessimism about the suitability of the site for supporting "the construction of a masonry dam of any form." Citing "water bearing" bedrock and "volcanic overflows separated by less stable material," Noble stated that construction of an "earth dam" was a "natural suggestion." In conclusion, he invited responses from Eastwood and Sinclair to all of his and Freeman's recommendations "so that we may see clearly where we differ."[69]

Within weeks, Eastwood attempted to compose a comprehensive response to the remedies and suggestions proposed during the previous five months. Starting with an analysis of the foundation, he denied that

there were any "strata of 'less stable material' underlying the river bed." Noting that he had accepted almost all advice related to reducing subsurface flow (in particular, grouting the foundations), he balked at "placing an earth fill to any great height against the upstream side of the dam," because "the dam is stable in itself" and use of excessive fill would be counterproductive. Characterizing the pro-posed placement of earthfill on the dam's downstream side as being "a rather expensive method of fooling the public," Eastwood in-dicated that his new spillway deck design would obscure "the apparent height of the structure" and should allay public fears about its strength and stability. And although he had already acceded to increasing the amount of concrete and steel in the structure, he concluded that, if Freeman and Noble "had made a study of the causes of earth-quake shocks in connection with volcanos," they would realize their comments "are very far fetched, and only intended to alarm the unwary and uninformed."[70]

In making his final defense, Eastwood ear-nestly attempted to present himself as a fair and reasonable engineer focused on provid-ing the GWPC with a low-cost, high-quality water storage structure. Echoing this view, Sinclair made his own spirited response to the Freeman/Noble recommendations.[71] None-theless, by February 1913, few members of the board of directors were disposed to accept such arguments, and the board adopted plans to abandon Eastwood's design. On Feb-ruary 8 the Railroad Commission held a hearing at which Sinclair testified that, to the best of his knowledge, the company had "adopted final plans in all respects for [East-wood's Big Meadows] dam." The day before, however, the Railroad Commission's chief en-gineer, R. A. Thompson, had undercut this position by pronouncing that, while "mathe-matical analysis appears to confirm the theo-retical safety of the [multiple arch dam] . . . its stability and safety depends on the abso-lute faithfulness with which the work is per-formed in placing the materials in the dam." Even more tellingly, he had referred to "gravity types of dams" as being "the safest and most lasting form of structure,"—a pronouncement that offered little encouragement to proponents of the multiple arch dam design.[72]

At the time of the hearing, Sinclair estimated that the completed 180-foot-high multiple arch dam would cost a total of $1,075,000, including approximately $500,000 already spent directly on the structure; less than two weeks later, however, the company prepared an "Amended Estimate" for the Big Meadows Dam outlining costs for a concrete gravity structure at over $1,600,000.[73] On March 11, the commission authorized a new GWPC bond issue of $3,900,000 with slightly more than $1,400,000 earmarked for a dam "of some suitable gravity type" at Big Meadows.[74] In a letter to Eastwood explaining its approval of the "change from the multiple arch to the gravity type," the Railroad Commission indicated that this "was authorized on application from the company." Alluding to unspecified complaints "questioning the safety of a [multiple arch dam] of so great a height and impounding so great a quantity of water," the commission revealed that it had urged the company to "change the type of structure" and indicated that "the company voluntarily accepted the suggestion."[75] Plans for building a multiple arch dam at Big Meadows had officially come to an end.

Freeman's interaction with the company and with the Railroad Commission from mid-October 1912 through March 1913 is undocumented. He unquestionably kept in communication with members of the board, however, because on March 5 GWPC secretary H. P. Wilson informed him "that due to reasons which I understand Mr. Burchard has fully explained to you, it has about been concluded to change the type of our Big Meadows Dam to the gravity section."[76] By the end of March, arrangements were being made for Freeman and Noble to visit the dam site and begin planning a new gravity structure. In the wake of their visit, they reported in late April that "the safest and best type of dam

for this situation" would be a hydraulic fill earth dam—a recommendation accepted by both the GWPC and the Railroad Commission.[77] During the summer, construction began on the new dam at a location slightly upstream from Eastwood's partially completed structure.

Although Freeman outlined the basic form of the new Big Meadows Dam, responsibility for the final design fell to Julius Howells, the engineer who in 1902 had filed water rights claims along the Feather River on behalf of the Guy Earl syndicate. Howells had been uninvolved in GWPC affairs for several years, but two factors contributed to his displacement of Freeman as designer of the new Big Meadows Dam: since 1905, Howells had traveled abroad extensively (he spent much of his time on a Puerto Rican sugar plantation project as Schuyler's colleague/assistant) and had only returned to California in the spring of 1913;[78] and Freeman left for an extended tour of Europe in early June 1913 and did not return until the end of August, preventing him from supervising construction of the new dam. Although he later expressed some dissatisfaction with Howells's work, Freeman seemingly was less concerned about receiving formal credit for the Big Meadows gravity dam than in ensuring abandonment of Eastwood's design.[79] Howells adhered to the massive tradition and was especially committed to building hydraulic fill dams; unlike Eastwood's, his designs did not challenge Freeman's stature as a leader in the field of hydraulic engineering.

During the 1913 construction season, the GWPC chose to conserve funds by limiting the height of the hydraulic fill dam at Big Meadows to about 70 feet above the streambed (that is, a spillway crest at 4,455 feet above sea level) (Fig. 6.10). Thus the capacity of the reservoir (called Lake Almanor) was reduced to 200,000 acre-feet—less than 20 percent of the volume that would have been impounded by Eastwood's dam. The structure retained its truncated dimensions until the mid-1920s (Fig. 6.11), when it was at last raised to the height of Eastwood's

6.10 *After the Great Western Power Company chose to build a hydraulic fill earth dam, the remains of Eastwood's design were visible for several years. The truncated multiple arch structure and the spillway for the earth dam (left background) are featured in this 1918 photograph. (Huber Papers, WRCA)*

aborted design (4,500 feet above sea level).[80] Although porous foundation conditions were cited by Freeman as a major justification for condemning the multiple arch design, Professor W. O. Crosby of MIT (the geological expert hired at Freeman's urging to study the site in the spring of 1913), declined to recommend any cement grouting to reduce subsurface flow.[81] Consequently, the same bedrock foundations that were labeled too dangerous and "leaky" to support a buttress dam were ultimately accepted as sufficient for a massive earthfill dam. How Eastwood's Big Meadows Dam would have performed under the pressure of a full reservoir cannot be demonstrated, but it seems probable that these same foundations (whether grouted or not) could just as successfully have supported a buttress structure.

For Eastwood, the GWPC's decision to abandon the multiple-arch design permanently ended his relationship with the company. Sinclair remained nominally associated with the GWPC after the spring of 1913, but his health steadily deteriorated and he died in September 1914.[82] Until his death, however, he continued to express confidence in Eastwood's engineering abilities. Indeed, during late March 1913, he sent the engineer to southwestern Wyoming to report on the viability of a proposed hydroelectric/irrigation project there. Had Sinclair remained healthy, the two men might well have found means to continue their professional relationship.[83]

In contrast, Freeman's influence on the corporate affairs of the GWPC (and its parent firm, the Western Power Company) began a long period of ascendancy. In 1915, he

129

6.11   *In the mid-1920s, the Big Meadows Dam was raised 40 feet, to the height of Eastwood's aborted design. This 1926 view shows the final stages of building the massive hydraulic fill embankment. Eastwood came to characterize these types of structures as "mud dams." The intake tower and Lake Almanor are on the far right. (Huber Papers, WRCA)*

was officially elected a member of the Western Power Company's board of directors—a position he retained until 1926, when the GWPC holdings were taken over by the North American Company, a nationwide electric utility holding company.[84] In the mid-1920s he lobbied vigorously to obtain the design commission for raising the Big Meadows Dam and to make his 32-year-old son Roger the contractor responsible for building the enlarged structure. The plan collapsed in January 1925 when his son unexpectedly died from appendicitis. After that event, Freeman's enthusiasm for active involvement in the GWPC waned. For more than a decade, however, he had served within the financial management of the GWPC; and in the words of historian Bruce Sinclair, he became a paradigm of his ideal: a member of the MIT-trained engineering elite filling "the top positions in America's corporations," where each would become "a gentleman, comfortable in the boardroom, a man who might also be elected a director of the firm."[85]

BIG MEADOWS IN RETROSPECT

A review of the events surrounding the Big Meadows Dam controversy verifies that nontechnical, "psychological" issues played a crucial role in the GWPC's decision-making process. Aside from making general comments about "thin clay seams" or subsurface water flow, no one ever enunciated a quantifiable, technical argument to suggest that the multiple arch dam was unsafe or inappropriate for the site. At most, structural criticisms called into question the long-term stability of reinforced concrete or the multiple arch dam's ability to resist seismic shocks.[86] In lieu of offering viable engineering arguments, critics denigrated the design largely because of its visual appearance; the nontechnical public was assumed incapable of appreciating theoretical vindications of the design.

Perhaps the most intriguing aspect of the controversy is that the two men who expressed the greatest concern about "psychological" issues were both leaders of America's engineering establishment, whereas the man promoting an innovative hydraulic technology was an engineer from the hinterlands of Fresno who had gained his knowledge of hydraulic engineering through practical work in western water resources development. If nothing else, the fate of Eastwood's Big Meadows design provides a striking counterexample to the notion that the breakthrough "scientific technologies" of the late nineteenth and early twentieth century always emanated from centers of academia in Eastern America and Europe. In this case, the eastern expert (Freeman) counseled adherence to a highly conservative philosophy of structural design. In admonishing the GWPC "to build a big massive lump of a dam," he championed an ideology of mass that contrasted strongly with Eastwood's ideal of material conservancy.[87] By any reasonable standard, Eastwood's approach to dam design was more mathematically rigorous and more "scientific," but this did not deter Freeman from characterizing Eastwood as a slightly crazed provincial engineer ("hair trimmed in scallops") who failed to appreciate the threat his new design posed to the innocent public.

All parties involved in the Big Meadows controversy appealed to the public interest to justify their positions. Thus the GWPC abandoned a new and supposedly controversial design in favor of a more traditional and costly technology that it became convinced would better satisfy public expectations about what a dam should look like. Noble sounded a re-

lated theme when he advised that "much weight should be given by a public service corporation to public opinion," while Freeman asked rhetorically, "But have we a right to build these thin structures [multiple arch dams] under heavy unit loads, where failure would have such a terrible effect?"[88] In turn, the Railroad Commission justified its decision to approve the much more expensive gravity design by asserting that "it is the best for the public to have the change made" because failure of Eastwood's design "would result in such great disaster to the people living below the reservoir."[89] On the other hand, Eastwood's basic rationale for developing the multiple arch dam lay in the public benefit it would foster. In lobbying the Railroad Commission, he argued that "the cost of storing water is of special interest to the people of this State and when this can be accomplished with equal or greater safety and at much less cost . . . they should not be deprived of these benefits through any misapprehension." He further stressed the public's long-term interest in reducing the expense of dam building, counseling that "as the rate payers must pay rates for [electric] service based on the cost of the works, any unnecessary increase in initial cost of works is a continuous injury to all rate payers of any utility."[90]

In an economic context, the ability of the GWPC to establish a Railroad Commission-approved rate schedule based on the amount of the firm's capital investment may have acted to mitigate (but not to eliminate altogether) its desire to reduce capital expenditure. After March 1913 the GWPC could rely on the commission to authorize higher rates to pay for a more expensive gravity dam at Big Meadows. Nonetheless, the company still needed to obtain capital from financial investors to pay for the improvements in the first place; and the company still needed to remain competitive with its rival, the Pacific Gas and Electric Company, as it sought to increase its share of the Northern California power market. Higher rates might be sanctioned by the Railroad Commission, but this did not mean that consumers would continue to use the same amount of power as prices increased. Thus, the decision to build a more expensive dam cannot be explained simply in terms of "guaranteed profits" derived from government regulatory power.

Ultimately, perceptions that the public feared the multiple arch dam more than they appreciated the economic savings it offered held sway with the GWPC leadership and the Railroad Commission. It is impossible, however, to gauge how much of this "public opinion" was generated spontaneously and how much was prompted by Freeman's agitation and by rumors spread by competing electric utilities. Certainly, no evidence exists that anyone thought of the psychological issue until Freeman planted the seed. If nothing else, the history of the Big Meadows controversy highlights the influence of nontechnical, social factors in technological development; it also underscores the difficulty of discerning the origins and validity of public opinion as it relates to technological development.

Clearly, both Freeman and Eastwood possessed personal financial interests in the Big Meadows Dam project. For his two years of work through March 1913, Eastwood received a little less than $16,000 ($4,687.50 for the plans, and $11,250 for construction supervision).[91] Because he worked on a "force account" basis, his salary was determined as a percentage of the total construction expenditure; thus, if his design had been completed, he probably stood to earn at least an additional $12,000.[92] In contrast, Freeman was paid approximately $4,000 for his one-day trip to the dam site and his consultations through the winter of 1913; he received further compensation for his work on the hydraulic fill dam design.[93]

But while both engineers were relatively well compensated, neither seems to have considered immediate financial gain paramount. The greater prize was to be responsible for impounding one of the largest reservoirs in the country. Eastwood hoped to use his success at Big Meadows as a means of promoting multiple arch dams for other sites and landing commissions for future projects. For Free-

man the payoff did not involve a dam design commission per se, but authority to dictate the basic form of the Big Meadows design and to extract general acknowledgment that a gravity dam (be it masonry or earth) was a safer, more conservative, and more desirable technology than a multiple arch dam. Both as a leading advocate of the massive tradition and as a highly paid hydraulic consultant, Freeman was particularly threatened by Eastwood's caustic criticism of gravity dam technology; his persistent opposition to multiple arch dams undoubtedly served his own long-term financial interests.

Before closing the chapter on Eastwood's ill-fated venture at Big Meadows, it is worthwhile to compare the types of treatment he received from the GWPC and Henry Huntington's Pacific Light and Power Corporation. In both instances, the corporate hierarchy ultimately rejected his entreaties to build multiple arch dams, but the events preceding this rejection followed significantly different trajectories. Whereas the leadership of the PL&P (Huntington, Kerckhoff, and Balch) never expressed any interest in Eastwood's dam design innovations, this was not true of the GWPC, within which both Edwin Hawley and H. H. Sinclair embraced the multiple arch concept. Although the GWPC ultimately lost faith in Eastwood after Hawley's death, nothing intrinsic in the nature of multiple arch dams led major capitalist/financiers automatically to dismiss the technology as foolish or inappropriate. The role played by East Coast engineers in influencing developments at both Big Meadows and Big Creek, however, appears to be remarkably consistent; uniformly, Freeman, Stone & Webster, and J. G. White & Company exhibited not the slightest interest in supporting Eastwood's work. Corporate leaders did not turn away from the multiple arch dam because conservative business practices required them to do so. Rather, their decisions were predicated on the engineers they chose to believe and on the technical prognostications these engineers endorsed. The fate of Eastwood's multiple arch designs was not a consequence of their technological viability (or lack thereof). Instead, it depended on choices made within a cauldron of emotion and reason fed by engineers, businessmen, and ill-defined (as well as self-serving) characterizations of public opinion.

Following his dismissal from the GWPC, Eastwood became almost completely separated from the world of large-scale hydroelectric power systems. In later life, he undertook some additional design work in the field, but never again did he occupy a position as prominent as the ones he had held at Big Creek and Big Meadows.[94] And although he originally accepted the Hume Lake and Big Bear Valley commissions as stepping-stones to future work in hydroelectric power develop-

ment, they soon served as vital precedents for the business he pursued during the final 11 years of his life. Freeman's assault on the "psychology" of the Big Meadows design may have seriously eroded his professional fortunes, but Eastwood maintained his resolve. In fact, during March 1913 he embarked on a detailed study of a prospective multiple arch dam design reaching a height of 300 feet.[95] Leaving behind memories of his work for both the GWPC and the PL&P, he soon began promoting himself as a specialist in "dams, dams only and only Eastwood Multiple-Arched Dams"—the designs that, in his characteristically immodest way, he considered to be "the last word in dams."[96]

CHAPTER 7

In Search of Patronage: The Business of a Dam Design Specialist (1913–1918)

Only by the use of a wide base can there be safety in a gravity dam, and a wide base means a big bond issue.

John S. Eastwood, October 1913

After a careful consideration of the various types the multiple arch type was accepted [for the Mountain Dell Dam]. One of the factors influencing this selection was the bedrock condition at the site. The bedrock is a calcareous shale not entirely watertight and of a nature to decompose somewhat under exposure to air and water. The advantages of the multiple arch type in this connection were considered to be the practical elimination of upward pressure, the practical impossibility of overturning or sliding on the base and the ready facilities for internal inspection of the dam at any time.

Sylvester Q. Cannon, September 1917

At one time, Eastwood's work planning the Big Creek project held out the promise of long-term financial security; but these hopes evaporated in 1912 when the Pacific Light & Power Corporation's $5-a-share assessment forced him to relinquish his stock holdings. The next year, his dismissal from the Great Western Power Company left him estranged from the world of hydroelectric power and facing an uncertain future. No longer a young man (he was 56 in 1913), Eastwood chose to shrug off his treatment by the electric power industry and to embark on a career as a specialist in multiple arch dam design. Upon completion of the Big Bear Valley Dam in late 1911, he had established an office in San Francisco's newly built Hearst Building.[1] After living for more than 25 years in Fresno, he and his wife Ella moved to Oakland, where they stayed the rest of their lives. This decision precipitated major changes in their personal life and reflected the importance Eastwood attached to his plans for promoting the multiple arch dam. Although he retained a small ranch on the banks of the Kings River until his death, after 1911 he no longer considered Fresno a suitable base of operations for his professional work.

At the time Eastwood moved away from Fresno, the West appeared to offer extensive opportunities for a dam design specialist. By 1913, several major regional water control projects (including municipal aqueducts for Los Angeles and San Francisco) either had been completed or were being planned. These efforts pointed the way for future large-scale development. In California, a new State Water Commission had been established; and although it was not instituted for the purpose of implementing reservoir projects, it was responsible for fostering more productive exploitation of water resources. Meanwhile, many of the U.S. Reclamation Service's first generation of (very expensive) projects were finally becoming operational. Despite the number of western water projects that had been completed by 1913, many more remained unbuilt, awaiting a time when promoters, financiers, and politicians would come to focus on their completion. In such an environment, it was reasonable for Eastwood to assume that his services would find a place in the western economy.

PROFESSIONAL ACTIVITIES

Starting in 1912–1913, Eastwood attempted to increase his professional visibility and to resume activities comparable to those he had undertaken in the Pacific Coast Electric Transmission Association. By this time, regionally based organizations were no longer in vogue, however, and national engineering societies exerted increasing influence in the West.[2] In the field of civil/structural/hydraulic engineering, the key organization was the American Society of Civil Engineers (ASCE). Initially formed in 1852 and reconstituted in 1867, the ASCE operated out of New York City, and its core membership resided in the Northeastern United States.[3] During the late nineteenth century the bulk of the society's activities focused on work east of the Mississippi River, but it still attracted some members from the Pacific coast; and by the time Eastwood began publicly championing his dams, the ASCE sponsored a San Francisco chapter.

In the summer of 1912, Eastwood sought to integrate himself into this chapter by presenting a talk on the Big Bear Valley Dam.[4] He also applied to join the national ASCE and in September 1913 became a full member.[5] Soon after notice of his membership appeared in the ASCE's *Proceedings*, however, he began to dissociate himself from the society. In terms of professional development, his ASCE swan song came during the International Engineering Congress convened in San Francisco in September 1915. At this ASCE-sponsored meeting, he participated in a panel discussion of a paper entitled "Dams" given by A. P. Davis (director of the U.S. Reclamation Service), and D. C. Henny (a frequent consultant to the Reclamation Service) which focused largely on gravity designs built by the federal agency. According to a published synopsis of his comments, Eastwood bluntly advised the audience that some of the authors' views on the effect of uplift were "based on doubtful assumptions" and that "the application of the correct principle of the design of masonry dams . . . must include the arch, in some form, for a water-face or deck." He also lectured the group "that the efficiency of the multiple arch dam increases and its comparative cost decreases with its height; and that multiple arch dams of 300 feet height are . . . entirely feasible."[6] Evidently, his outspokenness was not widely appreciated: after attending this prestigious conference, Eastwood ceased to participate in ASCE activities. Most notably, when articles on multiple arch dam construction began to appear in the ASCE *Transactions* after 1917 he provided no comments for the "Discussion" sections following each piece. He never gave a

reason for this self-imposed professional isolation but it probably related to the eminence
of Freeman (ASCE vice president in 1904 and
president in 1922) and other gravity dam advocates in the society's hierarchy. In fact,
given Freeman's prominence in the society
and his criticism of Eastwood's Big Meadows
Dam, it is remarkable that Eastwood applied
for ASCE membership in the first place.

In later years, Eastwood acknowledged
that he was probably not "politic" enough in
his professional affairs, but he expressed no
remorse over this.[7] Certainly his life might
have been easier if he had been more graceful
in his interactions with other engineers. But if
being politic meant compromising his ideas
on dam design, he was not interested. Apparently Eastwood soon realized that ASCE
membership would do little to help him increase his technical knowledge or gain new
clients. And as long as men such as Freeman
exerted influence on the society's affairs,
there was little chance that Eastwood's ideas
would receive the attention he believed they
merited.

After dropping out of the ASCE, Eastwood
chose not to ally himself with other professional organizations. But neither did he completely lose interest in reaching more generalized technical audiences. He remained
committed to his own vision of technological
progressivism, and in 1914 he expressed his
views in two public forums. The first was the
Journal of Electricity Power and Gas, where
he commented on the relationship of electric
power systems to state regulation.[8] Asserting
that "the public can be best, and most
cheaply served by a single public service concern," he recommended that "all rival [elec-
tric power] plants in the same territory should
be consolidated for efficiency of operation
. . . [and that] public service should be commission regulated because it tends towards efficiency and economy." In light of his treatment by the Great Western Power Company
and the Pacific Light and Power Corporation, it might seem logical for Eastwood to
have favored disaggregating large utility systems. Similarly, after his difficulties with the

Railroad Commission at Big Meadows, he
might have been expected to evince a distrust
of state regulation. Instead, however, he held
fast to the progressive belief that efficient
public service could flourish under government supervision.

Eastwood also promoted his vision of technologically rational economic development
by addressing the problem of navigation on
the Sacramento and San Joaquin Rivers.[9] In
objecting to public support for California's
river-borne transportation industry, he took
his message directly to the opposition camp.[10]
At a 1914 meeting of the Internal Waterways
Congress in San Francisco he introduced his
talk with the self-penned homily; "The California slogan e're should be, that 'tis a crime
to let our rivers reach the sea." Noting that
California's railroads had obviated the need
for transportation on internal waterways, he
argued that funding to keep rivers navigable
constituted "an economic waste." And as long
as there was insufficient water "to irrigate all
of the arable land . . . [there should be] no
fresh water to spare for navigation." Eastwood's speech probably had little impact on
the Internal Waterways Congress. But the
fact that he delivered it at all reflects a larger
commitment to what he considered the efficient development of western resources and
indicates that his interest in such development was not limited to "nuts and bolts" issues of water storage technology.

PROMOTION OF THE MULTIPLE
ARCH DAM

Eastwood had curtailed general publicity
about his designs when construction started
on the Big Bear Valley Dam, and this self-imposed silence continued throughout work at
Big Meadows. After the summer of 1913,
however, he began publishing letters, articles,
and a promotional "Eastwood Bulletin." The
campaign included several articles in West
Coast engineering journals and a letter

printed in the New York–based *Engineering News*. Publication of this letter, commenting on a recently published piece by George Holmes Moore entitled "Neglected First Principles of Masonry Dam Design," enabled Eastwood to advance his professional agenda before a national audience.[11]

In a critique of contemporary approaches to dam design, Moore counseled that all gravity dam profiles are "merely variations of a simple triangle, a triangle whose base dimension is two-thirds of its height." He also noted the vulnerability of gravity dams to "uplift" forces along the foundation. After advocating "dams which are as far removed as possible from dependence on simple gravity," Moore challenged civil engineers to "face squarely and openly certain inherent weaknesses of [gravity dam] design, weaknesses long known to exist by those in the profession, but never honestly admitted to the public." In his letter of supportive praise, Eastwood termed Moore's article a "most concise and lucid exposition . . . [revealing the] difficulties that are inherent in the 'gravity dam'." Proclaiming that "when all other types have reached their limitations, either through cost or stresses, the multiple-arched type is still in the running," Eastwood criticized the great expense of massive dams and admonished: "Only by the use of a wide base can there be safety in a gravity dam, and a wide base means a big bond issue."

In composing his letter to *Engineering News*, Eastwood recognized the opportunity to address a national audience of engineers; therefore, in the limited space available, he highlighted the economic advantages of the multiple arch dam. But in a longer article titled "The Ultimate Dam," published in the September 1913 issue of *Western Engineering*, he focused his attention on technical issues related to safety.[12] The two discourses reflect a basic dichotomy in how Eastwood advocated the superiority of his designs. In asserting that the multiple arch dam was both cheaper and safer than its competitors, Eastwood risked straining the credibility of

his argument. To a public that often associated greater expense with better quality, Eastwood's claim that a less expensive, less massive design was also a better design seemed counterintuitive. Consequently, at times he concentrated on describing the structural merits of the multiple arch dam and, relatively speaking, downplayed its economic advantages. "The Ultimate Dam" is a good example of his effort to emphasize issues of safety and permanence rather than cost.[13]

Paraphrasing George L. Dillman's "Great Hydraulic Principle" as "construct one impervious surface and build the rest of the structure to support that surface," Eastwood averred that the major problem of dam engineering was that maxim's "execution in actual practice."[14] Characterizing concrete as "the most stable material we know," he provided a litany of reasons why concrete multiple arch dams were best at resisting "undercutting of the foundations, sliding, overturning, uppressure, temperature cracks, [and] settlement of foundations"; in conclusion, he related his use of the arch and pyramid (that is, the buttress) to "arched bridges built across the Tiber by the Romans" and the "Pyramids of Egypt." Conscious that Freeman had castigated the multiple arch dam because of its newness, Eastwood sought to associate his designs with both classical antiquity and "the shapes of structures that have withstood the ravages of time." He had learned a lesson from the Big Meadows experience, and "The Ultimate Dam" attempted to address some of the "psychological" issues associated with his work. He soon published a follow-up article in *Western Engineering* that focused specifically on construction of the Big Bear Valley Dam, reinforcing the idea that his design concepts were already providing practical service to western water users.[15]

The multiple arch dam was most actively promoted in a four-page "Eastwood Bulletin" published in concert with the March 1915 issue of *Western Engineering*. This was the only time that Eastwood publicly advertised for business (aside from small business cards printed in the *Journal of Electricity Power and Gas*), and it came at a time when he had no active projects. Much of the "Bulletin" was redundant, repeating both itself and previously published articles. Nonetheless, it is an intriguing document because it markets "The Eastwood Multiple-Arched Dam" in an overt manner that might seem better suited to selling cars than to selling large hydraulic structures.[16] Presumably, an advertising agent/copywriter took some statements made by Eastwood and transformed them into a promotional leaflet designed to grab readers' attention, offering such memorable slogans as "bulk does not mean strength," "each one a monument, a monolith, and a unit of the terrain," "these are the last word in dams," and "why build any other type of dam when you can get the best for less money?"

Perhaps the most revealing aspect of the "Bulletin" involves the claim that "there is nothing experimental about the Eastwood Multiple-Arch Dam," since "four are in actual service in California." Evidently, Eastwood was concerned that people would consider his designs theoretically interesting but not particularly practical. Photographs of all four dams that had been completed by March 1915 were included in the "Bulletin" (no mention was made of Big Meadows), and the physical reality of these structures was reinforced by the inclusion of data on their dimensions. In addition, their costs were contrasted with estimates for comparable gravity structures built using "Wegmann Profile No. 1." Finally, Eastwood implored prospective clients to "ask those who are using them."

THE STRUCTURE OF EASTWOOD'S CONSULTING PRACTICE

Preparing written discourses and promotional material was important to Eastwood, but it was secondary to designing and building mul-tiple arch dams. The structures themselves constituted the most meaningful proof of his abilities as an engineer; and in the post–Big Creek era, design commissions constituted his major source of income. In setting up for business, he designated his service as the "Eastwood Construction Company."[17] This impressive name implies that Eastwood's business employed a large staff of assistants, but the Eastwood Construction Company never operated as anything more than a one-man outfit, with logistical help from a few junior engineers who served as draftsmen and survey assistants.[18] Initially Eastwood used the company name for official correspondence, but by 1916 he did most business under his own name. Although this change in nomenclature may have been undertaken on whim, it also coincided with an evolution in the way he interacted with clients.

During the 1913–1915 period, he advertised his availability for dam design and construction work on the basis of three different financial arrangements:

1. "a lump sum contract for the completed work"
2. "cost plus a fixed sum for engineering and superintendence"
3. "a fixed fee for the plans and specifications."[19]

In the first case, Eastwood would provide designs for multiple arch dams and take complete responsibility for their construction, as he had at Hume Lake and Big Bear Valley. In the second, he would provide plans and take responsibility for supervising the work of another contractor. And in the third, he would simply provide a design to the client, who would then handle all matters related to construction. During 1914, his firm erected a dam for the Kennedy Mining Company in Jackson, California; but this was the last construction project that Eastwood personally directed. Despite always retaining some degree of supervision over the building of his dams (as well as an interest in developing innova-

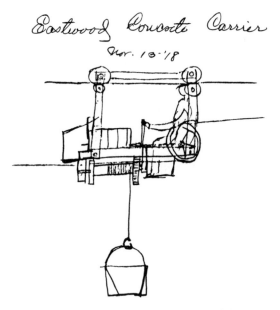

Eastwood Concrete Carrier
Nov. 10 '18

7.1 *Sketch (drawn in 1918) by Eastwood for a proposed "Eastwood Concrete Carrier," in which a cableway operator would move with—and control—a large concrete dump bucket. Although Eastwood concentrated his energies on developing dam designs, he never lost interest in innovative construction techniques. (Eastwood Papers, WRCA)*

tive construction techniques), after 1915 he concentrated his energies on design issues (Fig. 7.1). Thus, the phasing-out of the name "Eastwood Construction Company" reflected the evolution of his work away from construction and more exclusively toward design. Eastwood recognized that other engineers and contractors could handle construction, but his own approach to design involved a highly personalized process of creation that could not be delegated to assistants. Aside from one collaboration with R. W. Hawley, a one-time hydraulic engineer for the California Railroad Commission, Eastwood never worked as part of any "design team."

Before considering Eastwood's successful commissions in the years following the collapse of the Big Meadows project, it is important to recognize the speculative nature of his consulting practice. Many projects that ab-

sorbed enormous amounts of time and energy ultimately went nowhere, and it was impossible for Eastwood to discern easily which enterprises would eventually reach the construction stage. The process of design usually commenced with an initial overture by a prospective client, providing preliminary data on the topography of a dam site. Eastwood would respond quickly with a preliminary design, including a crucial cost estimate. If the project had not foundered in the meantime and if the client remained interested in Eastwood's proposal, further work would ensue, leading to a more detailed and complete design. Developing this involved making field trips to the site, generating more complete data on foundation geology, investigating alternative dam locations (in many cases), and performing subsequent design revisions. Then the project might be suspended while the client grappled with issues such as financing, legal problems over water rights, and objections by engineers who did not appreciate the structural character of multiple arch dams. And while particular projects might be held in abeyance for months or years, Eastwood would continue to propagate designs for other clients, always searching for a venture that would lead to a completed dam. Thus, he needed to tend to as many prospective projects as possible simultaneously, in order to maximize chances that some designs would actually be built.

LOS VERJELS DAM

During the summer of 1913, Eastwood began negotiating with a small company in the Sacramento Valley for construction of his first dam following the Big Meadows fiasco—a dam intended to store irrigation water for olive orchards east of the community of Loma Rica. The Los Verjels Land and Water Company's dam site was on Dry Creek near where the Feather River entered the Central Valley.[20]

Eastwood had often traveled through this region on his trips to Big Meadows, and company president V. T. McGillicuddy became aware of Eastwood's ability to design inexpensive, as well as controversial, water storage structures. In later years, McGillicuddy averred that plans to engage Eastwood's services initially encountered resistance from "our directors, outside engineers and the State Railroad Commission." Despite this opposition, McGillicuddy persevered; and by September 1913, negotiations with the Chico Construction Company were under way to build a multiple arch dam.[21]

Compared with Big Meadows, the Los Verjels Dam was a minor structure, and it cost only $21,500 to build. Out of this total, Eastwood received approximately $1,000 as a design fee.[22] Many years would pass before his commissions again approached the scale commanded by designers of world-class structures costing several hundred thousand dollars. But although designing larger dams meant greater professional exposure and bigger commissions, Eastwood rarely shrank from a potential project because it was too small, especially during the 1913–1915 period when he needed work. In fact, in 1914 he actively lobbied an ice company in Nevada to adopt a dam design (never built) that would have cost less than $10,000.[23]

The 350-foot-long Los Verjels Dam features sixteen arches supported on buttresses spaced 20 feet apart (Fig. 7.2). The deepest arches are 13 inches thick, while the upper portions taper to a thickness of only 6 inches. The structure was originally built to a height of 60 feet with the intention (never fulfilled) of eventually raising it another 30 or 40 feet; because of these plans, steel reinforcing bars were left protruding from the buttresses' downstream edge to facilitate a strong connection between the original structure and any subsequent addition. Eastwood did not use ferro-inclave sheets for the arches' upstream face as he had at Big Bear Valley and Big Meadows. Instead, he used wooden forms for both the intrados and the extrados, and

7.2   *Upstream side of Los Verjels Dam, shortly after completion of construction in 1914.* (Western Engineering, *1915)*

he reinforced the arch with "electric-welded mesh" (a metallic web similar to chicken wire).[24]

Construction began in mid-October 1913 and continued through June 1914. Heavy winter storms disrupted work on the structure; but aside from introducing minor delays for debris cleanup, they had no lasting effect. Eastwood provided the contractors with an eight-page "Description and General Specifications" for the dam, and he corresponded with them in regard to erection procedures. He viewed these recommendations as a guide, not an absolute requirement, and encouraged the contractor to use other methods if they were found to be "more simple and economical for the same work." While demanding a "first-class" effort, Eastwood recognized that "the experience of the . . . contractor on the ground" could prove useful in finding methods "conducive to better work and more economical work." Despite a distaste for engineers who wanted to alter his designs, he actively encouraged contractors to improve construction techniques.[25]

The Los Verjels construction plant was similar to the one at Hume Lake, as no cableway transported material around the site. Eastwood described the contractor's facility as "extremely simple, the only power being for running the concrete mixer and for operating a pump to raise water from the creek for concrete mixing and washing the foundations, forms, etc." Wet concrete was conveyed in "buggy barrows" wheeled over a tramway running lengthwise across the top of the buttresses. Screened outlet gates were built in two central arches to allow release of water during the irrigation season; but because of the long-term plans to raise the structure, no formal spillways were built. Instead, two arches were left at slightly lower elevations to carry off minor floods. For larger floods, Eastwood anticipated that water would pour over all of the arches; he welcomed this eventuality because it would clear the downstream bedrock of "overburden" and thus facilitate "extending the dam when it is desirable to build it to the full height."[26]

During construction, an incident took place that related only peripherally to the dam itself but highlighted a change in the Railroad Commission's attitude toward Eastwood's dams. In early 1913, the commission had expressed little confidence in Eastwood's Big Meadows Dam; but by early 1914, a new hydraulic engineer for the agency, R. W. Hawley, began to express support for multiple arch designs.[27] The controversy was sparked by the denunciations of a local resident who complained that the dam was being built "using improper methods and materials" and that a buttress had failed during construction. Eastwood acknowledged to the commission that a winter storm had knocked over "the base of a newly placed buttress," with the result that the contractor had "lost a few yards of freshly poured concrete." After stating that "there was no damage done to any part of the work now in place," Eastwood suggested that the resident's agitation may have stemmed from the drowning of his son in an accident unrelated to the dam's construction.[28] After Hawley inspected the dam in early March 1914, the Railroad Commission reassured the complainant that this "type of dam and its design have been tested in other places, notably [the Big Bear Valley Dam] near Riverside, which is 90 ft. high and has been filled to the crest." In addition, the commission advised Eastwood that work at Los Verjels was "being prosecuted satisfactorily." This represented a major reversal of the agency's earlier attitude and provided a timely endorsement of Eastwood's first dam since Big Meadows.[29]

The Los Verjels Dam reached completion during the summer of 1914, after the contractors had poured a total of 1,360 cubic yards of concrete.[30] The structure impounded a 2,600-acre-foot reservoir and quickly proved its integrity under extreme conditions. During the winter of 1914–1915, McGillicuddy reported that flood waters "pass[ed] over its entire length to a depth of three feet, carrying over logs and debris with no injury or cost for repair."[31] Although never raised to its full planned height, the dam enabled

Eastwood to regain momentum he had lost at Big Meadows. It also allowed him to remind businessmen and financiers interested in economic growth that the multiple arch dam was viable under financial conditions that ruled out more expensive gravity designs. As he wrote in an article on Los Verjels Dam for *Western Engineering:*

There are many irrigation projects that cannot stand the cost of storing water with the older types of dam because the investment would be beyond the possibility of profit on the venture, but by the use of this type of construction there are many projects that would otherwise be unprofitable or doubtful which are immediately removed into the class of profitable investments.[32]

The olive trees nourished by water from the Los Verjels Dam were cultivated by small-scale farmers who controlled irrigated tracts of, at most, several dozen acres. Eastwood's third completed dam did not serve the interests of a large corporation seeking to develop a large-scale agricultural project. Instead, McGillicuddy's initiative in financing an inexpensive Eastwood dam fostered the growth of locally owned and operated orchards that served as a good example of how small-scale irrigation systems could offer an alternative to more heavily capitalized and more bureaucratically controlled reclamation projects.

KENNEDY DAM AND
THE THREE-HINGED ARCH

As work at Los Verjels came to a close, Eastwood received a contract from the Kennedy Mining and Milling Company of Jackson, California, for a dam to store debris and tailings from the firm's gold-mining operation. The impetus for building this dam arose from a desire by farmers and navigation interests in Northern California to control, if not eliminate, the rock and earthen detritus that mining companies dumped into riverbeds after extracting the valuable material from it. In the 1880s, California farmers had blocked

further development of unregulated hydraulic mining operations; and in 1893, the U.S. Congress, invoking its constitutional authority to regulate navigation, established a California Debris Commission. Acting under the auspices of the War Department's Corps of Engineers, this commission regulated mining operations that might affect stream flow along the Sacramento and San Joaquin rivers and oversaw the construction of "debris dams" specially designed to hold back detritus.[33]

Although the Kennedy Mining and Milling Company's underground mines at Jackson did not produce huge amounts of waste rock, the firm could not allow any debris to pass into local streambeds; as a result, in 1914 the company retained Eastwood to build a debris dam of his own design. Eastwood encountered no difficulties in obtaining authorization from the Debris Commission, as in February of that year Major S. A. Cheney pronounced that the multiple arch dam, "when appropriate to the site and designed in accordance with good engineering practice is entirely satisfactory to the Commission." In addition, Eastwood later reported, Colonel W. H. Heuer, a former president of the commission, personally approved the dam "after a very thorough analysis of the stresses in the design and the suitability of this type of structure for [debris storage]."[34] This ready acceptance of the multiple arch design can perhaps best be explained by the relatively low height of the structure and the fact that, aside from debris delivered from the mine processing plant, little stream flow led into the impounding reservoir.

Located about 40 miles southeast of Sacramento and 80 miles east of Oakland, the 455-foot-long Kennedy Dam was built by the Eastwood Construction Company between June and December 1914. Originally erected to a height of 30 feet above the ground surface, the structure was raised to its final height of 50 feet in 1916 (Fig. 7.3).[35] Consisting of eleven arches with 40-foot spans, the original design deviated from Eastwood's earlier works in two respects. The first of these

7.3   *Kennedy Dam after being raised to its full height in 1916. (Historic American Engineering Record, Library of Congress)*

related to the dam's function as a barrage for mine tailings. Because the density of saturated debris exceeded that of normal water, Eastwood calculated the dam's dimension based on a loading of 75 pounds per cubic foot rather than the usual water load of 62.5 pounds per cubic foot.[36] The heavier loading did not significantly alter the shape of the design except that it slightly increased the thickness of the arches and buttresses.

The second distinctive aspect of the Kennedy Dam involved Eastwood's use of three-hinged arches for the upstream face, to help alleviate temperature or "rib-shortening" stresses (Fig. 7.4). By building the upstream edge of the buttresses with special circular "sockets" and coating these with asphaltum (a heavy, oily lubricant), he was able to construct a "hinge" that would allow slight rotation of the arch around the buttress; a third

hinge was placed at the arches' top (or "crown") to allow the two sides to rotate in relation to one another. Eastwood explained that, during construction, the buttresses were "finished to the full height, after which the arch rings were poured . . . in alternate halves for a small height." By using metal forms for the hinge sockets, he produced "smooth work" capable of facilitating rotation. After hardening, the buttress concrete received a coating of asphaltum that provided "an even and polished surface . . . against which the arch ring was cast." Eastwood believed that his three-hinged design would eliminate "all bending in the arch ring" because, if any bending moments existed in the arch, the hinges would move slightly and relieve the stresses. Clearly, Eastwood had taken serious notice of Alfred Noble's earlier comments regarding the possibility of temperature and "rib-shortening" stresses occurring in his arch designs and sought means to prevent their creation. He felt that uncontrolled cracking in the arches would present a significant problem; so in response, he developed a special method of construction. Eastwood did not invent three-hinged arches, but his use of the technology in dams was unprecedented.[37]

Construction of the Kennedy Dam utilized a simple construction plant. Following the pattern established at Hume Lake and Los Verjels, Eastwood's construction crews did not employ a cableway to transport material around the site. Instead, the 1,233 cubic yards of concrete were mixed using locally quarried sand and gravel and then "conveyed to the forms in concrete buggies and depos-

ited through homemade portable chutes." The initial Kennedy Dam cost $25,658, with Eastwood receiving approximately $2,000 for his services as both designer and contractor.[38] Later, he received some additional compensation for his design when the structure was raised to a height of 50 feet.

As a result of his success with the Kennedy Dam, in 1916 Eastwood received a commission from the Argonaut Mining Company in 1916 to design (but not build) a second debris dam in Jackson. Originally planned to be 80 feet high, the 420-foot-long Argonaut Dam was initially built to a height of 46 feet and never raised above this level. Utilizing fourteen arches with spans of 32 feet, the Argo-

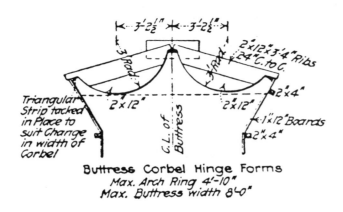

Buttress Corbel Hinge Forms
Max. Arch Ring 4'-10"
Max. Buttress width 8'-0"

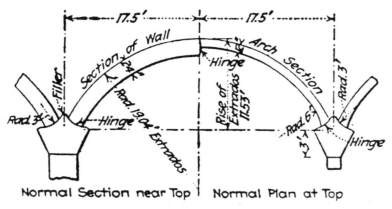

Normal Section near Top   Normal Plan at Top

7.4 *The technology of Eastwood's three-hinged arches. These drawings (depicting his 1915 design for Mountain Dell Dam) show how concave pockets formed along the edge of the buttresses could facilitate arch rotation; the crowns of the arches feature a similar form of concave/convex hinge. (Engineering News, 1918)*

naut Dam generally resembles the Kennedy design but does not feature three-hinged arches. The contracting firm of Bent Brothers (who would later build other multiple arch dams, including Lake Hodges and Littlerock) built the structure for approximately $23,000, with Eastwood receiving a design commission of slightly more than $1,000.[39] Although Eastwood's association with California's gold-mining industry did not yield any large structures nor generate much income, it did provide a convenient venue for him to demonstrate the versatility of his designs.

MOUNTAIN DELL DAM

Following completion of the original Kennedy Dam, Eastwood entered a period that held out no immediate prospects for design commissions. Not coincidentally, during this time he arranged for distribution of his newly published "Eastwood Bulletin" in concert with the March 1915 issue of *Western Engineering*. In early April, presumably as a result of the advertisement, Sylvester Q. Cannon, city engineer for Salt Lake City, wrote to Eastwood concerning plans for a 70-foot-high dam at Twin Lakes, high in the Wasatch Mountains.[40] Eastwood quickly prepared a preliminary design estimate, but he apparently became involved in the project at a fairly late date, and soon afterward the city selected a curved gravity design.[41] The Twin Lakes Dam, however, was part of a larger system under development by the municipality, and in July 1915, Cannon again approached Eastwood—this time about a storage dam planned for Parleys Canyon (Fig. 7.5).[42]

Located in foothills only a few miles east of the city, the dam in Parleys Canyon (soon known as the Mountain Dell Dam) was to serve as a major distribution reservoir. Although Cannon had not pursued Eastwood's design for Twin Lakes, he was intrigued by the safety attributes of multiple arch dams; in

his first letter to Eastwood regarding the Parleys Canyon project, he stressed the city's desire to build a particularly safe structure because "this damsite is located about 8 miles above a portion of the city that is rather thickly settled."[43] In response, Eastwood prepared a preliminary design for the Mountain Dell site complete with cost estimates for a 110-foot-high base and a completed 150-foot-high structure (see Chapter 8). He submitted his Parleys Canyon proposal to the Salt Lake City engineer in late July and offered to provide complete plans and specifications for "5% of the contract price for building the structure" or to take charge of construction completely for "10% of the net cost of the dam."[44]

In mid-September, Cannon informed Eastwood that the city would invite bids for both a 110-foot-high "base" structure and a complete 150-foot-high dam. Municipal leaders wanted to procure a cost-effective design but, not anticipating any immediate need for the full-sized reservoir, they planned to build the Mountain Dell Dam in two phases. Bids would be accepted for a concrete curved gravity dam and, "pending approval by [the] State Engineer," for both an Eastwood dam and an Ambursen flat-slab structure. No proposals were sought for earthfill or rockfill designs. Cannon would provide photographs of Parleys Canyon, blueprints of the site's topography, and a log of bore holes indicating the depth of bedrock; for his part, Eastwood (like other bidders) was to furnish inked drawings of his design and data on "the quantity of excavation of loose material and of trenching into solid rock, the quantity of reinforced concrete . . . and the approximate amount of steel" required. This information would allow contractors to develop their bids in terms of "unit prices" based on the estimated quantities.[45] During the early fall, Eastwood developed final plans; and in November, they were made available to prospective bidders. Nine different contractors (mostly from Utah, but Bent Brothers came from California) submitted bids for at least one of the designs, and most firms submitted offers on all three. The

7.5 *View of Parley's Canyon, circa 1914, looking downstream, before construction of the Mountain Dell Dam. The horizontal lines in the left background show two levels for the proposed dam; this photograph was supplied to Eastwood by Salt Lake City engineer Sylvester Q. Cannon to aid him in preparing a preliminary design. (Eastwood Papers, WRCA)*

bids were opened on November 24 and entered into the public record (Fig. 7.6).[46]

The Mountain Dell competition is of particular historical interest because it was openly administered by an independent authority and because it offers compelling evidence to verify Eastwood's claims for the multiple arch dam's economic efficiency. Low bids for both the 110-foot-high and 150-foot-high multiple arch designs were submitted by Parrott Brothers Co. of Salt Lake City and came to $75,298.20 and $138,839.47 respectively. Low bids for the Ambursen flat-slab designs were $117,052.25 and $216.587.11 for the two heights; and low bids for the curved gravity designs were $88,670.10 and $226,212.00. A comparison of the multiple arch and flat-slab designs reveals that the former required less excavation (approximately 30,000 cubic yards versus 36,000 cubic yards) and less concrete (approximately 14,750 cubic yards versus 21,000 cubic yards). The excavation required by the gravity design (approximately 35,500 cubic yards) was comparable to the buttress dam's but its 45,000 cubic yards of concrete was three times that required for the multiple arch design and twice that of the flat-slab structure. Although the gravity design required much greater quantities of concrete, the "unit cost"

147

- SUMMARY OF BIDS -

MOUNTAIN DELL DAM   November 24, 1915.

Contractor	Partial Height	Days to Complete	Full Height	Additional Days
TYPE 1 (Arched Concrete) *105 x 330*			*150 x 660*	
Jas. Stewart & Co. - - - - -	-$155812.40	300	$356117.00	300
The Utah Construction Co. -	134624.20	151	336551.00	110
Abrams & Ehrhart - - - - -	125499.20	250	302010.00	125
Bates & Rogers Constr. - - -	128968.50	Not stated	290577.50	Not stated
Bent Bros. - - - - - - - - -	113962.00	225	287600.00	325
Campbell Building·Co. - - -	109491.00	270	279200.00	180
Alston & Hoggan - - - - - -	111107.80	Not stated	273737.10	Not stated
Parrott Bros. Co. - - - - -	88670.10	150	229368.00	90
P.J. Moran, Contr., Inc. - -	94256.05	200	226212.00	150
TYPE 2 (Ambursen Reinf. Conc.)				
Jas. Stewart & Co. - - - - -	-$201359.65	300	$358924.50	300
Bates & Rogers Constr. Co. -	168629.50	Not stated	308620.63	Not stated
-Alston & Hoggan - - - - - -	-133780.41	do.	264229.81	do.
Campbell Building Co. - - -	123283.97	270	230488.18	180
Abrams & Ehrhart - - - - - -	125781.15	250	227295.90	125
Bent Bros. - - - - - - - - -	117247.50	225	219910.25	325
P.J. Moran, Contr., Inc. - -	117052.25	200	216587.11	150
TYPE 3 (Reinf. Multiple Arch)				
Jas. Stewart & Co. - - - - -	-$158844.33	300	$315034.50	300
Bates & Rogers Constr. Co.	129129.46	Not stated	245952.40	Not stated
Campbell Building Co. - - -	115531.10	270	215354.68	180
-Alston & Hoggan - - - - - -	108582.73	Not stated	208992.96	Not stated
Abrams & Ehrhart - - - - - -	97339.13	250	176021.06	125
Bent Bros. - - - - - - - - -	89373.50	200	168523.93	325
P.J. Moran, Contr. Inc. - -	89039.23	200	152929.74	150
Parrott Bros. Co. - - - - -	75298.90	150	138839.47	90

7.6 *Copy of official bids submitted for constructing Mountain Dell Dam, as recorded by the Salt Lake City Engineer's Office on November 24, 1915. (Eastwood Papers, WRCA)*

(that is, the cost per cubic yard) was substantially less for it than for the buttress dams. For example, the low bid on the gravity dam stipulated a unit cost of $4.64 per cubic yard of concrete, whereas low bids for pouring and placing the concrete in the two buttress structures exceeded $7.00 per cubic yard. This reflected the economic efficiency of pouring "mass concrete" versus placing concrete into tightly dimensioned formwork.

Of the eight bids on Eastwood's design, six were less expensive than the low bids for both the flat-slab and gravity designs, indicating that the multiple arch design did not attract just one "low-ball" bidder. The results of the competition left little doubt about which was

the most economic design. The only issue that remained was whether the multiple arch dam would meet the safety standards of Cannon and the state engineer. During December Eastwood visited Utah to provide further reassurance about the safety of his design, and it soon received all necessary approvals. Finally, more than a year after finishing the first stage of the Kennedy Dam, Eastwood had a new commission in hand.[47]

Construction of the initial 110-foot-high portion of Mountain Dell Dam began in April 1916 and concluded in August 1917 (Fig. 7.7).[48] The basic methods of erection conformed to earlier Eastwood dams, except that a "distribution tower" was used to deliver concrete to the various parts of the dam site. Concrete was mixed in the middle of the site, placed in a hopper, and then lifted by an electrically driven hoist up the 125-foot-high tower. From the tower, it flowed to the forms via a gravity-powered system of chutes. In 1916, the "chuting" of concrete was a new—but hardly unprecedented—technology designed to reduce the cost of transporting concrete on site.[49] The only major drawback of this method involved the tendency of contractors to use "wet" concrete that would flow easily without clogging. Because the strength of "wet" concrete is usually less than the strength of a drier mix that uses the same amount of cement, chuted concrete did not always result in the strongest material.[50] Nonetheless, it was more than adequate to meet the requirements of Eastwood's design.[51] The remainder of the construction process did not involve any innovative procedures. All

formwork was composed of wood, except for the steel sheeting that supplied smooth surfaces for the arch hinges. In line with the technique developed for the Kennedy Dam, the arches featured three hinges to accommodate the release of temperature or "rib-shortening" stresses.

Evidently, the contractors completed the initial structure in accordance with the "unit costs" of their initial proposal, and their work confirmed the economy of multiple arch construction. Between the time when bids were submitted in November 1915 and the time of completion of the dam in mid-1917 (after the United States had formally entered World War I), however, the price of timber in Salt Lake City doubled, thus increasing overall expenses. Parrott Brothers initially contracted to build the 105-foot-high structure for $75,000; the rise in timber prices resulted in a final cost of $90,000.[52] The Ambursen de-

7.7 *Downstream side of Mountain Dell Dam after completion of the structure to a height of 110 feet. It remained at this level until 1925. The hoisting tower (at right) and chuting system for transporting concrete for construction are still in place.* (Engineering News, *1918*)

7.8 *Mountain Dell Dam, 1971. (A) Upstream side under loading of a full reservoir more than 50 years after completion of the original dam. The arches do not feature a "vertical head" as called for in Eastwood's 1915 design. (B) Downstream side. (Historic American Engineering Record, Library of Congress)*

sign required comparable amounts of form-work and probably would have experienced a similar cost increase. The gravity design, however, required less wood, making construction less susceptible to fluctuations in the timber market (but not to changes in the cement market). The gravity dam would have almost certainly cost substantially more than the multiple arch dam, but the increase in timber prices highlighted an economic weakness of buttress dams; within a few years, Eastwood began developing a type of multiple arch dam that took advantage of the cheaper unit costs of "mass concrete" and thus was less sensitive to the cost of formwork.

Following completion of the 110-foot-high Mountain Dell Dam in 1917, Salt Lake City could store substantial amounts of water near its population center, thus providing an impetus to further civic development. Within a few years, water demand had increased sufficiently to impel the city to raise the dam to its full height of 150 feet. The decision to raise the dam was made in late 1924, shortly after Eastwood's death. In developing final construction plans for the 150-foot-high structure, his successors introduced one major change into his original design. Rather than complete the dam with the characteristic "vertical head" evident in other Eastwood dams, the city simplified the process of fabricating the formwork by building the arches on a continuous slope to the top of the structure.[53] This modification did not materially affect the stability of the dam but it did alter Eastwood's original plan (Fig. 7.8).

EASTWOOD AND CANNON

Although not as large as San Francisco, Salt Lake City occupied an important position within the economic structure of the American West, and the city's adoption of an Eastwood design provided the California-based engineer with a valuable and highly visible endorsement. In addition to the $3,168 he received at completion of the 110-foot-high dam, Eastwood gained enhanced credibility within western business and engineering circles.[54] In an article for the *Utah Society of Engineers Monthly Journal*, Cannon reported that "one of the factors influencing [the selection of the multiple arch design] was the bedrock condition at the site."[55] Because the bedrock was a "calcareous shale not entirely watertight and of a nature to decompose somewhat under exposure to air and water," Cannon considered the multiple arch dam to offer the best and safest design for the site. He also expressed the belief that Eastwood's design provided "practical elimination of upward pressure, the practical impossibility of overturning or sliding on its base and the ready facilities for the inspection of the dam at any time." Pointing to the size of the Big Meadows Dam and the character of its foundations, Freeman had counseled the Great Western Power Company not to build anything other than a gravity dam. In contrast, Cannon indicated his preference for the multiple arch design precisely because of the less than ideal foundation conditions in Parleys Canyon. And whereas Freeman would not acknowledge that buttress dams could obviate the deleterious effects of "uplift," Cannon exhibited a decidedly different point of view.

As Cannon had noted in his first letter to Eastwood, the site of the Mountain Dell Dam lay only a few miles "above a portion of the city that is rather thickly settled . . . [and] a break in the dam would be very serious."[56] Consequently, he warned that "extraordinary care" had to taken in selecting the design. In addition, a branch of the Denver and Rio Grande Railroad passed directly by the site, so the dam would be readily visible to many people. Despite the foundation conditions, the proximity of downstream settlements, and public accessibility to the site, questions about the multiple arch design's "psychological" suitability never arose between Eastwood and Cannon. Within the context of Utah's water resources development, the Mountain Dell Dam occupied a position generally comparable to that of the Big Meadows Dam in

7.9   *Malad Dam in southern Idaho, shortly after its completion in 1917. Eastwood's success at Mountain Dell helped him find clients among Mormon farming interests in the Great Basin and the Snake River Valley. (Eastwood Papers, WRCA)*

California. But the concern for "public misapprehension" that led to abandonment of Eastwood's Big Meadows design was conspicuously absent during planning for the Mountain Dell Dam.

Cannon's inclination to deviate from conservative engineering traditions (as exemplified by gravity dam designs) reflected both the independent spirit of Mormon culture and his own educational background. Born and raised in late nineteenth-century Utah

(his father was George Q. Cannon, a prominent Mormon leader), he matriculated to the Massachusetts Institute of Technology and graduated with a B.S. in mining engineering in 1899.[57] His sojourn at an a elite eastern university was part of a movement encouraged by Mormon leaders in the 1890s for younger church members to learn state-of-the-art technical skills and thus help further Utah's economic development. After serving as a church missionary in Europe, he returned to Utah and worked on several engineering projects before becoming city engineer for Salt Lake City in 1913. Sylvester Cannon was neither Eastwood's personal friend nor a close professional colleague; his interest in multiple arch designs rested on dispassionate analysis of their technological and economic attributes. Not beholden to the opinions of East Coast engineers such as Freeman or Stone & Webster, he projected an independent view of the multiple arch dam and of the character of the technology's most outspoken proponent. Under his authority, the *Salt Lake City Municipal Record* proclaimed Eastwood to be "an engineer of high reputation [who would exercise] advisory supervision over the construction of the great dam for the Mountain Dell reservoir."[58]

Salt Lake City's acceptance of his design gave Eastwood increased standing within the larger Mormon community, and he subsequently received commissions to design two dams for Mormon interests in southern Idaho. The first of these was the 70-foot-high

Malad Dam on the Malad River (Fig. 7.9), built in 1916–1917 (negotiations for this project actually started in 1915).[59] The second was the 90-foot-high, 2,600-foot-long Fish Creek Dam built near Carey, Idaho, in 1919–1920 (Fig. 7.10).[60] Both structures were erected with little fanfare and Eastwood did not have to undertake lengthy correspondence to justify their safeness. In fact, Idaho State Engineer J. H. Smith endorsed a preliminary design for the Malad Dam by stating that he was "glad to see this type of dam going in as I feel satisfied that it is a very good design"; and when final plans were submitted to him in December 1916, he reviewed and approved them within a few days.[61] Built as part of local irrigation developments, these dams did not receive the attention lavished on the highly visible Mountain Dell Dam. Still, they provided Eastwood with additional opportunities to hone his design skills, and they supplied him with income that did not require a major commitment of time or energy.[62]

7.10 *Upstream side of the Fish Creek Dam, near Carey, Idaho, September 1920. Although it was more than 2,000 feet long, this structure attracted little attention outside Idaho. Nonetheless, it was the longest Eastwood dam ever built. (Author's collection)*

Cannon's implicit endorsement enabled Eastwood to develop a source of support within the Mormon community and, for the first time, to expand his practice outside California. As it turned out, Eastwood and Cannon never worked together again, since Salt Lake City did not require any additional dams during the 1910s and early 1920s. Cannon continued to serve as city engineer until 1925, when he became a presiding bishop of the Mormon Church; in 1939, he ascended to the religion's highest council, the Quorum of Twelve, where he served until his death in 1943. Although never officially recognized as a monument to Cannon's service to Salt Lake City, the Mountain Dell Dam remains a vital part of the city's water supply system.

SAN DIEGO AND ED FLETCHER

Prior to receiving commissions for Mountain Dell and Malad, Eastwood was feeling financial pressure due to a lack of work. For example, in the fall of 1915, he pleaded for funds from the Malad Reservoir Company to help cover the expense of his design work. He explained:

There has been a strike at all the Mother Lode mines and this has affected the payment for the work on [raising] the Kennedy [Dam], and what with the extension of the Mountain Dell [bidding process] for 60 days, the failure of the Malad to come through has placed me in very straightened [*sic*] circumstances, and while I am always willing to assist to the best of my ability by having my compensation deferred, there is a limit which has been reached.[63]

Although the Mountain Dell and Malad projects ultimately bore financial fruit, the preceding letter highlights Eastwood's need for a patron who could free him from fear of imminent destitution. In this context, Colonel Ed Fletcher of San Diego, a businessman who came to embrace Eastwood's multiple arch

designs, proved to be his savior and most influential supporter.

In 1888, 16-year-old Ed Fletcher arrived in San Diego from Massachusetts and for the next eight years worked as a grocer's assistant, marketing fruit throughout San Diego County.[64] In 1896, he formed his own business and continued to expand his operations in the rolling terrain north and east of the port city. Through his travels, he learned about the region's rivers and about opportunities to extend his fortune beyond the realm of a dry-goods merchant. By careful husbanding of profits derived from the grocery trade, he accrued a modest amount of capital to invest in real estate ventures.

After the turn of the century, Fletcher (who gained the title of colonel from service in the state militia) began pursuing projects that promised to catapult him into the upper echelons of the county's leadership. In 1905, for example, he signed a contract with William G. Kerckhoff to act as an agent for the South Coast Land Company. In this capacity, he was to assemble land options in the San Luis Rey River Valley as part of a scheme involving the extension of Henry Huntington's electric railway system into San Diego County.[65] The South Coast Land Company foundered after Huntington abandoned direct competition with the Southern Pacific Railroad. For Fletcher, however, the project expanded his contacts with prominent capitalists and presaged future work in the field of water resources and real estate development.

To comprehend Fletcher's entrepreneurial activities, one must have a basic understanding of San Diego's regional geography (Fig. 7.11). San Diego County encompasses more than 5,000 square miles, including a coastline that stretches for more than 70 miles beginning at the Mexican border. The county is split by a range of mountains that divides the dry, sparsely settled desertland to the east from more populous districts on and near the Pacific coast. No single river system dominates the county. Instead, a series of modest-

7.11   *San Diego County rivers and dam sites, circa 1922. (Author's collection, courtesy of Richard K. Anderson)*

size streams flow westward out of the Laguna/Cuyamaca Mountains and provide most of the region's surface water supply. The city of San Diego lies close to the county's southern border, near where the San Diego River meets the Pacific Ocean. To the south lie the Sweetwater River, the Otay River, and Cottonwood Creek (which, near the border with Mexico, flows into the Tijuana River). About 20 miles north of the city, the San Dieguito River flows into the Pacific; another 5 miles north lies Escondido Creek (also called San Elijo Creek); and another 15 miles north (but still some 15 miles south of the border with Orange County) the San Luis

Rey River enters the ocean. None of these streams is more than 60 miles long, and at times each carries very little water. But during heavy rains, they swell into raging torrents capable of filling large reservoirs and serving the needs of tens of thousands of people.

In the early nineteenth century, the mission, pueblo, and presidio of San Diego drew some surface water from the San Diego River. By the beginning of the twentieth century, however, municipal supplies came from the privately owned Southern California Mountain Water Company. Controlled by local business magnate John D. Spreckels, this company operated an extensive system of reservoirs and canals that delivered water to the city from the Cottonwood Creek and Otay River watersheds.[66] The Spreckels interests tightly controlled San Diego's utility franchises. Thus, to fulfill any hopes of building a rival financial empire, Fletcher needed to explore business opportunities in the county's hinterlands, using knowledge gained during his extensive travels. By 1910, he began to concentrate his attention on three specific water development projects, two of which led to the completion of Eastwood dams.

In 1911, Fletcher became associated with William G. Henshaw, a San Francisco–based businessman who owned the Riverside Cement Company and who had recently purchased the Warner Ranch at the headwaters of the San Luis Rey River. Development of the Lake Henshaw project (as it later came to be known) had begun in 1905, when Fletcher served as an agent for Henry Huntington's South Coast Land Company.[67] When Huntington abandoned his own plans for this scheme, Fletcher arranged for Henshaw to buy Warner Ranch; in turn, Fletcher assumed management of the newly formed Volcan Land and Water Company, to develop water rights along the San Luis Rey River that were tied to the ranch. The Lake Henshaw project proved more complicated than originally envisaged and remained incomplete for more than a decade. In 1914, however, Fletcher and Henshaw approached Eastwood for a dam design. This initiative foundered, but it was soon followed by plans for another multiple arch dam along the nearby San Dieguito River.[68]

Like the San Luis Rey River, the San Dieguito River arises in the mountainous region of north-central San Diego County. In 1911, Fletcher surveyed the latter river and purchased options on several reservoir locations for Henshaw, the most important being a site owned by James Carroll. Located approximately 7 miles upstream from the river's mouth, the Carroll site could store more than 70,000 acre-feet of water for use in irrigating the "frostless belt" near the Pacific coast.

Contemporaneously with this early work for Henshaw, Fletcher had learned that the Atchison, Topeka & Santa Fe Railway was experiencing problems with its 12,000-acre San Dieguito Ranch (later known as Rancho Santa Fe) which straddled the lower sections of the San Dieguito River. Acting through the Santa Fe Land and Improvement Company (a wholly owned subsidiary), the railway had purchased this ranch in order to grow eucalyptus trees for railroad ties. The company knew little about tree farming, however, and the investment proved troublesome. Discussing these problems with Santa Fe vice president W. E. Hodges in 1911, Fletcher offered to manage the ranch in return for 20 percent of the annual gross receipts.[69] The railroad agreed and Fletcher soon transformed the ranch into a profitable enterprise that included 80 acres of irrigated vegetable gardens. This success pointed the way for future development.

In addition to his work for Henshaw and the Santa Fe Railway in the early 1910s, Fletcher had joined with James Murray, a wealthy capitalist from Montana, in purchasing the San Diego Flume Company.[70] Organized in 1886 to divert water out of the upper San Diego River, this company operated a 37-mile-long wooden flume that served farmers in El Cajon and Lemon Grove at the eastern edge of San Diego.[71] For twenty years, the flume functioned with limited success, largely because of maintenance problems. By the time Fletcher and Murray's Cuyamaca Water Company assumed ownership in 1910, the flume needed extensive rebuilding, forcing Fletcher and Murray to delay plans to expand the system's storage capacity.

In the headwaters of the San Diego River, the Cuyamaca company drew on Lake Cuyamaca, a storage reservoir located in the Laguna Mountains. Water released from the lake flowed through the 37-mile-long flume to a distributing reservoir on the outskirts of San Diego. Formed by a 65-foot-high hydraulic fill dam that had been completed in 1898 under the direction of Julius Howells, the La

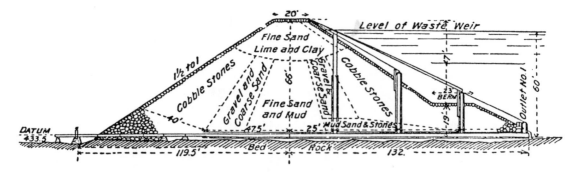

7.12 *Schematic cross section of the hydraulic fill La Mesa Dam, built by Julius Howells in the 1890s to store water for what became the Cuyamaca Water Company.* (Wegmann, The Design and Construction of Dams, *1911*)

Mesa Reservoir provided important insurance against breaks in the flume that could disrupt water delivery (Fig. 7.12).[72] In January 1916, however, the heavy rains that resulted in the overtopping of Eastwood's Big Bear Valley Dam also produced flooding that came within a foot of overtopping (and destroying) the earthen La Mesa Dam.[73] Impressed by this near calamity, and eager to increase the reservoir's storage capacity, Fletcher and Murray acted to replace the hydraulic fill design with a larger and safer structure.

As manager, starting in 1910–1911, of the holdings of two important capitalists (James Murray and William Henshaw) and one large landowning/transportation company (the Santa Fe Railway) in San Diego County, Fletcher understood that any substantive increase in the value of these projects — the Cuyamaca Water Company, the Volcan Land and Water Company, and the San Dieguito Ranch — depended on expanding the available water supply by building storage reservoirs. Thus, Fletcher approached Eastwood in early 1916 about plans to replace the Cuyamaca Water Company's La Mesa Dam; shortly afterward, the Oakland-based engineer also began preparing estimates for a structure at the Carroll dam site.[74]

Although the success of both projects depended on Fletcher's political/managerial skills, their financing and organization differed dramatically. The Cuyamaca Water Company was controlled by James Murray, a wealthy capitalist who could fund construction with little outside support; and the firm operated as a public utility under the supervision of the State Railroad Commission. In contrast, William Henshaw's financial resources were stretched thin during the 1915–1917 period, largely because of problems with his Warner Ranch holdings. In 1916, the Santa Fe Railway offered to sell him the San Dieguito Ranch so that he could develop the Carroll Dam as part of a major irrigation project, but Henshaw's financial circumstances forced him to turn down the offer. Fletcher quickly conceived a counterproposal under whose terms the Santa Fe Railway — through its subsidiary, the Santa Fe Land and Improvement Company — would finance the dam directly. Under laws limiting the ability of railroads to control nontransportation developments, the Carroll Dam/San Dieguito Ranch project could not be undertaken by a organization regulated by the Railroad Commission. Consequently, Fletcher suggested that the dam be built by a mutual water company legally distinct from the Santa Fe subsidiary. Although much of the work on the Murray Dam and the Carroll Dam (later called Lake Hodges Dam) occurred simultaneously during 1917–1918, the two projects were carried out with relatively little administrative overlap.

THE MURRAY DAM

Following the scare caused by the 1916 floods, Fletcher and Murray realized that the Cuyamaca Water Company could be devastated by failure of the 65-foot-high La Mesa Dam; in addition, they realized the advantage of increasing the reservoir's storage capacity. A taller dam, if economically feasible, would foster more agriculture and residential development in the company's service area and would increase income from water sales. In light of the partners' relatively limited financial resources, Eastwood's skills were exactly what Fletcher and Murray needed, and they soon asked him to work on a replacement for the earthen La Mesa Dam. The record documenting Eastwood's development of this project is sketchy; but by March 1917 he had completed a design for a 990-foot-long, 117-foot-high dam featuring thirty arches with spans of 30 feet. The top 12 feet of the arches were only 9 inches thick, making them the thinnest for any Eastwood dam except Los Verjels. In addition, for the first time since Big Meadows, Eastwood specified using siphon spillways to regulate the reservoir during floods.[75]

Plans were forwarded to the Railroad Commission, and by the end of April 1917 R. W. Hawley was urging authorization "for the construction of [an] Eastwood Multiple Arch Dam." The commission accepted Hawley's recommendation and, on April 28, directed the Cuyamaca Water Company "to proceed with the construction of the dam as planned." Approval incurred practically no delay, largely because of Hawley's familiarity with Eastwood's work. In fact, excavation for the buttresses was under way when the commission officially approved the design.[76] In digging the foundations, construction crews encountered an unanticipated problem: the upstream "toe" of the multiple arch dam cut into the downstream edge of the older earthen structure; and as Eastwood reported, "the sandy material of the filled dam began

to flow as quicksand after all these years, merely the same quicksand it was when placed." The problem was solved by building "timbered trenches" to protect foundation excavations for the new dam, and the event had no long-term consequences. Nonetheless, the fact that, after more than twenty years, portions of the La Mesa Dam remained in a semiliquid state confirmed to Eastwood the inherent instability of hydraulic fill structures.[77]

Construction of the Murray Dam took place under the field supervision of Frederic Faude, assistant manager of the Cuyamaca Water Company, and was carried out by the contracting firm of Sharp & Fellows. Eastwood had offered to take personal responsibility for building the dam on a cost plus fixed fee basis (similar to his arrangement at Kennedy and Big Bear Valley), but Fletcher and Murray preferred to engage him simply as a "supervisory engineer" with general authority over the work.[78] Foundation preparation was complete by August, and concrete began being placed via a "chuting system" soon afterward (Fig. 7.13). Construction continued through the rest of the year; and by the time the dam was completed in January 1918, slightly more than 8,220 cubic yards of concrete had been poured (Figs. 7.14 and 7.15). Despite hearing a few unsubstantiated reports about poor construction, Hawley and the Railroad Commission considered the dam to be well built.[79] Within a year after Eastwood submitted a final design, Murray Dam became operational (the reservoir came close to filling in the spring of 1918), and it has remained in service for more than 75 years. In the mid-1920s, Murray Dam—along with most of the Cuyamaca Water Company's other holdings—was sold to the La Mesa, Lemon Grove, and Spring Valley Irrigation District. Eventually, as the city expanded eastward, Eastwood's dam became integrated into San Diego's municipal water supply system.

7.13 *Murray Dam under construction in December 1917, using a hoist and chuting system to distribute concrete. The road on the right runs across the crest of the hydraulic fill La Mesa Dam. (Huber Papers, WRCA)*

7.14 *Upstream side of the completed Murray Dam in March 1918. (Huber Papers, WRCA)*

7.15 *Downstream side of the crest of Murray Dam, circa 1918. Eastwood is resting his foot on the walkway rail and Fletcher is to the right. (Historic American Engineering Record, Library of Congress)*

THE LAKE HODGES AND SAN DIEGUITO DAMS

Contemporaneously with his work on the Murray Dam, Eastwood developed plans for the Carroll site on the San Dieguito River. During 1916, Henshaw, Fletcher, and the Santa Fe Railway had pooled their interests into the newly formed San Dieguito Mutual Water Company as a way to facilitate con-

struction of the project. Fletcher became company president, Henshaw served on the board of directors, and (commensurate with its financial contribution to the new company) the Santa Fe Railway placed three employees on the board, including W. E. Hodges, the railway's vice president, and E. O. Faulkner, manager of the railway's "Timber and Tie Department" in Los Angeles. In 1918, a more symbolic acknowledgment of the Santa Fe's investment occurred, when

160

"Carroll Dam" was officially designated Lake Hodges Dam.

In May 1916, Eastwood visited the Carroll site. After studying the location initially selected by Fletcher (called site A), he expressed concern over the amount of earthen overburden covering the bedrock. He suggested that two other sites slightly downstream (known as B and C) be surveyed for comparison.[80] In June 1916, Eastwood worked up preliminary estimates, but the project languished for several months while Fletcher, Henshaw, and the railway worked out financing arrangements.[81] Finally, in early 1917 Eastwood was asked to compare the construction costs associated with the three sites; he soon recommended site C because of its larger storage capacity and shorter conduit.[82] The San Dieguito Mutual Water Company accepted Eastwood's recommendation; but before agreeing to build his design, the firm solicited competing offers from other engineers.

The most important alternative proposal came from Lars Jorgensen, who worked up estimates for both a single arch design and a multiple arch design; both exceeded the proposed cost of Eastwood's design, and neither was accepted.[83] During the spring of 1917 George L. Davenport, an engineer for the Santa Fe Railway, analyzed Eastwood's method of design and, while declining to endorse all claims of superiority for the multiple arch dam, offered a positive appraisal. Davenport urged slight increases in the thickness of the arches and the addition of a few struttie beams — recommendations reminiscent of comments made at Big Meadows five years earlier.[84] This time, however, they did not precipitate abandonment of the project, and indeed Davenport's approval convinced the Santa Fe of the efficacy of multiple arch technology. By mid-May, railway officials authorized Bent Brothers, the firm responsible for building Argonaut Dam the previous year, to serve as contractors; construction commenced in the late summer of 1917.[85]

Although the two were developed contemporaneously, the 550-foot-long, 136-foot-high Lake Hodges Dam design is not identical to the one used at Murray. In part this is attributable to Davenport's urging that the twenty-one arches constructed at Lake Hodges have a minimum thickness of 12 inches (the minimum at Murray was 9 inches), and in part it is because Eastwood calculated the maximum compressive stress on concrete at Lake Hodges at 300 pounds per square inch (psi) as compared with 325 psi at Murray. In addition, relatively little excavation was required at Carroll site C, prompting the use of narrower arches (24 feet versus 30 feet per span at Murray). The slightly bulkier dimensions and greater average height of the Lake Hodges arches resulted in a structure that required more than twice as much concrete as the Murray Dam (approximately 18,600 cubic yards versus 8,200 cubic yards).[86]

Aside from variations in structural dimensions, the biggest difference between the Lake Hodges and Murray dam designs involved their spillways. At Murray Dam, Eastwood used siphon spillways to regulate the reservoir level (Figs. 7.16 and 7.17). These siphons did not require a large discharge capacity, because (not counting discharge from the flumes) the watershed feeding into Lake Mur-

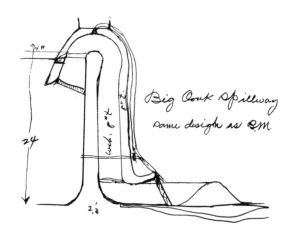

7.16 *Sketch by Eastwood of a siphon spillway design proposed for use at Big Meadows and Big Creek, drawn in spring 1912. Five years later he successfully integrated the technology into his design for Murray Dam. (Eastwood Papers, WRCA)*

A

B

7.17 *Murray Dam siphon spillway (A) with reservoir empty; (B) with water stored to the crest in late spring 1918, showing how siphons could help maximize the storage capacity of a reservoir. (Huber Papers, WRCA)*

ray was small and not susceptible to heavy flooding. In contrast, the lower San Dieguito River can experience heavy floods; so for the Lake Hodges Dam Eastwood stipulated the use of a large overflow spillway that could discharge a flow of 71,000 cubic feet per second. This spillway was to include a "rollway and rear deck . . . terminating in a smoothly curved apron" at the dam's downstream base.[87] The design proposed by Eastwood, however, was significantly modified before construction was completed—an action that displeased him and served as a harbinger of future frustrations.

The change in spillway design was prompted by a new dam safety law enacted by the California state legislature in May 1917. Because the San Dieguito Mutual Water Company was not a public utility subject to supervision by the State Railroad Commission, the new law mandated that construction at Lake Hodges be overseen by the state engineer, Wilbur F. McClure. McClure approved much of Eastwood's design without alteration; but acting on advice from consultant Walter L. Huber, he demanded that the spillway be redesigned. Eastwood deplored this change, and he later gave full credit "to the state engineers' office for the spillway as I would not even accept a fee for it though it was part of the contract."[88] McClure moved the spillway to the dam's northern abutment and extended it for 360 feet, modifications that involved extensive additional excavation into bedrock. But the increased cost was not Eastwood's chief criticism of the new spillway. The top of Lake Hodges Dam is 330 feet above sea level and Eastwood originally designed the spillway crest to conform closely to this height so that the reservoir could impound as much water as possible. When McClure relocated the spillway he also lowered its crest 15 feet, thus reducing the storage capacity from 75,000 to less than 45,000 acrefeet. Eastwood considered this an enormous economic waste and lamented that "the whole plant [water supply system] is . . . penalized as the storage is the measure of the efficiency of the whole investment."[89]

Changes in the spillway design caused delays, but by November 1917 excavation was largely complete and Bent Brothers began pouring concrete (Figs. 7.18 and 7.19).[90] The Lake Hodges construction plant featured a large chuting system similar to that used at Mountain Dell. Concrete was mixed on the northern edge of the site, hoisted up a tower, and then distributed to the formwork via adjustable chutes. Because the dam was more than 700 feet long, substantial quantities of concrete had to be chuted several hundred feet. The construction plant did not meet Eastwood's standards and he later complained about "clogging" and the fact that "it was always giving trouble by breaking down in one part or another."[91]

Despite problems with the construction facility, the dam dramatically demonstrated its structural integrity even before it was completed. In early March 1918, when most of the central arches extended 50 feet above the streambed, a severe rainstorm hit the San Dieguito River watershed. Water quickly built up behind the dam and began pouring through the opening for arch No. 17, which was only completed to the 30-foot level. The water level ultimately rose to 16 feet above the arch (46 feet above the streambed) and flowed through the opening for several days. The May 1918 issue of *Western Engineering* reported that "stumps and logs up to 12 inches diameter and 24 feet long . . . [moving] at a speed of 30 feet per second" had passed through the opening, but caused no damage. The journal also termed the "excellence of the concrete . . . particularly laudable" because most of the arches were found to be watertight, even without a cement coating on the upstream face.[92]

The most interesting aspect of this flood relates to the structural performance of the buttresses adjacent to arch No. 17. Engineers had long asked what would happen if one of the arches of a multiple arch dam were somehow removed suddenly. Would the arches collapse on one another like dominoes, or would water simply flow through the opening and slowly empty the reservoir? The *Western En-*

7.18 *Construction view of Lake Hodges Dam in December 1917, showing arch formwork (with steel reinforcement) and the placement of jagged "plum" stones in the concrete buttresses to help bond successive "lifts" of concrete. In contrast to the arches, the buttresses were not to be given any steel reinforcement. (Huber Papers, WRCA)*

7.19 *Construction of Lake Hodges Dam nearing completion in 1918. The extensive excavation necessary to build the overflow spillway (on the left) is reflected in the large pile of rockfill in the center/left foreground. (Huber Papers, WRCA)*

gineering article alluded to "reputable engineers [who] claim that, if one arch of a multiple-arch dam should fail, the entire structure would go out." But the unexpected flood during construction of Hodges Dam served "to show that the multiple-arch type has not been given sufficient credit for strength in this particular."[93]

The March 1918 flood demonstrated the stability of the structure and helped quell any move to prevent storage in Lake Hodges. Later reports acknowledged that hairline cracks were visible along many buttresses even before the dam was completed (Fig. 7.20). But in the immediate aftermath of construction, these cracks were simply accepted as minor manifestations of concrete shrinkage that did not reflect any safety problems. Not until a few years later did the cracks generate interest among engineers generally unenthusiastic about multiple arch dam technology; and by that time, the Lake Hodges Dam had already proved its serviceability as a water storage structure (Fig. 7.21).

The San Dieguito Mutual Water Company's irrigation plans included construction of an auxiliary "distribution" reservoir about 2 miles downstream from the Lake Hodges Dam. This structure provided the system with additional storage capacity and was to be filled via a concrete conduit (or canal) connected to the main reservoir. Bent Brothers began building the structure, known as the San Dieguito Dam, after Lake Hodges was well under way.[94] Because of its height and the shape of the dam site, Eastwood patterned the San Dieguito design closely after the Hume Lake Dam (Fig. 7.22).[95] Slightly more than 600 feet long, with a maximum height of 52 feet, the dam consists of twelve 50-foot-span arches. As at Hume Lake, the arches encompass an arc of 120 degrees and are inclined upstream at an angle of slightly less than 60 degrees.[96] No strut-tie beams are used to connect the buttresses.

In his original design for the San Dieguito Dam, Eastwood wanted a minimum arch thickness of 9 inches. Based on a maximum

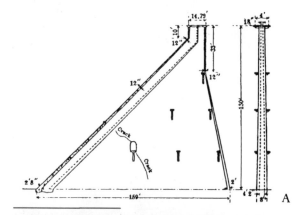

A

B

7.20   *(A) Cross section showing the general location of temperature cracks that appeared in the buttresses of Lake Hodges Dam. This drawing does not show the crack widths to scale. (*Proceedings of the American Society of Civil Engineers, *1922) (B) Diagonal "temperature crack" extending across a buttress at Lake Hodges. This photograph was taken in June 1931, after the structure had operated successfully for 13 years. (Huber Papers, WRCA)*

7.21   *Lake Hodges Dam in operation, circa 1930. This postcard view shows how the overflow spillway reduced the amount of water that could be stored behind the dam. It also documents how the dam as originally built (with no steel in the buttresses) safely functioned under full water load. (Author's collection)*

7.22   *Downstream side of the San Dieguito Dam in September 1918. This structure bears a strong resemblance to the Hume Lake Dam (both are about 60 feet high, utilize 50-foot-arch spans, and do not rely on strut-tie beams to assist with lateral stability). (Huber Papers, WRCA)*

allowable stress of 325 psi, this would have been identical with the top dimensions of the Murray Dam. State Engineer McClure balked, however, and demanded an increase in the minimum thickness. He initially wanted a minimum arch thickness of 15 inches, but eventually Eastwood convinced him that a 12-inch-thick water face at the top ("where there is no load to speak of") did not threaten the structure.[97] Although the controversy did not cause any major delay, it, like the redesign of the Lake Hodges spillway, foreshadowed future problems with McClure.

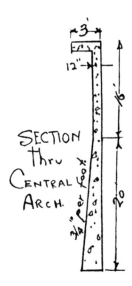

7.23 *Schematic cross section of the main arch of the Eagles Nest Dam. This structure, which was less than 40 feet high, featured a maximum arch thickness of little more than 2 feet. (Huber Papers, WRCA)*

EAGLES NEST DAM AND THE PATRONAGE OF ED FLETCHER

In addition to the three major dams he built for the Fletcher interests in 1917–1918, Eastwood designed a small dam for the Fletcher family retreat ("Eagles Nest") about 65 miles northeast of San Diego, in the hills east of Warner Springs.[98] Despite being less than 40 feet high, the Eagles Nest Dam is significant because of its "triple arched" design and because, in contrast to earlier structures, it does not feature a series of arches with equal spans. Instead, harkening back to ideas Eastwood considered in his preliminary Hume Lake proposal, the design features "a large center arch" spanning 70 feet, with "the remaining gap to the edge of the canyon being filled with two smaller arches" with spans of 25 feet each. Because of its limited height, the dam does not feature an inclined upstream face; thus no vertical component of water is utilized to help stabilize the structure. Despite this, the arches possess a maximum thickness of less than 2.5 feet (Fig. 7.23). The entire dam reportedly used only 184 cubic yards of concrete to close an opening 125 feet wide.[99] Using the cylinder formula, Eastwood calculated the maximum stress to be only 267 psi, which demonstrated

"that there is no need of mass for strength if the design is scientific."[100]

Because of its small size, the Eagles Nest Dam received little publicity, but the structure underscores the unique relationship that was developing between Eastwood and his San Diego patron. In Eastwood, Fletcher found an ally who offered the possibility of developing major water projects with a minimum of capital outlay. Specifically, the Murray Dam only cost the Cuyamaca Water Company $118,905 (for a structure 900 feet long and with a maximum height of 117 feet), while the Lake Hodges Dam (550 feet long and 137 feet high) cost a total of $328,463 (including a special $68,376 cement freighting expense billed to the Santa Fe Railway and $38,138 spent to excavate the McClure/Huber spillway).[101] Subsequently, the two men continued to collaborate on San Diego County projects and on projects associated with the Santa Fe Railway in Arizona and New Mexico. Eastwood dams provided Fletcher with an entrée into a new level of regional economic development. From Eastwood's perspective, Fletcher constituted an ideal client: a man who offered valuable design commissions (Eastwood earned over $13,000 for his Lake Hodges and Murray designs), supported the development of future projects, and—perhaps most significantly—unabashedly endorsed the efficiency of his designs to the western financial/development community. Eastwood's credibility benefited enormously from Fletcher's reputation as a successful businessman and opponents found it increasingly difficult to dismiss Eastwood's claims of developing "The Ultimate Dam" as empty rhetoric.

CHAPTER 8

Theory and Practice in Dam Design

It is undoubtedly the proper procedure to fit theory to practice but the factors of the theory must be based on the actual physical conditions as they are in practice or else theory will lead us astray.

John S. Eastwood to Paul Downing, 1916

The primary uncertainties in reinforced concrete behavior have never been removed by mathematical analysis however rigorously consistent.

David Billington, 1983

Historians, like other members of society, are often reluctant to abandon the notion that engineering is an exact science capable of developing ideal responses to technological quandaries. In concert with this, many people believe that mathematically based, theoretical approaches to technical problem solving are more rigorous, and hence more valid, than methodologies that emphasize qualitative considerations based on practical experience. The distinction between a mathematically complex but not necessarily imaginative method of engineering design and a more visually intuitive approach was discussed by David Billington in his recent book *The Tower and the Bridge: The New Art of Structural Engineering*. In developing his concept of "structural art" based on the ideals of material conservancy, economic efficiency, and visual elegance, Billington makes some important observations about the evolu-

tion of modern engineering design in the period following World War I:

[During this period] everything from factory management to the unconscious sex drive was thought to be amenable to scientific analysis. The truths of life were bound up in formulas which great minds, in academic settings, were carefully setting about to refine and solve . . . In structural engineering this faith in formula led to an emphasis on mathematical analysis which . . . seemed to require that designers justify their works by sophisticated calculation.[1]

Although they do not focus on hydraulic engineering or on specific issues surrounding the development of multiple arch dams, Billington's thoughts on the evolution of thin-shell concrete design are directly relevant to the history of American dam building:

As the 1920s wore on, science-based formulas gained prestige. The major results of these formulas were to create a scientific discipline of analysis isolated from design . . . this was not a question of

169

intuition versus rigor, or of approximate and uncertain estimates versus precise and scientific predictions. The primary uncertainties in reinforced concrete behavior have never been removed by mathematical analysis however rigorously consistent.[2]

Billington appreciates that mathematical analysis can help generate safer and more efficient designs, but he spurns the notion that it unerringly leads to the creation of innovative structural forms. In his mind, the engineers whose work best exemplifies the ideals of structural art resisted an overarching "faith in formula [and] . . . sought rather to base design on simplified calculations and on observations of physical behavior." Whereas America's twentieth-century engineering establishment has embraced the idea that mathematically sophisticated analysis inevitably fosters more accurate methods of design, Billington considers mathematics as simply a tool in the overall design process.[3] Eastwood's work with multiple arch dams closely adheres to Billington's views; in rejecting reliance on mathematical theory as an absolute determinant of structural design, Eastwood resisted pervasive trends in the civil engineering community. His methodology, in which experience guided and supplemented the use of mathematics, frequently was greeted with apathy or active opposition. But in his ongoing search for more efficient structural forms, Eastwood never exhibited any qualms about deviating from the technological status quo.

PATENTS AND COMPETITORS

Despite extensive efforts to associate himself with multiple arch dam technology, Eastwood never patented his designs nor attempted to prevent others from erecting structures of this type. In fact, he went so far as to state publicly in his 1915 "Eastwood Bulletin" that "there are no royalties charged on the Eastwood Multiple-Arched Dam."[4] The reason underlying this separation from the patent

system is clear: in 1911–1912, after completing the Hume Lake Dam, he was forced to contest a nuisance patent infringement complaint brought against him by George Ladshaw of Spartanburg, South Carolina.[5] In 1906, Ladshaw had received a patent for what he termed a "multi-differential" dam; and although he appears never to have built any structures based on this patent, Ladshaw subsequently claimed that any builder of a multiple arch dam infringed on his rights.[6] Given that Henry Goldmark's detailed description of a multiple arch dam in the 1897 ASCE *Transactions* antedated Ladshaw's patent by almost ten years, Eastwood reasonably considered the infringement charge to be groundless. Ultimately, court rulings vindicated Eastwood's position, but the suit constituted an unproductive drain on his time, energy, and finances. It was not an experience he wished to repeat.[7]

In the Eastwood Papers at Berkeley, a set of circa 1913 draft specifications exists for an "invention relat[ing] to certain improvements in multiple arched dam[s]."[8] Eastwood's interest in submitting a patent application quickly faded, however, and by 1915 he considered all dam designs basically unpatentable.[9] In later life, Eastwood often criticized the efficiency or the suitability of other engineers' multiple arch dam designs, but he never claimed that they infringed on his rights as an inventor. Rather than attempting to take credit for all multiple arch designs, he chose to promote the "Eastwood Multiple-Arched Dam" as a specialized design superior to all others and sought thereby to distance himself from the world of patent law and patent lawyers. His strategy proved successful; after the Ladshaw incident he avoided further entanglement in patent disputes.

Eastwood did not wish to place legal restraints on potential competitors, but it disturbed him that other, seemingly less qualified engineers might enter the field and take advantage of his pioneering efforts. In 1914, he expressed this concern by averring that "the perfection of the design of dams . . . can only result from long study, intimate analysis, and practical experience in their erection." Conversely, Eastwood denounced engineers who "through the lack of practice and experience . . . hold to the traditions of design and copy works that are standing."[10] Arguing that "the rarity of the use of this kind of structure [dams] leaves most engineers novices through lack of practice and experience in their design and construction," he asserted that "the subject is too large to be consummated in the time [nonspecialists] have to give it." Despite such admonitions, other engineers entered the field; and in truth, the adoption of multiple arch designs by some of these competing engineers helped give credence to his effusive claims for the technology.

After Eastwood, the most prolific designer of multiple arch dams was Gardiner S. Williams, a professor at Cornell University and later the University of Michigan.[11] Williams first experimented with the form while preparing designs for an arch dam near Ithaca, New York, in 1902. His plan called for a small multiple arch structure to close a shallow ravine near the main dam.[12] This auxiliary dam was never built, however, and Williams waited another eight years before constructing his first multiple arch dam, as part of a hydroelectric plant in Sturgis, Michigan. Completed in 1910–1911, the Sturgis Dam was 22 feet high and featured fourteen arches with spans of 20 feet.[13] During the next twenty years, Williams built nine more multiple arch dams, most as part of hydroelectric plants in Michigan and Minnesota. None was taller than 40 feet.[14] Shortly before his death, he designed his most interesting dam for an unusual client: the Soviet Union. During the economic/diplomatic thaw between the United States and the U.S.S.R. in the early 1930s, Williams designed a 40-foot-high, 3,000-foot-long multiple arch dam across the Ural River as part of the new industrial center of Magnitogorsk being built under the direction of American engineers.[15]

Williams devoted only a portion of his professional energies to dam design, and in addition to his university duties, he worked on a wide variety of engineering projects. But de-

spite Williams's diverse professional interests, Eastwood considered him to be his only true colleague in the design of multiple arch dams. In part, this professional comradery probably stemmed from a shared distaste for Ladshaw, who had attempted to exact patent royalties from Williams in 1912.[16] Eastwood wrote to Williams in September 1915 and confided that "I feel you and I are the only engineers in this U.S. that have done what we preach as the thing to do."[17] In the early 1920s, he again had reason to speak kindly of Williams, after becoming embroiled in a conflict over buttress stresses in his design for the Cave Creek Dam near Phoenix. In a letter to the *Engineering News-Record*, Williams supported Eastwood's position, stating that "there can be little question that the method of computation employed by the designer of the dam [Eastwood] was the better one to employ for a rock foundation."[18] Not surprisingly, Eastwood was quick to acknowledge Williams's expertise, describing him as outranking "all other authorities on the subject [of multiple arch dam stresses], he being both practical and highly trained technically."[19] While Eastwood's admiration for Williams was genuine, it was helped by the fact that the two men operated within different regions and never competed for the same clients or design commissions.

Along with Gardiner Williams, a few other Americans built multiple arch dams in the early 1910s, the most prolific of these being William Barclay Parsons, his brother Harry de Berkeley Parsons, and their colleague Walter J. Douglas. This group collaborated on multiple arch designs for Pecks Lake Dam (45 feet high) and Garoga Dam (60 feet high) in upstate New York in 1910–1911.[20] The Parsons brothers and Douglas did not specialize in dam design work, but Harry Parsons subsequently designed three more multiple arch dams across the upper Hudson River in New York for the International Paper Company. In 1913, he built the Palmer Falls Dam (38 feet high) and the Glens Falls Dam (26 feet high); then, after a hiatus of almost ten years, he returned to the field to design the Sherman Island Dam (80 feet high) for use in generating hydroelectric power. Because of its soft foundations, the dam attracted considerable attention—especially after Parsons described it in the 1925 ASCE *Transactions*.[21] In general, the Parsons/Parsons/Douglas multiple arch dams constituted a relatively isolated group of structures that, aside from the Sherman Island Dam, remained largely unknown to the profession. Nonetheless, their work provided early evidence that multiple arch designs were suitable for conditions outside the West and might prove economically viable in the northeastern United States.

Gardiner Williams and the Parsons/Parsons/Douglas collective were content to work on multiple arch dams when suitable opportunities arose; their professional reputations were not closely tied to this specialized form of hydraulic technology. In their stead, formal publications on multiple arch dam design largely fell to three European-trained engineers who emigrated to the United States in the early twentieth century. During the period 1910-1930, Lars Jorgensen, Fred Noetzli, and Bernhard F. Jakobsen practiced engineering in California and became major theoreticians in the design of single arch and multiple arch dams. Each authored articles published in the ASCE *Transactions* and participated in professional discussion related to large-scale dam design. Eastwood's relationship with these engineers was at best ambivalent, and he generically characterized them as "imitators" who were capitalizing on his earlier efforts to promote the technology.[22] Eastwood declined to comment publicly on their professional articles, but in private correspondence he off-handedly referred to them as "discussing in a very learned manner the stresses in multiple-arched dams . . . [in order to] try to set up a reputation for a thing they have not done in practice."[23] Nonetheless, in comparison with the opposition presented by gravity dam advocates such as John R. Freeman, the three unsought allies gave Eastwood little reason for complaint; Jorgensen, Noetzli, and Jakobsen were firmly committed to using the arch principle in dam de-

sign, and all three engineers resisted design philosophies associated with the massive tradition.

Lars Jorgensen was born in Denmark in 1876 and received his technical education in Germany.[24] He came to America in 1901, working first as a draftsman for the General Electric Company in New York, and a few years later moving west to work for both the Edison Electric Company in Los Angeles and the Pacific Gas and Electric Company in San Francisco. While with PG&E, he attracted the attention of Frank G. Baum, a hydroelectric power engineer in Northern California; and between 1907 and 1914, he served on the staff of F. G. Baum & Company. In 1911, Jorgensen (in conjunction with Baum) received a patent for the constant-angle arch dam (mentioned in Chapter 2). The theoretical priority and legal validity of the Jorgensen/Baum patent are dubious since Eastwood had previously published a similar design in *Engineering News*. But in a professional context, the patent served as an important stepping stone for Jorgensen's future work in dam design. In 1913, he designed the world's first constant-angle arch dam, for a hydroelectric project on Salmon Creek near Juneau, Alaska. Later he helped establish the Constant Angle Arch Dam Company.[25]

Jorgensen also considered multiple arch dams as part of his bailiwick, and in 1915 he received a commission to build two structures of this type for the Pacific Power Corporation in the Sierra Nevada west of Bodie, California. The Gem Lake (Fig. 8.1) and Agnew Lake dams (112 feet high and 50 feet high, respectively) expanded the storage capacity of two natural lakes in order to increase the productivity of the company's hydroelectric system (this was similar to what Eastwood had proposed to do for the Mammoth Power Company in 1901). Jorgensen described his design procedure for the Gem Lake and Agnew Lake dams in the 1917 ASCE *Transactions,* and his approach echoed Eastwood's method in its reliance on the cylinder formula. Interestingly, the Gem Lake and Agnew Lake structures were the only multiple

8.1　*Gem Lake Dam, California, completed in 1916 from a design by Lars Jorgensen. Along with a similar dam at nearby Agnew Lake, this structure was widely publicized in the engineering press. After constructing these two multiple arch designs, however, Jorgensen concentrated almost exclusively on single-arch "constant-angle" structures. (Huber Papers, WRCA)*

arch dams ever built from Jorgensen's designs; after 1916, he concentrated on building single arch structures. Nonetheless, his article remained a standard reference on multiple arch dam design and attracted attention for many years.[26]

Like Jorgensen, Fred Noetzli and B. F. Jakobsen received their technical education in Europe before emigrating to California as young men to pursue careers in hydraulic engineering.[27] Shortly after the end of World War I, they began publishing a series of theoretical treatises on arch dam design in the ASCE *Transactions*. Two of these articles, printed in 1924, were analyses of multiple arch dams that seemed to demonstrate hitherto unappreciated theoretical problems with the technology.[28] As of this time, neither Noetzli or Jakobsen had ever built a multiple

arch dam—a fact that prompted Eastwood to express exasperation with their criticisms. But after his death, their view of multiple arch dam design became the accepted standard (Fig. 8.2). Although both Noetzli and Jakobsen eventually did have dams of their own design built, the extent of this practical work never reached the level that their publication record might suggest.[29]

Besides Jorgensen, Noetzli, and Jakobsen, a few other engineers participated in designing of multiple arch dams during Eastwood's lifetime. They included H. C. Vensano, who designed the Rock Creek Dam for the Pacific Gas and Electric Company in 1916, and R. P. McIntosh, who designed a small multiple arch dam as part of San Francisco's Hetch Hetchy project in 1919. In addition, the U.S. Reclamation Service built two multiple arch

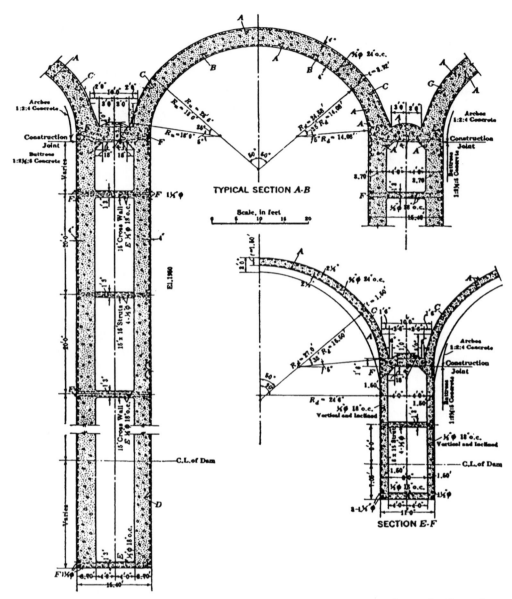

8.2   *Drawings of a double-walled, hollow buttress design developed by Fred Noetzli. The arch encompasses an arc close to 180 degrees, revealing Noetzli's reliance on the elastic theory.* (Transactions of the American Society of Civil Engineers, *1924*)

structures (each less than 35 feet high) between 1911 and 1914, one of which actually served as a large spillway for an earthfill diversion dam. However, none of these engineers or their designs had any lasting impact on the development of the technology.[30]

EASTWOOD'S METHOD OF DESIGN

Three basic principles underlie the operation of all multiple arch dams:

1. The water in the reservoir exerts hydrostatic pressure perpendicular to the upstream face of the arches.
2. The hydrostatic pressure compresses the arches and is transferred from the arches to the upstream face of the buttresses.
3. From the upstream face of the buttresses, the hydrostatic pressure is carried down through the body of the buttresses and distributed onto the bedrock foundations.

In other words, the arches concentrate the hydrostatic pressure on the buttresses, and the buttresses distribute this pressure on the foundation. While questions about multiple arch dam design can become quite complicated, at its core the technology rests on this basic concept.

The closest Eastwood ever came to a public description of his dam design method was in the 1914 article "The Eastwood Multiple-Arched Dam" published in *Western Engineering*. This discourse did not explicate a step-by-step process; instead, it presented a variety of "factors" and "influences" that are "interrelated and interdependent, and for that reason each dam site requires a design especially adapted to it."[31] Beyond this general discussion, Eastwood never published a detailed description of his design procedure. In part this was because he considered his procedure to be proprietary information, and in part it reflected the fact that he had little time to devote to such an exercise, especially during the final years of his life, when he was inundated with work.[32]

Eastwood did not operate in a world of academic or research engineering, where publications constituted a primary component of an individual's professional identity. The dams themselves provided the ultimate verification of his design concepts, and theoretical descriptions held little interest unless they directly related to practical construction issues. Thus, a detailed examination of the evolution of one specific structure (the Mountain Dell Dam, about which substantial design-related data survive) will be used to document how Eastwood reconciled

practical and abstract considerations in developing a final design for a particular site.

At the most elementary level, Eastwood considered stress—usually expressed in pounds per square inch (psi) or tons per square foot (tsf)—to be the key factor in determining the dimensions of his designs. Adhering to standard practice in the early twentieth century, he assumed that concrete could withstand a compressive stress of 3,000 psi before being crushed (in other words, that it possessed an "ultimate strength" of 3,000 psi). He then arranged to work with a maximum allowable stress of about 300 psi, or approximately one-tenth of the ultimate strength, thus allowing him to claim a "safety factor" of 10 for the design. Most frequently, he used a maximum allowable stress of exactly 300 psi, although at times he prepared designs with maximum allowable stresses varying from 350 psi to as low as 225 psi. The key point is that Eastwood developed his dams in accordance with stress limits that did not even remotely approach the ultimate compressive strength of concrete.

After selecting a maximum compressive loading, Eastwood determined the basic shape of his design, including the span of the arches, the arc of the arches, and the upstream slope of the buttresses. He considered all these features to be interrelated, but he believed that the arch span (the width of the arch) was central to determining all other dimensions. He listed six factors as being among the "influences affecting the economic [arch] span":

1. The site configuration (that is, the topography)
2. The structure's height
3. The amount of excavation required to reach bedrock
4. "Unwatering difficulties" (that is, the ease of controlling surface water flow during construction)
5. The cost of building formwork
6. The cost of transporting materials (such as cement) to the dam site

Arches with shorter spans require less concrete to build, but they also involve more excavation and more formwork for the buttresses. Thus, for a site where the bedrock foundations lay close to the surface, it might be relatively more economical to utilize arches with a span of only 24 feet; but for a similar site where the bedrock lay 30 feet below the surface, it might be desirable to increase the arch span in order to reduce the number of buttress foundations that would have to be excavated. By balancing such "positive and negative influences at each site," he sought to determine the arch span that would result in the least expensive structure to build.[33]

The cylinder formula provides a simple method for determining the thickness of arches based on three variables: allowable stress, span width, and the arc encompassed by the arch. By this formula, the thinnest possible arch is one encompassing a full semicircle (or an arc of 180 degrees); conversely, the shortest possible arch is a very thick one that virtually describes a straight line between the two endpoints of the arc. Because the volume of an arch is calculated by multiplying its length (that is, the path of the arch) times its thickness, an important question becomes: what arc dimension requires the least amount of concrete to build? Clearly, both a deep 180-degree arc (creating a long thin arch) and an extremely flat arc of approximately 90 degrees (creating a short thick arch) require substantial material to erect. The "arc of minimum quantity" lies somewhere between these two extremes (in fact, it can be shown mathematically to be equal to 133 degrees 34 minutes) and provides for both a relatively short and a relatively thin arch.

Theoretically, Eastwood could have minimized the amount of concrete in his arches by designing them all with an arc of 133 degrees 34 minutes; and indeed, for some of his designs, he actually used this dimension. But diverging slightly from the "arc of minimum quantity" does not result in a great increase in volume, and other factors might make deviation from the theoretical ideal desirable. Mindful of this, Eastwood realized that the

most economically efficient arc must reflect pragmatic considerations related to construction. For example, since the crest of his arches carried essentially no water load, he could theoretically (although not practically) have made them infinitely thin. But as a practical matter, Eastwood specified a minimum thickness for his arches (usually about 12 inches) that would ensure watertightness and facilitate the easy placement of concrete in the formwork.[34] As a result, the upper 20 feet or so of his designs were "top-heavy" in the sense that they contained more concrete than they theoretically needed for stability. This, in turn, prompted him to use wider arch spans and flatter arcs, in order to minimize concrete quantities in realistic structures that were prudent to build and operate. The use of "top-heavy" arches also meant that his designs would not require a vertical component of water pressure in order to ensure stability near the crest. Consequently, Eastwood built his dams with "vertical heads" that eliminated the vertical component of water pressure in the upper sections, reduced the overall diagonal length of the arches, and hence decreased the overall amount of concrete required to complete the structure.

MOUNTAIN DELL DAM: A CASE STUDY

Having received basic information about the shape and geological features of the Parleys Canyon site from Sylvester Cannon in mid-July 1915, Eastwood immediately prepared a preliminary design for purposes of formulating an estimate. In handwritten notes dated July 15, he jotted down that "deep overburden [and] difficult unwatering calls for wide spans, say 40 feet."[35] Acknowledging the need for a "very strong dam," he selected a maximum allowable loading of 18 tons per square foot (or 250 psi). He then summarily stipulated the use of three-hinged arches with arcs of 133 degrees 34 minutes. Despite seeming to start the project arbitrarily, Eastwood actually relied on previous experience in formulating the initial design. He reasoned that the "influence [of] deep overburden" would lend economy to the relatively wide arches specified, because using them would reduce the amount of excavation required for the buttresses. In selecting an arc of 133 degrees 34 minutes (the "arc of minimum quantity"), he stipulated the same dimension used for the Kennedy Dam. The three-hinged arches reflected a continuing concern with the potential effect of temperature and rib-shortening stresses.[36]

By the time Eastwood responded to Cannon in late July, he had already revised the plans outlined in his initial notes.[37] For the time being, the arches remained three-hinged, with an arc of 133 degrees 34 minutes; but other aspects of the design had changed. The biggest alteration involved increasing the maximum allowable loading from 250 psi to 350 psi (25.2 tons per square foot). In addition, the arch spans were reduced from 40 feet to 35 feet, in order to lessen the amount of concrete necessary. Even at 35 feet, Eastwood considered the arch span to be quite substantial and indicated that such a change would help lower excavation expenses by "accommodat[ing] the structure to the heavy overburden in the channel." After preparing this preliminary design and cost estimate, Eastwood did little further work on the project until mid-September. At that time, Cannon informed him that a multiple arch design would be put out for bids and asked Eastwood to submit a detailed proposal.[38] During the next few weeks, Eastwood prepared a new design that closely resembled his July prospectus except that the arch angle was reduced to 120 degrees (a dimension similar to the 118 degrees used at Hume Lake).

Arch Design

The cylinder formula offered Eastwood an easy means of proportioning arch thickness. For the work at Mountain Dell, he proceeded as follows: taking the arch span as 35 feet and the arc as 120 degrees, he found the theoretical maximum radius for the extrados of the arch to be 20.20 feet.[39] To facilitate connecting the arches to the buttresses and ensure enough space for the formwork, however, he reduced the radius by 14 inches to 19.04 feet. Representing the arch thickness by T and the depth below the dam crest by H, the cylinder formula indicates the following relationship:

$$T = \frac{P \times R}{Q}$$

where

P = Pressure of water acting radially against the arch water density × Depth $[H]$ below surface

   = .03125 tons per cubic foot [tcf] × H

R = radius of arch = 19.04 feet

Q = Maximum allowable loading = 350 psi = 25.2 tsf

Thus,

$$T = \frac{H \times .03125 \times 19.04}{25.2}$$
$$= H \times .0236$$

Let $H = 150$ feet; then

$$T = 150 \times .0236$$
$$= 3.54 \text{ feet}$$

In other words, at a depth of 150 feet below the water surface of a full reservoir, this design called for arches to have a thickness of slightly more than $3^{1}/_{2}$ feet.

By using the simplified equation for T for a series of calculations with $H = 10$, $H = 20$, $H = 30, \ldots, H = 150$, Eastwood could calculate the arch dimensions from the top to the bottom of the design. And if it became necessary later to adjust the design to accommodate a different maximum allowable stress, the recomputation could be accomplished easily. For example, when Cannon subsequently requested that the maximum compressive stress be reduced to 300 psi (or 21.6 tsf), the formula became:

$$T = \frac{H \times .03125 \times 19.04}{21.6}$$
$$= H \times .0275$$

For example, let $H = 150$ feet; then, at 300 psi,

$$T = 150 \times .0275$$
$$= 4.125 \text{ feet}$$

Again, by setting $H = 10$, $H = 20$, and so on, Eastwood could readily calculate arch dimensions for the entire design.

Buttress Design

Eastwood's method for determining the thickness and the length of his buttresses at different elevations ($H = 10$, $H = 20$, and so on) was almost as simple as his technique for determining arch thickness. But instead of relying on the cylinder formula as a mathematical guide, he used calculations related to "shearing stress" to help determine structural dimensions. In the context of Eastwood's dams, *shearing stress* refers to forces acting to shear or rupture the structure along generally horizontal planes. Thus shearing is similar to sliding along a foundation, except that it occurs within the concrete itself and is internally resisted. In his 1914 article "The Eastwood Multiple-Arched Dam," Eastwood did not mention shearing stresses, but when work began on the Mountain Dell project a year later this concept constituted a critical factor in his formulation of the final design.

In developing a buttress design, Eastwood assumed the density D of water to be .03125 tons per cubic foot (or 62.5 pounds per cubic foot); in addition, he considered the vertical weight of the water in the reservoir to push down on the upstream face of a buttress. Hence, at a depth H of 140 feet, the water pressure P would equal:

$$P = H \times D$$
$$= 140 \times .03125 = 4.375 \text{ tons per cubic foot}$$

Because the water pressure acting on the full width of the arches was concentrated on the upstream face of the buttresses, this factor had to be included in the calculations. At Mountain Dell, the arches were to have a span W of 35 feet. Consequently, at a depth of 140 feet, the upstream face of a buttress would support a vertical force of:

$$W \times P = 35 \times 4.375 = 153.125 \text{ tons per lineal foot}$$

To determine the buttress thickness (in this example, at a depth of 140 feet), Eastwood took this figure and divided it by the maximum allowable stress Q of 350 psi (or 25.2 tsf):

$$\frac{W \times H \times D}{Q} = \frac{35 \times 140 \times .03125}{25.2}$$
$$= \frac{153.125}{25.2} = 6.07 \text{ feet}$$

Thus, at $H = 140$, the buttress was to have a thickness of slightly more than 6 feet for its entire length. Similar calculations were performed for elevations $H = 10$, $H = 20$, $H = 30$, and so on, to determine the required buttress thickness at various heights.[40]

The preceding calculation provided a way to calculate a buttress's thickness but not a way to calculate its length. For the latter task, Eastwood considered it necessary to ascertain shearing stresses. Dividing the dam into a series of 10-foot horizontal sections, he determined the total horizontal thrust of the water pressure at each elevation, using the formula:

$$\text{Horizontal thrust} = .03125 \times W \times H \times \frac{H}{2}$$

where:

W = Arch span = 35 feet
H = Height or elevation of water
.03125 = Water density (tons per cubic foot)

For example, at an elevation of $H = 10$ feet, the horizontal thrust of the water pressure is:

$$.03125 \times 35 \times 10 \times 5 = 55 \text{ tons}$$

Similarly, at $H = 50$, the horizontal thrust is:

$$.03125 \times 35 \times 50 \times 25 = 1,367 \text{ tons}$$

At this point in the design process, Eastwood knew the thickness of the arches (from the cylinder formula) and the thickness of the buttresses. From previous experience, he chose to build the arches and buttresses with an upstream slope of 45 degrees. Based on this slope, he stipulated a preliminary length for the buttresses at various elevations. Knowing the thickness and the length of the arches and the length and the width of the buttresses, he could calculate the horizontal surface area of concrete at any elevation from $H = 10$ to $H = 150$.[41] And by dividing the surface area of the concrete by the horizontal thrust of the water, he could determine the maximum possible shearing stress along a horizontal section. At the start of the design process, Eastwood had arbitrarily decided that shearing stresses were not to exceed 100 psi (or 7.2 tons per square foot) — a conservative figure that he selected based on the knowledge that plain (that is, unreinforced) concrete could easily withstand tensile stress of this magnitude. Now he simply needed to make sure that the buttresses possessed sufficient surface area at each horizontal cross section to keep the shearing stress below this limit.

For example, in the initial design for the Mountain Dell Dam the horizontal thrust at an elevation 20 feet below the water surface was determined to be 218.8 tons, while the surface area of concrete equaled 96.73 square feet. Dividing 218.8 tons by 96.73 square feet, Eastwood calculated the shearing stress to be 2.26 tons per square foot (or 31 psi). As it turned out, the initial design did not include sufficient surface area in the lower parts of the dam to keep the calculated shearing stress below 100 psi. For example, at $H = 120$, Eastwood calculated the stress to be 103.5 psi (7.45 tons per square foot). But because this shearing stress exceeded the maximum allowable loading by only a small amount, he did not feel compelled to rework the design totally. Instead, he increased the length of the buttresses by a small amount (2 feet at the deepest elevations) in order to provide a slightly larger horizontal surface area;

this reduced the shearing stress induced by the horizontal thrust of the water below the 100 psi maximum.

Eastwood recognized that his method of calculating shearing stresses was not truly accurate, because it made no attempt to consider two other forces: the vertical weight of water pressing against the structure, and the vertical pressure exerted by the weight of the concrete itself. By neglecting these forces, he developed a kind of "worst-case" scenario that exaggerated the magnitude of the actual stresses.[42] In his work, Eastwood extensively used mathematical calculations, but he did not do so in order to develop an absolutely accurate method of design based on theoretical concepts. In calculating the shearing stresses, he was content to use a simple, conservative method that erred on the side of safety and ensured a solid structure.

At the end of October 1915, Cannon directed Eastwood to reduce the maximum allowable compressive stress in the design from 350 psi to 300 psi.[43] Because the calculations involved were simple, this did not constitute a major problem; Eastwood merely inserted the new stress value into the cylinder formula in place of the old one and reworked all of the calculations for different values of H. The result was specification of a design with slightly thicker arches. In reducing the maximum allowable stress to 300 psi, he also found it necessary to increase the thickness of the buttresses. This he accomplished by using the same formula as before but substituting 21.6 tsf (300 psi) for 25.6 tsf (350 psi). At a depth of 140 feet, for example, the calculated buttress thickness for the new design increased from 6.07 feet to 7.08 feet. The additional thickness for both the arches and the buttresses meant that the buttresses did not need to be as long in order to provide sufficient surface area to limit shearing stresses to 100 psi. Accordingly, Eastwood modified the upstream slope of the buttresses from an angle of 45 degrees (a length:height ratio of 1:1) to one of slightly more than 50 degrees (a length:height ratio of 10:12), thus permitting a decrease in buttress length.[44]

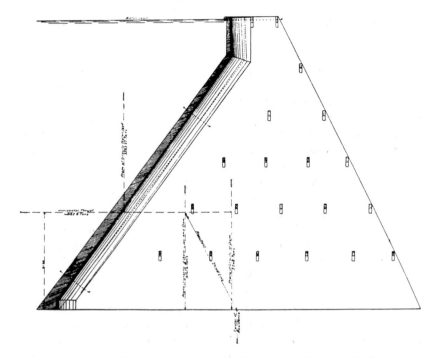

8.3   *Cross section of a large buttress design showing "resultant force" of water pressure and dam weight. This diagram, drawn in 1910, documents Eastwood's understanding of how the inclined upstream face acted to keep the resultant force at the center of the buttress.* (Journal of Electricity Power and Gas, *1910*)

In designing the Mountain Dell Dam, Eastwood devoted little overt attention to the overall stability of the structure and to the question of whether or not a full reservoir might "tip" the dam over. He apparently provided Cannon with drawings (which unfortunately do not survive) showing where the "resultant force" acted on the base of the buttresses; however, calculations to discern the magnitude and location of this "resultant force" were not a primary determinant in developing a suitable design. He understood that the sloping upstream faces of his designs ensured that the "resultant" would fall somewhere very near the center of the buttresses (Fig. 8.3), and consequently, he was not particularly worried about whether the upstream slope was 45 degrees or 50 degrees or some other roughly equivalent inclination. Instead, he developed designs through analysis of compressive stresses in the arches and shear-

ing stresses in the buttresses; once a design was conceived in this manner, he checked to make sure that the "resultant force" fell close to the center of the buttresses, thus providing what he termed "balanced loading."[45]

Steel Reinforcement and Strut-tie Beams

Cannon believed that the placement of steel bars within the buttresses would help counteract temperature stresses, and he urged Eastwood to adjust his Mountain Dell design accordingly. Eastwood thought that it was structurally unnecessary to place reinforcement in the buttresses except where they were intersected by the strut-tie beams, but he quickly acceded to Cannon's wishes and recommended that the reinforcement be "placed as nearly as possible at right angles with the resultant thrust [of the water pressure]." In addition, recalling his experience in constructing the Hume Lake Dam, he suggested that the reinforcing steel "consist of large members, as for instance, old lightweight railroad rails."[46]

To the average observer, the strut-tie beams that run between buttresses are the most visually prominent feature of many Eastwood dams. As he noted on several occasions, strut-tie beams were intended to support or brace the buttresses in the event of an earthquake or some other seismic disturbance. Eastwood never undertook any formal calculations to demonstrate the actual structural value of the strut-tie beams.[47] He did, however, assert that they broke the buttresses up into a series of "short columns" that were stable against lateral toppling. Lateral stability could also be enhanced by placing thick counterforts perpendicular to the downstream edge of the buttresses. The issue of how many (or even whether) strut-tie beams should be included in the Mountain Dell design is unmentioned in surviving correspondence between Cannon and Eastwood. Nonetheless, from the earliest preliminary proposals through the final design, strut-tie beams were included as an integral part of the structure. In the end, Eastwood incorporated a series of twenty-two strut-tie beams into the 150-foot-high design, each "spaced 20 feet apart vertically and 29 feet horizontally."[48] Cannon considered these braces to be quite important; and in December 1915, he requested that Eastwood adjust the plans one last time to increase the amount of steel reinforcing placed where the strut-tie beams passed through the buttresses.[49] In complying with this request, Eastwood arrived at the final Mountain Dell design.

EASTWOOD'S RELATIONSHIP WITH MATHEMATICAL THEORY

Having received training within a university environment, Eastwood became skilled in using mathematics to facilitate his hydroelectric power and dam design work. But despite his ability to manipulate algebraic formulas and the trigonometric relationships important in surveying, he never employed calculus as an aid in the design process; while many other engineers focused attention on using more mathematical[ly] sophisticated models, Eastwood declined to participate in this movement. Adhering to the approach that David Billington associates with the creation of structural art, Eastwood viewed mathematical theory as a tool, not as an unequivocal determinant of a design's dimensions. Rather than attempting to calculate the exact stresses within a structure, he was content to develop approximate methods of analysis that erred on the side of safety.[50]

In the early 1920s, while embroiled in a dispute over stresses in his Cave Creek Dam design, Eastwood drafted a revealing memo entitled "Limitations to Formulae."[51] In this discourse, he vented frustration over the notion that mathematical theory always provided exact answers to problems involving the physical environment. Noting that "all formulae are based on assumptions . . . [but] these assumptions may be true or in error depending on the range of departure from the conditions for which they were assumed," Eastwood acknowledged the utility of mathematical formulas but emphasized that this utility depended on how realistic the assumptions underlying them were. In particular, he rejected the idea that a formula useful in one context could be extrapolated to apply to extreme conditions and still be considered valid. He forcefully expressed these thoughts with regard to a formula used to calculate waterflow in canals and streams when he pleaded: "Where does it lead if one takes the Kutter formula for stream discharge applied to the Mississippi River, or [to] the Gulf Stream for coef[ficient] 'N' of roughness? Einstein is Right! All lines are curves and all things mundane are relative."[52]

The specific theoretical dilemma that prompted Eastwood to draft "Limitations of Formulae" related to techniques for calculating how the resultant force acts upon a multiple arch dam. The question at issue involved whether the cross-sectional area of the arch was to be combined with the buttress or whether the buttress area alone was to be considered as resisting the resultant force. Eastwood chose what he believed to be the most conservative method and stipulated that the "entire load" was to be "distributed on the buttress only." Excluding the arch limited the area that the resultant acted upon and thus increased the calculated compressive stress. At one point, he went so far as to acknowledge that his method of calculating the forces acting on buttresses "is not correct for any portion of the structure as is no formula based on assumptions, but it gives a criterion of the ultimate safety of the structure as to its foundation loadings and this is always on the safe side."[53]

The issue took on special meaning when S. M. Cotten, a disgruntled local engineer, attempted to stop construction of the Cave Creek Dam near Phoenix. Cotten branded Eastwood's design unsafe on the basis of calculations in which he assumed that the resultant acts on a combined arch/buttress unit. Specifically, Cotten determined that, at the top of the dam, substantial tensile stresses would form along the downstream edge of the buttress, causing the dam to tip upstream into the full reservoir. This scenario constitutes a logical impossibility, and Eastwood considered it a good example of how rigid adherence to a seemingly precise method of mathematical analysis could lead to untenable conclusions. A letter submitted by Gardiner Williams to the *Engineering News-Record* helped him refute Cotten's contentions, but the incident reinforced his belief that mathematical theory must be tempered with common sense in order to be useful.[54] Eastwood did not desire to develop structural theories that were universally valid and unerring. Instead, he sought to create safe, economical, real-world structures. For him, mathematical formulas offered useful guidance, but careful consideration of how theory related to physical reality was the way to achieve the true ideal of "scientific" design.

ARCHES AND THE ELASTIC THEORY

In proportioning arch dimensions, Eastwood relied on the simple cylinder formula. This formula is absolutely accurate for an infinitely thin arch encompassing an arc of 180 degrees and resting on a rigid foundation. As a structure diverges from this ideal, however, the theory becomes less precise and less reliable as an indicator of actual stresses. Most of the early single arch dam designs, including F. E. Brown's 1884 Bear Valley Dam, were based on the cylinder formula—a circumstance that aroused the interest of engineers who hesitated to accept the safety of thin arch dams. Several concrete arch dams built in Australia in the early twentieth century were plagued by cracks that formed as the result of temperature fluctuations; and although these dams remained functional, their cracks were viewed as evidence of the cylinder formula's inadequacy.[55]

The cylinder formula considers arches to exist in an idealized physical state in which external forces cannot cause deformations that might alter the distribution of stresses. In the real world, all materials are elastic to some degree (that is, they bend under pressure or as a result of temperature change), and this can effect the performance of any structure, including a dam. In 1854, the French theoretician Jacques Bresse first formulated an elastic theory of arches that considered the effect of deformations on arch stresses. Bresse did not limit his theory to dams and, in fact, considered the structural mechanics of arches within a broad mathematical context. For many years, the elastic theory played little role in dam construction; but by the early twentieth century, attempts were under way to integrate the theory into hydraulic engineering. Although the elastic theory of arches is based on its own set of idealized assumptions that affect its relevance to how actual structures perform, it nonetheless appears to offer an accurate means of analyzing stresses; by the 1920s, many engineers had adopted it as a useful improvement over the cylinder formula.[56]

Eastwood first revealed his knowledge of the elastic theory during construction of the Big Meadows Dam in 1912. When questions arose over the arches' ability to resist temperature and rib-shortening stresses, Eastwood drew on methods outlined in Ira Baker's 1909 edition of *A Treatise on Masonry Construction* to analyze the effect of these stresses mathematically, using elastic theory.[57] In applying the theory to his Big Meadows design, he discerned that stresses could be reduced (at least theoretically) by using arches encompassing deep, wide arcs. In other words, stresses in an arch of 180 degrees were calculated to be less than those in an arch of 120 degrees. When Eastwood designed the Los Verjels Dam in 1913 (the first built after the Big Meadows debacle), he used arches of over 140 degrees, the largest in any of his designs. For the next two dams, Kennedy and Mountain Dell, he employed three-hinged arches that were designed specifically to move and/or rotate in order to relieve all potential temperature or rib-shortening stresses. In the period 1912–1915, Eastwood took the existence of "secondary" arch stresses quite seriously and, using elastic theory as a guide, formulated designs to accommodate them.

During construction at Mountain Dell, however, his thoughts on temperature and rib-shortening stresses underwent major changes. After 1915, he never again specified the use of three-hinged arches, and his arch designs began to feature flatter arches. Before 1915, most of his designs (including Big Bear Valley, Big Meadows, Los Verjels, Kennedy, and Mountain Dell) featured arches with arcs greater than 120 degrees; by 1920, he was using arches as shallow as 100 degrees—a move that ran directly counter to the dictates of elastic theory. Although no surviving document specifies the exact reason for his disenchantment with the theory, it almost certainly resulted from observation of how his dams performed under actual use.

In one of two letters Eastwood wrote in 1916–1917 expressing dissatisfaction with the elastic theory, he claimed that his views were "the result of experience and many trials."[58] He had personally supervised construction of the three-hinged Kennedy Dam in 1914; and when the dam was raised 30 feet in height in 1916, he had a good opportunity to evaluate the structural performance of the three-hinged arches. The nature of what he learned can almost certainly be found in published observations made in the mid-1920s regarding the performance of Mountain Dell Dam. Specifically, Fred Noetzli acknowledged that, based on a field inspection undertaken in 1925, the Mountain Dell arch hinges had never moved in almost eight years. He informed the engineering community:

In 1925 a careful inspection was made of the [Mountain Dell Dam structure built in 1916–1917 and] . . . a remarkable thing was observed. When the dam was built the upstream face of the arches was cement washed. This left a thin layer of cement . . . across the joints of the hinges. It was found that in the seven years of operation of the dam and reservoir none of the hinges had moved a sufficient amount to break the thin coating of cement wash . . . The hinges were pointed with asphalt and probably offered little resistance to rotation due to deformation of the arches. It appears, therefore, that the deformation of the arches was too small to break the cement coating. These conditions were obtained for the hinges at the abutments, as well as for those at the arch crown.[59]

In other words, even when special efforts were made to build hinged arches that would physically respond to the effects of temperature and rib-shortening stresses, no movement could be induced. This conflicted with prognostications derived from the elastic theory and demonstrated that the theory was deficient, at least in regard to multiple arch dams. In Eastwood's own words: "It is undoubtedly the proper procedure to fit theory to practice but the factors of the theory must be based on the actual physical conditions as they are in practice or else theory will lead us astray."[60] Eastwood made no attempt to assess the inaccuracy of the elastic theory quantitatively. Rather, he simply switched to using the simpler cylinder formula and designed thin arches that provided reasonably good (but not absolutely precise) compatibility with the formula.

Eastwood had demonstrated serious interest in the use of sophisticated mathematical analysis to help him with the design of arches. But when the elastic theory led to conclusions incompatible with performance, he recognized the limitations of the theory and did not feel bound to its dictates. In adopting his design methodology, he struck a logical—yet easily misunderstood—middle ground between highly abstract, academic approaches to structural design and so-called "old-fashioned" engineering based on practical experience.

Buttresses and Principal Stresses

In designing buttresses, Eastwood worked from two different perspectives. First, he considered the issue of "shear stresses" to be of great importance. Second, he made sure that the resultant of all forces acting on the dam fell at or near the centerline of the buttresses. At Mountain Dell, Eastwood considered "shear stresses" to be the critical design factor, and he seemingly devoted little attention to calculating the location and magnitude of the resultant force. At other times, he analyzed this latter aspect of his designs more closely.

In analyzing the general stability of the buttresses, Eastwood divided the structure into a series of horizontal sections each 10 feet high. During the 1920s, engineers with more mathematical training began criticizing the widespread use of horizontal sections and proposed analyzing buttress stresses along inclined, or nonhorizontal, sections.[61] Most often employed to determine what were called "principal stresses," analytical techniques focusing on nonhorizontal sections did not interest Eastwood. Although the analysis of "principal stresses" did not find its way into Eastwood's design lexicon, impetus for other engineers to analyze multiple arch dams along non-horizontal sections arose when Lake Hodges Dam developed small diagonal

buttress cracks.[62] These cracks were observed to have formed before the reservoir was filled, thus eliminating the possibility that they were caused by hydrostatic loading. As water accumulated behind the dam, measurements of the cracks' width were made. No correlation could be found between the changes in widths of the cracks and the hydrostatic pressure exerted by the reservoir, however. Instead, monitoring revealed that variation in crack size depended on changes in temperature.[63] During warm weather the cracks narrowed, while in cold weather they expanded. In essence, they merely expanded and contracted in response to temperature fluctuations (see Fig. 7.20).

Although the formation of these temperature cracks did not indicate any serious structural problems, it did reflect a limitation in how Eastwood conceived of the forces acting on multiple arch dams. In November 1915, he had reassured Cannon that steel reinforcement in the buttresses was unnecessary because "shrinkage cannot take effect in a vertical cracking for the combined reasons of a compressive loading to offset [it] and a tapered or truncated pyramidal shape that is free to contract on all sides." Based on the Lake Hodges experience, however, this was not necessarily true. In any case, acceding to Cannon's wishes, he recommended that the reinforcement be "placed as nearly as possible at right angles with the resultant thrust" of the water pressure, demonstrating a prescient understanding of where temperature cracks were, in fact, most likely to occur.[64]

Most importantly, the ability of Lake Hodges Dam to store water safely was not affected by hairline buttress cracks. In fact, during the 1920s, other multiple arch structures such as the Big Dalton Dam near Los Angeles were purposely built with inclined expansion joints.[65] These joints provided an artificial means of relieving temperature stresses within the buttresses, and helped eliminate the possibility that natural cracks might appear. Man-made expansion joints also helped dispel the psychological disquiet caused by unwanted cracks forming in a dam, no matter how "safe" or inconsequential they might be. For his part, Eastwood remained committed to the view that the temperature cracks at Lake Hodges were structurally insignificant; and when given the chance, he continued to specify that only a minimal amount of reinforcement be placed in the buttresses. For example, the Anyox Dam (completed in 1923) contains steel only in the arches, in the strut-tie beams, and in places where the strut-tie beams extend through the buttresses; no significant buttress cracks were ever reported to afflict the 156-foot-high design.

OTHER PRACTITIONERS OF THE STRUCTURAL TRADITION: JORGENSEN, NOETZLI, AND JAKOBSEN

Eastwood's disenchantment with mathematical theory did not place him in the mainstream of the civil engineering profession. In contrast, the other key proponents of multiple arch technology during the 1920s relied heavily on mathematical analysis—and especially on the use of elastic arch theory—during the design process. Lars Jorgensen, Fred Noetzli, and B. F. Jakobsen actively promoted the use of multiple arch dams in several articles published in journals such as the ASCE *Transactions.*[66] The design approach underlying these articles supports Billington's observations that in the 1920s, "faith in formula led to an emphasis on mathematical analysis which . . . seemed to require that designers justify their works by sophisticated calculation."[67] For these three engineers, the elastic theory functioned as a powerful predictive tool that was to be heeded, not questioned.

Although Jorgensen was the first of the three to build a multiple arch structure (Gem Lake Dam in 1916), he soon focused almost all of his efforts on large, constant-angle arch dams. Evidently, in the early 1920s, Jorgensen planned a few dams (never built) that fea-

tured a large main arch supplemented by a few smaller arches. In general, however, his work seems not to have evolved much beyond the basic type of design he first used at Salmon Creek, Alaska, in 1913.[68] Jorgensen's designs offered significant savings in material over comparable gravity dams, but his interest in developing their structural form further seems to have stagnated by the mid-1920s. Perhaps not coincidentally, at this time his firm (the Constant Angle Arch Dam Company) began to threaten to sue other builders of constant-angle dams on grounds of patent infringement—a program that bordered on legal extortion. In the late 1920s, the Salt River Valley Water Users' Association in Phoenix agreed to a pay a cash settlement to Jorgensen's firm rather than fight an expensive courtroom battle over the alleged patent infringement represented by their Mormon Flat dam design.[69]

In lieu of Jorgensen, Noetzli (and to a lesser extent, Jakobsen) took the lead in advocating multiple arch dam construction in the 1920s. Noetzli's contributions to the technology are perhaps best evidenced in the development of wide-span, "double-wall" buttress designs. This type of structure did not offer any material savings over Eastwood's designs, but it did present a more massive and conservative appearance than Eastwood's so-called "lace curtain" structures. One of the earliest of Noetzli's "double-wall" designs to reach construction was the Big Dalton Dam (Fig. 8.4), a structure that featured diagonal expansion joints in the buttresses analogous to the natural cracks in Eastwood's Lake Hodges Dam (Fig. 8.5).[70] Noetzli based the design of these expansion cracks on his analysis of "principal stresses" within the buttresses; in this context, advanced mathematical techniques enabled him to justify a design feature that was ultimately more cosmetic than functional.

In addition to promoting the use of "double-wall" buttresses, Noetzli and Jakobsen both spurred the proliferation of multiple arch dams with arches that featured a semicircular (or 180-degree) extrados. The elastic

8.4 *Big Dalton Dam in southern California, completed in 1929; a good example of a double-walled, hollow multiple arch dam. (A) Downstream side. The buttresses project a solid, massive appearance, at least in comparison with designs such as Eastwood's Lake Hodges Dam. (B) Upstream side, showing the wide-span arches with their 180-degree arcs. (Huber Papers, WRCA)*

structural dams came to a different, though equally premature end. In the early 1930s he was censured by the American Society of Civil Engineers for having publicly criticized another ASCE member in the course of reporting the existence of fraud during construction of a flood control dam in Los Angeles County. Jakobsen subsequently sought professional refuge in the Army Corps of Engineers, where his skills in designing multiple arch dams went unused for the duration of his professional life; he retired in the 1950s.[72]

U.S. RECLAMATION SERVICE

The U.S. Reclamation Service (which in 1923 became the Bureau of Reclamation) adopted an approach to dam design that, to some degree, incorporated elements of both the structural and massive traditions; eventually the latter tradition came to dominate the agency's construction activities, resulting in some of the most prominent gravity dams built in the West. Prior to the 1930s, the Reclamation Service/Bureau was only one of several important participants in the development of the arid region's hydraulic infrastructure. The agency maintained such a high profile, however (in part due to its own promotional efforts), that its work in dam design was perceived as significant and influential by the general public as well as by the engineering community. In this context, it is important to understand the agency's approach to dam design, especially as it contrasts with the methodology developed by Eastwood.

8.5 *Detail view of Big Dalton Dam, showing the diagonal expansion joint purposely built into a buttress wall. This "artificial crack" serves exactly the same structural function as the naturally formed temperature cracks that appeared in the Lake Hodges Dam buttresses. (Huber Papers, WRCA)*

theory had indicated that using a 180-degree arc is the best way to reduce rib-shortening and temperature stresses. Remarkably, however, Noetzli continued to advocate this design feature even after directly observing the unmoved condition of the three-hinged arches at Mountain Dell. Evidently, Noetzli did not view the physical behavior of a functioning structure as offering reason enough to modify his reliance on mathematical theory. Noetzli remained an active advocate of structural dams until his untimely death in 1933, but he seems never to have transcended a "faith in formula."[71] Jakobsen's outlook resembled Noetzli's, but his career as a designer of

The Reclamation Service's first director and chief engineer, Frederick Haynes Newell, graduated as a mining engineer in 1885 from the Massachusetts Institute of Technology. Starting in 1888, Newell helped John Wesley Powell administer the federal Irrigation Survey; and in the early 1890s, he was appointed the U.S. Geological Survey's chief hydrographer.[73] Allied with Gifford Pinchot, the first forester of the U.S. Forest Service, Newell became a leader in the self-styled "conservation movement" whereby he came to believe that "nearly all the [western] land which is available for irrigation by individual effort or which affords profitable opportunities for comparatively small investments has been utilized."[74] As historian Lawrence Lee notes: "The predominant theme that ran through Newell's writings and Reclamation Service publications was that the West had given up on private enterprise and depended exclusively upon the federal government to build the large water storage and distribution works necessary for further irrigation advancement in arid America."[75]

When Newell was appointed chief engineer of the Reclamation Service in 1902, he had already achieved standing as a prominent irrigation advocate. His skills, however, were largely those of an administrator based in Washington, D.C., rather than of a practicing engineer. To ameliorate his lack of experience, he looked to his assistant chief engineer (Arthur P. Davis) and a system of "engineering boards" for technical expertise.[76] As John Wesley Powell's nephew, Davis attracted favorable attention, but he too did not bring a great deal of practical knowledge to his work. After graduating from George Washington University in Washington, D.C., in 1888, he joined Powell's Irrigation Survey and spent the 1890s as a federal employee.[77] Although more active in field work than Newell, Davis shared the characteristic of never having built or operated an irrigation system prior to the formation of the Reclamation Service. To substitute for a strong engineering presence at the top of the service's organizational chart, Newell devised a system of consulting "engineering boards" (usually consisting of three or four men) charged with preparing, reviewing, and/or approving major plans.[78]

Seeking an engineer to provide advice on large-scale dam design, Newell turned to George Y. Wisner, a 63-year-old hydraulic engineer from Detroit, Michigan, who had no previous experience in dam design, irrigation, or western construction work. Prior to

1903, Wisner's professional interests focused on issues such as sanitary engineering, harbor development, and water-borne transportation along the Great Lakes and the Mississippi River.[79] Despite his marginal experience in directly relevant areas, Wisner served on the engineering boards of several Reclamation Service projects, and (until Wisner's death in 1906) Newell relied on him for expertise in the mathematical analysis of dam designs.[80] For two of the most dramatic dam sites in the West, Wisner helped develop thin arch designs that utilized smaller quantities of concrete and masonry than would have been necessary for massive gravity structures. Both the Pathfinder Dam site in southeastern Wyoming and the Shoshone Dam site in northwestern Wyoming featured narrow, hard-rock gorges that were ideal for supporting arch structures; the steep canyon walls were perfectly suited to absorbing the thrust of an arch under hydrostatic load (Fig. 8.6).[81] Using a cross section that was similar in shape to James Schuyler's 1888 Sweetwater Dam, Wisner and his assistant Edgar Wheeler mathematically analyzed their two arch designs, applying methods related to those used on the recently completed curved gravity Cheeseman Dam near Denver.[82] Given the remarkably deep and narrow topographical shapes of the Pathfinder and Shoshone sites, the arch dams built by the Reclamation Service were not particularly daring; and in fact, Eastwood criticized the bulky dimensions of the Shoshone Dam in a letter published in a June 1910 issue of *Engineering News*.[83] Wisner's efforts did, however, establish a precedent within the agency for constructing thin arch designs, and this eventually helped foster the building of other structural dams in the 1920s.

In terms of the publicity it received, the Roosevelt Dam near Phoenix constituted the agency's most prominent early project, and its massive configuration became much more emblematic of the agency's approach to engineering design than either the Pathfinder Dam or Shoshone Dam. Built with locally quarried sandstone, the Roosevelt Dam uti-

8.6 *Shoshone (Buffalo Bill) Dam, located in a narrow canyon of the Shoshone River in northwestern Wyoming. Completed by the U.S. Reclamation Service in 1909, this is one of the federal agency's earliest thin arch dams. (Historic American Engineering Record, Library of Congress)*

lized a massive curved gravity design derived from the DeSazilly/Delocre/Wegmann tradition (Fig. 8.7). This type of profile, in the late nineteenth century, became the standard for metropolitan water systems such as those supplying New York (Croton Dam), Boston (Wachusett Dam), and San Francisco (San Mateo Dam). Attempting to establish the prestige of the Reclamation Service, Newell wanted the agency's most visible dam to project an aura of permanence similar to those built by major municipalities. While Reclamation Service officials never explicitly stated that the Roosevelt Dam was to mimic the prominent metropolitan system structures of the period, little thought was given to using anything other than a curved gravity design.[84]

The agency's propensity for using gravity

designs for all but the most remarkable dam sites (such as Pathfinder and Shoshone) was expressed in a letter written by Newell in 1912:

We [the Reclamation Service] have been inclined to adhere to the older, more conservative type of solid dam, largely perhaps because of the desire not only to have the works substantial but to have them appear so and recognized by the public as in accordance with established practice.[85]

Newell relished the idea of leading a scientific organization, but he was equally concerned with adhering to a status quo defined by "established practice." Newell's interest in appearance and its effect on public perceptions was particularly acute in relation to storage dams:

Plans for the construction of storage works, while they must be prepared with regard to reasonable

189

8.7 *Construction view of Roosevelt Dam in 1908. This massive curved gravity dam was built by the U.S. Reclamation Service. (Author's collection)*

economy, must be [undertaken] with a view to being not merely safe but looking safe. People must not merely be told that they are substantial, but when the plain citizen visits the works he must see for himself that there is every indication of the permanency and stability of a great storage dam . . . he must feel, to the very innermost recesses of his consciousness, that the structure is beyond question.[86]

The emphasis Newell placed on the visual attributes of dam design closely resembles that expressed by John R. Freeman. In fact, Freeman was a close friend and colleague of A. P. Davis and corresponded frequently with him and with Newell in the period 1910–1912.[87] Although Freeman never formally sat on any of the service's "engineering boards," he was responsible for inducing the Great Western Power Company to retain Davis as a consultant for the Big Bend Dam project in 1909. In the fall of 1912, at the height of his attacks on the "psychology" of Eastwood's Big Meadows design, Freeman used Davis as a sounding board and sympathizer, as when he proselytized: "The psychology of these airy arches and the lace curtain effect of [Eastwood's] stiffening props is not well suited to inspire public confidence."[88] Significantly, Newell's statement of confidence in "the older, more conservative type of

solid dam" came in response to an inquiry about the construction of buttress dams.[89]

Davis replaced Newell as director of the service in 1914. Thereafter, the agency embraced the massive tradition, forgoing more materially efficient structural dams. The financial condition of the agency eventually disintegrated, however, and Davis was fired in 1923.[90] The renamed Bureau of Reclamation soon adopted a more open attitude toward thin arch dams (but not toward multiple arch designs); the agency resuscitated the basic idea behind Wisner and Wheeler's designs for the Pathfinder and Shoshone dams and developed the "trial-load" method of arch dam design using techniques derived from the elastic theory.[91]

The "trial-load" method represents a theoretical approach to arch dam design that developed out of the elastic theory. First proposed in the late nineteenth century, this method recognized that an arch dam resists hydrostatic load in part by "gravity action," especially in the lower parts of the structure where the arch is relatively thick. The "trial-load" method conceives of an arch dam as consisting of an interrelated set of horizontal arches and vertical cantilever sections that coexist within the structure. By specifying that the structure be designed so that deflections of the two systems under the same hydrostatic load (calculated according to elastic theory) are identical in various parts of the dam, the method postulates a way to determine stresses in arch dams with seemingly great mathematical precision.[92]

First proposed in 1889 by Luther Wagoner and Herbert Vischer as a way to analyze stresses in the Bear Valley Dam, the "trial-load" technique received wider publicity in 1904 when Silas Woodward used it as an aid in designing Denver's Cheeseman Dam.[93] The method's name relates to the use of a trial-and-error approach in determining the relationship between the dam's deformation and the distribution of the hydrostatic load within the structure. Rather than attempting to solve complicated equations as a basis for creat-

ing a completely new design, engineers found it easier to hypothesize a design, analyze how much compatibility existed between the arch and cantilever deflections, and then hypothesize another design that would presumably provide better compatibility. After three or four iterations (or trials), the designer could formulate an arch design in which stresses could be forecast fairly accurately. These designs were not necessarily efficient in their use of materials, however, and they could assume profiles as thick as that of a simple gravity dam. Thus, while some of the designs developed by the Bureau of Reclamation with this technique featured cross sections that were substantially thinner than those required for a gravity profile (such as the Gibson Dam in western Montana), others were curved dams of such ample proportions that no arch action was necessary for stability (such as the Owyhee Dam [Fig. 8.8]

8.8 *Owyhee Dam in eastern Oregon, built by the Bureau of Reclamation in the 1920s, using the "trial-load" method of design. This curved gravity design was considered by the bureau to be a precedent for the later design of Hoover Dam. (Library of Congress)*

8.9   *Bartlett Dam, north of Phoenix, Arizona, completed in 1939. This double-walled, hollow buttress structure was the only major multiple arch dam ever built by the Bureau of Reclamation. (Salt River Project Archives)*

in eastern Oregon and Hoover Dam on the Nevada–Arizona border).[94]

The "trial-load" method encouraged designers to presume that they could rigorously calculate stresses in a structure. As such, the method held considerable appeal for many engineers of this era, as well as for a bureaucracy in which individual initiative was subordinated to group consensus. Working through a system of consulting boards left over from the Newell era, a collective of engineers found it relatively straightforward to agree to results derived from the application of a seemingly precise mathematical formula. And with the increased reliance on federally subsidized water projects after 1930, the committee approach to hydraulic design gained influence throughout the West, leaving little room for the more individualistic techniques championed by Eastwood. Only once, in the late 1930s, did the Bureau of Reclamation design and build a multiple arch dam. Constructed for the Salt River Valley Water Users' Association in Phoenix, Arizona, the bureau's Bartlett Dam closely emulated the "double-walled" hollow buttress designs pioneered by Noetzli and Jakobsen in the 1920s (Fig. 8.9).[95] At Bartlett, the bureau proved that it could build large multiple arch dams; but aside from this one project, it never did so.

CHAPTER 9

Evolution of a Structural Artist (1918–1924)

Prove them all wrong, and there will be another crop of dunces to rally for a little State money and favors, till we are exhausted, and delay is what he [State Engineer McClure] wants, delay and still more delay.

John S. Eastwood to Burt Cole, July 1920

My joy in life is in doing each one a bit better than the one just completed. At Anyox I had no "critics" and built it as it should be, and was able, by reason of my getting a "free hand" to give my clients . . . the best service and the most complete dam in every particular in the world.

John S. Eastwood to Ed Fletcher, April 1924

After 1918, although Eastwood's designs remained controversial among certain influential engineers, his success in reducing the cost of water storage fostered a growing list of prospective clients. During the final six years of his life, he developed new forms of the multiple arch dam that promised ever greater economic savings for western water users. Significantly, David Billington's analysis of the careers and accomplishments of the engineers he characterizes as "structural artists" reveals that all of them developed their most creative designs at a relatively late stage in life.[1] In this respect, Eastwood closely fits the professional template of a structural artist: rather than stagnating once he turned 60 years old, his designs underwent significant evolution.

In his later years, Eastwood developed three basic structural innovations:

1. "Curved face" multiple arch dams that resembled his standard designs except that the "vertical head" was replaced by a gentle curve. The Cave Creek Dam and the Anyox Dam were both structures of this type.
2. "Radial plan" multiple arch dams, in which the upstream edges of the buttresses lay relatively close together while the downstream edges were spread apart. As a result, the dam's deepest sections had narrow span arches while the crest featured wide arches. Eastwood proposed "radial plan" designs for several projects (most

193

prominently the Littlerock Dam), but these were never built.

3. "Radial cone" and "triple arch" designs that featured a few (usually three or four) large arches. Many were designed with constant-angle arches (giving the appearance of inverted cones), while smaller structures were designed with constant-radius arches. These designs permitted the placement of less expensive "mass concrete," using techniques similar to those used for large gravity dams. One large "triple arch" design was built (Webber Creek Dam) and several "radial cone" structures were on the verge of being constructed when Eastwood died.

The most obvious motivation underlying Eastwood's innovations was a desire to reduce construction costs. But his inspiration to pursue projects sprang from a deeper urge to build and create; nothing gave him greater pleasure than seeing a design pass from the drawing board into a physical, functioning structure. As he wrote about his dam at Anyox, British Columbia: "My joy in life is in doing each one a bit better than the one just completed. At Anyox I had no "critics" and built it as it should be."[2] Eastwood certainly welcomed the financial rewards that came when his dams reached the construction stage, but profit maximization was not a primary goal of his consulting business. His commission usually constituted 5 percent of construction costs, giving him little motivation to undertake numerous revisions in order to reduce concrete quantities by a couple of hundred cubic yards and save a prospective client a few thousand dollars. Instead, the thrill of showing the world what he could do provided the central incentive for his constant design refinements. In this context, Billington describes all structural artists in terms appropriate for Eastwood: "At the heart of the technology they found their own originality, they created personal styles without denying any of the rigor of engineering."[3]

DAM SAFETY

After World War I, western water projects continued to grow and incorporate ever larger schemes for storing and transporting water. Among the most prominent were expansion of Los Angeles's Owens Valley aqueduct system, completion of San Francisco's Hetch Hetchy dam and aqueduct, plans for a federally supported storage dam across the Colorado River to assist farming interests in California's Imperial Valley (and eventually to aid real estate interests in greater Los Angeles), settlement of state-sponsored irrigation colonies near Sacramento, and a proposal for a California "State Water Plan" to capture water in the northern part of the state and transport it to more arid regions in the south.[4] Support and planning for these projects involved municipal, state, and federal authorities and reflected increasing government control over water resources development. In concert with this, government officials began to influence privately financed endeavors through enforcement of dam safety laws.

The issue of dam safety came to the fore as part of the Progressive movement of the early twentieth century, and it received increased public attention after the collapse of the Austin Dam near Austin, Pennsylvania, in 1911. The failure of this concrete gravity dam resulted in seventy-seven deaths and prompted an outcry for protective legislation; state regulation was considered to be a way to guard the public from ignorant or unscrupulous dam builders. Any detrimental effect that bureaucrats and their advisers might have on innovative yet sound design work went unacknowledged.[5]

State regulation of dams in California began in earnest with passage of the Public Utilities Act of 1911. Prior to this, a few mining dams came under the supervision of the federally sponsored Debris Commission; but otherwise, dams in the state were essentially unregulated.[6] The 1911 law only applied to dams built as part of enterprises regulated by the State Railroad Commission (such as the Great Western Power Company's Big Meadows Dam). It did not cover structures built by irrigation districts, mutual water companies, municipalities, or small private water users that lay outside the commission's jurisdiction. In late 1913, the commission appointed as its hydraulic engineer R. W. Hawley, a graduate of Colorado State College who had previously served with the U.S. Reclamation Service.[7] Serving in this capacity, Hawley first encountered Eastwood during construction of the Los Verjels Dam. Hawley remained with the commission for several years and oversaw many projects before resigning in 1919 to establish a private consulting business. In his wake, other engineers such as Frederic Faude served as hydraulic engineer and continued the work of regulating dam construction. The hydraulic engineer did not unequivocally speak for the commission on dam safety issues; all final decisions were officially made by the five-member commission. Nonetheless, the engineer's recommendations carried great weight, and unless countered by strong outside political pressure, they were usually adopted.

Prior to World War I, the Railroad Commission's work in dam regulation proceeded with little controversy, but many dams fell outside the commission's purview. In 1915, the California legislature empowered the state engineer to collect design data on other water storage structures in the state.[8] At this time, however, the state engineer (a position first authorized in the 1870s) possessed no authority to force the alteration or abandonment of existing structures or of proposed designs. In January 1916, interest in expanding the state engineer's role in dam safety increased dramatically after the collapse of the Lower Otay Dam near San Diego. This rock-fill dam had functioned safely for almost twenty years; but following a series of heavy rainstorms, water overtopped the structure and washed it away (Fig. 9.1). As expressed in *Western Engineering*, the Otay Dam failure led to calls for "laws of some sort establishing State supervision over the design and construction of dams."[9]

Although the Lower Otay disaster accelerated efforts to enact new state dam safety regulations, legislation on the subject languished for more than a year.[10] Finally, in May 1917, a new law granted the state engineer authority over the construction of all dams in California that were more than 10 feet tall or impounded more than 10 acre-feet of water.[11] Only three types of structures that met the height and capacity requirements were exempt: dams built to store mining tailings that were under the supervision of the Debris Commission; dams built under the supervision of the State Railroad Commission; and dams built by municipal corporations that had their own department of engineering. The dams in the first and second categories were already under some form of government supervision. The third category, however, constituted a class of dams totally outside state and federal control. The reasons behind this exemption help explain why the 1917 law was delayed for more than a year after the Lower Otay Dam failure.

The politically sensitive office of state engineer was held by Wilber F. McClure between 1912 and 1926. In the 1880s, McClure worked as a civil engineer for various railroads, but he left the world of engineering in 1893 to serve as a Methodist lay missionary in northern California.[12] In 1900, he recommenced technical work and supervised the removal of several large rocks that were impeding navigation in San Francisco Bay. Between 1906 and 1911 he served as City Engineer/Commissioner of Public Works for the city of Berkeley. Apparently because of McClure's experience in managing an engineering bureaucracy, Governor Hiram Johnson appointed him state engineer in 1912. Although skilled as an administrator, McClure had little experience in dam design or construction. Nonetheless, in 1917 he officially became responsible for overseeing California's new dam safety initiative.

The men who controlled municipal engineering organizations in Los Angeles and San Francisco considered it professionally demeaning to have to submit their dam designs

9.1 *A dam no more: Lower Otay Dam after being overtopped during floods of January 1916. This disaster was a major catalyst for the enactment of a new dam safety law in California in 1917. The intact dam is shown in Figure 2.1. (Eastwood Papers, WRCA)*

to the state engineer for review and approval. Consequently, they lobbied the state legislature to exclude them from the 1917 law. M. M. O'Shaughnessy, San Francisco's city engineer between 1912 and 1932, later wrote: "I had our City Attorney present objections to the State legislative body in Sacramento in 1917, against allowing Mr. McClure to have anything to do with our dams at Hetch Hetchy."[13] O'Shaughnessy claimed that he took this position because "I did not think from [McClure's] previous experience and knowledge, [that] he had the requisite experience to pass on such a subject and I did not care to be subject to his capricious rulings." While other engineers and water user organizations may have possessed similar skepticism concerning the state engineer — to say nothing of

their interest in autonomy, regardless of the state official's competence — they lacked the political clout necessary to exempt themselves from the new law.

The state engineer's office did not immediately assert its power to regulate dam construction. By 1918, however, McClure began drawing advice from a select group of consulting engineers on matters involving dam safety.[14] Why McClure sought advice from these particular men is unknown (nothing in the 1917 legislation required him to engage outside consultants), but they soon exerted great influence on his actions. For multiple arch dams, McClure's most important adviser proved to be Walter L. Huber, a 1905 graduate of the University of California at Berkeley who eventually served as president of the

American Society of Civil Engineers.[15] Huber obtained experience in water supply engineering and hydroelectric power work as a district engineer for the U.S. Forest Service in 1910-1913 and later as a junior colleague of John D. Galloway—another engineer who advised McClure on matters of dam design.[16] In 1918 Huber assisted the state engineer in the handling of Eastwood's Lake Hodges spillway design, and his interest in multiple arch dams continued for another twenty years. There is no record that Huber ever personally designed any multiple arch dams; instead, he became an expert on the technology by scrutinizing the work of Eastwood, Jorgensen, and others. The generally skeptical view that Huber and Galloway exhibited toward Eastwood's designs may perhaps be understood more clearly in light of John Freeman's 1925 statement that "Galloway and Huber also have for a good many years past been numbered among my good friends."[17]

Besides Huber and Galloway, many other engineers interacted with Eastwood on issues of design and safety during the final years of his life. But one of these men warrants special notice. Joseph B. Lippincott is well known to historians interested in western water resources development because of his controversial work with the U.S. Reclamation Service before becoming assistant chief engineer for Los Angeles's Owens Valley Aqueduct.[18] Less well known is his work as a consultant specializing in "water supply for irrigation and municipal uses," in which he provided advice for the financial/investment community and other interested parties, including the state engineer. In this capacity he became involved with the Littlerock Dam in Los Angeles County (ostensibly as a consultant for Shelton and Lancaster Investment Brokers) and with Eastwood's work in San Diego County. Like Huber, Lippincott concentrated most of his efforts in the area of dam construction on evaluating and assessing other engineers' designs.

After 1917, the opinions of the State Railroad Commission and the state engineer's office (and the consultants these officials listened to) became vitally important to Eastwood as he sought to expand his business within the West's most economically prominent state. Stricter dam safety laws were ostensibly enacted to protect the public from man-made floods, but government supervision could also impede the development of new and innovative methods of storing water. Prior to 1917, the actual performance of Eastwood's dams had given no one any cause to question their safety or serviceability. In fact, the Big Bear Valley Dam had received national publicity for remaining intact despite being overtopped during the same episode of flooding that destroyed the Lower Otay Dam in 1916.[19] Most dam failures involved either earthfill or rockfill embankment structures, so it might logically be expected that these technologies would attract the most scrutiny following passage of the 1917 law.[20] Instead, Eastwood's work generated much more concern than comparable embankment dams—a fact that frustrated his efforts to develop innovative design forms. Lacking the political clout necessary to obtain exemption from state supervision, Eastwood had to endure the rulings of California authorities if he wished to keep his business alive within the state.

During 1917-1918, Eastwood had experienced radically different bureaucratic responses from the Railroad Commission and the state engineer in connection with his dams in San Diego County. While the design for Murray Dam was actively endorsed by the Railroad Commission and its hydraulic engineer, R. W. Hawley, the Lake Hodges design received less than enthusiastic support from State Engineer McClure and his advisers. California's two major dam safety agencies held divergent views on the merits of Eastwood's designs, and a confrontation between the two soon developed over a proposed dam in northern Los Angeles County.

LITTLEROCK DAM

Flowing northward into the Antelope Valley (a geographical designation comprising the western end of the Mojave Desert), Little Rock Creek drains a watershed of more than

60 square miles in the San Gabriel Mountains. Irrigation on tracts adjacent to the creek began by the early 1890s, when the Littlerock Creek Irrigation District was organized under authority of the 1887 Wright Act. Encompassing more than 2,000 acres of desert land, the district struggled for many years, relying on seasonal surface flow and pumping to keep a few hundred acres in production. By 1910 there were 250 acres of pears, 200 acres of apples, and 50 acres of almonds under cultivation, supporting a population of at most a hundred people.[21] Meanwhile, the landowners in the district watched spring floods sweep down Little Rock Creek and sink into desert lake beds. As J. B. Lippincott stated in 1915:

Little Rock Creek, like all Southern California streams, is flashy in character. The summer flows are low and frequently the stream bed is dry. In the winter and early spring, due to heavy rains in the mountainous portion of the basin, large floods frequently pass the headworks, which are of short duration. The maximum demand for water in the irrigation season is about July 1st, at which time the stream flow is usually very low. For this reason it is necessary to store the winter floods in order to have sufficient water to supply the demand during the irrigation season, which lasts from June 1st through September 15th.[22]

Local farmers understood the value of storing "spring runoff" for irrigation use throughout the summer. Their major problem involved the cost of building a dam large enough to impound most of Little Rock Creek's annual flood flow. Unfortunately for them, no site was available that would permit a dam of modest size to create a reasonably large reservoir. In fact, to store approximately 5,000 acre-feet of water (not very much by western standards), they would need a dam at least 150 feet high.

The Littlerock Creek Irrigation District and the Palmdale Irrigation District (a secondary water appropriator on Little Rock Creek that served farmers and residents in nearby Palmdale) faced a classic western water dilemma.[23] They needed capital to build a dam in order to increase agricultural production, but the structure's cost could not exceed

their ability to pay off the construction debt with revenue made possible by the additional storage capacity. In essence, the project was financially viable only if the districts' investment in the dam could be kept low. This was exactly the type of economic scenario that propelled Eastwood's advocacy of the multiple arch dam; he wanted to minimize water storage costs in order to facilitate maximum economic development. Once the two districts seriously began to pursue implementing a water storage project, they visited several of Eastwood's existing dams and then sought out his services.[24]

Plans for a large dam on Little Rock Creek were announced in late 1917. On April 5, 1918, Eastwood agreed to provide the districts with "full and complete plans . . . [for a] multiple arch type [dam] of a height of approximately 182 feet."[25] The design was based on the Lake Hodges Dam and featured 24-foot-span arches and a minimum arch thickness of 12 inches. In May, plans were forwarded to McClure. During the summer, the state engineer expressed concern about the thinness of the proposed arches, indicating that he would not approve any dams exceeding 50 feet in height unless all "water-face members" were more than 18 inches thick.[26] Learning of this pronouncement, Hawley wrote McClure to protest that all structural requirements should "be based purely upon scientific reasoning . . . [and that] I am not to any extent in accord with you. . . . I am opposed to any arbitrary provision or requirement that may make it impossible for the development of resources when the funds available are limited."[27] Whether as a conciliatory gesture in response to Hawley's complaint or not, McClure lopped 3 inches off his previously announced minimum acceptable arch thickness and in September 1918 notified Burt Cole, engineer for the Palmdale Irrigation District, that he would "be pleased to approve plans for your proposed multiple arch type dam in Little Rock Canyon with minimum thickness of 15 inches for the top members."[28] A 3-inch differential in arch thickness remained between Eastwood's specified minimum (12 inches) and McClure's adjusted minimum (15 inches), but McClure's amicable note to Cole offered hope for resolving the impasse.

During that fall, however, McClure had second thoughts about Eastwood's design and, without warning, arbitrarily acted to limit the height of all future multiple arch dams built in California. In late November, McClure wrote Cole that, on the basis of a "short statement" from an employee in his department and a report by an anonymous "engineer of marked ability" (who was never publicly identified), he was "fully persuaded that no [multiple arch dam] should be built to a greater height than from 140 to 150 feet."[29] He also asserted that, if a multiple arch dam were built approximately 180 feet high "and proper stability provided, the cost would amount to as much as a gravity section concrete dam." In other words, he categorically ruled out building any large multiple-arch dam that cost less than a gravity dam. Whatever the source of McClure's antipathy toward Eastwood's designs, his intention was clear: to stop the construction of large multiple arch dams in California.

Eastwood appealed to the state engineer to rescind the height limit, and he offered technical arguments justifying this action. He also became extremely irate, informing McClure that "in all my long life of practice I have never been injured as much by any man as I have by you[r opposition to] . . . my efforts to give the world something better." Eastwood ridiculed McClure for asking a "draughtsman in your employ . . . to make a report on a subject as foreign to him as Sanskrit" and caustically observed: "Did anyone ever hear of an engineer of marked ability who made an anonymous report?"[30] Although it was probably counterproductive, his anger is understandable when the ramifications of McClure's decision are fully considered. After a decade of promoting multiple arch dams, Eastwood was finally attracting design commissions for structures costing several hundred thousand dollars. And now, just as he was reaching his goal of creating large, inex-

pensive storage dams, he encountered the opposition of a bureaucrat empowered by a new state law. In this light, the accusation that McClure had "injured" him is reasonable, as the "150-foot height limit" presented a serious threat to his consulting business in California.

Eastwood counseled Cole that the rejection of his Littlerock design was "apparently all a trumped [up] and inspired thing to knock out your districts."[31] He then hit on the real economic significance of the state engineer's decision: "If you do not build a multiple arched dam, you cannot build any kind of dam, for no type can be built within the economic limits of your bonding limit." The irrigation districts had not selected a multiple arch design merely to save a little money. They had chosen it because they simply could not afford to adopt any other design.

THE "RADIAL PLAN" DESIGN AND THE RAILROAD COMMISSION

Following McClure's imposition of a 150-foot height limit on multiple arch designs, the two districts sought means of excluding the state engineer from the approval process for Littlerock Dam. A scheme was devised whereby the Palmdale Water Company—a public utility regulated by the Railroad Commission— would build the Littlerock Dam and, upon completion, transfer ownership of the structure to the two irrigation districts.[32] As a result, the Railroad Commission (and not the state engineer) would exercise authority over the dam construction process. Upon learning of the switch in tactics, Eastwood decided to propose a new and even less expensive design for Little Rock Creek. The second design represented a new type of structure he called a "radial plan" multiple arch dam (Fig. 9.2). As he told William Petchner, attorney for the Palmdale Irrigation District, he would have used this type of design from the beginning;

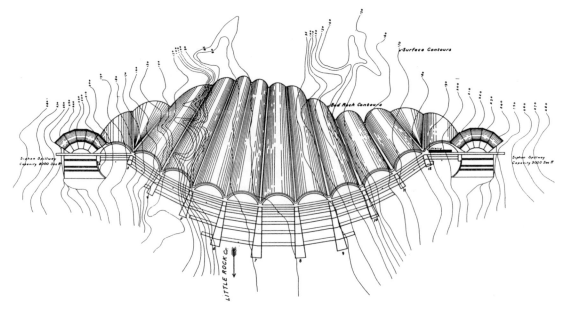

9.2   *"Radial plan" design for Littlerock Dam, drawn in 1919. The overall plan of the structure appears to arch downstream. (Retraced by Richard K. Anderson from an original in the Littlerock Creek Irrigation District files)*

but because of its "intricacies," he considered it impractical to "educate one so dense" as McClure.[33]

In a radial plan design the arches are not cylinders; instead, they taper toward the bottom in a conical shape. To support arches with a conical shape, the buttresses are placed with their upstream edges closer together than their downstream edges. Specifically, for Eastwood's second Littlerock design, the arches and buttresses were to be 50 feet apart at the downstream edge and only 25 feet apart at the front of the structure. The structural concept underlying the design is the same as that used for constant-angle arch dams: the amount of concrete necessary for construction can be minimized by reducing the arch span (and hence the radius) in the deepest parts of the dam. In addition to its lower cost, Eastwood claimed, the radial plan design provided structural advantages. Noting that the "buttresses become struts that carry their loads into the sides of the canyon," he compared this to "a man bracing himself against the door jambs instead of against the

door. He is harder to put out when thus braced." Aside from its economic and structural features, a radial plan design presents a rather strange appearance in that it seems to be arched in the wrong direction. Eastwood explained that the downstream curvature of the crest "must not be confused with curvature for arch action, for there is no arch action [extending between buttresses] in the curved crest." He further noted that "each buttress takes its loading from the adjacent arches exactly as in the straight crested type [of multiple arch dam]."[34]

In December 1918, the Palmdale Water Company informed the Railroad Commission of its intention to construct a multiple arch dam on Little Rock Creek; a month later Eastwood submitted his radial plan design to Hawley.[35] During February, Eastwood's proposal was reviewed by Frederic Faude, the engineer who helped supervise construction of Murray Dam and was now on the commission staff.[36] In reporting to Hawley, Faude noted that "a new feature . . . is introduced in the proposed structure, [it] being curved downstream." But instead of criticizing this innovation, he called it "a distinct advantage." Noting that the design "works for decided economy in quantities," Faude recited the advantages of multiple arch dams in their "freedom from hydrostatic uplift" and their use of "thin walls to secure a structure almost free from internal stresses." Concluding that Eastwood's design promised a "safe and economical structure" and constituted "no experiment," he averred that the dam's unprecedented height "need cause no uneasiness, as increased height is only a question of proper design."[37]

In early March 1919, the Railroad Commission held a public hearing on the Littlerock Dam application, at which Hawley advised "that there can be none other reasonably built that will be as safe" and, like Faude, recommended approval of Eastwood's radial plan dam.[38] In separate testimony, Eastwood described at length his engineering experiences and approach to design. At one point, the matter of McClure's refusal to approve the original Littlerock design arose, but Eastwood claimed that only "psychology or imagination" had motivated the state engineer's rejection. During the remainder of March, the Railroad Commission considered the application but hesitated to issue a formal opinion. Apparently, Eastwood's comments on the original Littlerock design prompted some concern, and commission members sought to learn more about McClure's views on multiple arch dams. Consequently, at the end of the month the commission requested the state engineer to review Eastwood's new proposal and participate in a "further hearing at a date agreeable to yourself."[39]

Within the commission, the decision to consult the state engineer had an immediate and dramatic effect; Hawley left his post after six years of service.[40] No official reason for his departure was ever given, but it undoubtedly related to the commission's reluctance to approve Eastwood's design. Hawley had unequivocally endorsed the "radial plan" dam at the public hearing; and when his recommendation was not accepted, he resigned. Chester

H. Loveland subsequently replaced him as hydraulic engineer, and Faude and M. E. Ready, another assistant engineer for the commission, handled most future work related to Eastwood's dams.

McClure readily agreed to the commission's request for aid and called upon Walter Huber and John Galloway to help analyze the new design.[41] On May 22, 1919, the three engineers, along with McClure's assistant C. H. Kromer, conferred in San Francisco. Within days, both Huber and Galloway provided written statements severely criticizing the radial plan proposal, urging that it be "radically altered" and "subjected to radical modification."[42] The major focus of their criticism was the downstream curve of the dam with Huber calling this a "dangerous feature since any cracks in the structure will tend to open under water pressure." Galloway also called the 300 psi maximum allowable compressive stress "too high," and Huber claimed that arch stresses "in excess of 310 [psi] . . . are higher than conservative engineering practice would dictate."[43] Acting on these recommendations, McClure testified on May 29 at a second hearing on the Littlerock application and strongly urged the commission to disallow the dam's construction.[44]

A few days later, the Railroad Commission issued an official opinion on Eastwood's radial plan design, permitting construction on the condition that "in the matter of the approval of further details" the commission would "invite the cooperation and suggestions of the State Engineering Office." On its face, the statement authorizes "the construction of a dam on Littlerock Creek."[45] But the nature of McClure's participation in working out the "details" proved to be far from merely advisory. In fact, the state engineer found himself in a position to dictate whether the structure would ever be built. On June 21, Huber urged McClure not to approve any details of the design, counseling that "you should [not] be compelled to assume such responsibility." The state engineer accepted this advice, and the dam project entered a bureaucratic limbo.[46] The Railroad Commission had no

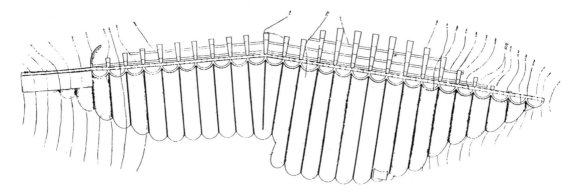

9.3 *Drawing of a "straight-crested" design (with angle) for Littlerock Dam, done in October 1919. This design served as the basis for the structure as built. (Littlerock Creek Irrigation District)*

statutory reason for allowing McClure a de facto veto over Eastwood's design; but evidently the commissioners either felt politically uncomfortable in ignoring the state engineer's recommendations or were unwilling to take the bureaucratic responsibility for approving an untested design over his explicit objections. Whatever the cause, the Railroad Commission's ruling meant that no radial plan dam would ever be built on Little Rock Creek.

A NEW SITE, A NEW DESIGN

Once the districts grasped the implications of the Railroad Commission's decision, they initiated a new course of action. On June 14, William Petchner wrote McClure to propose building a straight-crested multiple arch dam at a site that had been surveyed by J. B. Lippincott in 1915.[47] Indicating that the new site (located a few miles downstream from where Eastwood's first two designs were to be built) would not require a dam extending more than 150 feet above the streambed, Petchner anticipated that McClure might be more disposed to approving a design that adhered to his earlier pronouncements on height limitations.

During the summer of 1919, Eastwood de-

veloped a design for the new site.[48] On September 17, C. I. Rhodes, assistant engineer for the Railroad Commission, visited the Antelope Valley and reported that he could see "no reason why this [new] site should not prove satisfactory"; he also characterized Eastwood's new design as featuring "an obtuse angle, open upstream, of about 165 degrees [with] . . . both sides of this angle [being] straight lines."[49] Eastwood finished the design on October 2 (Fig. 9.3). For the next three years, these plans would form the focus of technical debate.

Eastwood delivered his new design to the Railroad Commission, and information on the project was also provided to two contractors, Bent Brothers and W. A. Kraner, Inc. In late October 1919, the Railroad Commission approved Eastwood's latest proposal but, in line with their earlier decision, specified that the state engineer approve "details" of the design.[50] In November, C. H. Kromer of the state engineer's office, C. H. Loveland, hydraulic engineer for the Railroad Commission, and his assistant M. E. Ready, met to discuss the straight-crested proposal. Little was decided except the obvious: maximum allowable stresses would have to be specified, and the design would then have to be checked formally to ensure that these stresses were not exceeded.

In January 1920, Kromer informed Mc-

Clure that stresses in the proposed dam were too high; following this, activity related to the approval process languished until spring.[51] In early 1920, the Littlerock and Palmdale Irrigation Districts dropped the tactic of using the Palmdale Water Company as a front (although the latter company still remained involved in the project), and they once again became the principal parties seeking approval for the dam. As a result, the state engineer's office now formally, as well as functionally, controlled the proceedings.[52]

In May 1920, C. H. Kromer indicated that the shearing stresses (or what Eastwood termed the "shear ratio") should be limited to half of the 118 psi that constituted the basis of Eastwood's design.[53] He took Eastwood's plans to Huber who, while expressing displeasure with certain design features, demurred on the question of the shearing stresses: although "the stresses in the structure are somewhat higher than I would myself make them in making a decision, and while probably a little beyond the limits of conservative engineering they cannot be classed as actually unsafe."[54] Grudging though it was, Huber's opinion indicated that the official view of the design might be changing. Shortly afterward, however, H. H. Wadsworth, another private engineer consulted by McClure, complained that shearing stresses in the proposal were too great.[55] This prompted McClure to write Burt Cole that "until corrections are made . . . [Eastwood's] plans cannot be approved."[56] Eastwood met directly with Wadsworth, but the meeting proved inconsequential, and Eastwood expressed to Cole his growing frustration. Referring to Wadsworth and Huber as experts who "do not know the first thing about the matters they discuss so learnedly for cash and future favors," he bluntly accused the state engineer's office of using dilatory tactics for ulterior motives:

If we succeed in showing that [they are] all wrong, there are always others to step in to try to down a competitor in business . . . [and] there will be another crop of dunces to rally for a little State money and favors, till we are exhausted, and delay

is what he [McClure] wants, delay and still more delay.[57]

In early August 1920, Donald Barker, president of the Palmdale Water Company, wrote to McClure asking how the irrigation districts could ever get approval for their dam.[58] Barker pointed out that the only type of dam that the districts could afford was a multiple arch dam. McClure responded by acknowledging that "we agree that the type of dam proposed is the only one which may be built within the [bonding] limits of the two districts."[59] In the fall of 1920, seeking to find an economically competitive alternative to Eastwood's design, McClure asked Lars Jorgensen to prepare an estimate for an arch dam at the new Little Rock Creek site. Jorgensen submitted a design for a large constant-angle arch supplemented by two small cylindrical arches that he estimated would require 54,000 cubic yards of concrete and cost $815,000.[60] Although Jorgensen's proposal was certainly far less expensive than a gravity design, it was nonetheless impossible for the irrigation districts to finance such a dam with their limited resources. The choice remained an Eastwood dam or no dam at all.

During the fall of 1920, continuing questions about shearing stresses appeared to constitute the state engineer's primary problem with Eastwood's design.[61] In November, Wadsworth reported to McClure that, although he still had disagreements with Eastwood, he believed that "shearing stresses of 100 lbs. per square inch should not be considered excessive" but that to be conservative, "80 or 85" psi would "produce satisfactory results." Without explanation, Wadsworth had abandoned his previous position that maximum shearing stresses of 60 psi were "proper."[62] Apparently Wadsworth's opinion held sway over McClure. The state engineer soon "consent[ed] to 85 pounds per square inch unit stress direct shear in buttresses," but simultaneously acknowledged that altering the original design specifications even to this extent would increase costs beyond the bonding limit of the districts.[63]

In December, the districts sought out Charles Derleth, a professor of engineering at the University of California, Berkeley, to appraise the stability of the design. Eastwood had what he termed a "very gracious" meeting with Derleth but believed that the academic engineer's comments only added to the "confusion." In one of Eastwood's last surviving letters relating to design approval negotiations, he recalled the story of "the donkey, the old man and the boy—no matter who rode or walked, man, boy, or donkey, there was always a critic of the act."[64] Ironically, just as Eastwood was on the verge of giving up hope, McClure chose to reassess (but not to reverse) his position on the Littlerock Dam. On January 18, 1921, the state engineer unobtrusively approved Eastwood's design except for "Sheet #5" of the drawings, which concerned the "section through the arch ring."[65] Once again, the minimum thickness of the arch was the main sticking point, as McClure would not relent on his requirement that all parts of the arch be at least 15 inches thick.[66] This seemingly small matter, in conjunction with the cost of adding steel to reinforce the buttresses, sufficed to frustrate the project.

McCLURE RELENTS

From February 1921 until the spring of 1922, no mention of activity related to the Littlerock Dam appears in the available records, although negotiations undoubtedly took place on a level far removed from Eastwood. J. B. Lippincott, whose exact influence on McClure is unclear, clearly provided important assistance on the project. In an April 12, 1922, letter to McClure, Lippincott referred to "your favor of April 5, in which you sent me copies of your correspondence relative to the multiple arch dam for Little Rock Creek."[67] Whatever this correspondence may have involved, it does not survive in Lippincott's papers or in the Department of Water

Resource's available files; evidently, some kind of political accommodation was being worked out between the irrigation districts and the state government. Lippincott had been requested by Shelton and Lancaster Investment Brokers to report on "the feasibility of the proposed irrigation projects of the Littlerock Irrigation District and the Palmdale Irrigation District" and to help them decide whether the Littlerock Dam would be a safe investment. In mid-April, Lippincott advised the brokerage firm that the dam and associated irrigation improvements were "worthy" and would "result in a valuable public improvement."[68]

During the spring of 1922, McClure changed his mind about Eastwood's design, and on May 18 the districts were notified that he had approved a compromise design worked out between Cole and Lippincott (Fig. 9.4).[69] As described in a memo to McClure by Kromer, the final design was for a dam 158 feet high with a maximum shearing stress within the buttresses of 109 psi.[70] The once intractable opposition of the state engineer to designs that permitted shearing stresses in excess of (first) 60 psi and (then) 85 psi evaporated, as did his refusal to approve any multiple arch design taller than 150 feet. Moreover, the approved design featured a minimum arch thickness of only 12 inches, thus confirming the structural dimension first proposed by Eastwood in 1918. McClure provided no explanation for his change of mind on arch thickness, although for years he had refused to modify his views on this issue. In fact, the compromise design's only major change to the plans Eastwood had submitted in October 1919 involved the addition of steel into the upstream face of the buttresses—evidently to reduce the chance that temperature cracks might appear.

With McClure's presumed final approval in hand, construction planning began in earnest. In June 1922, Bent Brothers signed a contract with the Palmdale Water Company that was quickly approved by the Littlerock and Palmdale Irrigation Districts;[71] and by early August, excavation work was under way.

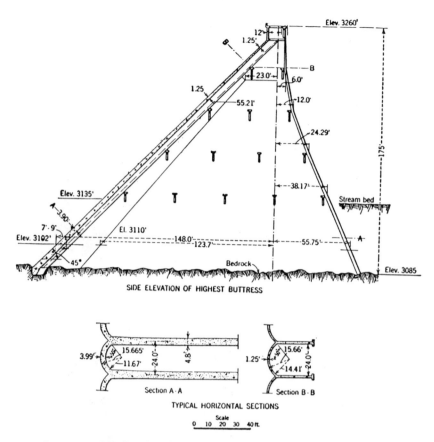

SIDE ELEVATION OF HIGHEST BUTTRESS

Section A·A   Section B·B

TYPICAL HORIZONTAL SECTIONS

Scale
0 10 20 30 40 ft.

9.4   *Drawings of Littlerock Dam as built. (Wegmann and Noetzli,* The Design and Construction of Dams, *1927)*

But one final obstacle remained. In preparing the drawings for the second dam site, Eastwood had worked from a general topographic map of the area. The data it provided were generally accurate, but slight adjustments proved necessary to produce the best fit of the structure to the site (Fig. 9.5). On August 7, the state engineer's representative ordered work stopped until the "changed plans are submitted to the State Department of Engineering and Irrigation for approval and action thereon."[72] Although no substantial alterations were made to the design, the revised plans still took almost three months to wend their way through the bureaucracy. Finally, on November 4, 1922, McClure gave final authorization for construction to proceed.[73] Bent Brothers recommended construc-

tion immediately and worked without interruption until May 1924. Building the dam proved generally uneventful, as the chuting system (used to pour 25,000 cubic yards of concrete) functioned without incident. Excavation to reach bedrock in the streambed, however, proved more laborious than originally anticipated and the structure reached a height of at least 170 feet measured from the crest to the deepest foundations.[74] Thus, despite all the haggling over McClure's attempt to limit multiple arch dams to a height of 150 feet, the structure as built came very close to matching the 180-foot dimensions of Eastwood's first proposed design.

After McClure accepted the completed dam in June 1924, it remained dry for almost two years before spring floods filled the reser-

A

B

C

9.5 *The Littlerock Dam, 1979. (A) View looking across the upstream side, showing the controversial angle opening upstream. (B) Detail view of the arches, showing their flat 100-degree arcs. (C) Downstream side, showing, on the right, where the original siphon spillway was removed and replaced with an overflow design. (Author's collection)*

206

voir.[75] Since that time it has been filled many times without incident. And in March 1938, it successfully weathered an especially severe test: during heavy late winter storms, the siphon spillways became clogged with timber brush, causing water to pour over the full length of the dam for several hours. Nonetheless, aside from localized damage to the spillway walls, the structure survived the pounding unscathed (Fig. 9.6).[76] In addition, no special problems have beset the two partially conical arches forming the Littlerock Dam's internal angle, an angle similar to those proposed for all the arches in Eastwood's "radial plan" design. In May 1919, Huber and Galloway voiced fears that the curve of the radial plan design would cause cracks in the arches; but in view of the performance of the arches forming the angle in the existing structure, their anxieties have proven baseless.

Despite the need to excavate an additional 22,000 cubic yards of "streambed material" beyond the amount originally anticipated, total expenditure for the structure came to only $435,000.[77] Recalling that Jorgensen's constant-angle proposal had been estimated at more than $800,000 in 1920 (and any gravity structure likely would have doubled this figure), the economic efficacy of Eastwood's design is little less than stunning. In terms of financing, by the early 1920s the Littlerock district had issued $368,000 worth of bonds (mostly at 6 percent interest for 40 years), while the Palmdale district had issued $445,000 worth of bonds under similar terms. In addition to paying for building the storage dam, bond proceeds were needed to refinance existing debt dating prior to 1910, to construct new distribution systems, and, most important, to reconstruct completely the 7-mile-long diversion canal and holding reservoir that served the lands in Palmdale.[78] The necessity of limiting the cost of Littlerock Dam was no mirage, and Eastwood's earlier prediction that "no type [other than a multiple arch dam] can be built within your bonding limit" seems accurate.

The districts may have operated with the attributes of a local government authority; but in light of their reliance on bonds purchased

9.6 *Littlerock Dam in March 1938, a few days after the siphon spillway became clogged with debris during heavy floods and water poured over the crest of the entire structure. Notice the wooden branches and debris that were left behind as residue after the floodwaters receded. (Huber Papers, WRCA)*

within the private investment market, they are best thought of as a private initiative representing the interests of their landholders. By the end of the 1920s, irrigation statistician Frank Adams reported that almost 2,000 acres of pear orchards in Littlerock were under cultivation, encompassing "85 holdings averaging about 32 acres. There is one large holding of 1000 acres, another of 160 acres, and a third of 80 acres. Eliminating the 1000 acre holding and the average is about 20 acres . . . the estimated population within the district is 250." In Palmdale, the "area reported for 1926 [was] 620 acres, and for 1927, 640 acres, principally in pears and apples, with some field crops. In August 1928, there were 50 irrigators, 165 domestic users, 275 town parcels, and 174 outside holdings . . . the total population for the district [is] 615."[79] As these data reveal, construction of the new storage reservoir did not precipitate any major social or economic restructuring of the two communities. Instead, drawing on a local agricultural heritage dating back to the 1887 Wright Act, the districts financed the dam without outside governmental assistance or subsidies, and retained long-term local control over the water resources of Little Rock Creek.

THE POLITICS OF APPROVAL

The Littlerock Dam was the last Eastwood design to receive approval from McClure. Although the two engineers retreated from the confrontational posture they adopted in 1918–1920, this was largely because they had relatively little interaction after 1921. Eastwood did maintain correspondence with the state engineer over several possible designs, but never with regard to any project that came close to reaching the construction stage.[80] McClure eventually permitted construction of the Littlerock Dam, but he nonetheless seriously impeded the development of multiple arch dams in California. In resisting efforts to approve multiple arch dams that extended higher than 150 feet, McClure acted (whether by design or not) to ensure that sparsely funded groups of water users would be constrained in their ability to store water. This, in turn, encouraged less diffused (and hence more centralized) control over the state's water resources. The reasons enunciated in opposition to Eastwood's Littlerock design may have been "technical," but in light of the structure's dramatically low construction cost, they resonated with political and economic significance.

Looking beyond official concerns about the safety of the proposed design for Littlerock, historians should consider whether McClure's opposition to it may have been influenced by larger economic/political interests. Eastwood alluded to this in late 1918, when he commented that unnamed people wanted to "knock out" the irrigation districts. In 1920, he again addressed the political dimensions of the problem when he wrote Chester Rowell, longtime editor of the *Fresno Republican*, to express his feeling "that I can be of great benefit to the cause of development in this state if I can have a free field, and am not shut out before the race begins" and to request "a letter of introduction to his Excellency, the Governor [William Stephens]."[81] A onetime protégé of famed progressive governor (and later U.S. senator) Hiram Johnson, Stephens had served as mayor of Los Angeles before Johnson hand-picked him as his lieutenant governor (and successor) in 1916. Unfortunately, Stephens's surviving papers at the California State Archives and at the Bancroft Library at Berkeley contain no evidence of any activities related to issues in the Antelope Valley (both are extremely small collections), and cast no direct light on any activity related to Littlerock Dam during his tenure as governor from 1917 through 1922.[82] Nonetheless, it is plausible that the fate of Eastwood's design was played out in a larger political arena.

In the early 1920s the City of Los Angeles was bringing water from hundreds of miles away through its Owens Valley Aqueduct and was beginning to formulate plans to tap into the Colorado River along the Arizona border. With the city exhibiting a voracious appetite for water resources, interests in the Southland had good reason to fear the effect of Eastwood's designs.[83] By minimizing the cost of water storage, Eastwood enabled a wider range of people and organizations to build dams. Appropriated water rights depend on actual use; and to obtain rights to floodwaters users must find a way to store them in reservoirs. Thus, storage dams provided a means for groups to lay legal claim to floodwaters that would otherwise have remained inaccessible to them.

Within the confines of an arid region, expanding municipalities and other well-financed organizations reasonably might have sought to force builders of large-scale dams to choose from among the more expensive types, as a way to limit the number of groups capable of controlling such resources. Available documents do not reveal any overt acts of collusion between McClure (or any of his engineering consultants) and well-heeled financial interests to undermine Eastwood and/or the two irrigation districts seeking to build the Littlerock Dam. But the record is clear that Eastwood's designs engendered intense opposition for more than three years and that the force of arguments offered by Huber, Galloway, and other advisers to McClure during this time ultimately evaporated without any compelling technical rationale. As such, McClure's final design approval represented a political decision, not an engineering judgment per se.

Given that the farmers of Littlerock held (and would continue to hold) control over the normal surface flow of Little Rock Creek, regardless of whether Eastwood's dam was built, it may be that any other parties interested in future use of the creek's (relatively limited) floodwaters came to perceive this as an impractical objective. Thus, direct impetus for opposing the Littlerock Dam gradually dissipated, and the districts' efforts to win political support (alluded to in Lippincott's April 1922 reference to "copies of [McClure's] correspondence") gained momentum in the face of more generalized opposition to tall multiple arch dams. In the end, Eastwood's dam fulfilled its purpose; and for the remainder of the twentieth century, all precipitation falling within the Little Rock Creek watershed has been controlled by local authorities within the Antelope Valley.

"CURVED FACE" DAMS

During the protracted Littlerock Dam negotiations, Eastwood pursued many other projects. Not content to consider development of the multiple arch dam complete, he sought further means of improving his designs; by 1921, this had led him to conceive of his "curved face" designs. Although Eastwood never explained how the idea of "curved face"

dams first occurred to him, he apparently developed the form through a lengthy process of trial and error, whereby he laboriously calculated the amount of concrete required for a wide range of arch/buttress design configurations.[84] Structurally, the "curved face" design functioned similarly to the "vertical head" that Eastwood had employed since his work at Hume Lake. But instead of having a sharp angle between the inclined and vertical sections of arch, his new design utilized a smooth, gradual curve. At the top of the dam, the arches are vertical; then they slowly curve until they reach a point where they maintain a constant inclination (usually an angle of about 45°). The new design did not represent a radical departure from Eastwood's previous work so much as a refinement of it.

Cave Creek Dam

The first "curved face" dam to be built was on Cave Creek, about 22 miles northwest of Phoenix, Arizona. During heavy rainstorms, Cave Creek (which is usually a dry arroyo leading out of the New River Mountains) becomes a raging torrent capable of inundating the city's central and western districts.[85] Cave Creek floods caused major problems: the Arizona State Capitol building lay in the path of the deluge; bridges and roads of Maricopa County and the City of Phoenix were washed out; the canals and lands of the Salt River Valley Water Users' Association and the proposed Paradise Verde Irrigation District were flooded; and the trackbed of the Atchison, Topeka and Santa Fe Railway suffered erosion. By 1921, a community consensus existed that a dam on Cave Creek would offer numerous benefits, so governmental groups at the state, county, and municipal levels formed the Cave Creek Flood Control Board.[86] In December 1921, the board requested bids for an earthen flood-control dam across Cave Creek. In addition, contractors were permitted to submit alternative designs that might prove more economical.

Eastwood first learned of the proposed

Cave Creek Dam in the fall of 1921, when George Davenport, assistant engineer for the Santa Fe Railway, forwarded data on the site and requested a preliminary design for a multiple arch dam.[87] Simultaneously, Eastwood received support from Ed Fletcher; in mid-November, Eastwood advised his San Diego–based patron that "[Arizona State Engineer Thomas] Maddock has requested me through the Santa Fe engineers to get up plans for the Cave Creek Dam, so you can count that your boosting has been doing a great deal of good and I thank you."[88] By December, Eastwood provided Maddock with estimates for his "latest design" with a "curved front slope" and 44-foot-span arches. Eastwood's design was subsequently given to Lynn S. Atkinson, a Sacramento-based contractor, for submission with an alternative bid.[89] Because Davenport had previously urged the flood control board to consider Eastwood's proposal, the Atkinson bid came as no surprise.[90] Only one bid for the earthen design was offered and it proved to be substantially higher than Atkinson's. The flood control board quickly moved to accept the multiple arch design so that construction could begin in early 1922.[91]

The project's only major stumbling block emanated from S. M. Cotten, an assistant engineer with the City of Phoenix who seemingly maintained close ties with the contractor who anticipated building an earth dam on Cave Creek. Cotten possessed no previous experience with multiple arch dams, but he soon began to prophesy that Eastwood's dam would fail if called on to impound a major flood.[92] Cotton's attacks came in two phases: the first occurred shortly after the flood control board accepted Atkinson's alternative bid in December 1921; the second came the next summer after construction had already begun.[93] On both occasions, his criticisms involved seemingly esoteric technical arguments that centered on whether the buttresses should be considered as taking the entire weight of the arches and the water. Eastwood consciously chose to consider the buttresses as taking all the weight of the adjacent arches.

He recognized that this assumption was not absolutely accurate; but to the extent that it was incorrect, it erred on the side of safety, and it certainly made design computations easier. Cotten proposed an alternative method of analysis in which the arches and buttresses were treated as sharing the arch weight and the water load at all elevations. At least superficially, this technique appeared to possess some validity. Cotten's approach led to totally illogical conclusions, however, since it predicted that the pressure exerted by a full reservoir would cause the upper portions of the Cave Creek design to suffer from tensile stresses at the downstream edge of the buttresses.[94] This meant, in defiance of all common sense, that the dam would tend to tip over upstream into the reservoir under full hydrostatic load.

In April 1922, Cotten published an anonymous letter in the *Engineering News-Record* (printed under the pseudonym "Enquirer") asking for support for his approach to buttress stress analysis.[95] Initially this appeared to aid his cause, but the gambit soured when Gardiner S. Williams submitted a convincing letter confuting Cotten's approach.[96] Eastwood was able to make good use of Williams's letter in defending his design to Arizona State Engineer Thomas Maddock, and Cotten's disruptive tactics ultimately proved ineffectual.[97] The controversy took a toll on Eastwood, however. In fact, Cotten's attacks are what prompted him to draft his memo on "Limitations to Formulae," which discussed the potential misuse of mathematical analyses.[98]

In February 1922, Lynn A. Atkinson signed a contract with the flood control board (Fig. 9.7); excavation began within a month.[99] The finished dam consists of thirty-eight arches, each spanning 44 feet, and stretches more than 1,692 feet across the expansive streambed. Despite possessing a maximum height of 120 feet in the central section, most of the structure is less than 90 feet tall. The dam proved to be much taller than the flood control board had initially believed necessary and caused the structure to exceed the pre-construction estimates of approximately

9.7   *The Cave Creek Flood Control Board in 1923, with Eastwood (upper right) and contractor Lynn Atkinson (upper left). The five men on the board include Thomas Maddock (state engineer), C. C. Cragin (Salt River Valley Water Users' Association), V. A. Thompson (Phoenix city manager), E. W. Mitchells (Paradise Valley Irrigation District), and Harry Vernon (Maricopa County Board of Supervisors). (Salt River Project Archives)*

$350,000.[100] However, the extra cost necessary to secure solid foundations would have been incurred for any type of dam built at the site. The arches are 12 inches thick for the top 20 feet of the structure and increase to a thickness of slightly more than 3 feet at the deepest elevations. They are reinforced with a grid of steel bars to help resist temperature stresses. Aside from some bars placed within the counterforts at the downstream edge of the buttresses, the only reinforcement in the buttresses consists of "four 25 pound steel rails 30 feet long in each buttress near the spring line of the intrados."[101] Notwithstanding the hairline buttress cracks at Lake Hodges, Eastwood continued to believe in the structural integrity of unreinforced concrete.

Construction of the dam proceeded along different lines than those employed on previous Eastwood structures. There was no ca-

bleway, no chuting system, and no trestle extending across the tops of all the buttresses. Instead, the lower parts of the Cave Creek buttresses were poured from movable concrete mixers that had been temporarily placed directly above the foundations. Sand and aggregate were obtained from "shallow washes" and transported by motor trucks to the mixers. After pouring the buttress foundations, Atkinson changed the original "mixing and placing system" to a "central mixing plant." From this central plant, concrete was carried to the various arches and buttresses via a "Ford truck." Then the "hopper was lifted from the rack on the truck by [a] Brown hoist crane" and the concrete placed in the formwork.

The *Southwest Builder and Contractor* reported that Atkinson saw the "lost motion involved in rigging chutes and building trestles or towers" and realized "the great advantage of the direct mixing and placing achieved by the crane method." Faced with constructing thirty-eight similar arch/buttress units, Atkinson developed a kind of motorized assembly line system for building the dam as it gradually extended across the streambed (Fig. 9.8). Ironically, the main factor impeding swift completion of the structure was a lack of water for mixing the concrete. In fact, it was reported that "for several weeks the production [of concrete] was controlled by the water supply and somewhat curtailed." Eventually a reliable water supply was obtained after "excavating a dug well over 100 feet in depth into bedrock and drifting for seepage."

The pouring of concrete began in March 1922 and was completed the following February (Fig. 9.9). Almost immediately it stopped a flood that "backed up against the dam for a height of 20 feet." For this the *Arizona Ga-*

zette reported that it had "already more than paid for itself."[102] The final cost of the structure slightly exceeded $555,000; the expense was borne by Cave Creek Flood Control Board members and several private firms including the Santa Fe Railway, Standard Oil Company, Union Oil Company, and Greenwood Cemetery.[103] The Cave Creek Dam protected the Phoenix area for more than fifty years before being replaced in the late 1970s by a larger earthfill dam (Cave Butte Dam) built downstream by the Corps of Engineers. Even so, Eastwood's dam remains in place and unaltered to this day.

From a historical perspective, one of the most noteworthy aspects of the Cave Creek project relates to how Eastwood became associated with it in the first place. If not for his previous involvement with the Santa Fe Railway at Lake Hodges, Fletcher and Davenport would never have brought him to the attention of officials in Phoenix. The idea of a

9.8 *Cave Creek Dam near Phoenix, while under construction in December 1922. Note the graceful curve of the buttresses' upstream face. (Salt River Project Archives)*

A

B

9.9   The completed Cave Creek Dam. (A) Upstream side, showing the
"curved face." Eastwood developed this type of design to replace the "vertical
head" of his earlier structures. (National Archives) (B) Downstream side,
showing how the structure extends for a length of more than 1,700 feet.
(Salt River Project Archives)

railroad helping disseminate new ideas in hydraulic technology during the post–World War I era may be surprising.[104] But in this instance the Santa Fe Railway unquestionably played a critical role in expanding Eastwood's practice eastward out of California.

Although no longer an active component of Arizona's hydraulic infrastructure, the Cave Creek Dam still stands as one of the most remarkable and materially efficient concrete structures ever built in the United States. Perhaps the best way to comprehend the sophistication of the "curved-face" design is to relate its length and its depth to the quantity of concrete in the structure. Almost 1,700 feet long, with an average height of 70 to 75 feet, the Cave Creek Dam contains only 19,000 cubic yards of concrete. This means that, on average, every lineal foot of the structure—each reaching up over 70 feet—requires only slightly more than 10 cubic yards of concrete. By comparison, a gravity dam of comparable size would utilize almost 60 cubic yards of concrete per lineal foot. It would be difficult to proffer a better example of material economy in a major water control structure.

Anyox Dam

Almost contemporaneously with his work at Cave Creek, Eastwood began developing designs for a large storage dam to be built in British Columbia, Canada. In October/November 1921, he traveled by ship to inspect a dam site for the Granby Consolidated Mining, Smelting and Power Company in Anyox, a remote copper mining facility about 25 miles from the southernmost tip of Alaska; in December, the company authorized him to prepare a design for its consideration. Eastwood's proposed dam was intended to provide supplemental storage capacity on Falls Creek for an already extant hydroelectric power plant serving local copper smelters.[105] For Anyox, Eastwood devised a structure approximately 150 feet tall. Slightly less than 700 feet long, it included twenty-six arches, each

spanning 24 feet and encompassing an arc of 100 degrees. Although the arc and span of the arches were identical to those of the Littlerock Dam, the Anyox design featured a "curved face" that was vertical at the crest and gradually assumed an upstream slope of 48 degrees in its lower sections. Water levels in the reservoir were to be regulated by a bank of siphon spillways.[106]

After having prepared the Anyox design in early 1922, Eastwood was called on by the Granby firm's New York office to attest to its safety in the face of disparaging comments from unnamed engineers. The issues related to shearing stresses, the thinness of the buttresses, and the structure's ability to resist earthquakes. Eastwood offered technical arguments to support his proposal; in addition, he spoke of the problems inherent in calling upon outside engineers to inspect the design. He flatly told the company that "if you begin trying to get plans passed on by men who . . . are not familiar with the design, nor the methods of practice related to it, you will never be done."[107] And if the "plans were altered to meet these objectors [and] then submitted to another set [of engineers] they . . . would criticize them as much as the first set ad infinitum." Recalling the Littlerock project, Eastwood was convinced that the net result of extended review would be needless delay and a final design inferior to the original.

To reassure the company, Eastwood pointed out that he designed multiple arch dams "as a specialist . . . drawing [my] revenue from the design of them on a percentage basis." As a result, there was no reason for him to do cheap, inadequate work, "for in the reduction of cost I [would] reduce the basis of my fee and by careless design would destroy my field of operations." As he put it, "there is no possible angle . . . wherein it would be profitable for me to skimp [on] a design or make any mistake on the side of approaching the danger line." Eastwood's comments helped assuage the company's worries; but before accepting the multiple arch design as safe, H. S. Munroe, the general manager of the Anyox facility, came to San Francisco to meet directly with Eastwood. A few weeks after this early March rendezvous occurred, the company dispatched a succinct telegram declaring "dam authorized."[108] Brushing aside criticisms from unnamed engineers in the East, the company accepted Eastwood's personal assurances and approved construction of a "curved face" multiple arch dam unaltered from the original design. The Anyox Dam represented an investment of over $350,000; and despite the site's remote location, the company would have been loath to take any unnecessary risks in its construction.[109] In this context, the Granby Company's development of the Anyox facility corresponds to the Hume-Bennett Lumber Company's expansion into the Ten-Mile Creek watershed; both firms operated relatively remote industrial facilities and, after a short period of uncertainty, opted to finance construction of a highly innovative, economically attractive, yet potentially controversial, multiple arch dam. And once again, Eastwood found support for his work from a corporate client operating completely within the financial confines of the private sector.

In April 1922, Eastwood sent George E. Holyoke — an engineer who worked on building the Lake Hodges Dam and who later assisted him as a draftsman — to Anyox as his personal representative to ensure that actual construction complied with the design specifications.[110] The company was to take responsibility for building the structure, but Eastwood wanted someone familiar with multiple arch dams to be on site at all times. Project planning was well under way by May 1922, but one final snag loomed: the design still needed bureaucratic approval from the Comptroller of Water Rights for British Columbia. Astutely, the Granby Company engaged the services of William Young, a Vancouver engineer who had previously worked in the comptroller's office. After Young cleaned up some drawings and endorsed Eastwood's design method, the company received authorization to start construction (Fig. 9.10).[111]

Excavation began in June 1922, and by August concrete was being poured via a cableway transportation system. The company initially planned to complete the dam within a year, but this schedule proved overly optimistic.[112] Work on the dam proceeded slowly, but it eventually resulted in the erection of a high-quality structure (Fig. 9.11). In December 1923, the dam proved its integrity when, prior to completion of the final arch, a major storm unexpectedly filled the reservoir and water began pouring through the arch opening at a rate of 1,700 cubic feet per second (Fig. 9.12).[113] The deluge overtopped the arch by more than 7 feet and lasted for several days; nonetheless, despite "the very severe vibration," Fred Noetzli later reported, the flood caused "no damage worth mentioning."[114]

Eastwood considered this incident dramatic proof of his design abilities and of the inherent strength of multiple arch dams. Referring to Anyox as "the most wonderful dam in the world," he called the plume of water splashing over the arch "the Bridesmaid of the dam." His pride in the structure was heightened because, as he wrote to Ed Fletcher, "At Anyox I had no 'critics' and built it as it should be."[115] Because he was not "hampered by any of the restrictions of ignorance" or by having to "pass the criticism of those who are in authority but without experience or vision," Eastwood was free to set the design parameters as he wished, without bureaucratic meddling. The dam featured arches with a minimum arch thickness of 12 inches and buttresses almost completely devoid of reinforcing steel, but no reports cast aspersions on the integrity of the completed structure or indicated any significant cracking in the buttresses.[116] In fact, a 1925 article on hydro-engineering in British Columbia praised the structure as "a particularly pleasing design" and considered it "a pity it is in such a remote place." With a maximum height of 156 feet, the Anyox Dam remained for many years Canada's tallest dam.[117]

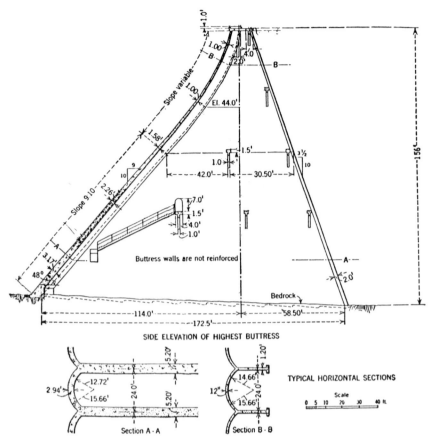

SIDE ELEVATION OF HIGHEST BUTTRESS

TYPICAL HORIZONTAL SECTIONS

Section A - A

Section B - B

9.10 *Drawings of Anyox Dam as built. (Wegmann and Noetzli,* The Design and Construction of Dams, *1927)*

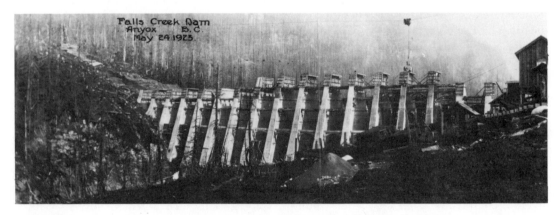

9.11 *Anyox Dam on Falls Creek, British Columbia, during construction, May 1923: downstream side. Note the cableway used to deliver concrete to the formwork. (Eastwood Papers, WRCA)*

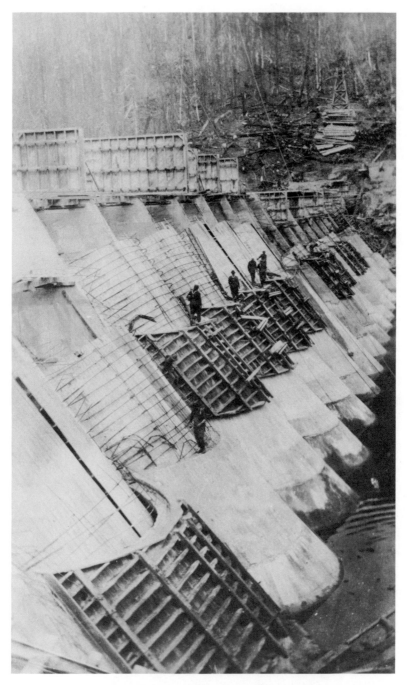

9.11, CONTINUED Anyox Dam: upstream face. The gentle slope of the
"curved face" is evident, as is the steel reinforcement being placed in
the arches. (Eastwood Papers, WRCA)

9.12   *As Anyox Dam approached completion, one arch remained*
unfinished. When a sudden storm filled the reservoir, water poured through
this arch opening to a depth of more than 7 feet, providing dramatic
evidence of the design's inherent strength. Eastwood was particularly proud
of this event, and he referred to the spray of water splashing off of the
strut-tie beams as "The Bridesmaid of the Dam." (Historic American
Engineering Record, Library of Congress)

WEBBER CREEK:
A "TRIPLE ARCH" DAM

The least economical aspect of the multiple arch designs previously discussed (whether straight-crested, "radial plan," or "curved face") involved the necessity of placing concrete in tightly dimensioned formwork. While the highly articulated shapes of these structures reduced concrete quantities, they simultaneously increased the cost of pouring concrete. This became evident in the bidding on Mountain Dell Dam, when the multiple arch design required very little material but unit costs for placing 1 cubic yard of concrete exceeded $7.00. In contrast, the curved gravity dam used large amounts of concrete, but the unit costs were only about $4.00 per cubic yard. More simply, gravity designs offered a degree of economy by limiting formwork costs and by allowing concrete to be easily dumped into the gaping space between the upstream and downstream faces.

Although the 150-foot-high multiple arch dam at Mountain Dell still proved dramatically cheaper than the curved gravity design, Eastwood appreciated the significance of the unit cost differential. At Eagles Nest in 1917–1918, he first demonstrated an interest in building dams with only a few large arches that called for simpler formwork. For wide sites, Eastwood continued to advocate more traditional straight-crested buttress designs (although they eventually featured a "curved face"). With his "triple arch" and "radial cone" designs Eastwood sought to minimize the amount of concrete for structures in more narrow canyons while simultaneously adopting more efficient construction techniques usually associated with gravity dams.[118] The phrase "radial cone" specifically referred to designs in which the radii of the arches varied at different elevations; "triple arch" designs featured three arches (sometimes supplemented by shallow auxiliary spans) designed with constant radii.[119] Eastwood's choice of which of the two design types to use depended on the configuration of the particular

dam site; for deep sites, he favored "radial cone" designs; whereas for shallower sites, he relied on "triple arch" designs.

Eastwood's interest in designing material-conserving dams that could be erected with "mass concrete" construction techniques dated to at least 1910, when he wrote to *Engineering News* about a variable-radius single arch design for the Shoshone Dam site in Wyoming.[120] A precursor of Jorgensen's "constant-angle" designs, this proposed structure reveals that Eastwood did not confine his early creative thought to multiple arch designs featuring relatively small arch spans. His 1917 *Journal of Electricity* article, "The Multiple-Arched vs. the Single-Arch Dam," criticized the latter for their tendency to develop vertical temperature cracks. It did not, however, mention "triple arch" designs as a possible alternative for narrow sites.[121] Evidently, development of his new design forms was too incomplete at that time to warrant public discussion; but by 1921 he was seriously advocating the use of "triple arch" and "radial cone" designs for many projects. Three years after his death, the 1927 edition of Wegmann's *Design and Construction of Dams* noted Eastwood's development of "Multiple-Cone Type" dams, but during his lifetime, he never publicly described these new designs in print.[122] In private correspondence, he referred to the process of designing these structures as "requir[ing] many repetitions and trials to arrive at the best final results" and termed "computing the [concrete] quantities [as] . . . quite an extended operation." Eastwood did not base his "triple arch" and "radial cone" designs on elastic analysis or theories of principal stresses. Instead, he relied on the cylinder formula to proportion the arch thickness, and he calculated horizontal shearing stresses as a way to determine proper dimensions for the massive buttresses.[123]

Only one of Eastwood's "triple arch" designs was actually built, and this structure developed out of a collaborative effort with R. W. Hawley. Relatively few records related to the history of Webber Creek Dam survive, and its origins remain frustratingly enigmatic. Nonetheless, the structure's distinctive form clearly emanated from Eastwood's vision of a new style of multiple arch dam.[124] After leaving the Railroad Commission in April 1919, Hawley established himself as a consulting engineer and soon requested Eastwood to prepare preliminary estimates for a small 20-foot-high dam in Northern California. Eastwood worked up a distinctive design with "a large center span and one small one to the left and three small ones of varying arcs at the right."[125] As in the Eagles Nest Dam, the arches were to extend vertically without any upstream inclination. Although work on this unnamed structure never proceeded past the initial planning stage, Hawley hinted to Eastwood in the course of corresponding on the project that there were "several other small dams in the same vicinity . . . [and] the little ones may grow."[126]

Slightly more than two years later, Hawley began planning a dam for the El Dorado Water Company on Webber Creek near the town of Placerville.[127] As the company's manager and engineer, he was responsible for increasing the water supply available for local pear and grape orchards, and in this capacity, he began promoting the need for a new storage dam. In early February 1922, Hawley filed preliminary plans with the Railroad Commission for a "three-arch structure" with a 160-foot-span central arch and two 90-foot-span side arches.[128] The design featured a 134-degree arc for the main arch, but Hawley indicated that "these plans should not be taken as final . . . [as it is] intended to have Mr. John S. Eastwood serve as consulting engineer and he has not yet been available." Two months later, Hawley submitted a second preliminary design for the Webber Creek Dam. In this design the arc of the main arch had been reduced to 130 degrees and the angle of its upstream inclination had been steepened from a height:length ratio of 10:6 to one of 10:4. In addition, he now proposed to "build the entire main arch on a water face radius of 77.3 feet," meaning that the structure was not to employ arches with a constant angle; thus, it did not constitute a "radial cone" design.[129]

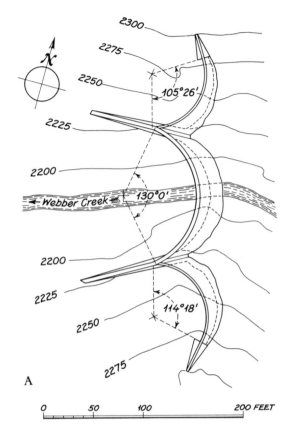

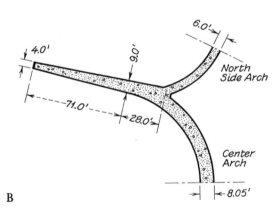

9.13 *Drawings of Webber Creek Dam near Placerville, California. (A) Plan drawing showing the "triple-arch" design. (B) Horizontal cross section. The maximum arch thickness is 12 feet. (C) Vertical cross section, as planned for a height of 120 feet. (Drawings by Richard K. Anderson from data in Wegmann and Noetzli,* The Design and Construction of Dams, *1927)*

220

In August 1922, final "triple arch" plans were submitted for the Webber Creek Dam; this design closely resembled the design proposed the previous April (Fig. 9.13).[130] It featured a maximum height of 115 feet and a 140-foot-span central arch with a horizontal radius of 77.2 feet. The two side arches spanned 105 and 115 feet, respectively. The central arch was to have maximum thicknesses of 12 feet at the bottom and 2.5 feet at the top. Although not a "radial cone" design, the "triple arch" structure was laid out on a radial plan, meaning that the arches were aligned along a slight downstream curve. In reviewing the plans for the Railroad Commission, Frederic Faude examined the site's foundations and counseled that "no fears need be entertained as to the safety and stability of a dam erected thereon." He also reported that "these plans have been checked and found to be consistent with good practice as to dimensions, loading, etc. . . . [and] the proposed dam will contain approximately 5500 cubic yards of concrete and is estimated to cost $79,000."[131] Faude's endorsement constituted sufficient assurance for the commission, and construction commenced in September 1922. The rapid approval of the design is particularly noteworthy in light of the intense scrutiny that State Engineer McClure had recently given to the Littlerock Dam. Had it been considered necessary to get McClure or his adviser Walter Huber to endorse the design, the Webber Creek Dam would probably

have never been built. But the Railroad Commission accepted Faude's recommendation and authorized construction without requesting that McClure consent to the "details," as it had at Littlerock.[132]

Erection of the dam took place between September 1922 and September 1923. Using a chuting system with a hoist tower placed in the middle of the site, construction crews built the dam to a height of 90 feet (Fig. 9.14). A few years later, Noetzli described the structure as having "no reinforcement in [the] arches and buttresses."[133] In other words, it is a completely unreinforced, plain concrete structure. Ever since his work on the Hume Lake Dam, Eastwood had expressed interest in building dams that were not subject to tensile stresses; he employed steel reinforcement only as a way of resisting tensile forces created by temperature stresses. At Webber Creek, he demonstrated that it was possible to build a dam without cracks, expansion joints, or steel reinforcement. With this design, Eastwood essentially achieved the ideal of a concrete dam subject only to compressive stresses.

Eastwood remained uninvolved in the construction process, due to Hawley's position with the water company, but he visited the site in March 1924 and observed the structure as it first began impounding water.[134] Hawley is not known to have been involved subsequently in the construction of any other dams, much less a "triple arch" design.[135] The Webber Creek Dam thus appears to represent

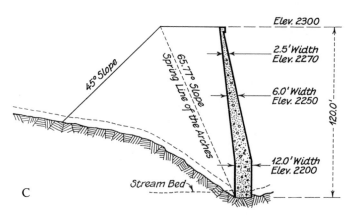

9.13 *Drawings of Webber Creek Dam, continued.*

A

B

9.14 *Webber Creek Dam in March 1924 after its completion to a height of 90 feet. (A)*
Downstream side. The concrete mixing plant and hoisting tower are still in place. (B) Upstream
face. Formwork for the arches is still partially in place, while the reservoir is more than
half-filled. The hoisting tower is visible behind dam. (Huber Papers, WRCA)

a collaborative effort between the two engineers, but credit for the structural design surely belongs to Eastwood. Although Hawley provided the field work and managerial expertise for the project, the form sprang from Eastwood's mind.

A few years after its initial construction, the owners proposed to raise the dam 25 or 30 feet to the original planned height. Huber was asked by the state engineer for his opinion on the proposal; and in early 1928, he advised that "increasing the height of this structure is of very doubtful feasibility."[136] The Webber Creek Dam has remained 90 feet high ever since. Aside from some small changes to the spillway and minor strengthening of one of the buttress foundations, it has not been substantively altered during seventy years of service. Although Noetzli later built a "triple arch" dam with a completely vertical upstream face (like the Eagles Nest Dam), the Webber Creek Dam stands as a unique and innovative structure within the lexicon of American hydraulic technology.[137] Eastwood's collaboration with Hawley gave him a valuable opportunity to demonstrate the stability of his large-scale "triple arch" dams. As such, the structure on Webber Creek offers compelling testimony that the numerous "radial cone" and "triple arch" designs that remained unbuilt at the time of Eastwood's death represented practical engineering proposals eminently capable of being constructed.

MAJOR UNBUILT PROJECTS

During the last five years of his life, Eastwood worked on many projects that never advanced beyond the planning stage. Some of these foundered for economic and/or political reasons unrelated to Eastwood, while others probably would have been completed if he had not died so suddenly. By the early 1920s, he was working out of his house in Oakland and, aside from some drafting assistance provided by George Holyoke, was handling all of the design work by himself. This put a great strain on his productivity, and at one point he lamented that "it is so easy in one written sentence to lay out work for a week or two or more . . . I can only get things out as fast as I can work."[138] The nature of Eastwood's consulting business demanded that he explore almost every possible commission that came to his attention. Because so many projects never reached fruition, and because his major source of revenue came from completed dams, he rarely let any prospect go by without making some type of effort to obtain the design commission. At times, he even submitted unsolicited proposals in hopes that his promise of providing a less expensive design might find receptive ears.[139] In sum, his ego, his entrepreneurial spirit, and (perhaps most importantly) his memories of times when no commissions were in hand spurred Eastwood to explore as many potential projects as possible, in hopes that some of them might pass from the design stage into actual construction.[140]

In the early 1920s, Eastwood explored several projects outside California, the most intriguing being a large dam proposed for construction in Sinaloa, Mexico.[141] He visited the Balojaque dam site near San Blas in mid-1923 and shortly thereafter prepared a design for a structure more than 3,000 feet long with at least one "radial cone" section exceeding a height of 300 feet.[142] Eastwood reported that "in all of my travels and investigations," nothing compared with the Balojaque venture "for the amount and cost of storage, for the extent and fertility of the lands possible to reach, and [for] the ease of diverting [the water] and distributing [it] on these lands."[143] Eastwood developed fairly complete preliminary plans for the Balojaque Dam (Fig. 9.15), but the ambitious project foundered during 1924, and his proposal never proceeded any further. Perhaps something would have happened if he had lived longer, but no dam seems to have been built at the site until many years later. Still, on another level, the Balojaque project indicates that Eastwood's

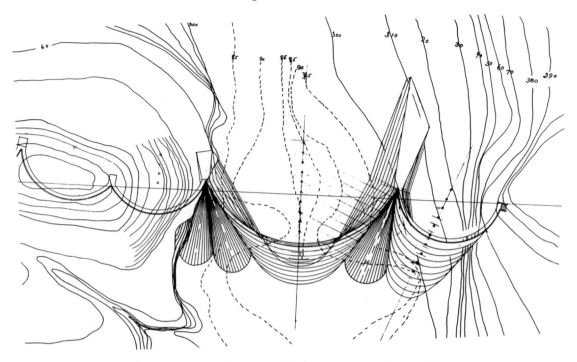

9.15 *Portion of a working drawing for the proposed Balojaque Dam in Sinaloa, Mexico—an example of the "radial cone" types of design that Eastwood began developing in the 1920s. (Eastwood Papers, WRCA)*

business was expanding into the Central/ South America market at the time of his death—a region that offered him fertile ground for practicing his trade without interference from dam safety bureaucracies.

Eastwood's success at Cave Creek may have engendered criticism from gravity dam proponents, but it also fostered interest in his designs among certain Southwestern groups. One such group was the Salt River Valley Water Users' Association in Phoenix. Although the full extent of his work on the Mormon Flat Dam project is unclear, Eastwood developed a preliminary design for a site on the Salt River.[144] The structure was to be built downstream from the U.S. Reclamation Service's Roosevelt Dam (a masonry gravity arch design completed in 1911). A large debt had been incurred from construction of the Roosevelt Dam, and the water users' association now sought to supplement their income by building a series of hydroelectric power

dams below Roosevelt. Whereas the Roosevelt Dam was financed by the federal government, Mormon Flat (like its companion structures, Horse Mesa and Stewart Mountain dams) was funded by bonds sold to private investors. Consequently, the SRVWUA was eager to find ways to reduce capital expenditures, and this prompted Eastwood's preparation of a two arch "radial cone" design for the site in 1923. As it turned out, a variable-radius arch dam designed by personnel within the SRVWUA was eventually built at Mormon Flat and Eastwood's proposal languished unused.[145]

Contemporaneously with his Mormon Flat proposal, Eastwood also prepared initial plans for a dam at the Diamond Creek site on the Colorado River (about 100 miles upstream from Las Vegas) in northwestern Arizona. Starting in 1916, published reports began discussing the feasibility of building a large dam that would flood sections of the lower Grand Canyon and provide huge quantities of hydroelectric power for regional use. Two years later, Arizona engineer James B. Girand was described in *Engineering News* as devoting "all his time to a big hydro-electric project in the Grand Canyon of the Colorado River."[146] The project stalled, and Girand later served as supervisory engineer for the Cave Creek Flood Control Board during construction of its multiple arch dam. Presumably, this connection led to Eastwood's subsequent proposal for a 400-foot-high three arch "radial cone" dam at Diamond Creek. Eastwood provided a brief description of his proposed design in January 1923, but the project never proceeded any further; no dam has ever been constructed across the Colorado at this site.[147]

Like the SRVWUA, the Santa Fe Railway had supported construction of Eastwood's Cave Creek design. In 1923, the railroad, working in concert with Ed Fletcher, sought Eastwood's help in developing an irrigation project in New Mexico.[148] The Santa Fe served the district around the town of Bluewater, about 100 miles west of Albuquerque, and wished to increase agricultural production as a way to help boost freight revenue. Beginning in mid-1923, Eastwood prepared a series of "curved face" and "radial cone" designs for the Bluewater-Toltec Irrigation District. At the time of his death, plans for a "radial cone" structure were essentially complete; and had he lived a bit longer, the design almost certainly would have been built.[149] As it turned out, in 1925 the district built a single arch dam at the site using plans prepared in part by W. S. Post, an engineer who had previously worked with Ed Fletcher on many irrigation projects in San Diego County.[150]

While continuing to work on a variety of individual dam designs, after 1918 Eastwood directed substantial amounts of energy toward several large projects in California involving more than a single dam.[151] Significantly, some of the most interesting of these endeavors promised to reinvolve him in the world of hydroelectric power development for the first time since his dismissal from Big Meadows in 1913. After the end of World War I, various utilities sought his assistance; and although none of these projects resulted in actual construction of a dam, they often played a role in furthering the growth of his design concepts. In 1919, for example, he developed one of his earliest "radial plan" designs (similar to his second design for Littlerock) for the "Sheeps Rock" site on the Pit River for the Pitt River Power Company; correspondence related to the project provides valuable documentation underlying development of this structural form.[152] Before it could begin construction, the company collapsed in the face of competition from the Pacific Gas and Electric Company, and Eastwood quickly moved on to other projects.

Undoubtedly, Eastwood's most expansive hydroelectric project of the 1920s involved the proposed system of the Sespe Light & Power Company (SL&PC) in Ventura County, about 70 miles northwest of Los Angeles. Beginning in 1920, the company engaged him as its "chief engineer" to design a series of dams and power plants along Sespe Creek and Piru Creek, two major tributaries of the Santa Clara River.[153] During the next four years, Eastwood developed numerous designs for several dam sites and devoted considerable time (much of it spent at the SL&PC offices in downtown Los Angeles) to conducting economic analyses of which dams and power plants should be built. Plans were drawn up for the 240-foot-high Topa Dam (named after a prominent nearby mountain); other proposed structures included the Brain Dam, Hammel Dam, and Buren Dam.[154] In spite of his intensive work, Eastwood was hampered by the company's reluctance (or inability) to fund construction work. In addition, local agricultural interests organized the Santa Clara River Protective Association in order to maintain control over the watershed.[155] When Eastwood died, the company still believed that at least some of the dams would be built; it was even reported that one would be named in his memory.[156] The company's plans ended in frustration, however, when the Federal Power Commission revoked its permit in early 1926. The hydroelectric power scheme was never revived.[157] Whether the SL&PC hydroelectric power system on Sespe and Piru Creeks would have been built if Eastwood had lived is debatable. But he certainly devoted many hours of effort to the project, using it to refine his approach to "radial cone" dam design.

Starting in late 1918, the San Joaquin Light & Power Corporation (SJL&PC) asked Eastwood to undertake work on hydroelectric power development that, for different reasons, ultimately proved as fruitless as his efforts for the Sespe and Piru interests.[158] The SJL&PC was, of course, the corporate descendent of the firm that had purchased the bankrupt San Joaquin Electric Company in 1903; through the mid-1920s the utility remained under the financial control of William Kerckhoff and A. C. Balch. In light of his unhappy association with these businessmen at Big Creek, Eastwood's willingness to pursue any further relationship with them is perhaps surprising. However, much of the SJL&PC's work was handled by its general manager, A. G. Wishon, a Fresno resident who had remained friendly with Eastwood for almost twenty years. Because of Eastwood's intimate knowledge of the Kings River (an area he explored during his early work for the Smith & Moore lumber interests and when he built Hume Lake Dam), Wishon approached him to help design hydroelectric power dams in the river's upper watershed.[159]

All of Eastwood's dealings with the company were handled through Wishon, and for a time the company seemed poised to utilize his multiple arch designs for several reservoirs. But after Eastwood expended considerable effort in developing designs for the Wishon, Cliff, Coolidge Meadows, and Dinkey Creek dam sites, the SJL&PC simply chose to ignore his proposals.[160] Interestingly, this rejection can in part be traced to the influence of Eastwood's nemesis, John Freeman. In early 1922, Wishon wrote to Eastwood requesting data on the Big Bear Valley

Dam that would help him demonstrate that "a thin dam is not necessarily a weak dam." At the same time, Wishon opined that "a gravity dam is sinful waste of money" and bemoaned that "it is a tremendous undertaking to sell the idea [of multiple arch and single arch dams] to the financier who slips behind your back and consults a man like John R. Freeman." Wishon even went so far as to assert "that the prominence of John R. Freeman in the engineering world and his influence with men of capital [has] delayed the storing of water for a period of ten or fifteen years."[161]

Wishon's comments may only have been a calculated appeal to Eastwood's distaste for Freeman, but they probably accurately reflect why no multiple arch dams were ever built by the SJL&PC. As the company's Fresno-based general manager, Wishon could exert some influence on major development plans. But the corporate managers in Los Angeles and the financiers in New York who controlled major expenditures of capital were doubtless inclined to consult (even if only informally) an engineer of Freeman's prominence and to heed his advice. During this period, Freeman was actively involved in managing the Great Western Power Company and he exhibited no hesitancy in deprecating Eastwood's skills as a dam engineer. In 1924–1925, for example, Freeman reminded the GWPC that "the company has had enough disastrous experiences . . . [such as] with Eastwood in trying to save expense injudiciously." He also alluded to the earlier efforts of H. H. Sinclair and Eastwood when "strange advice was followed."[162] In this light, Wishon's comments have the ring of truth and provide a plausible reason for the SJL&PC's rejection of Eastwood's plans. Without question, Freeman's antipathy for the Oakland-based engineer became manifest in the politicking that surrounded Ed Fletcher's hopes of utilizing Eastwood dams in a major expansion of San Diego's water supply infrastructure in the 1920s.

THE FINAL CONTROVERSY:
FLETCHER AND FREEMAN IN
SAN DIEGO

Eastwood worked with a variety of clients during his career, but none was more supportive than Ed Fletcher. The Southern California businessman sponsored construction of four Eastwood dams in San Diego County during 1917–1918, advocated use of Eastwood designs at Cave Creek, Arizona, and at Bluewater, New Mexico, and provided highly positive recommendations endorsing Eastwood's engineering skills and personal integrity.[163] Fletcher's interest in building dams extended beyond the promotion of Eastwood designs, and he did not confine his interest solely to multiple arch structures.[164] Nonetheless, he exhibited a special affection for Eastwood, and at one point assured him that "I want to see your type go in [for a project on the San Diego River] and I am going the limit to see that it goes in."[165] For his part, Eastwood felt that Fletcher deserved special attention because he offered the one thing Eastwood cherished above all else: the opportunity to see his ideas transformed into three-dimensional concrete structures. The San Diego developer provided him with a major venue for exercising his design skills, and he rewarded this support with unswerving loyalty. This was most directly expressed during Fletcher's protracted political maneuvering to develop dams on the San Diego River when Eastwood affirmed: "[While] awaiting further news from the battle line, I am yours to the end."[166]

In the post–Lake Hodges era, Eastwood prepared designs for several sites in San Diego County, most of which were located on the San Diego River. However, one of the sites was situated on Escondido Creek (also called San Elijo Creek), north of the San Dieguito River not far from the Lake Hodges Dam.[167] Although the San Elijo Dam remained a prospect for many years, funding through the San Dieguito Mutual Water Company never solidified, and the project failed to reach the con-

struction stage. Despite the ultimate dormancy of the San Elijo proposal, in 1923 Eastwood developed an excellent set of plans for a 140-foot-high "radial cone" design (Fig. 9.16). These are among the best drawings of this structural type to survive in the Eastwood Papers at Berkeley.[168]

The biggest prize in San Diego's water struggles was control of the San Diego River. The initial Spanish settlements at the San Diego Mission and Presidio utilized the river; but by the early twentieth century, the city largely depended on the Southern California Mountain Water Company's Cottonwood Creek and the Otay River system for its municipal water supply. While Fletcher and Murray's Cuyamaca Water Company diverted considerable water flow from the upper San Diego River into its lengthy flume, the Cuyamaca system (which included the off-stream Murray Dam) used only a portion of the river's annual flow, allowing large quantities of floodwaters to escape into the sea.

The battle for control of the San Diego River pitted Fletcher against the business interests and associates of John D. Spreckels. The latter group controlled the municipality's existing water supply system and was led by City Engineer Hiram Savage, a firm advocate of the massive tradition. In the early 1920s, he directed construction of the city's curved gravity designs for Barrett Dam on Cottonwood Creek and the new Lower Otay Dam, which replaced the rockfill dam destroyed by floodwaters in 1916 (Fig. 9.17). Clearly, he had no interest in multiple arch dams.[169] With the support of San Francisco City Engineer M. M. O'Shaughnessy and John R. Freeman, Savage consistently pressed for construction of gravity designs regardless of cost considerations.[170]

The struggle between Fletcher and the Spreckels interests involved not only the choice of dam technology, but also the reservoir site locations. The controversy revolved around five key points:

1. The owners of the different dam sites and reservoir areas.

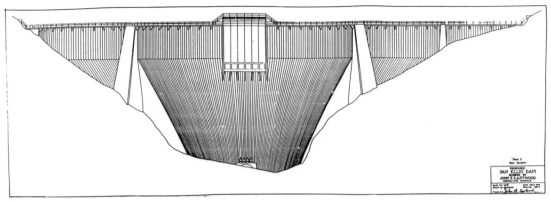

A

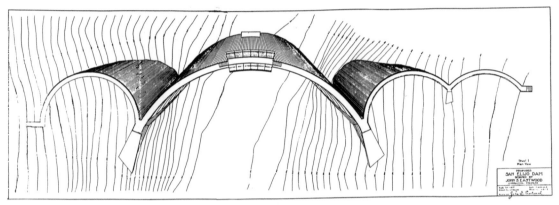

B

9.16 *Drawings of the proposed San Elijo Dam, on Escondido Creek near Encinitas, drafted in 1923. (A) Elevation drawing of the downstream side. A siphon spillway is located at the center of the main arch. (B) Plan drawing showing its "radial plan." (C) Cross section of the main arch. The arch includes a siphon spillway, and Eastwood intended it to be built with a slightly inclined face. The 140-foot-high design featured a maximum thickness of approximately 12 feet. (Eastwood Papers, WRCA)*

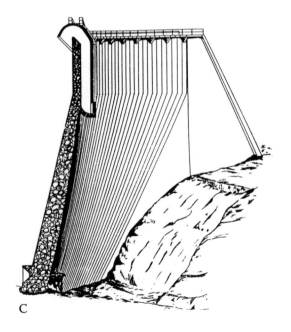

C

228

9.17   *The new Lower Otay Dam, completed in 1921 to replace the rockfill structure washed out by the 1916 floods. This concrete curved gravity design was constructed under the direction of Hiram Savage. It served as a model for gravity structures that Savage and John Freeman soon advocated for proposed dam sites along the San Diego River. (Huber Papers, WRCA)*

2. The cost of storing various amounts of water (a factor that depended on the dam height chosen).

3. How much water would be lost to evaporation (a physical phenomenon directly related to reservoir surface area and elevation above sea level).

4. The geographical areas easily supplied with water from various proposed reservoirs.

5. Foundation conditions at different sites.

San Diego's political and business leaders all recognized that Mission Gorge offered a valuable reservoir location, but the exact location for the dam became a major bone of contention. Three specific dam sites (Nos. 1, 2, and 3) were located at Mission Gorge, with the battle soon focusing on Nos. 2 and 3 (Fig. 9.18). Fletcher owned Mission Gorge Site No.

3 and tirelessly promoted it as the best reservoir site. Savage was just as adamant in his advocacy of Mission Gorge Site No. 2.[171] The physical differences between the two sites primarily concerned the amount and quality of land to be inundated by the reservoir and the quantity of water that would be lost through evaporation.

With a dam approximately 220 feet high (up to "contour 330 ft."), Mission Gorge No. 3 offered a reasonably large reservoir site (45,000 acre-feet) in return for flooding a relatively small amount of land (approximately 1,400 acres). The deep reservoir would have limited the water's surface area, thus minimizing evaporation losses. In contrast, a dam of comparable size at Mission Gorge No. 2 offered construction of an extremely large reservoir (285,000 acre feet) that would require flooding out more than 6,500 acres of land.

229

9.18 *View of the San Diego River in flood during December 1922, looking upstream at Mission Gorge Dam Site No. 3. (Huber Papers, WRCA)*

Mission Gorge No. 2 provided six times as much storage capacity, but the annual flow of the San Diego River might never have filled the reservoir, especially because of excessive evaporation losses.[172]

Attention also focused on two other potential reservoir sites farther upstream. The larger of the two was called El Capitan, while the smaller was known as the Fletcher dam site. Both were controlled by Fletcher and he considered them valuable properties. Because of their distance from the city proper, however, he considered it more prudent to concentrate on getting a dam built at Mission Gorge No. 3 and later to supplement its storage capacity by building at the El Capitan and Fletcher sites.

Between 1921 and 1924, Eastwood worked on designs for the Mission Gorge No. 3, El Capitan, and Fletcher dam sites.[173] Most of

this effort focused on Mission Gorge No. 3, and Eastwood developed a series of designs that constantly evolved as he conceived of less expensive alternatives. Initially, he proposed constructing a radial plan multiple arch dam similar to his second proposal for Littlerock.[174] By March 1922, however, he had adopted a "radial cone" design, determining that the use of mass concrete would further reduce the structure's cost (Fig. 9.19).[175] As early as 1918, Eastwood had prepared a 1,200-foot-long design for the Fletcher site, utilizing a design based on the dimensions of the Lake Hodges structure. By 1924, however, this had evolved into a "curved face" design similar to the one used at Anyox; at El Capitan, he proposed a "radial cone" structure.[176]

Although they did not lead to any completed dams, Eastwood's San Diego River projects are particularly interesting because they once again brought him into direct conflict with John Freeman. Since their confrontation at Big Meadows in 1912–1913, the two engineers had not officially been involved in any projects together. But in 1923, the City of San Diego hired Freeman to study the city's municipal water supply and make recommendations on its future development.[177] The selection of Freeman to occupy this post came at a time when the hairline cracks in the Lake Hodges buttresses were first beginning to attract attention. The ability of the Lake Hodges Dam to impound a full reservoir had been demonstrated several times by 1922, and Fletcher made a point of celebrating this accomplishment.[178] But regardless of their structural significance (or lack thereof), the cracks could easily be exploited in efforts to discredit Eastwood or multiple arch dams in general. During the summer of 1922, S. M. Cotten attempted to do exactly that, hoping to stop construction at Cave Creek. Fletcher wrote the Arizona state engineer to assure him that anonymous "rumors" concerning the Lake Hodges Dam were "entirely unfounded."[179] Noting that "the cracks are only hair cracks, which are usually found in all concrete structures," he protested that "some-

one is maliciously knocking and I would like to know how you got your information." Fletcher's response satisfied the Arizona state engineer, but the incident foreshadowed future public relations problems in connection with the Lake Hodges cracks.

In August 1923, Freeman visited San Diego to undertake an intensive survey of the county, inspect existing dams and potential dam sites, and meet with the panoply of politicians and business leaders who held a primary interest in regional water development. During his three-week visit, Freeman maintained a fieldbook/diary in which he jotted down many of his observations on engineering issues as well as on the personalities of various actors in the civic drama; as he subsequently observed: "Down at San Diego their questions developed into broader dimensions than at first proposed and I got into one of the most lively exhibitions of vigorous human nature and opposing views that I have seen anywhere."[180] Freeman did not make any specific reference to Eastwood's character or his impassioned advocacy of multiple arch technology in his fieldbook. But while describing Fletcher as an "honest optimist whose success has been due [to] energy and optimism . . . a real builder — up for San Diego," he obliquely

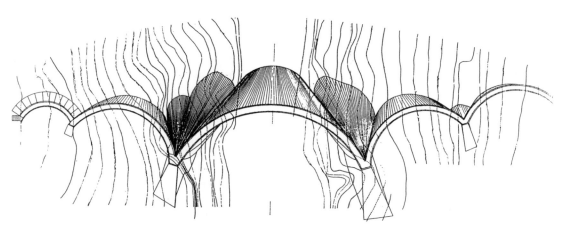

9.19 *Plan drawing of the proposed Mission Gorge No. 3 Dam, drawn in 1922. With Ed Fletcher's support and encouragement, Eastwood continued to develop increasingly refined "radial cone" designs for this project until his death. (Institute Archives and Special Collections, Massachusetts Institute of Technology)*

referred to Eastwood by opining that Fletcher "gets misled by those who desire to please him and secure his patronage."[181]

In the company of Fletcher (and others, including his son Roger Freeman and J. B. Lippincott), Freeman examined the Lake Hodges, San Dieguito, and Murray dams but was taciturn about the Eastwood structures. In fact, Fletcher soon informed Eastwood, "[Freeman] told his son in my presence that each of them were o.k. and were functioning 100% . . . [and that he] actually approved them and was particularly stuck on Lake Hodges . . . he isn't unfriendly at all to you — at least he hasn't said one word against you."[182] Observations recorded in Freeman's fieldbook reflect a similar positive assessment of the Lake Hodges cracks as he reported: "Nearly all piers show shrinkage cracks diagonal-parallel to thrust, just as one might expect. No danger I tell Lippincott, even if cracks had been built an inch wide in this location . . . dam now about 5 or 6 years old and I find no appearance of deterioration as yet." Freeman's longstanding distaste for multiple arch technology surfaced, however, as he added: "Nevertheless, I concur that these pure [unreinforced] walls are dangerously unsupported . . . if I were responsible I would sooner or later fill [in between the buttresses] with rubble like a rock fill but hand placed in 5 foot horizontal layers."[183]

Soon afterward, Lippincott reported in private correspondence that Freeman believed "the cracks [do] not endanger the structure at all except so far as a vibratory or lateral motion might shake down the buttresses." This was not quite as laudatory an opinion of the structure as Fletcher had reported and, in line with the fieldbook entry that hypothesized placement of "rock fill" between the buttresses, provides evidence that Freeman was not inclined to endorse Eastwood's dam. Lippincott also revealed that Freeman had "talked over the situation with me as a professional friend," and that the comments were not to be used in "a report for any kind of publication."[184] In informal comments to Fletcher and Lippincott, Freeman

seemingly approved of the Lake Hodges design, but he carefully kept such comments off the public record. He thus did not foreclose any options when it came time to make a formal report. Within a few weeks, Fletcher came to fear that Freeman's friendly attitude might be a smoke screen; in September 1923, he applied to Lloyd's of London for insurance covering the Murray and Lake Hodges dams. As he told the Railroad Commission, this was done for "political reasons."[185] Presumably, Fletcher sensed that the Lake Hodges Dam was likely to come under attack by Freeman. By insuring the structure with such an internationally renowned firm, he hoped to engender public respect for the structure's integrity.

After his visit to San Diego in the late summer of 1923. Freeman left the city and did not submit a final report for several months. In the meantime, the failure of a so-called multiple arch dam in Italy provided an opportunity for critics to cast aspersions on the technology in general. On December 1, 1923, the Gleno Dam in Northern Italy collapsed shortly after the reservoir filled for the first time. As Noetzli later observed, the Gleno Dam was built under the direction of "an Italian cotton industrialist," who provided "no trained engineering supervision of any kind during the construction."[186] Originally the Gleno Dam was to have been a masonry gravity structure, but halfway through construction the owner decided to complete it as a multiple arch dam. Thus, in the deepest part of the dam, the multiple arch structure was placed on top of a masonry substructure more than 50 feet tall (Fig. 9.20).

The Gleno failure was directly attributed to the "faulty foundation" and the "unbelievably poor quality of the masonry." In Noetzli's words: "when the dam failed, all the buttresses built on top of the masonry base went out, while the buttresses founded on rock remained in place." To label the catastrophe a multiple arch dam failure was a gross distortion; and after Eastwood heard about it, he wrote Fletcher that the Gleno Dam was "no more like one of my dams than

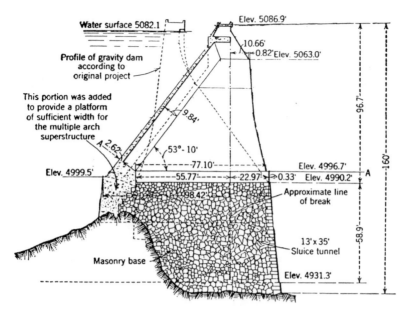

Water surface 5082.1'
Elev. 5086.9'
10.66'
0.82' Elev. 5063.0'
Profile of gravity dam
according to
original project
96.7'
This portion was added
to provide a platform
of sufficient width for
the multiple arch
superstructure
9.84'
A 2.62'
53°- 10'
77.10'
Elev. 4996.7'
Elev. 4999.5'
55.77'
22.97'
0.33'
Elev. 4990.2'
A
98.42'
Approximate line
of break
160'
13' x 35'
Sluice tunnel
58.9'
Masonry base
Elev. 4931.3'

9.20   *Cross section of Gleno Dam, which failed in late 1923. Notice the
massive masonry base on which the multiple arch structure stood. Failure
occurred within the masonry and not within the multiple arch section.
(Wegmann and Noetzli,* The Design and Construction of Dams, *1927)*

is a gravity dam."[187] Nonetheless, the dam possessed characteristics of a multiple arch structure, and opponents such as Freeman could now use the collapse to condemn the entire technology as unsafe.

In May 1924, Freeman finally returned and presented his findings to the city council, at which time he also responded to council members' oral questions. These informal, yet "on-the-record," comments were soon published in the Spreckels-controlled newspaper, the *San Diego Union.* Taken together, Freeman's written and spoken observations constituted a major assault on Fletcher and Eastwood's dam construction plans for the county.

In suggesting a course of action for the city's water resources development, the written report concurred almost 100 percent with Savage's proposals.[188] Freeman recommended construction of a dam at Mission Gorge No. 2, dismissing all of Fletcher's alternative proposals. In addition, he strongly advised that the city build "massive gravity concrete" structures similar to "the standard adopted by

. . . the cities of Boston and New York for their high dams." In the entire 240-page report, Freeman made only one direct reference to multiple arch dams, when he casually remarked that "the additional cost" of gravity designs over "dams similar to those recently erected at Lake Hodges and at the Murray Reservoir" was "abundantly justified by reason of [their] increased durability and safety."[189] No detailed documentation or argument was offered to support this assertion.

Although his written report ignored the subject of multiple arch dams, Freeman's verbal comments to the city council directly criticized the technology. He drew attention to the Gleno Dam disaster with the glib remark, "one of these failed in Italy some time ago and killed a lot of people"; and he proclaimed that "you can save on [multiple arch dams] by skimping them down, until they have not the proper degree of safety. You have seen those seams in Hodges Dam."[190] Freeman considered it possible to strengthen multiple arch dams by using more materials, "but then

233

your expense is not much less than in other construction." In other words, the councilmembers were led to believe that multiple arch dams could only be safe if they cost as much as gravity designs. Of course, in characterizing the expansion cracks at Lake Hodges as dangerous "seams" he directly contradicted his own comments made to Lippincott and recorded in his fieldbook the summer before. Evidently, however, the purpose of his public report was to heighten the city council's appreciation of massive dams by denigrating dams adhering to the structural tradition.

Both Fletcher and Eastwood reacted sharply to Freeman's public statements. Fletcher's rejoinder was the less emotional of the two, although he started out by commenting that "any engineer of the old school fights any new idea if he does not originate it or he never had any experience in construction of multiple arch dams." Fletcher provided a calm explanation of why the Gleno Dam failed and why "Mr. Freeman only hurts himself when he calls the Italian disaster a multiple arch failure." He added that "there has never been a failure of a multiple arch type of dam as such" and that Lloyd's of London had insured Lake Hodges and Murray Dam "at its lowest rate of insurance of any dam insurance in the United States that we have any record of."[191]

In his response to Freeman, Eastwood did not temper his anger with diplomatic phrasing. In a letter to the *San Diego Sun*, he reproached Freeman for his "vindictive spirit" in magnifying "haircracks in the buttresses [into] . . . those seams in Hodges Dam" and accused him of being "an expert who is so certain of the futility of the work of others." Characterizing Freeman as "a hopeless back number, a has been," Eastwood further challenged Freeman's understanding of dam construction costs and the Gleno Dam disaster. And referring to several recent successes (including the Big Bear Valley Dam's overtopping in 1916, its weathering of the April 1918 earthquake, and the Anyox Dam's unexpected flooding in December 1923), he proclaimed his multiple arch designs to be "the

true and ultimate scientific type of dam" now beginning to achieve worldwide acclaim.[192] Twelve years after his first encounter with Freeman at Big Meadows, Eastwood was once again engaged in an engineering/public relations battle over the relative merits of gravity and multiple arch dams. Neither engineer had mellowed with age, and—just as Eastwood continued to explore new ways of building less expensive dams—Freeman remained fervently committed to the same gravity designs he had promoted a decade earlier.

After Freeman submitted his report, questions about the type and location of new dams on the San Diego River remained unresolved. Fletcher continued to pursue implementation of Eastwood's designs and to focus public attention on the excessive cost of gravity dams. For example, he wrote Eastwood on June 9, 1924:

Your letter covering [Mission Gorge] No. 3 to the 330 ft. contour is just what I want. Now, please write me another letter giving the estimated cost of a dam to the 350 ft. contour. We have a real fight on here but we are going to win out. I assume it will be around $700,000 or $800,000 . . . Freeman in his report says it will cost over $4,000,000. He is figuring an earth dam, and $5,000,000 for a gravity arch. I want your letter to turn over to the water committee of the Chamber of Commerce just as soon as I can get it.[193]

Despite Fletcher's desire to settle the political and technological questions related to development of the San Diego River by winning a clearcut victory in a "real fight," the issue remained in legal limbo for several years until a lingering water rights controversy was finally resolved by the California Supreme Court.

The dispute centered on the original Spanish grant for the San Diego Mission, with the City of San Diego arguing that this eighteenth-century grant gave it a "paramount right" to all water in the San Diego River. The issue developed out of the City of Los Angeles' successful effort in the late nineteenth century to assert legal control over the entire flow of the Los Angeles River based on a supposed "pueblo right" granted to the settlement by the king of Spain in 1781. In his recent book *The Great Thirst,* Norris Hundley debunks the historical validity of any "pueblo rights" that supposedly date to the Spanish era. Nonetheless, as Hundley details, such rights were granted full legal status by the California Supreme Court (and are still enforced in the 1990s).[194] In the 1920s, the Spreckels interests, acting through the San Diego city government, sought to follow the Los Angeles precedent. After gaining a "paramount right" over the entire flow of the San Diego River, they would be in a position to negate all existing riparian and appropriated rights that might impede the city's growth. Fletcher vigorously opposed this action; he knew that it would threaten rights claimed by the Cuyamaca Water Company and would obviate any political support he might drum up for dam construction at Mission Gorge No. 3 and the Fletcher dam site. During the early stages of litigation in August 1923, Freeman recognized the problems confronting Fletcher when he observed in his notebook: "I judge [that] Fletcher Dam can't be financed in face of the Pueblo suits." No major financier would be willing to invest in a dam construction project that might be found to lack the legal right to store water.[195]

Legal maneuvering dragged on for years, with Fletcher claiming that San Diego was primarily a military presidio during the Spanish era and so did not qualify for any supposed "pueblo rights."[196] To his dismay, in 1930 the California Supreme Court rejected this view and ruled that the city controlled the river through a preexisting "paramount right."[197] With this ruling, Fletcher's hopes for building storage reservoirs at Mission Gorge No. 3 and the Fletcher dam site met an ignominious end. The water rights of the Cuyamaca Water Company—then controlled by the La Mesa, Spring Grove, and Spring Valley Irrigation District—were not completely abrogated, but the district was forced to meld its interests into those held by the City of San Diego. Fletcher's rights to the El Capitan dam site were sold to the municipality; and in 1934, an earthfill gravity dam rose at the site, ending any hope that an Eastwood dam would one day impound the San Diego River.[198]

Although Eastwood worked for several years on the various San Diego River projects, he died long before the civic drama surrounding the "paramount right" issue reached its final act. In fact, his response to Freeman's May 1924 report constituted Eastwood's last major public defense of the multiple arch dam. Nothing was resolved in the final bitter exchange between the two engineers, but it provided a fitting denouement for Eastwood's often frustrating career. For his part, Fletcher did not consider the obstacles and objections raised by Freeman to be anything more than self-serving political sniping. He never lost faith in Eastwood, and in the latter part of July he reaffirmed his support when he wrote Harry Chandler, influential editor of the *Los Angeles Times:*

I believe [Eastwood] has rendered a remarkable service to the country in that he has increased the factors of safety and cut the cost of construction nearly one-half by the new principle of scientific design, either a multiple arch or radial cone type. I see Los Angeles is considering flood control dams, and I know that he can render service to your community . . . and anything that you can do to assist him in getting his design in competition with others will be personally appreciated. You will then be rendering a service to your county.[199]

If nothing else, Eastwood's efforts to advance the ideals of efficiency and economy found an appreciative advocate in Ed Fletcher. The final phase of his career did not culminate in any dramatic accomplishment or embarrassing disaster. With Fletcher's support, he simply continued to develop designs that reduced capital expenditures to a minimum.

CHAPTER 10

The Multiple Arch Dam After Eastwood

*[John S. Eastwood] has put multiple arch dams on the map on this Pacific
Coast, and given some new ideas for the world to copy. . . . To give you an
idea of what Lloyd's of London feels toward Eastwood's dams, [I] will say that
they have put a $600,000 insurance policy on Lake Hodges Dam and
$200,000 on Murray Dam in San Diego County at 75 cents on the $100,
probably the lowest rate of insurance in the United States on concrete dams.*

Ed Fletcher to Harry Chandler, 1924

*The multiple-arch dam is a relatively new type of structure and experience
with the design is correspondingly limited . . . it is to be hoped that [Lake
Hodges Dam] will never be surpassed in the matter of frailty and instability,
defects that will soon be made a matter of the past by completion of the
rehabilitation work now in progress.*

Editorial in Engineering News-Record, 1936

During the summer of 1924, Eastwood kept busy on numerous designs for Ed Fletcher in San Diego, the Sespe Light & Power Company in the Santa Clara River Valley, and the Bluewater–Toltec Irrigation District in New Mexico. On August 9, he wrote H. H. Garstin, president of the Bear Valley Mutual Water Company, that he had "just completed the estimates [for] the El Capitan Dam for the City of San Diego, at 140,000 cu. yds. to cost about $1,660,000.00."[1] At the same time, he expressed exasperation over being "so pressed for time that I do not know where to turn, or [how] to get off my necessary correspondence." Eastwood told Garstin that he was ea-

ger to witness the ongoing construction of the highway bridge atop Big Bear Valley Dam. This would have to wait, however, until he completed "things that are the most pressing for time." The next day—Sunday, August 10—he was relaxing at his small ranch on the Kings River east of Fresno and, while swimming, suffered a heart attack that resulted in death by drowning. After a life unencumbered by health problems, Eastwood's death came swiftly and without warning at the age of 67.[2] Notice of his passing appeared in a few newspapers and engineering journals but only one major obituary was published. In January 1925, the *Southwest Builder and*

Contractor printed a two-page description of his career and noted that Eastwood "constant[ly] endeavor[ed] to give the most economical design for a given location." While acknowledging "considerable opposition [he encountered] . . . from members of the engineering profession," the piece eulogized him for being "always the seer, the prophet of things to be, the dreamer who saw far into the future, and who, happily for us, was able to make some of his dreams come true."[3]

Eastwood's creative powers had flourished until the end of his life. Had he lived a few more years, he would almost certainly have overseen the construction of several "radial cone" dams. But following his death, none of these designs reached fruition; their form was so closely tied to Eastwood's vision of structural design that they died with their creator. Subsequently, no other engineer ever adopted his "radial plan," "curved face," or "radial cone" multiple arch dams, although straight-crested designs continued to be built for several years after 1924.[4] These later structures usually featured double-walled buttresses and wide-span arches encompassing 180-degree arcs, thus following the form promoted by Fred Noetzli in his 1924 ASCE *Transactions* article.[5] In 1927, the eighth edition of Edward Wegmann's book *The Design and Construction of Dams* presented a lengthy new chapter providing "a mathematical discussion and description of multiple arch dams." Written by Noetzli, this discourse in the world's most prestigious book on dam engineering seemed to signal the emergence of multiple arch design as a major form of hydraulic technology. But a few specific events, conjoined with broader patterns of New Deal economic development, soon brought multiple arch dam construction to a halt.

The decline of the multiple arch dam in California (and by extension, in the West in general) can be traced to three separate controversies: problems with the concrete at Gem Lake Dam, one of Lars Jorgensen's multiple arch designs, built in 1915–1916; the cataclysmic collapse of the St. Francis Dam in March 1928; and temperature cracks in Eastwood's Lake Hodges Dam and

efforts to "repair" them in the 1930s. When Eastwood died in 1924, the professional critics and engineering bureaucracies who had opposed his work did not pass away; instead, their influence steadily grew, and they eventually controlled both the resolution of these controversies and the historical assessment accorded Eastwood's work. But beyond particular incidents and issues, larger political and economic forces that began to predominate during the 1930s strongly militated against the proliferation of multiple arch dams.

GEM LAKE DAM

Beginning in the early 1920s, concrete in the arches of Jorgensen's Gem Lake Dam began deteriorating. This disintegration attracted the attention of Walter L. Huber, who coauthored an article on the subject in the ASCE *Transactions*.[6] The exact cause of the deterioration was never definitively ascertained, but it seems to have been related to the quality of sand used in the concrete rather than to the design or construction technology used. In addition, the extreme elevation of the dam (more than 9,000 feet above sea level) and the fluctuation of the reservoir level exacerbated the problem by exposing the structure to a severe "freeze-thaw" cycle. Huber perceived this situation as evidence of the frailty of multiple arch dams—a theme echoed by his mentor John D. Galloway, who urged: "too much emphasis cannot be given to the Gem Lake failure. It teaches that under such severe climatic and operating conditions, the multiple arch dam with its relatively thin concrete should not be used." Noetzli argued that the Gem Lake Dam's condition did not evidence a flaw in multiple arch technology, but he found himself in the minority of engineers who commented publicly on Huber's article.[7]

In absolute terms, the damage to the Gem Lake arches was minimal. Rehabilitation work was required, but the structure did not collapse and did not have to be completely replaced (Fig.

10.1   *Gem Lake Dam after repairs. This 1931 view shows that a protective coating has been applied to the upstream face. The dam remains in service more than 75 years after it was constructed. (Huber Papers, WRCA)*

10.1). As an engineering report prepared in the 1960s phrased it: "[despite] imperfections, [Gem Lake Dam] has been continuously in service (except for the one season of repairs) for nearly half a century in about the most severe exposure it is possible to find."[8] In light of the poor safety record of earthfill and rockfill dams, the problems at Gem Lake hardly warranted condemnation of all multiple arch dams. But this "failure" was readily exploited by engineers who opposed the technology.

ST. FRANCIS DAM

Late in the evening of March 12, 1928, the 220-foot-high St. Francis Dam—a concrete

10.2   *The remains of the St. Francis Dam after its collapse in March 1928. The structure was designed by William Mulholland without any outside review by or approval from the state engineer's office or the State Railroad Commission. (*Western Construction News, *1928)*

gravity structure—collapsed and unleashed a raging flood through the heart of the Santa Clara Valley in Southern California, killing at least 400 people and causing millions of dollars in property damage (Fig. 10.2).[9] Built by the Los Angeles Department of Water and Power, this curved gravity dam had impounded more than 40,000 acre-feet of water drawn from the city's Owens Valley Aqueduct. Officially designed by William Mulholland, chief engineer for the department, the dam did not require the approval of the state engineer or any other authority due to a loophole in California's 1917 dam safety law that exempted major municipalities from state supervision of such projects. Eastwood encountered years of delay before the Littlerock Dam finally received the state engineer's sanction; but Mulholland's St. Francis Dam, built

almost simultaneously at a location fewer than 50 miles away from Littlerock, passed from design to construction and operation without any comparable review.

The public and professional response to the tragedy was an impassioned outcry demanding that such a disaster never be allowed to recur. Within a matter of weeks after Mulholland's dam failed, the engineering community reached two primary conclusions concerning the St. Francis disaster. First, the structure was built on an inferior rock foundation that softened when exposed to water. Second, responsibility for its design and construction had been concentrated in the hands of a single engineer.[10] Practically no one criticized the use of a curved gravity dam at the site (although "uplift" acting along parts of the base almost certainly contributed to the failure).[11] Generally, the disaster was treated as a freak accident that did not reflect on the suitability of gravity dams in any larger sense. As Walter Huber stated to Freeman less than 10 days after the collapse: "Briefly the whole story is clearly one of lack of suitable foundation . . . the central section of the dam which reached to a firmer rock stands intact. It is the one great witness of the stability of a gravity section founded on a solid foundation."[12]

While Mulholland was forced to assume full responsibility for the design, the singular nature of his authority came to be perceived as the real culprit behind the disaster. Thus, an *Engineering News-Record* editorial entitled "The Human Factor" soon exhorted that: "the indictment [for the collapse should be on] . . . the organization policy which made it possible for decisions depending entirely upon human judgment to rest in one man."[13] The legislative response to the disaster was to pass a new law placing all of the state's dams (both old and new) that fell outside of federal control under the supervisory authority of the state engineer. Enacted in 1929, the new law was drafted to eliminate the exemption that had excluded large municipalities from coverage under the 1917 act. It also removed the Railroad Commission, which had served as a major supporter of Eastwood's work in the late 1910s and early 1920s, from any role in the dam safety review process.[14] Although impetus for the 1929 act derived from a gravity dam failure, the law produced a more hostile bureaucratic environment for structural dams. Whereas concrete, rockfill, and earthfill designs continued to receive approval from the state engineer (for example, Los Angeles replaced the destroyed St. Francis Dam with an earthfill structure in nearby Bouquet Canyon), multiple arch and single arch designs were viewed with extreme skepticism. In fact, after 1929 the building of structural dams in California nearly ceased, while construction of massive designs flourished.[15]

In particular, the abandonment of multiple arch designs as a viable hydraulic technology was hastened by a special study initiated by State Engineer Edward Hyatt in the spring of 1931. Hyatt, who attained his position after Wilbur McClure's death in 1926, appointed Huber to head a "Multiple Arch Dam Advisory Committee" that was to provide guidance on how to enforce the 1929 dam safety law.[16] After extensive field examinations of California's existing multiple-arch dams (Fig. 10.3), followed by mathematical analyses (based on elastic arch theory) of these same structures, Huber's committee reported that:

Although the multiple arch dam has its place . . . it should not be regarded as a cheap substitute for

10.3 *After the St. Francis Dam disaster, Walter L. Huber was appointed head of a Multiple Arch Dam Advisory Committee charged with investigating the safety of multiple arch dams throughout California. Here the committee gazes up at the imposing downstream face of Eastwood's Littlerock Dam, during a visit on June 6, 1931. (Huber Papers, WRCA)*

241

all other types. . . . [the] committee was impressed with the fact that certain defects were common in a number of these structures [and] . . . it is appropriate to call attention to these undesirable features. . . . [I]t is a naturally slender [type of] structure, with integral members of relatively thin concrete . . . some of them have been designed under competitive conditions resulting in structures successfully answering certain mathematical requirements, but [are] hardly adequate from other points of view.[17]

The safety record of Eastwood's dams over the previous twenty years was not entirely ignored during the committee's deliberations. For example, in August 1931, committee member Harry Dennis confided to Huber that "you refer specifically to the Little Rock Dam in particular, and while I agree with your observations as to high stresses, thin buttresses, and geology in general, I cannot overlook the fact that the dam has been loaded above spillway elevation with water and has not shown any distress except some scour at the spillway."[18] Nonetheless, the committee's final report expressed little confidence in the structural merits of multiple arch technology in general (especially the "slender structure[s] . . . designed under competitive conditions" that Eastwood advocated). In California, this report (and its acceptance by State Engineer Hyatt) marked the end of an era in which multiple arch dams could be considered as a realistic option for new water storage projects.[19]

LAKE HODGES DAM

In the wake of the St. Francis Dam collapse, Eastwood's Lake Hodges Dam became the primary object of condemnation and treatment during California's dam safety crusade of the early 1930s. Specifically, the temperature cracks that had formed in its buttresses during construction began to fuel inquiries into the structure's overall stability. Studies of the cracks' structural significance were first undertaken in the early 1920s by Charles Derleth, a professor at the University of California and a friend of J. B. Lippincott.[20] Although his commentary did not reach a definitive conclusion about the dam, Derleth expressed concern over the possible effect of "heavy vibrations from flood or earthquake."[21] Without explaining why, he also voiced misgivings about the "slender" buttresses and the "inadequate" bracing provided by the strut-tie beams. Derleth's analysis had little impact for several years. After passage of the state's new dam safety law, however, the Lake Hodges Dam received renewed attention. And although the Lake Hodges Dam had provided exemplary service as a water storage structure, its design was soon stigmatized as dangerous.

In 1929, a special board of consultants recommended to the state engineer that the Lake Hodges Dam was "safe to carry loads excepting in the case of a major earthquake [or] . . . overtopping." The *Engineering News-Record* reported the story with the headline, "High Multiple Arch Dam Declared Safe Except from Earthquake."[22] Although the performance history of multiple arch dams gave no indication of structural instability in the face of seismic shocks, the board found an appreciative audience for the report among the community of gravity dam advocates.[23] Several years passed before state authorities and the City of San Diego (owner of the Lake Hodges Dam since 1925) agreed on a way to "strengthen" the structure. Finally, in 1936 work began on a series of heavily reinforced vertical frames between alternate buttresses (Fig. 10.4).[24] The extent to which these massive frames increased the strength and stability of the dam may be debatable. But they certainly altered the appearance of the downstream face, making the structure seem cluttered and (more important) massive (Fig. 10.5). This change, whether structurally meaningful or not, was sufficient to placate the state's dam safety bureaucracy.

When the new "vertical frames" at Lake

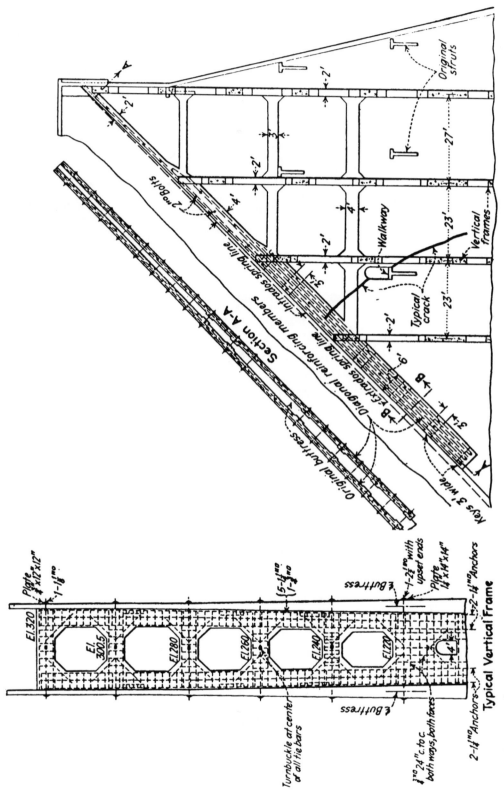

10.4 *Drawings depicting alterations intended to "repair" the buttresses of Eastwood's Lake Hodges Dam. (Engineering News-Record, 1936)*

243

10.5   *Lake Hodges Dam in 1937, after implementation of "repairs." The new "braces" tend to make the design look more like a solid, massive construct. (Huber Papers, WRCA)*

Hodges were completed, the *Engineering News-Record* enunciated what became the standard official critique of Eastwood's dams by the American engineering establishment. In a 1936 editorial entitled "Unsafe Dam Design," the journal reported that "the caution appropriate to a new type of design was not always observed in building multiple arch dams."[25] Referring to the Lake Hodges Dam's "frailty and instability," the editorial cited the buttress cracks as evidence of a "weakened and perhaps dangerous condition." But the major deficiency of the dam was not the existence of eighteen-year-old hairline temperature cracks. Instead, the structure's putative lack of stability against seismic forces was asserted as the key safety issue.[26] Earthquakes were touted as the principal threat facing multiple arch dams; the *Engineering News-*

Record editorial invoked the "Long Beach earthquake of three years ago" and proclaimed that "out of our catastrophes thus are coming safer designs and higher construction standards."

The 1933 Long Beach earthquake had not caused any dam failures and certainly had not precipitated the collapse of any multiple arch dams, but the editors of *Engineering News-Record* cited it nonetheless. To them, the central (albeit conjectural) point was that multiple arch dams were essentially unsafe—despite the dams' exemplary safety record, despite the fact that some were actually built with artificial expansion joints to take the place of natural hairline cracks, and despite their ability to conserve material and eliminate the hazards of hydrostatic uplift. Multiple arch dams, especially the radically thin

244

10.6 *Upstream side of the 4,000-foot-long Grand River Dam in northeast Oklahoma, shortly after its completion in 1940. This represents one of the last major multiple arch dams built in the United States. (Author's collection)*

structures championed by Eastwood, simply did not conform to what dams were expected to look like in the New Deal era. A few major structures, such as the Hamilton Dam in Texas (now known as the Buchanan Dam), the Bartlett Dam near Phoenix, and the Pensacola Dam in Oklahoma (also known as the Grand River Dam) were erected in the 1930s (Fig. 10.6).[27] But compared with concrete gravity and earthfill designs, multiple arch dams were only rarely constructed in America after 1930; and since the end of World War II, no new multiple arch dam has been built in the United States.

LEGACIES: FREEMAN'S OPPOSITION AND THE NEW DEAL

Given the failure of the multiple arch dam to secure a continuing role in American water resources development, what is the significance of John S. Eastwood and his life's work? Is he merely a minor engineer who built a few unusual dams, designed some hydroelectric power systems in the Sierra Nevada, and had an unfortunate tendency to alienate leaders of the American civil engineering establishment? Or does his story help elucidate more elemental issues concerning both technological development and the history of the modern American West?

Leaving aside for a moment the economic circumstances surrounding the New Deal, historians might be tempted to interpret the brief flowering and subsequent demise of the multiple arch dam as an example of "technological momentum" at work. According to this view, the momentum of gravity dam design simply proved too powerful to permit the technology promoted by Eastwood to survive, so after a few years of fitful experimentation the latter quietly faded into obscurity. On the surface, this explanation might appear plausible. But the multiple arch dam's failure to achieve an enduring place in the world of hydraulic engineering was not the result of some predetermined technological imperative; rather, in large part, the technology was abandoned by the profession because important engineers consciously opposed it in the pre–New Deal era and worked hard to prevent its construction wherever possible.

In this regard, the rivalry between Eastwood and John R. Freeman acquires paramount significance. Beginning at Big Meadows in 1912–1913, Eastwood encroached on the professional and financial interests of Freeman and earned a powerful enemy for the rest of his life. In the 1920s, Freeman interfered with prospective plans for the San Joaquin Light & Power Corporation and, most important, publicly opposed Eastwood's designs for impounding the San Diego River. Simultaneously, Freeman championed gravity dams as the only suitable designs for major water projects (reflecting a faith that remained unshaken even by the St. Francis catastrophe) and, until his death in 1932, used his influence to promote the massive tradition. Guided by the New England engineer's refusal to consider multiple arch dams as anything more than cheap, inferior substitutes for gravity structures, the American engineering profession found it easy to erase Eastwood's "Ultimate Dam" from its collective consciousness.[28] Thus, when Walter Huber and others set out in the 1950s to write the history of dams in the American West, multiple arch designs were largely ignored. By the 1990s, the technology came to be treated as little more than a quaint artifact that most hydraulic engineers know nothing about.[29]

Viewed in the context of Freeman and his opposition to the multiple arch dam, Eastwood's experiences as an engineer highlight the social nature of the technological decision-making process. While the structural form of Eastwood's designs emanated from a highly personalized engineering vision, the activities that determined whether his dams would be built involved a complex interplay among engineers, businessmen, bureaucrats, and (to a far lesser degree) the general public. The major performers in each drama were not numerous; in the aggregate, they numbered a few score. However, the social interaction surrounding the construction (or rejection) of Eastwood's designs was intense.

The social context of technological development is especially well illustrated in Eastwood's dealings with the state engineer's office and with the State Railroad Commission in

California. In the 1920s, his ability to build a dam in the most economically important state in the West hinged on which bureaucracy retained supervisory authority over the project. The basic structural form of a design may not have differed, but formal approval for construction largely depended on which particular engineers were asked to evaluate it. Hawley, Faude, Fletcher, and others formed a community of Eastwood supporters; but McClure, Huber, Galloway, and others constituted an informal (but hardly accidental) group of engineers opposed to his designs. Although technical arguments ostensibly formed the basis for decisions surrounding multiple arch dams, the strict application of reasoned and impartial analysis did not determine the technology's fate. The story of Eastwood's dams is as much a history of professional ambitions, personal jealousies, and corporate financial machinations as it is a technological history of hydrostatics and structural design.[30]

Effects of Freeman's and Huber's opposition to multiple arch dam technology would have been felt in the 1930s even in the absence of the Great Depression, but the economic woes of this period played a significant social role themselves in hastening the cultural demise of Eastwood's "Ultimate Dam." The New Deal era is often associated with gargantuan public works projects that captured America's imagination, if only because they helped palliate the economic misery afflicting the country by putting vast numbers of people to work—at least temporarily. Dams were among the most prominent of these projects, especially the ones built by the Bureau of Reclamation, the Tennessee Valley Authority, and the Army Corps of Engineers. The vast majority of dams built by these federal agencies were gravity structures, including the Hoover Dam (actually authorized in 1928 by Calvin Coolidge but constructed in 1931–1935), Grand Coulee Dam, Friant Dam, Shasta Dam, Fort Peck Dam, Bonneville Dam, and Norris Dam (Fig. 10.7).

During the New Deal, the "celebration of mass" became the dominant ideology associ-

10.7   *Downstream side of Norris Dam, built by the Tennessee Valley Authority (TVA) in the 1930s, using a design prepared by the Bureau of Reclamation. Many TVA dams exhibit a stylish surface treatment; but underneath this "skin," they consist of unremarkable gravity profiles harkening back to DeSazilly's mid-nineteenth-century "profile of equal resistance." (Library of Congress)*

ated with dam construction: the more material a dam required, the more acclaim and adulation it received (Fig. 10.8). In an era of limits and diminished expectations, American culture apparently derived psychological satisfaction from creating something big in the face of adversity. Thus, the Grand Coulee Dam drew praise for being the first masonry structure in more than three millennia to use more material than the largest Egyptian pyramid. Similarly, no one complained that the Hoover Dam would have been grossly overbuilt even without its pronounced upstream curve (Fig. 10.9). Citizens were encouraged to applaud the role of gravity dams in conserving America's water resources, but attention rarely focused on the extravagant use of materials necessary to the massive tradition.

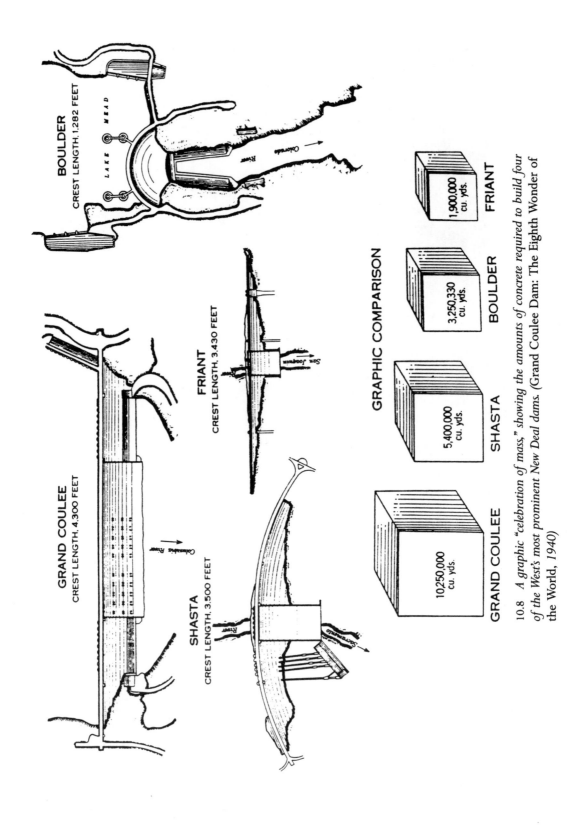

BOULDER
CREST LENGTH, 1,282 FEET

LAKE MEAD

Colorado River

GRAND COULEE
CREST LENGTH, 4,300 FEET

Columbia River

FRIANT
CREST LENGTH, 3,430 FEET

San Joaquin

SHASTA
CREST LENGTH, 3,500 FEET

River

Sacramento River

GRAPHIC COMPARISON

FRIANT
1,900,000
cu. yds.

BOULDER
3,250,330
cu. yds.

SHASTA
5,400,000
cu. yds.

GRAND COULEE
10,250,000
cu. yds.

10.8 *A graphic "celebration of mass," showing the amounts of concrete required to build four of the West's most prominent New Deal dams. (Grand Coulee Dam: The Eighth Wonder of the World, 1940)*

A

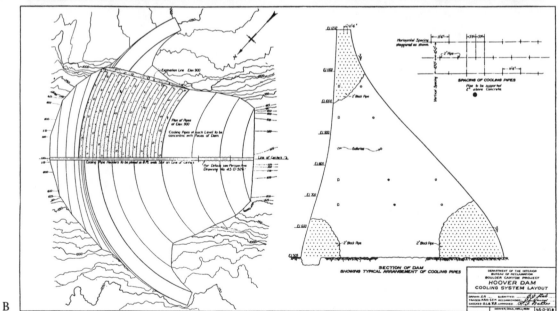

B

10.9   *Mass and domination: Hoover (Boulder) Dam. (A) The downstream side at night. This view highlights the imposing appearance of the curved gravity design. (Library of Congress) (B) Schematic cross section depicting both the dam's bulky dimensions and the system of pipes built into it to remove heat emitted by the concrete as it hardened. Without this cooling system (cold brine flowed constantly through these pipes), engineers estimated, it would have taken 700 years for the interior of the structure to cool down. (Western Construction News, 1930)*

249

Rather than being related to economy in the quantities of construction material, the term *efficiency* was used exclusively in connection with standardized design and the development of new methods of material conveyance—such as employing mechanized bulldozers to distribute earthfill or utilizing huge movable cranes to distribute concrete (Fig. 10.10).[31]

A complete discussion of the technical, social, and political significance of New Deal dams lies beyond the scope of this book. Clearly, however, the methods of publicly financing these massive structures soon smothered any interest in (or appreciation for) material-conserving methods of dam design. During the 1930s, dam building encompassed

more than just the impoundment of floodwaters: it became integrally involved with efforts to alleviate the effects of the Depression.[32] The social function of dam construction underwent a transformation that still resonates within the American political economy as dam projects became a key vehicle for dispensing the largess of "pork-barrel" politics. Not coincidentally, the ascendance of massive earthfill, rockfill, and concrete gravity dam technology accompanied the rise of publicly financed (or subsidized) water projects in the West.

Conversely, Eastwood's work as an engineer occurred within a capitalist milieu that required construction costs to be recouped in strict accord with the financial demands of a

10.10 *Friant Dam under construction across the San Joaquin River, near Fresno, circa 1940. The huge movable cranes facilitated the pouring of concrete along the length of the gravity structure; in the post–World War II era, American dam engineers devoted much of their creative energy to designing material-handling systems that facilitated the construction of massive dams. (Author's collection, courtesy of John Snyder)*

market economy. Broadly speaking, his dams may have been "public works," but all of them except the Mountain Dell Dam and (in part) the Cave Creek Dam were funded by essentially private entities that received no governmental subsidies. Unlike federal agencies (and their beneficiaries), Eastwood could not depend on public appropriations and political maneuvering to extend a project's repayment schedule. Bearing this in mind, it is easier to comprehend why interest in multiple arch dams faded so quickly. The economic and cultural justification for their construction simply disappeared as dam financing became as much a vehicle for distributing federal funds as it did a fiscal basis for undertaking a water storage project. While criticism of the technology may have been couched in terms of safety (as in the Lake Hodges controversy), Eastwood's goal of promoting economic growth through construction of inexpensive dams ran counter to what became status quo in the world of western water development. Within less than twenty years of his death, the material-conserving character of multiple arch technology bore scant relevance to the economic, social, and political environment surrounding large-scale water projects.[33]

EASTWOOD AND THE CONTROL OF WESTERN WATER

In *Rivers of Empire* and in articles such as "Hydraulic Society in California" and "Hoover Dam: A Study in Domination," Donald Worster portrays twentieth-century water development in the West as being subject to the control of a centralized bureaucracy (termed an "elite of water bearers") oriented toward serving the economic interests of a select group of landowners and powerful businessmen.[34] Working through the politically attuned (and largely subservient) Bureau of Reclamation, the West's authoritarian "hydraulic society" has, in Worster's view,

guided water development from a singular, self-serving perspective. In so doing, it has established "a coercive, monolithic and hierarchical system, ruled by a power elite based on the ownership of capital and expertise."[35] In *The Great Thirst*, Norris Hundley challenges Worster's argument by asserting that "a so-called 'water establishment' [in California] . . . has never been a monolith driven by a single purpose or vision, save the idea that water (and nature generally) exists to serve mankind. Rather . . . it has consisted of many discrete groups, both in and outside the state, each with its own (frequently changing) agenda that has sometimes led to conflict."[36] Which of these two perspectives best describes what Eastwood experienced in promoting the multiple arch dam?

On one level, Hundley's argument that myriad forces have contributed to the growth of the region's contemporary water supply systems is reflected in Eastwood's experiences. As an engineer, he worked with an enormous range of water-based projects involving logging, mining, flood control, irrigation, hydroelectric power, and municipal development and with a complex array of patrons, supporters, opponents, and regulatory officials allied with scores of "local agencies." The growth of large-scale water projects occurred in a historical environment rife with significant conflicting interests; and this seemingly refutes any simple prognostication that a "power elite based on the ownership of capital and expertise" bears primary responsibility for the region's modern hydraulic infrastructure. But on a deeper level, Eastwood's experiences are fully compatible with the thesis Worster has outlined: development of the West's hydraulic technologies was controlled by a small number of engineers, businessmen, and administrators who prescribed a handful of potential solutions to problems that they were instrumental in defining. Above all, Eastwood challenged the "water establishment" by attempting to expose the region to new technologies that could diffuse the advantages of water storage to a wide range of ambitious, yet financially limited, water users who were otherwise shut out from dam building. The opposition to (and ultimate suppression of) multiple arch technology bolsters arguments that portray the West's modern "hydraulic society" as a closed caste.

In drawing attention to centralized and hierarchical facets of western water development, Worster has adopted a view that parallels the concept of structural art proposed by David Billington. Billington perceives structural art (distinguished by the ideals of efficiency, economy, and elegance that characterized Eastwood's designs) as exhibiting "a lightness, even a fragility, which closely parallels the essence of a free and open society," whereas massive masonry design reflects "autocratic" values. Billington's relational assertions may appear ingenuous, but in view of Eastwood's experiences opposing the hegemony of the massive tradition of dam design, such insights become more persuasive.[37] Significantly, Worster implicitly allies himself with Billington's perspective by portraying the massive curved gravity Hoover Dam as a "study in domination" and not (as Joseph Stevens rhapsodized in his book *Hoover Dam: An American Adventure*) an "engineering marvel . . . [that allows one to feel] that the future is limitless . . . that we have in our grasp the power to achieve anything if we can but summon the will."[38] As Worster states, "it is not 'man' who has achieved mastery over western rivers, but *some men,* while the rest of us have looked on in passive wonder."[39] The economic savings that Eastwood's designs offered to prospective clients do not obviate the relevance of this view; as with the Littlerock Dam, they simply opened up the field to a wider number of players. In this way, the multiple arch dam supported what Billington characterizes as a "free and open society" by acting to constrain the influence of Worster's "elite of water bearers."

In this context, a clear delineation separating "public works" and "private interests" becomes impossible to sustain when dealing with western water development. Although almost all of Eastwood's work was accomplished within the private sector, he nonetheless per-

ceived himself as serving a larger public good associated with increased use of the region's water resources. In this regard, the so-called "public works" undertaken by local, state, or federal authorities were no less involved in serving the interests of (as Worster terms it) "some men," than Eastwood was in designing dams to serve the desires of either Ed Fletcher and the Santa Fe Railway or small-scale farmers cultivating pear orchards alongside Little Rock Creek. Even the seemingly selfless acts of Sylvester Cannon in bringing the financial benefits of multiple arch dam technology to Salt Lake City can be interpreted as serving the private interests of an insular Mormon culture. Similarly, historians may wish to distinguish Henry Huntington's Pacific Light and Power Corporation (centered on Eastwood's Big Creek system) from the municipally owned Los Angeles Department of Water and Power system or from the Bureau of Reclamation's power plant at Hoover Dam, but these entities differ little in many respects. And while New Deal projects may be glorified as the ultimate evidence of the American people's strength in overcoming adversity, the massive dams that symbolize these projects do not necessarily represent the "public interest" (or a free and open society) any better than the first Eastwood dam built for the Hume-Bennett Lumber Company.

FINAL THOUGHTS

In the past seventy-five years, technical arguments and disagreements surrounding multiple arch dams built in the early twentieth century have remained essentially the same, although computers have introduced a new (but not always edifying) element into the analytical process. An engineer who seeks to demonstrate the safety and strength of an Eastwood design can do so relatively easily, but it is equally feasible to show that the design comprises a dangerous structure that should have collapsed years ago.[40] And while the long-term safety record of the multiple arch dam can be taken as evidence of its inherent strength, engineers can readily point to studies that "prove" its instability. Adopting the latter view, the state bureaucracy charged with enforcing California's 1929 dam safety law (now known as the Division of Safety of Dams) has continued to castigate multiple arch technology, using the "strengthening" of the Lake Hodges Dam as a precedent for later alterations to the Murray, Big Bear Valley, and Littlerock dams. In 1993, for example, the state's protracted effort to transform the Littlerock Dam into something different from what Eastwood designed in 1919 finally bore fruit; as reported in *Engineering News-Record,* "a $12.2 million buttressing . . . essentially will convert [Littlerock Dam] from a multiple concrete arch structure to a gravity dam . . . [a local official reported that] 'the basis for doing the work at all is that the state Division of Safety of Dams has determined that the dam has a couple of problems.' "[41] In contrast, Salt Lake City considers the Mountain Dell Dam to be a stable and valuable part of its water supply system and the U.S. Forest Service is satisfied with the condition and performance of the Hume Lake Dam. As Eastwood well understood, the validity of any structural assessment rests on its underlying assumptions. And as always, these assumptions reflect a wide range of subjective interpretation.

Were Eastwood still in practice as a civil engineer, he would be chagrined that the profession has forgotten "The Ultimate Dam" and ignored his 1924 pronouncement that "anyone who tries to slur them [multiple arch dams] now is a hopeless back number, a has been, for engineers throughout the whole world have come to recognize the type as the true and ultimate scientific type of dam."[42] Nonetheless, Eastwood might take a modicum of satisfaction in knowing that the most noteworthy recent dam failures in the West have all involved massive earthfill dams.[43]

More problematic would be his reaction to a society in which the values of unrestrained economic and technological growth have begun to be questioned by a significant portion of the citizenry. In promulgating a vision in which "California's slogan e're should be, that 'tis a crime to let our rivers reach the sea," Eastwood distilled a point of view common among westerners of his era. Perhaps the most intriguing aspect of Eastwood's efforts to minimize the cost of storing water involves their rejection by a regional culture intent on creating a pervasive "second nature" based on large-scale reservoirs and water control systems. For historians of the modern American West, this apparent incongruity presents the story of John S. Eastwood as a challenge to any easy interpretation of water resources development in the region. It also lies at the heart of why Eastwood's professional experiences as a hydraulic engineer continue to hold meaning seventy years after his death.

Sources

Technical journals and books such as *Western Engineering,* the *Journal of Electricity Power and Gas, Engineering News,* the *Transactions of the American Society of Civil Engineers,* Edward Wegmann's *The Design and Construction of Dams,* and James D. Schuyler's *Reservoirs for Irrigation, Water Power and Domestic Water Supply* provide pertinent data and important contextual evidence, but a study of John S. Eastwood and the place of the multiple arch dam in western water history can only be accomplished through extensive use of primary sources. Seventeen of Eastwood's dam designs reached the construction stage and at least forty more were seriously considered by various clients. In addition, he made major contributions to the economic growth of greater Fresno and played a key role in developing hydroelectric power systems in the Sierra Nevada. His multiple arch dams were located throughout the West—in California, Utah, Idaho, Arizona, British Columbia, and Mexico—and each project had a distinctive history. Thus, a study of Eastwood's career involves research into a daunting range of endeavors whose only common feature is a perceived need for water storage.

The John S. Eastwood Papers at the Water Resources Center Archives, University of California, Berkeley, provide the foundation for this book. These papers contain Eastwood's surviving business records from the last fifteen years of his life (along with a few earlier reports), and they include correspondence, essays, design specifications, calculations, drawings, and photographs. After Eastwood's death, this material was sold by his widow to Mr. Chester H. Loveland, an engineer associated with the California Railroad Commission and with water projects in San Diego County. In 1961 these files, minus some material that had inadvertently been discarded, were donated to the Water Resources Center Archives by the California Water and Telephone Company (a firm organized in the 1920s by Loveland and Eastwood's colleague Frederic Faude). The Eastwood papers are divided into more than 60 separate folders that cover distinct projects or contain general correspondence and data related to dam design. The amount of information in each folder varies, and (unfortunately) the more significant projects are not necessarily the best documented. Despite having some frustrating lacunas, however, the Eastwood Papers contain a wealth of information and constitute the main source of information on Eastwood's dam-building career.

The Eastwood Papers are supplemented by a much smaller collection of material at the

Bancroft Library, University of California, Berkeley, donated by Eastwood's niece, Mrs. Marguerite E. Welch, in the late 1960s. Most of the Eastwood material in the Bancroft Library consists of published material that can be found elsewhere, but it also includes copies of a few letters otherwise unavailable: the entire file is duplicated in Folder 62 in the Eastwood Papers at the Water Resources Center Archives. Mrs. Welch desired that the accomplishments of her uncle be remembered; therefore, around 1970 she commissioned Mr. Charles Allen Whitney, an engineer and technical writer who had previously worked in the licensing and right-of-way division of the Southern California Edison Company, to prepare a biography of Eastwood. Tentatively titled "The Life and Times of John S. Eastwood," this manuscript was never finished, and Whitney only wrote about Eastwood's career through the first years of the twentieth century. Despite its nonscholarly format, however, Whitney's manuscript provides valuable material on Eastwood's early work in the Fresno region and is based on many personal sources including Ella Eastwood's diary. A copy of the manuscript is on file at the Fresno City and County Historical Society. Unfortunately, the location of much of the primary source material used by Whitney is currently unknown. Whitney published a short article on Eastwood for *Montana, the Magazine of Western History* and also prepared a draft article on Eastwood's involvement in the design of the Big Creek hydroelectric power project, entitled "Dollars and Genius Built Southern California: The Story of Henry Huntington and John S. Eastwood." A copy of the latter manuscript is on file at the Water Resources Center Archives.

Other important primary sources can be broken down into two basic categories: manuscript collections of engineers or businessmen who were involved in projects associated with Eastwood; and records from various public and private entities that became involved with Eastwood on dam projects or inherited control of projects he had helped to develop. Sources in the first category include

several engineers who represented interests unsympathetic—and at times openly hostile—to Eastwood's design ideas. Among them are John R. Freeman and Walter L. Huber, two prominent engineers who served as presidents of the American Society of Civil Engineers and who opposed Eastwood's ideas on a number of occasions; their surviving records provide a valuable counterpoint to Eastwood's own correspondence. Eastwood also had some prominent advocates, such as Colonel Ed Fletcher of San Diego and Great Western Power Company vice president H. H. Sinclair, and manuscript sources reflect their support. In corporate records, perhaps the most important data related to Eastwood are retained by the Southern California Edison Company as part of its files documenting the legal history of water rights associated with the Big Creek hydroelectric power project.

The search for records documenting Eastwood's work is often frustrating, since many relevant files have disappeared or been destroyed. For example, despite a wealth of records in the Henry E. Huntington Library related to the history of this remarkable institution's benefactor, relatively little primary source material survives in connection with Henry E. Huntington's, William G. Kerckhoff's, and Allan C. Balch's management of the Pacific Light and Power Company and the Mammoth Power Company in the period 1902–1910. Similarly, the activities of the Eldorado Water Company in commissioning the innovative triple-arch Webber Dam in 1923–1924 are only very sketchily documented in existing archives. In other instances, valuable material has almost miraculously survived, perhaps the best example being an album of more than 100 photographs documenting the construction of the Hume Lake Dam. These unique photographs are unavailable in California but are maintained as part of the Hackley-Hume Collection at the Michigan State University Archives and Historical Collections in Lansing, Michigan.

Eastwood never worked for the federal government; consequently, the records of agencies such as the Reclamation Service (renamed the Bureau of Reclamation in 1923) and the U.S. Army Corps of Engineers are not particularly fruitful sources of information on his professional activities. But dam safety became an important public issue during the early twentieth century, especially in California, and records of the California State Railroad Commission (later renamed the Public Utilities Commission) and the California Department of Engineering contain important data on several Eastwood projects. The Railroad Commission's records are maintained within the California State Archives, while the latter files are maintained as part of the still-active Division of Safety of Dams. In some cases, these records are remarkably complete; but in others, "gaps" obscure complete understanding of historical events. Other sources of information in the California State Archives include the records of the California Supreme Court (specifically in regard to Eastwood's involvement with Big Creek, as documented in *Herminghaus v. Southern California Edison Company*) and official "Articles of Incorporation" filed by businesses with the Secretary of State.

In spite of intensive research efforts, the author recognizes that relevant information on Eastwood's career undoubtedly exists in unexamined repositories. Nonetheless, sufficient data on his work in fostering development of the multiple arch dam is available to allow meaningful analysis of this aspect of America's civil engineering heritage and its place in western water development.

Manuscript Collections

Derleth, Charles. Papers. University of California Water Resources Center Archives, Berkeley, California.

Eastwood, John S. Papers. Water Resources Center Archives, Berkeley, California.

Fletcher, Ed. Papers. Library and Special Collections, University of California, San Diego, California.

Fletcher, Ed. Papers. San Diego Historical Society, San Diego, California.

Freeman, John R. Papers (MC51). Institute Archives and Special Collections, Massachusetts Institute of Technology, Cambridge, Massachusetts.

Hackley and Hume Papers. Michigan State University Archives and Historical Collections, East Lansing, Michigan.

Huber, Walter L. Papers. Water Resources Center Archives, Berkeley, California.

Huntington, Henry E. Papers. The Huntington Library, San Marino, California.

Lippincott, Joseph B. Papers. Water Resources Center Archives, Berkeley, California.

O'Melveny, Henry W. Papers. The Huntington Library, San Marino, California.

Savage, Hiram N. Papers. Water Resources Center Archives. Berkeley, California.

Sinclair, Henry H. Papers. The Huntington Library, San Marino, California.

Williams, Gardiner S. Papers. Ayres, Lewis, Norris & May, Inc., Ann Arbor, Michigan.

Public and Private Archives and Files

Articles of Incorporation Files. California State Archives, Sacramento, California.

Bear Valley Mutual Water Company Files. Redlands, California.

California Supreme Court Records and Transcripts. California State Archives, Sacramento, California.

Division of Engineering and Industry: Dams File. Museum of American History, Smithsonian Institution, Washington, D.C.

Division of Safety of Dams Files. Department of Water Resources, the Resources Agency. Sacramento, California.

Fresno City and County Historical Society: Newspaper Clippings and Photograph Files. Fresno, California.

Fresno County Recorder's Office. Fresno, California.

Littlerock Creek Irrigation District Files. Littlerock, California.

Madera County Recorder's Office. Madera, California.

Palmdale Water District Files. Palmdale, California.

Peters, A. W., Photograph Collection. Fresno City and County Historical Society. Fresno, California.

Public Utility Commission Records: Files of the Hydraulic Division, State Railroad Commission. California State Archives, Sacramento, California.

Salt River Project Archives. Salt River Project. Tempe, Arizona.

Sequoia National Forest Files. U.S. Forest Service. Porterville, California.

Southern California Edison Company Files. Rosemead, California.

Special Collections. California State University, Fresno, California.

United States Bureau of Reclamation [U.S. Reclamation Service] Records. Record Group 115, National Archives, College Park, Maryland.

United States Forest Service Records. Record Group 95, National Archives, College Park, Maryland.

Notes

Chapter One

1. Walter Prescott Webb, *The Great Plains* (Boston: Ginn, 1931), pp. 3–44.

2. Lawrence B. Lee, *Reclaiming the American West: An Historiography and Guide* (Santa Barbara, Cal.: ABC-Clio Press, 1980); Donald J. Pisani, "Deep and Troubled Waters: A New Field of Western History," *New Mexico Historical Review* 63 (October 1988): 311–31; and Lawrence B. Lee, "Water Resource History: A New Field of Historiography?" *Pacific Historical Review* 57 (November 1988): 457–67. Notable recent books include Donald J. Pisani, *From Family Farm to Agribusiness: The Irrigation Crusade in California, 1850–1930* (Berkeley: University of California Press, 1984); Donald J. Pisani, *To Reclaim a Divided West: Water, Law, and Public Policy 1848–1902* (Albuquerque: University of New Mexico Press, 1992); Donald Worster, *Rivers of Empire: Water, Aridity and the Growth of the American West* (New York: Pantheon, 1985); Donald Worster, *Under Western Skies: Nature and History in the American West* (New York: Oxford University Press, 1992); Norris Hundley, *Water and the West: The Colorado River Compact and the Politics of Water in the American West* (Berkeley: University of California Press, 1975); Norris Hundley, *The Great Thirst: Californians and Water, 1770–1990* (Berkeley: University of California Press, 1992); Stanley Davison, *The Leadership of the Reclamation Movement: 1875–1902* (New York: Arno Press, 1979); and James Earl Sherow, *Watering the Valley: Development Along the High Plains of the Arkansas River* (Lawrence: University Press of Kansas, 1990).

3. These include Worster, *Rivers of Empire;* Marc Reisner, *Cadillac Desert: The American West and Its Disappearing Water* (New York: Viking Press, 1986); William A. Warne, *The Bureau of Reclamation* (New York: Frederick Praeger, 1973); Michael Robinson, *Water for the West* (Chicago: Public Works Historical Society, 1979); Karen Smith, *The Magnificent Experiment: Building the Salt River Project, 1870–1917* (Tucson: University of Arizona Press, 1986); Joseph Stevens, *Hoover Dam: An American Adventure* (Norman: University of Oklahoma Press, 1988); William L. Karhl, *Water and Power: The Conflict over Los Angeles' Water Supply in the Owens Valley* (Berkeley: University of California Press, 1982); Abraham Hoffman, *Vision or Villainy: Origins of the Owens Valley–Los Angeles Water Controversy* (College Station, Tex.: Texas A&M University Press, 1981).

4. State of California Department of Public Works, *Flow in California Streams* (Sacramento: California State Printing Office, 1923), p. 72. *Building the Ultimate Dam* adopts a definition of the American West that encompasses the transMississippi region lying west of the 98th meridian. One of the most distinctive environmental characteristics of this region is the relative lack of water. Aridity is not universally evident in western America, however (witness the temperate rain forests of the Pacific Northwest); and it is inappropriate to adopt a doctrinaire view that water-related conditions are the only way to define the region. For recent discussion of different definitions of the West, see Stephen Aron, "Lessons in Conquest: Towards a Greater Western History," *Pacific Historical Review* 63 (May 1994): 125–48; David M. Emmons,

"Constructed Province: History and the Making of the Last American West," *Western Historical Quarterly* 25 (Winter 1994): 437-60; and Susan Rhoades Neel, "A Place of Extremes: Nature, History, and the American West," *Western Historical Quarterly* 25 (Winter 1994): 489-506.

5. Water rights issues are discussed in M. Catherine Miller, *Flooding the Courtrooms: Law and Water in the Far West* (Lincoln: University of Nebraska Press, 1993); Robert G. Dunbar, *Forging New Rights in Western Waters* (Lincoln: University of Nebraska Press, 1983); Wells A. Hutchin, *The California Law of Water Rights* (Sacramento: California State Printing Division, 1956); Wells A. Hutchin, *Water Rights Laws in the Nineteen Western States* (Washington, D.C.: Government Printing Office, 1974); Michael C. Meyer, *Water in the Hispanic Southwest: A Social and Legal History, 1550–1850* (Tucson: University of Arizona Press, 1984); Samuel C. Wiel, *Water Rights in the Western States* (San Francisco: Bancroft-Whitney, 1905); A. E. Chandler, *Elements in Western Water Law* (San Francisco: Technical Publishing, 1912); and S. T. Harding, *Water Rights for Irrigation: Principles and Procedures for Engineers* (Palo Alto, Calif.: Stanford University Press, 1936). Charles Dumas et al., *Pueblo Indian Water Rights: Struggle for a Precious Resource* (Tucson: University of Arizona Press, 1984), provide data on the status of Native American water rights; George Thomas, *The Development of Institutions Under Irrigation with Special Reference to Early Utah* (New York: MacMillan, 1920), describes unique features of Utah water law in effect from 1852 through 1880. In California, so-called "Pueblo rights" also have been granted to the cities of Los Angeles and San Diego so they can completely control use of the Los Angeles and San Diego rivers. Hundley, *The Great Thirst*, pp. 45-58, 126-35, explains the origins of California's Pueblo rights and their dubious historical (but not legal) validity.

6. John Wesley Powell, *Report on the Lands of the Arid Region of the United States* (Washington, D.C.: Government Printing Office, 1879), was first submitted to Congress in 1878 [45th Cong., 2d sess., House Executive Document 73 (1878)]. The importance of dam building in the West is further reflected in James D. Schuyler, *Reservoirs for Irrigation, Water Power and Domestic Water Supply*, 2d ed. (New York: John Wiley & Sons, 1909), William G. Robbins, *Colony and Empire: The Capitalist Transformation of the American West* (Lawrence: University Press of Kansas), 1994.

7. Robert Gottlieb and Margaret Fitzsimmons, *Thirst for Growth: Water Agencies as Hidden Government in California* (Tucson: University of Arizona Press, 1991), pp. xviii, 2.

8. Donald Worster, *Dust Bowl: The Southern Plains in the 1930s* (New York: Oxford University Press, 1979); Sherow, *Watering the Valley;* William Cronon, *Nature's Metropolis: Chicago and the Great West* (New York: W. W. Norton, 1991); and William G. Robbins, *Colony and Empire: The Capitalist Transformation of the American West* (Lawrence: University Press of Kansas, 1994).

9. Worster, *Dust Bowl,* p. 6.

10. See, e.g., "Eastwood Bulletin," distributed in concert with *Western Engineering* 5 (March 1915).

11. John R. Freeman to Arthur P. Davis, September 26, 1912; and John R. Freeman and Alfred Noble to H. P. Wilson, October 17, 1912; Box 63, John R. Freeman Papers (MC51), Institute Archives and Special Collections, Massachusetts Institute of Technology, Cambridge, Massachusetts [hereafter Freeman Papers, MIT].

12. Reisner, *Cadillac Desert;* Arthur Morgan, *Dams and Other Disasters: A Century of the Army Corps of Engineers in Civil Works* (Boston: Port Sargent, 1971); and Martin Russell, *Glen Canyon and the Struggle for the Soul of the American West* (New York: Henry Holt, 1989). Other books in this vein include Tim Palmer, *Stanislaus: The Struggle for a River* (Berkeley: University of California Press, 1982); Arthur Maass, *Muddy Waters: The Army Engineers and the Nation's Rivers* (Cambridge, Mass.: Harvard University Press, 1951); Constance Elizabeth Hunt and Verne Huser, *Down by the River: The Impact of Federal Water Projects and Policies on Biological Diversity* (Washington, D.C.: Island Press, 1988); and Edward Goldsmith and Nicholas Hild Yard, *The Social and Environmental Effects of Large Dams* (San Francisco: Sierra Club Books, 1984).

13. Cronon, *Nature's Metropolis,* pp. 56-62, 263-69.

14. Donald Worster, "Transformations of the Earth: Toward an Agroecological Perspective in History," *Journal of American History* 76 (March 1990): 1089-90. See also Richard White, "American Environmental History: The Development of a New Historiographical Field," *Pacific Historical Review* 54 (August 1985): 297-335.

15. "Huntington Lake: San Joaquin & Eastern R.R.," promotional brochure published circa 1926 [author's collection].

16. Preliminary designs for a dam to flood the lower Grand Canyon are discussed in Diamond Creek Folder (#28), John S. Eastwood Papers, Water Resources Center Archives [hereafter, JSE, WRCA]. Also see "Surveying Dam Sites in the Grand Canyon," *Engineering News* 76 (August 17, 1916): 306-7; and "Hunt Re-Election Enlivens Colorado River Problems," *Engineering News Record* 93 (November 13,

1924): 805. Diamond Creek Dam was never built. (Also see p. 290, note 10.)

17. Sherow, *Watering the Valley*, p. 167.

18. See Daniel Rodgers, "In Search of Progressivism," *Reviews in American History* 10 (December 1982): 113-32.

19. George E. Mowry, *The California Progressives* (Berkeley: University of California Press, 1951); William Deverell and Tom Sitton, eds., *California Progressivism Revisited* (Berkeley: University of California Press, 1993).

20. JSE to Railroad Commission of California, March 17, 1913, in Great Western Power Company Application No. 357, Public Utility Commission Records, California State Archives, Sacramento, California.

21. Samuel D. Hays, *Conservation and the Gospel of Efficiency: The Progressive Conservation Movement, 1890-1920* (Cambridge, Mass.: Harvard University Press, 1959), pp. 2-7. Publications emphasizing the technical work of the Reclamation Service/Bureau of Reclamation include Ellis Armstrong et al., eds., *History of Public Works in the United States, 1776-1976* (Chicago: Public Works Historical Society, 1976) and Michael Robinson, *Water for the West* (Chicago: Public Works Historical Society, 1979). The agency's dams receive prominent notice in Carl Condit, *American Building Art: The Twentieth Century* (New York: Oxford University Press, 1961). This issue is discussed in Donald C. Jackson, "Engineering in the Progressive Era: A New Look at Frederick Haynes Newell and the U.S. Reclamation Service," *Technology and Culture* 34 (July 1993): 539-74.

22. Joseph B. Lippincott, "A National Reclamation Policy: Explanatory Statement Regarding Report of the Committee of the Irrigation Committee," *Transactions of the American Society of Civil Engineers* 95 (1931): 1307-20, confirms the Fourteenth Census (1920) report that only 2 million out of 27 million irrigated acres in the West involved funding from the federal government.

23. "A Survey of Hydroelectric Developments," *Electrical Engineering* (July 1934): 1087-94, covers the entire United States, but the statistics provided here refer only to power plants west of Denver. The one major pre–New Deal plant built by the Reclamation Service was at Roosevelt Dam near Phoenix, Arizona.

24. The Lenin quotation comes from Jonathan Coopersmith, *The Electrification of Russia, 1880-1926* (Ithaca, N.Y.: Cornell University Press, 1992), p. 3. It first appears in "Communism and Electrification," report of December 22, 1920, to the Eighth Congress of Soviets. The context for the statement is given in the excerpt from this report reproduced in Robert C. Tucker, *The Lenin Anthology* (New York: W. W. Norton, 1975), pp.

492-95. The Bloch quotation comes from Marc Bloch, *The Historian's Craft* (New York: Random House, 1953), p. 66.

25. Thomas P. Hughes, *Networks of Power: The Electrification of Western Society, 1880-1930* (Baltimore: Johns Hopkins University Press, 1984). See also David Nye, *Electrifying America: Social Meanings of a New Technology* (Cambridge, Mass.: MIT Press, 1991); and Harold Platt, *The Electric City: Energy and the Growth of the Chicago Area, 1880-1930*, (Chicago: University of Chicago Press, 1991). Before Hughes's book, the most important work on the history of the electric power industry was Harold Passer, *The Electrical Manufacturers: 1877-1900* (Cambridge, Mass.: Harvard University Press, 1953).

26. Charles M. Coleman, *P. G. and E. of California: The Centennial Story of the Pacific Gas and Electric Company* (New York: McGraw-Hill, 1952); William A. Myers, *Iron Men and Copper Wires: A Centennial History of the Southern California Edison Company* (Los Angeles: Trans-Anglo Books, 1984). For example, in *The Great Thirst*, Hundley mentions hydroelectricity only as it relates to government initiatives; he offers little more than passing reference to privately financed electric power development. Worster's *Rivers of Empire* only briefly discusses hydroelectric power.

27. See Hughes, *Networks of Power*, pp. 106-39, for discussion of the battle between Edison and others over the introduction of AC technology. It is now possible to transmit high-voltage DC power over long-distance transmission lines, but this technology was not developed until the latter part of the twentieth century.

28. Silvanus P. Thompson, *Polyphase Electric Currents and Alternate-Current Motors* (London: E. & F. N. Spon, 1895) pp. 43-110; Thomas P. Hughes, "The Science-Technology Interaction: The Case of High Voltage Power Transmission Systems," *Technology and Culture* 17 (October 1976): 646-62; and Charles F. Scott, "Long Distance Transmission for Lighting and Power," *Electrical Engineer* 13 (June 15, 1892): 601-3. Single-phase motors were operated at Telluride, but they were difficult to start and proved unworkable for general usage.

29. Louis C. Hunter, *A History of Industrial Power in the United States, 1780-1930: Waterpower*, vol. 1 (Charlottesville: University Press of Virginia, 1979); Louis C. Hunter and Lynwood Bryant, *A History of Industrial Power in the United States, 1780-1930: The Transmission of Power*, vol. 3 (Cambridge, Mass.: MIT Press, 1991); Terry Reynolds, *Stronger Than a Hundred Men: A History of the Vertical Water Wheel* (Baltimore: John Hopkins University Press, 1983).

30. *Mining and Scientific Press*, October 8,

1887, as quoted in Coleman, *P. G. and E. of California*, p. 103.

31. David P. Billington, *The Tower and the Bridge: The New Art of Structural Engineering* (New York: Basic Books, 1983).

32. Ibid., pp. 4-6, 24, 53.

33. Engineers interested in dam design theory are directed to Eric B. Kollgaard and Wallace L. Chadwick, eds., *Development of Dam Engineering in the United States* (New York: Pergamon Press, 1988). Published under the auspices of the United States Commission on Large Dams, this book offers a wealth of technical data but provides little historical background or social context. Readers desiring detailed mathematical analysis of multiple arch dam design should consult Glenn L. Enke, "Investigation of Elastic Behavior of a Multiple Arch Dam" (Ph.D dissertation, Utah State University, 1972). Written in the 1970s while Enke was a professor of civil engineering at Brigham Young University, this investigation formed the basis of a report presented to Salt Lake City concerning the structural safety of John Eastwood's Mountain Dell Dam.

34. Norman Smith, *A History of Dams* (Secaucus, N.J.: Citadel Press), pp. 124-25, 213-15. Also see Lars Jorgensen, "The Record of 100 Dam Failures," *Journal of Electricity* 44 (March 15 and April 1, 1920): 274-76, 320-21.

35. David G. McCullough, *The Johnstown Flood* (New York: Simon & Schuster, 1968); Harlan D. Unrau, *Historic Structure Report: The South Fork Dam* (Denver: National Park Service, 1979) contains an extensive bibliography.

36. For example, in John S. Eastwood to J. T. Crabbs, February 12, 1922 Anyox Dam Folder (#9), JSE, WRCA. Eastwood states: "As the designer of these [multiple arch] dams as a specialist and as a man drawing his revenue from the design of them . . . [a] careless design would destroy my field of operation." Hereafter, this source will be referenced as JSE [Folder #], WRCA.

Chapter Two

1. S. W. Helm, "Jawa, a Fortified Town of the Fourth Millennium B.C." *Archaeology* 27 (1974): 136-37; and S. W. Helm, *Jawa: Lost City of the Black Desert* (Ithaca, N.Y.: Cornell University Press, 1981). Key secondary sources in early dam history include: Norman Smith, *A History of Dams* (Secaucus, N.J.: The Citadel Press, 1972); Norman Smith, "The Roman Dams of Subiaco," *Technology and Culture* 11 (1970): 58-68; Norman Smith, *Man and Water: A History of Hydro-Technology* (New York: Charles Scribner's Sons,

1975). Nicholas J. Schnitter, *A History of Dams: The Useful Pyramids* (Rotterdam, Netherlands: A. A. Balkema, 1994), incorporates data drawn from his articles "The Evolution of the Arch Dam," *International Water Power and Dam Construction* 28 (October and November 1976): 34-40, 19-21; "The Evolution of Buttress Dams," *Water Power and Dam Construction* 36 (June and July 1984): 38-42, 20-22; and "Roman Dams," *Water Supply and Management* 3 (1979): 29-39. J. A. Garcia-Diego, "The Chapter on Weirs in the Codex of Juanelo Turriano: A Question of Authorship," *Technology and Culture* 17 (April 1976): 217-34; and "Old Dams in Extramadura," *History of Technology* 2 (1977): 95-124. See also Nicholas Adams, "Architecture for Fish: The Siennese Dam on the Bruna River—Structure and Designs, 1468-ca.1530," *Technology and Culture* 25 (October 1984): 768-97; and Peter Molloy, "Nineteenth Century Hydropower: Design and Construction of Lawrence Dam, 1845-1848," *Winterthur Portfolio* 15 (Winter 1980): 315-43.

2. Embankments built parallel to a river to prevent the inundation of nearby bottomland are often called *levees;* these earthen structures represent a type of flood control dam. On some rivers, low dams have been built in order to increase the depth of water so that boats and barges can navigate the stream more easily. Often these navigation dams are built with movable crests that allow the height of the dam to be reduced during periods of heavy floods so that the flow can more quickly pass downstream. Movable dams are primarily relevant to humid regions and will not be discussed in this book. An excellent early twentieth-century reference on these types of technology is B. F. Thomas and D. A. Watt, *The Improvement of Rivers* (New York: John Wiley & Sons, 1909).

3. George L. Dillman, "A Proposed New Type of Masonry Dam," *Transactions of the American Society of Civil Engineers* 49 (1902): 95.

4. James Leffel, *Leffel's Construction of Mill Dams* (Springfield, Ohio: self-published, 1881 [reprinted Park Ridge, N.J.: Noyes Press, 1972]), pp. 126-29, describes a mid-nineteenth-century "Log and Plank Dam" in Lycoming County, Pennsylvania, in which "round timbers are used throughout . . . [and] the whole interior of the dam was filled with stone and gravel."

5. The other main problem (besides overtopping) with earthfill and rockfill dams relates to water seeping through the structure and causing it to weaken and collapse. Seepage can result from water infiltrating the dam upward from the foundation or from water entering the upstream face of the structure from the reservoir. Seepage is impossible to prevent completely in earth and rockfill dams, but it can be controlled by using facing on

the upstream side or by constructing "impervious" corewalls made of concrete or densely packed clay in the structure's interior.

6. Smith, *History of Dams*, pp. 117–20. Any hydrostatic analysis is based on an understanding of how to calculate the position and intensity of an applied water load. In 1586, Simon Stevin first discussed this problem when he observed that "the water pressure acting against a vertical surface varies uniformly from zero at the top to a maximum at the deepest point." Analyzing stresses in dams is often neither simple nor straightforward. However, the manner in which water pressure exerts itself was widely understood prior to the nineteenth century. See Smith, *History of Dams*, pp. 192–93, for a discussion of Simon Stevin's 1586 treatise *De Beghinson des Waternichts*.

7. J. E. Gordon, *Structures: Or Why Things Don't Fall Down* (New York: Penguin Books, 1978), pp. 33–44, provides a good discussion of how the late seventeenth-century work of Newton and Hooke influenced the theoretical development of structural mechanics.

8. For complete references to dam design publications by Belidor, Bossut, Smeaton, Coulomb, and Moseley, see Molloy, "Nineteenth Century Hydropower," and Smith, *History of Dams*. In particular, Belidor utilized a simple method of structural analysis to calculate the amount of masonry required in a rectangular wall to prevent it from being tipped over by hydrostatic forces acting on one of its sides.

9. Edward Wegmann, *Design and Construction of Dams*, 3d ed. (New York: John Wiley & Sons, 1900), pp. 222–23.

10. Joel Justin, William Creager, and Julian Hinds, *Engineering for Dams*, vol. 3 (New York: John Wiley & Sons, 1945), p. 655. Similarly, James Sherard, Richard Woodward, Stanley Gizienski, and William Clevenger, *Earth and Earth Rock Dams* (New York: John Wiley & Sons, 1963), p. 46, states: "No specific rules can be given for selecting the inclination of the outside slopes of the embankment [for an earth dam]." Of course, ongoing research into the science of soil mechanics since the 1930s has (through techniques such as "slip-circle analysis") provided guidance on what types of soil are best suited for earthfill dams.

11. M. DeSazilly, "Sur un type de profil d'égale résistance proposé pour les murs des réservoirs d'eau," *Annales des Ponts et Chaussées* (1853): 191–222; and M. Delocre, "Mémoire sur la forme du profil à adopter pour les grande barrages en maçonnerie des réservoirs," *Annales des Ponts et Chaussées, Mémoires et Documents* (1866): 212–72. Both of these references are taken from Smith, *History of Dams*.

12. Smith, *History of Dams*, pp. 197–200. For

later structures such as the Ternay Dam (1865–1868) and the Bon Dam (1867–1870), Delocre selected maximum compressive stresses of 100 psi and 114 psi; but by modern standards, even these were extremely conservative.

13. Wegmann, *Design and Construction of Dams*, p. 69.

14. W. J. M. Rankine, "Report on the Design and Construction of Masonry Dams," *Engineer* 33 (January 5, 1872): 1–2.

15. In his article on the Lawrence Dam, Molloy reports that Moseley recognized the importance of the "middle third" in the early nineteenth century. However, when Rankine discussed the significance of the middle third in the 1870s, there is no evidence that anyone considered it a reiteration of previously discussed ideas. Smith makes no mention of Moseley in his *History of Dams*.

16. Smith, *History of Dams*, pp. 205–6; and Wegmann, *Design and Construction of Dams*, pp. 81–90.

17. This gravity "profile" was originally developed for a design for a structure termed the "Quaker Bridge Dam" that was to be built across the Croton River. In the 1890s, the planned structure was relocated to a new site in the river valley and renamed the "Croton Dam." However, the cross sections of the Quaker Bridge and Croton designs are essentially identical.

18. P. S. Bulson, J. B. Caldwell, and R. T. Severn, eds., *Engineering Structures: Developments in the Twentieth Century* (Bristol, U.K.: University of Bristol Press, 1983), pp. 229–59. Chapter 8 ("The Analysis and Design of Dams") offers an extended discussion of late nineteenth- and early twentieth-century British engineers' concerns about the theory of gravity dam design and "uplift."

19. George Holmes Moore, "Neglected First Principles of Masonry Dam Design," *Engineering News* 70 (September 4, 1913): 442–45.

20. Robert F. Leggett, "The Jones Falls Dam on the Rideau Canal," *Transactions of the Newcomen Society* 31 (1957–1959): 205–18.

21. Smith, *History of Dams*, pp. 181–83. Schnitter, "Evolution of the Arch Dam," notes that the Zola Dam was first described in an engineering journal in 1872.

22. Schnitter, "Evolution of the Arch Dam," provides a brief analysis of the structural nature of the Zola Dam. An examination of the profile of the Zola Dam reveals that the cylinder formula was not used as a rigid means of proportioning the structure. Rather, Zola used it as a guide to assist him in increasing the thickness of the arch as it descended into the canyon. Schnitter, *A History of Dams*, pp. 195–96, also notes construction of the

40-foot-high arch Parramatta Dam in Australia built in 1856-1857.

23. James Dix Schuyler, *Reservoirs for Irrigation, Water Power and Domestic Water Supply*, 2d ed. (New York: John Wiley & Sons, 1909), pp. 246-56, provides a good description and photograph of the original Bear Valley Dam. See also F. E. Brown, "The Bear Valley Dam," *Engineering News* 19 (June 23, 1888): 513-14.

24. Schuyler, *Reservoirs for Irrigation*, pp. 213-37. As the designer of this important dam, Schuyler provided an extensive description of it in his book. See also James D. Schuyler, "The Construction of the Sweetwater Dam," *Transactions of the American Society of Civil Engineers* 19 (1988): 202-3.

25. Albert Pelletreau, "Barrages cintrés en forme de voûte," *Annales des Pont et Chaussées* (1879). This reference is included in Schnitter, "Evolution of the Arch Dam."

26. Gardiner Williams, discussion of "Lake Cheeseman Dam and Reservoir," *Transactions of the American Society of Civil Engineers* 53 (1904): 183; and John S. Eastwood, "An Arch Dam Design for the Site of the Shoshone Dam," *Engineering News* 63 (June 9, 1910): 678-80.

27. Lars Jorgensen, "The Constant-Angle Arch Dam" *Transactions of the American Society of Civil Engineers* 78 (1915): 685-733. The Salmon Creek Dam was not, strictly speaking, a constant-angle structure; instead, it incorporated a "juggled radius" in order to fit the dam to the site and prevent "overhanging." For acknowledgment of this, see William Creager, *Engineering for Masonry Dams* (New York: John Wiley & Sons, 1917) p. 166. See also Nancy Farm Mannikko, "Seattle City Light's Constant Angle Arch Dam at Diablo Canyon." *IA: Journal of the Society for Industrial Archeology* 17 (1991): 17-31.

28. Schnitter, *A History of Dams*, pp. 147-48, describes several eighteenth-century masonry buttress dams in Mexico with vertical upstream faces.

29. Leffel, *Leffel's Construction of Mill Dams*, pp. 16-19; Schuyler, *Reservoirs for Irrigation*, pp. 502-4, illustrates the Faucherie Dam in Northern California (built in the 1870s)—a particularly large example of an all-timber buttress dam. Most designs of this type were restricted in size because of wood's limited strength and durability.

30. F. H. Bainbridge patented a steel dam on April 16, 1895 (No. 537,520), and this later served as the basis for the Ash Fork Dam. Henry Goldmark, "The Power Plant, Pipe Line and Dam of the Pioneer Electric Power Company at Ogden, Utah," *Transactions of the American Society of Civil Engineers* 38 (1897): 302-5, provides a description of a "structural steel dam" similar to Bainbridge's design. See also "Steel Dam at Ash Fork, Arizona, A.T. and S. F. Ry." *Engineering News* 39 (May 12, 1898): 299-300.

31. "The Redridge Dam," *Engineering News* 46 (August 15, 1901): 101-2. Complete descriptions of the earliest steel dams can be found in F. H. Bainbridge, "Structural Steel Dams," *Journal of the Western Society of Engineers* 10 (September, 1905): 615-37.

32. "The Hauser Lake Steel Dam in the Missouri River Near Helena, Montana," *Engineering News* 58 (November 14, 1907): 507-9; and F. L. Sizer, "The Break in the Hauser Lake Dam, Montana," *Engineering News* 59 (April 30, 1908): 491-92. Otis Ellis Hovey, *Steel Dams* (New York: American Institute of Steel Construction, 1935), provides a complete treatise on steel dam technology including the use of steel for facings and corewalls of rockfill and earthfill dams. This book was published to promote new markets for the U.S. steel industry during the depression of the 1930s. For insightful analysis of the technology and its demise, see Terry S. Reynolds, "A Narrow Window of Opportunity: The Rise and Fall of the Fixed Steel Dam." *IA: Journal of the Society for Industrial Archeology* 15 (1989): 1-20.

33. "A Hollow Concrete-Steel Dam at Theresa, N.Y.," *Engineering News* 50 (November 5, 1903): 403. The 1904 Ambursen Dam at Schuylerville is described in "A Hollow Reinforced Concrete Dam at Schuylerville, N.Y.," *Engineering News* 53 (April 27, 1905): 448-50.

34. The Division of Engineering and Industry, National Museum of American History, Smithsonian Institution, retains several early trade catalogs published by the Ambursen Company that describe the company's dams and methods of operation. These include *Relating to Concrete-Steel Dams* (ca. 1905); *Album for 1906* (1906); and *The Succeeding of Success* (ca. 1910). Of these, the first provides the best account of the design principles used by the Ambursen Company, and the third provides the best illustrated descriptions of the firm's early flat-slab dams. This literature provides no formulas for calculating the thickness of the upstream face, but presumably this involved three steps: calculating the bending stresses in the flat slabs, based on the distances between buttresses; selecting a maximum allowable stress low enough to preclude cracking; and determining the proper slab thickness, by relating the bending stresses to the maximum allowable stress. This type of simple analysis for determining the dimensions of a flat slab for the upstream face would have been well within the capabilities of many early twentieth-century civil engineers.

35. "La Prele Dam," *Engineering Record* 59 (April 3, 1909): 373-75; and "The La Prele Dam: A 130-Ft Hollow Reinforced Concrete Dam Near

Douglas, Wyoming," *Engineering News* 64 (November 10, 1910): 499–501. The latter article indicates that construction began in the spring of 1908 but was not finished until "late 1909." Although in isolated instances early Ambursen dams failed because of undermining of their earthen foundations, these collapses did not lead to abandonment of the technology. For a description of the Ashley Dam failure in Pittsfield, Massachusetts, see "The Undermining of a Reinforced-Concrete Dam at Pittsfield Mass.," *Engineering News* 61 (April 1, 1909): 345–47. The failure of the Stony River Dam in West Virginia in 1914 is described in F. W. Scheidenhelm, "The Reconstruction of the Stony River Dam," *Transactions of the American Society of Civil Engineers* 81 (1917): 907–1024. Other designs for flat-slab dams are given in Edward Wegmann, "Four Alternate Designs of Hollow Concrete Dams for Stony River Dam, Grant Co., W. Va.," *Engineering News* 68 (September 5, 1912): 446–49; J. F. Jackson, "Some Observations on the Stability of Dams," *Engineering News* 62 (July 29, 1909): 120–22; and Frank C. Osborn, "The Reversed Dam: A Hollow Concrete Dam of a New Type," *Engineering News* 68 (December 19, 1912): 1142–43.

36. See Schnitter, *A History of Dams*, pp. 118–20, for a description of these structures; on p. 65 he notes that portions of the Roman buttress dam at Esparragalejo in Spain feature a curved upstream face, making it a partial multiple-arch dam.

37. Ibid., p. 151.

38. Goldmark, "Dam at Ogden, Utah," pp. 246–314. Because Goldmark implies that his dam is actually in the process of being built, some later historians have incorrectly surmised that the design became a physical reality. For example, see Carl Condit, *American Building Art, The Nineteenth Century* (New York: Oxford University Press, 1960), p. 240.

39. Because Goldmark's arch rings were to be inclined at a steep angle of 65 degrees, there was a relatively small vertical component of water load. Consequently, the resultant fell near the downstream end of the buttresses' center third. Goldmark also determined that no overturning along the downstream axis of the dam would be possible and that, because of the angle of the resultant, the dam would not slide along any horizontal plane. To ensure against excessive leakage, Goldmark proposed covering the upstream faces of the arch rings with 1/4-inch-thick steel plates. He acknowledged, however, that it might be just as beneficial—and that it certainly would be much cheaper, to coat the arch-rings with asphalt instead.

40. "The Belubula Dam, New South Wales,"

Engineering News 40 (September 8, 1898): 148; the structure was built by the Lyndhurst-Goldfields Company to support mining operations. The only major dam of similar design was the Aziscohos Dam in Maine, completed in 1910. See Seth Moulton, "The Aziscohos Dam, Rangeley Lake Region, Maine," *Engineering News* 65 (March 9, 1911): 288–91.

41. Dillman, "New Type of Dam," pp. 94–111; Edward Wegmann's comments appear on pp. 103–6, where he further opined that "the design of such structures would have to be based upon the results obtained by actual construction, low dams being built at first, and others of greater height when the lower dams had stood successfully for some years."

42. Early irrigation by Native Americans is described in R. Douglas Hurt, *Indian Agriculture in America: Prehistory to the Present* (Lawrence: University Press of Kansas, 1987), pp. 19–26; Norris Hundley, *The Great Thirst: Californians and Water, 1770–1990* (Berkeley: University of California Press, 1992), pp. 16–24, discusses irrigation in California prior to Spanish settlement.

43. Water use in the Spanish era is described in Michael C. Meyer, *Water in the Hispanic Southwest: A Social and Legal History, 1550–1850* (Tucson: University of Arizona Press, 1984). For a photograph and brief description of the 1743 Espada Dam in San Antonio, Texas, see T. Lindsay Baker, *Water for the Southwest* (New York: American Society of Civil Engineers, 1973) pp. 121–23; Schuyler, *Reservoirs for Irrigation*, pp. 213–14, describes the eighteenth-century Spanish mission dams at San Diego and San Gabriel, and includes a good photograph of the San Diego Dam.

44. For more on Mormon irrigation efforts, see Charles Brough, *Irrigation in Utah* (Baltimore: Johns Hopkins University Press, 1898); George Thomas, *The Development of Institutions Under Irrigation with Special Reference to Early Utah* (New York: Macmillan, 1920); and Leonard J. Arrington and Thomas C. Anderson, "The 'First' Irrigation Reservoir in the United States: The Newton, Utah Project," *Utah Historical Quarterly* 39 (Summer 1971): 207–23.

45. John Wesley Powell, *Report on the Lands of the Arid Region of the United States* (Washington, D.C.: Government Printing Office, 1879). This report was first submitted to Congress in 1878 [45th Cong., 2d sess., *House Executive Document 73* (1878)] and published for general distribution in 1879. Powell's career is recounted in Wallace Stegner, *Beyond the Hundredth Meridian* (Boston: Houghton Mifflin, 1953). In the 1850s and 1860s, other Anglo-American groups followed the Mormons and established their own irrigation-based settlements. For example, German farmers established the Anaheim

Colony in southern California in the 1850s while the Union Colony in Greeley, Colorado, was settled in the late 1860s. See Richard D. Bateman, "Anaheim Was an Oasis in the Wilderness," *Journal of the West* 4 (January 1965): 1-20; and David Boyd, *Greeley and the Union Colony* (Greeley, Colo.: Tribune Press, 1890).

46. See Everett Sterling, "The Powell Irrigation Survey, 1888-1893," *Mississippi Valley Historical Review* 27 (1940): 421-34; and John T. Ganoe, "The Origin of a National Reclamation Policy," *Mississippi Valley Historical Review* 18 (June 1931): 34-52. The best historical analysis of the Powell Irrigation Survey and its demise in 1893 appears in Donald J. Pisani, *To Reclaim a Divided West: Water, Law, and Public Policy 1848-1902* (Albuquerque: University of New Mexico Press, 1992), pp. 127-168.

47. One of the best sources on early rockfill mining dams is A. J. Bowie, *A Practical Treatise on Hydraulic Mining in California* (New York: D. Van Nostrand, 1905), pp. 94-113. Schuyler, *Reservoirs for Irrigation*, pp. 497-509, also includes descriptions and photographs of these early California mining dams. A large timber mining dam that was built without rockfill is described in E. M. Chandler, "High Timber Dams in California," *California Journal of Technology* 12 (November 1908): 32-34.

48. The Shaver Lake Dam was built by the Fresno Flume and Irrigation Company to supply water for a lumber flume. It was later taken over by Southern California Edison Company as part of their Big Creek hydroelectric power system and replaced with a concrete gravity dam. See Edwin M. Eaton, *Vintage Fresno* (Fresno, Calif.: Huntington Press, 1965), pp. 26-30, for a brief description of the company and a photograph of the dam under construction in 1892. The Escondido Dam is described as "the first rock-fill dam built in California for irrigation purposes" in "Rock-Fill Dams in California," *Engineering News* 40 (July 28, 1898): 62-64.

49. See Schuyler, *Reservoirs for Irrigation*, pp. 53-54; "The Walnut Grove Dam," *Engineering News* 20 (October 20, 1888): 303-4; "The Walnut Grove Dam Disaster," *Engineering News* 22 (March 8, 1890): 229-30; and "The Walnut Grove Dam Failure," *Engineering News* 22 (April 26, 1890): 389-90.

50. See Randall E. Rohe, "Hydraulicking in the American West: The Development and Diffusion of a Mining Technique," *Montana, the Magazine of Western History* (Spring 1985): 18-35.

51. Succinct descriptions of all these dams can be found in Wegmann, *Design and Construction of Dams*, pp. 237-39. See also Burr Bassell, *Earth Dams: A Study*, 2d ed. (New York: Engineering

News Publishing Company, 1907), for an excellent review of turn-of-the-century earth dam technology. Much of the data in the book originally appeared in various articles Bassell previously wrote for *Engineering News*.

52. James D. Schuyler, "Recent Practice in Hydraulic-Fill Dam Construction," *Transactions of the American Society of Civil Engineers* 57 (1907): 196-277, provides a detailed description of several hydraulic dams built in the American West; most were constructed under the direction of Julius Howells.

53. Bassell, *Earth Dams*, pp. 17-32 includes a good description of the 1902 Tabeaud Dam (120 feet high) built in California by the Standard Electric Company. The earthen structure was built up by "four-horse teams" pulling "dump-wagons holding 3 cu[bic] yds each."

54. Schuyler, *Reservoirs for Irrigation*, pp. 237-46; 256-74. The Folsom Dam was used for hydroelectric power generation, while the Hemet and La Grange dams were built for irrigation.

55. Charles L. Harrison and Silas H. Woodward, "Lake Cheeseman Dam and Reservoir," *Transactions of the American Society of Civil Engineers* 53 (1904): 89-209.

56. Schuyler, *Reservoirs for Irrigation*, pp. 342-43; and "The Five Dams and Wood Stave Conduit of the Southern California Mountain Water Co.," *Engineering News* 51 (April 7, 1904): 335-38. Schuyler notes a significant circumstance that helped prompt a bold design for the Upper Otay site: "If the [arch] dam should break under full reservoir pressure no very serious consequences could ensue, on account of the large size of the Lower Otay reservoir, into which the water would be discharged." The Upper Otay design is credited to E. S. Babcock, president of the Southern California Mountain Water Company; it is the only dam he is known to have designed.

57. Schuyler, *Reservoirs for Irrigation*, pp. 502-4.

Chapter Three

1. Charles Allen Whitney, "The Life and Times of John S. Eastwood" [Unpublished manuscript, circa 1970, on file at Fresno City and County Historical Society, Fresno, California], chapter 2, p. 2; and Charles Allen Whitney, "John S. Eastwood: Unsung Genius of the Drawing Board," *Montana, the Magazine of Western History* 19 (Summer 1969): 41. Eastwood was born with the Dutch name "Van Oosterhout," but as a young man he anglicized it. In an application "For Admission" to the American Society of Civil Engi-

neers in 1913, he reported his birthplace as Jordan, Minnesota; see Box 63, Freeman Papers, MIT.

2. Privacy laws prevent the release of Eastwood's University of Minnesota transcript; however, annual catalogs published in 1878–1881 do not list him as receiving a degree. In a public hearing before the California Railroad Commission in 1919, he referred to the University of Minnesota as his "Alma Mater." See files of the Hydraulic Division, State Railroad Commission, "Application No. 4319, Palmdale Water Company; Reporter's Transcript, March 3, 1919," p. 5, Public Utility Commission Records, California State Archives, Sacramento. Whitney, "Unsung Genius," p. 41, indicates that he attended the State Normal School at Mankato, Minnesota, prior to 1878. In "For Admission [to ASCE]" Eastwood stated that in "1877 and 1878 (between school terms) asst. to George W. Cooley, Minneapolis, as chainman and rodman.; 1878 and 1880 attended State Univ. of Minnesota." Box 63, Freeman Papers, MIT.

3. "For Admission [to ASCE]" reports Eastwood's early railroad experience as: "1880 and 1881 instrumentman and asst. res. engr for six months, then res. eng. in charge of construction on Pacific Extension, Minneapolis & St Louis R.R.; spring 1881 to 1882 first in charge of a construction division as asst., and later as res. engr., on Oregon California Railroad; then took charge of a division of Oregon Ry. & Navigation Co. having charge of bridges, track changes and yard location; winter 1882 leveler with party in Blue Mts. of eastern Oregon, summer 1883 had charge of construction of logging railroads near Kalama, Wash., Oct. 1883 began private practice as an engr. at Fresno, Cal." Box 63, Freeman Papers, MIT.

4. W. Turrentine, Rand F. Herbert, and Stephen R. Wee, eds., *Report of the Board of Commissioners on the Irrigation of the San Joaquin, Tulare, and Sacramento Valleys of the State of California, 1873* (Washington, D.C.: Government Printing Office, 1990), pp. 3–18, provide a description of early irrigation in the Central Valley. Although some mining activity occurred along the San Joaquin River, it was minor compared with the "bonanza" strikes to the north.

5. Edwin M. Eaton, *Vintage Fresno* (Fresno: Huntington Press, 1965) p. 17; and *Description of Fresno County* (Fresno: Fresno Land Office, 1886), p. 24. Of course, "boosterism" was hardly confined to Fresno; for an analysis of this phenomenon, see William Cronon, *Nature's Metropolis: Chicago and the Great West* (New York: W. W. Norton, 1991), pp. 34–46; and Glenn Dumke,

The Boom of the Eighties in Southern California (San Marino, Calif.: Huntington Library, 1944).

6. Donald J. Pisani, *From Family Farm to Agribusiness: The Irrigation Crusade in California and the West, 1850–1931* (Berkeley: University of California Press, 1984) pp. 121–28; and Virginia Thickens, "Pioneer Agricultural Colonies of Fresno County," *California Historical Quarterly* 25 (March/June 1946): 138, 169–77. An excellent map of colonies and canals surrounding Fresno appears in Elwood Mead, *Report of Irrigation Investigations in California* (Washington, D.C.: Government Printing Office, 1901), p. 260 [plate xxiv]. Fresno's early history is also discussed in Charles W. Clough and William B. Secrest, *Fresno County: The Pioneer Years from the Beginning* (Fresno, Calif.: Panorama West Books, 1984); Wallace Elliot, *History of Fresno County* (San Francisco: W. W. Elliot, 1882); and *Imperial Fresno* (Fresno, Calif.: Fresno Republican Publishing, 1897); Paul Vandor, *History of Fresno County* (Los Angeles: Historic Record, 1919); Lilbourne Alsip Winchell, *History of Fresno County and the San Joaquin Valley* (Fresno, Calif.: A. H. Cawston, 1933). A popular history of the San Joaquin River is provided in Gene Rose, *San Joaquin: A River Betrayed* (Fresno, Calif.: Linrose Publishing, 1992).

7. Kevin Starr, *Inventing the Dream: California Through the Progressive Era* (New York: Oxford University Press, 1985), pp. 128–75, provides background on California's agricultural development in the late nineteenth century. Donald J. Pisani, *To Reclaim a Divided West: Water, Law and Public Policy 1848–1902* (Albuquerque: University of New Mexico Press, 1992), pp. 69–108, documents irrigation and agricultural development throughout the West during this era.

8. Miss Ella Tabor came to Fresno in 1884 to assist in organizing "a young people's program" for the Baptist Church. John Eastwood taught Sunday school at the church, and the two fell in love. They were married in the fall of 1885. They never had children. See Whitney, "Life and Times," chapter 1, pp. 24–28, for more on their romance.

9. The July 12, 1884, *Fresno Morning Republican*, reports Eastwood opening an office as "civil engineer and surveyor." Whitney, "Life and Times," chapter 1, pp. 3–4, indicates that Eastwood's first stationery letterhead advertised him as a "Civil Engineer, Surveyor and Draughtsman" capable of "Land Surveying, Canal and Irrigation Work, Subdividing of City Lots" in "Fresno and adjoining Counties." A business card circa 1884 in the administration files of the Water Resources Center Archives, Berkeley, California, advertises Eastwood as a "Deputy County Engineer." One of Eastwood's early forays into the Sierra Nevada is

documented in an 1884 photograph by W. R. Rodd, showing Eastwood at the "Smith and Mc-Cradle Millyard." See photo box "Mountain Scenes: Big Trees and Others," Fresno City and County Historical Society.

10. The October 7, 1885, *Fresno Weekly Expositor* reported approval of the city's incorporation by a vote of 277 for to 185 against. Eastwood's appointment as city engineer is noted in the November 7, 1885, *Fresno Expositor* (see newspaper clipping file, Fresno City and County Historical Society). Ben Randal Walker, *Fresno: 1872–1885, A Municipality in the Making* (Fresno, Calif.: Fresno County Historical Society Publications, 1934), p. 15, notes that he started his duties on November 2, 1885. His appointment to the city's health board in January 1886 is documented in Vandor, *History of Fresno County*, p. 415.

11. Winchell, *History of Fresno County and the San Joaquin Valley*, p. 145, indicates that the original pay in 1885 for Fresno's street superintendent and for the city attorney was in each case $25 per month. Eastwood's salary as engineer is not listed in this source, but it was probably comparable.

12. California State Mining Bureau, *Tenth Annual Report of the State Mineralogist* (Sacramento: State Office, 1890), pp. 183–85. Eastwood's numerous mining and mineral claims in Fresno County during the late 1880s and 1890s are referenced in "Mining Claims Index"; for example, see his December 13, 1889, claim to "Alcalde Oil Claim No. 1" in the Coalinga district in "Mining Claims," Book G, p. 377; and his February 13, 1896, claim to the "San Joaquin Placer Mine" in "Mining Claims," Book J, p. 53. Deed records for land transactions document several purchases by Eastwood, including a ranch along the Kings River in 1890 (Book 82, p. 222, July 30, 1890) that eventually was the site of his death. All sources in Fresno County Recorder's Office, Fresno, California. In "For Admission," Eastwood reported: "1890 and 1891 laid out and built logging railroads (about $50,000); summer 1892 located and built logging railroads (about $50,000) for Smith & Moore Lumber Co.," Box 63, Freeman Papers, MIT.

13. See Hank Johnston, *They Felled the Redwoods* (Los Angeles: Trans Anglo Books, 1966). Also see Vandor, *History of Fresno County*, pp. 157–61; and Marley Brown and Michael Elling, "An Historical Overview of Redwood Logging Resources Within the Hume Lake Ranger District, Sequoia National Forest, California" (May 1981), on file at the Sequoia National Forest headquarters, Porterville, California.

14. Hank Johnston, *Thunder in the Mountains* (Los Angeles: Trans Anglo Press, 1968), pp. 16,

30–33, provides descriptions of the Madera Flume and Trading Company's 52-mile-long flume between Soquel Mill and Madera, the Kings River Lumber Company's (later the Sanger Lumber Company's) 54-mile-long flume from Millwood to Sanger, and the Fresno Flume and Irrigation Company's 46-mile-long flume from Shaver Lake to Clovis. See also J. P. Martin, "The Design of Log Flumes," *Engineering News* 68 (November 14, 1912): 908–13.

15. The October 21, 1887, *Fresno Morning Republican* cites Eastwood as surveying the "Moore and Smith Flume." Field notebook #5/20 "1886–1888," JSE 11, WRCA, records data from this flume survey dating to December 1886; this same notebook also contains an undated survey of more than 2,000 sequoia in the Converse Basin, recording the number of trees per section (for example, in section 5, Township 13 S, Range 28 E, he inventoried 240 trees) and estimating the aggregate timber to be worth $5,475,000. His March 22, 1889, patent from the federal government for 160 acres of land in the Boulder Creek sequoia groves is documented in "Patents," Book X, p. 75, Fresno County Recorders Office. "A California Flume for Transporting Lumber," *Engineering News* 25 (April 11, 1891): 356, credits J. M. Graham with building the Sanger flume.

16. See Harold K. Steen, *The U.S. Forest Service: A History* (Seattle: University of Washington Press, 1976), pp. 24–25; and M. Nelson McGeary, *Gifford Pinchot: Forester–Politician* (Princeton, N.J.: Princeton University Press, 1960), pp. 34–40.

17. John Muir's reverence for the giant sequoia is well known and need not be documented at length; it is worth noting, however, that the Boulder Creek sequoia groves within which Eastwood surveyed and purchased 160 acres of land were specifically noted by Muir in *Our National Parks* (San Francisco: Sierra Club Books, 1991), p. 222 [originally published 1894], and in a journal entry made on June 13, 1891, when he traveled through the Kings River region and commented "many grand sequoias along Boulder Creek, young and old, particularly fine and perfect on the right hand as we go up the trail nearly to the summit of the basin." See Linnie Marsh Wolfe, ed., *John of the Mountains: The Unpublished Journals of John Muir* (Madison: University of Wisconsin Press, 1938), p. 333.

18. Whitney, "Life and Times," chapter 1, pp. 37–38, reports that Eastwood's "services were largely in connection with the construction of levees and land reclamation associated with the irrigation division of the company. He had, however, built the mainline logging railroad for the lumber division whose headquarters were at Shaver Lake."

19. A good history of logging in the Pine

Ridge/Shaver Lake District is provided in Gene Rose, *Reflections of Shaver Lake, Center of Activities on Pine Ridge for More Than One Hundred Years* (Fresno, Calif.: Panorama West Publishing, 1987); Eaton, *Vintage Fresno,* pp. 26–30, includes an 1892 construction photograph of the rockfill dam at Shaver Lake.

20. Pisani, *Family Farm to Agribusiness,* pp. 250–82; and Thomas E. Malone, "The California Irrigation Crisis of 1886: Origins of the Wright Act" (Ph.D. dissertation, Stanford University, 1965). The location of the proposed Sunset Irrigation District is illustrated in F. H. Newell, *Report on Agriculture by Irrigation in the Western Part of the United States at the Eleventh Census: 1890* (Washington, D.C.: Government Printing Office, 1894), pp. 38–40. The district was formally organized in March 1891.

21. Whitney, "Life and Times," chapter 1, pp. 42–44; "An Irrigation Job," *San Francisco Chronicle,* February 3, 1894, indicates that Schussler prepared the initial plans for the project. When no contractors would bid on these plans, they were turned over to Eastwood, who completed them in April 1893; see Sunset Irrigation District Folder (#61), JSE, WRCA. See also "Hermann Frederick August Schussler," *Transactions of the American Society of Civil Engineers* 83 (1919–1920): 2329–30. The *San Francisco Call,* February 3, 1894, accuses T. L. Reed (a local real estate promoter) of attempting to defraud the district. Eastwood is noted as engineer but is not mentioned as being involved with Reed's manipulations. The district's problems are described in Frank Adams, *Irrigation Districts in California, 1887–1915* (Sacramento: California State Printing Office, 1916), pp. 35–37. Pisani, *Family Farm to Agribusiness,* pp. 264–70, discusses difficulties afflicting many Wright Act districts.

22. *Fresno County Centennial Almanac* (Fresno, Calif.: Fresno County Centennial Committee, 1956), p. 151. In this compendium, notice is given of the Fresno Gas Company (1881), the Fresno Gaslight Company (ca. 1883), the Fresno Electric Light and Power Company (1886), and the Fresno Gas and Electric Light Company (1888); see *Fresno Daily Evening Expositor,* August 17, 1894, for quotation on "Doused the Glim"; the *Fresno Daily Evening Expositor,* December 25, 1895, describes the city's gas works and notes that "one of the hindrances to the supply of cheap gas was the excessive freight charges for coal and materials to manufacture [it]."

23. See *Electrical World* 20 (July 2, 1892): 3–4; *Electrical World* 21 (January 21, 1893): 45; and "The Oerlikon Three-Phase Alternator," *Electrical Engineer* 12 (August 26, 1891): 231–32. Scholars desiring an in-depth discussion of California's early

hydroelectric power development should consult William Allen Myers, "Electricity in Orange County, California, 1890–1940: A Case Study of the Socio-economic Impact of Technology," M.A. thesis, California State University, Fullerton, 1991.

24. All material on Decker's life is taken from George Low, "Biographical: Almerian William Decker," *Journal of Electricity Power and Gas* 13 (January 1903): 96–98. During the late 1880s, Decker worked for Charles F. Brush (a pioneer in electric arc lighting) and for the Forest City Electrical Works in Cleveland.

25. C. G. Baldwin, "The Heretofore Unpublished Facts of the Pomona Case," *Journal of Electricity* 7 (February 1899): 23, describes how William Stanley of Pittsfield, Massachusetts, helped convince Westinghouse to design a 10,000-volt system at Pomona. See also *Electrical Engineer* 13 (March 23, 1892): 314; *Electrical Engineer* 14 (August 3, 1892): 100; and George P. Low, "10,000 Volt Alternating Current Long Distance Transmission at Pomona, California," *Electrical Engineer* 16 (August 2, 1893): 97–99. Later alterations are described in Robert Sibley, "The Pacific Light and Power System," *Journal of Electricity Power and Gas* 28 (February 24, 1912): 168.

26. George P. Low, "Edison Electric Company of Los Angeles," *Journal of Electricity Power and Gas* 13 (January 1903): 11–13.

27. Low, "Almerian William Decker," p. 98. Low also notes that Decker was working on the Mount Lowe Railway at this time.

28. When discussing the introduction of polyphase technology to the United States, most recent authors have stressed the importance of Westinghouse. See Harold Passer, *The Electrical Manufacturers, 1875–1900* (Cambridge, Mass.: Harvard University Press, 1953), pp. 296–345; and Thomas P. Hughes, *Networks of Power: The Electrification of Western Society, 1880–1930* (Baltimore: Johns Hopkins University Press, 1984), pp. 106–40.

29. Low, "Edison Electric Company of Los Angeles," pp. 11–12, indicates that bids for the Redlands were called for February 5, 1893. Three companies submitted proposals. Westinghouse offered to build a two-phase system, while the Electrical Engineering Company of San Francisco offered to build a direct-current system. Only General Electric complied with Decker's specifications for a three-phase system.

30. In J. W. Hammond's official company history, *Men and Volts: The Story of General Electric* (Philadelphia: J. B. Lippincott, 1941) pp. 231–32, the Redlands plant is referred to as GE's first three-phase installation. In the engineering press, Redlands was also referred to as the first commercial polyphase system in the United States. See "The

First Three-Phase Transmission Plant in the United States," *Electrical Review* 23 (November 29, 1893): 179; and "The First Three-Phase Transmission Plant in the United States," *Electrical World* 34 (February 16, 1894): 171. However, in a typewritten note labeled "Extracts from GE Catalogue #5 — August 1894" contained within the GE historical file at Schenectady, New York, reference is made to an 1893 three-phase GE installation in Hartford, Connecticut. In 1897, *Electrical World* briefly mentioned a three-phase 300-kw GE generator that transmitted power to a motor in the company's Hartford substation and helped power a DC generator used in a street railway system. The three-phase power was used only as a means of supplementing an existing DC generator and did not constitute a commercial transmission system in its own right. See William S. Robb, "Long Distance Transmission of Power at Hartford," *Electrical World* 29 (February 13, 1897): 227-29. Following Redlands, the next commercial three-phase systems installed by GE were at Concord, New Hampshire, Taftville, Connecticut, and Columbia, South Carolina, which began operation in late 1893 and early 1894. In 1933-1934, the Redlands plant was slightly modified to increase productivity and to meld more easily with later development of the regional system.

31. The origins of General Electric's Pacific coast operations are discussed in a biographical note on James Lighthipe, the first chief engineer of the company's San Francisco office. See *Journal of Electricity* 6 (July, 1898): 21. See also Low, "Almerian William Decker," p. 96.

32. "The Folsom-Sacramento Power Transmission," *Journal of Electricity* 1 (September 1895): 55-63. The Livermore family had hopes of developing water power at the site as early as the 1860s but not until convict labor from nearby Folsom Prison was used to construct the massive gravity dam did the dream become reality.

33. Charles M. Coleman, *P. G. and E. of California: The Centennial Story of Pacific Gas and Electric Company, 1852-1952* (McGraw-Hill, 1952), pp. 116-27, describes the history of the Folsom development from the 1850s through its use in generating AC power for Sacramento in the 1890s.

34. A California "style" of hydroelectric power systems is described in Thomas P. Hughes, "Regional Technological Styles," in *Technology and Its Impact on Society* (Stockholm: Tekniska Museet, 1979), pp. 211-34.

35. The Folsom-Sacramento system also operated at 11,000 volts, as did the Niagara Falls-Buffalo transmission line that became operational in late 1896.

36. George P. Low, "The Fresno Transmission Plant," *Journal of Electricity* 2 (April 1896): 79-89, p. 81. The National Tube Works of McKeesport, Pennsylvania, also fabricated parts of the penstock.

37. In the *Fresno Daily Evening Expositor*, December 25, 1895, Eastwood revealed that he first appreciated the possibility of a power plant along the North Fork of the San Joaquin in 1885, when he observed the terrain during survey work in the Pine Ridge region on the southern bank of the main San Joaquin. See also Whitney, "Life and Times," chapter 1, pp. 52-55.

38. On November 13 and November 15, 1893, Eastwood and Frank Thresher (a man whose name appears nowhere else in documentary material related to Eastwood or the SJEC) filed claims for a total of 20,000 miners inches (or 400 cfs) of water from the North Fork of the San Joaquin River; these claims were superseded on January 13 and May 18, 1894, when Eastwood and J. J. Seymour filed claims for a aggregate of 30,000 miners inches (600 cfs) from both the "South Fork of the North Fork" and the "North Fork of the North Fork" of the San Joaquin River; *Water Rights Book No. 1*, pp. 19, 31, 40, 42, Madera County Recorder's Office, Madera, California. Whitney, "Life and Times," chapter 1, pp. 52-56, describes the origins of Eastwood's hydroelectric power plan for Fresno as reflected in Ella Eastwood's diary for 1894. Unfortunately, the present location of this diary is not known. The partnership undertaken between Eastwood and Seymour on January 15, 1894, is noted in the *Fresno Daily Evening Expositor*, December 25, 1895.

39. "San Joaquin Electric Company: Articles of Incorporation," dated March 30, 1895; California State Archives. All seven members of the company's original board of directors resided in Fresno. Seymour graduated from Illinois State University in Civil Engineering in 1877; after performing mining work in California and Colorado, he became president of the Fresno Water Company in 1890. In 1895, the water company merged many operations with the SJEC, and Seymour became president of the latter firm. See *Journal of Electricity* 5 (June 1898): 180-81. See also *Fresno Daily Evening Expositor*, April 2, 1895.

40. See "Electric Power Transmission at Fresno, California," *Electrical Review* [London] 41 (July 23, 1897): 108, which states that "The Municipal Investment Company of Chicago and London took an interest in the company and advanced the necessary capital." The same firm is identified as supporting the Fresno plant in *Journal of Electricity* 3 (July 1896): 37. At this time, Howells was an "Engineer-Inspector" with the Municipal Investment Company.

41. *Fresno Daily Evening Expositor,* July 13, 1895.

42. The most complete article describing the San Joaquin Electric Company's initial system is Low, "The Fresno Transmission Plant." The system's electrical equipment is described in C. E. Dutcher, "Some Details of the Fresno Plant," *Journal of Electricity* 4 (April 1897): 1–9. In Frederick Hall Fowler, *Hydroelectric Power Systems of California and Their Extensions into Oregon and Nevada* (Washington, D.C.: Government Printing Office, 1923), pp. 454–58, the date for beginning construction is given as April 5, 1895.

43. By the mid-1890s, numerous books on electricity were available. Many of these books, such as T. O'Conor Sloane's *Electricity Simplified: The Theory and Practice of Electricity* (New York: Norman W. Henly Publishing, 1891) and E. T. Bubier's *Questions and Answers About Electricity* (Lynn, Mass.: Bubier Publishing, 1892) were intended for the educated general public. Books for engineers and academics either discussed electrical phenomena from a highly theoretical perspective or addressed issues related to the design of dynamo-electric machinery; examples include Silvanus Thompson, *Lectures on the Electromagnet* (New York: W. J. Johnston, 1891), and Francis B. Crocker and Schuyler S. Wheeler, *The Practical Management of Dynamos and Motors* (New York: D. Van Nostrand, 1894). During the late 1890s, books specifically oriented to problems involved in large-scale commercial power and light projects began to appear. Perhaps the most important of these was Louis Bell, *Electric Power Transmission: A Practical Treatise for Practical Men* (New York: Electrical World Engineer, 1897). Bell's text contained information relevant to hydroelectric power development, but it was published too late to assist Eastwood's design efforts. Eastwood could have drawn some guidance from journals and similar sources, but even they would have been of minimal use in planning the high-head Fresno plant.

44. Johnston, *Thunder in the Mountains,* describes logging operations in the area upstream from Eastwood's system. See also A. G. Wilson, "Reminiscences of Power Development on the San Joaquin," *Journal of Electricity* 45 (September 15, 1920): 268–69, for a brief description of the Quartz Mountain Mining Company's "Old French Ditch," which was built in 1875. Although Eastwood made no use of this ditch, parts of it were later used to support hydroelectric power development.

45. During the summer of 1895, the work crew numbered "about 150 men"; by October it had dropped to "about a 100 men." See *Fresno Daily Evening Expositor,* September 2, 1895, and Octo-

ber 18, 1895. Low, "The Fresno Transmission Plant," p. 87, indicates that 23 men worked on the "line corps" that constructed the transmission line to Fresno.

46. Johnston, *Thunder in the Mountains,* provides a map showing the general area of the SJEC system. "The 35-Mile Three-Phase Transmission at Fresno Cal.," *Electrical World* 27 (May 30, 1896): 661, reports that the diversion canal dropped at a rate of 5.28 feet per mile.

47. Construction progress on the SJEC system is documented in the *Fresno Daily Evening Expositor,* July 13, 1895; November 23, 1895; December 25, 1895; and February 24, 1896.

48. *Fresno Daily Evening Expositor,* April 4, 1896.

49. *Fresno Daily Evening Expositor,* April 15, 1896; and Whitney, "Life and Times," chapter 1, p. 21. Eastwood adhered to the social conventions of the late Victorian era, and having his wife start the new power system would have been considered quite appropriate.

50. Initial problems with "faulty" electrical apparatus are noted in the *Fresno Daily Evening Expositor,* April 27, 1896. In addition, some secondary sources report that an unnamed "German engineer" made a mistake when first operating the penstock valves and allowed water to pour into the powerhouse. The "engineer" then reportedly left the Fresno area, never to return. Although a minor incident of this type did occur, it did not cause any serious damage. The reference to a "German engineer" who supposedly caused the accident and then departed the area is apparently completely fallacious. For a succinct telling of this tale, see Coleman, *P. G. and E. of California,* p. 187. A version based on Coleman's account is repeated (with some embellishment) in Todd A. Shallot, "Water and the Rise of Public Ownership on the Fresno Plain, 1850 to 1978" (City of Fresno Public Works Department, October 1978), pp. 47–48.

51. *Fresno Daily Evening Expositor,* June 25, 1896; Low, "The Fresno Transmission Plant," pp. 88–89. To receive the street lighting franchise and encourage private customers to utilize their system, the SJEC offered rates that were described as "remarkably low." For example, operation of "dusk-to-dawn" street lights cost the city $6.45 per month per light; power for motors cost $64.00 per horsepower per year for "24-hour" service; residential charges were $.30 per month for "setting room" lamps, $.25 for kitchen, dining room, and hall lamps, $.15 for parlors, pantries, and barn lamps, and $.10 for bedrooms, bathrooms, and cellars. There was no discount or surcharge for use of current during periods of light or heavy demand. The City Trustees' award of the city lighting franchise to the SJEC over a competing offer by the Fresno

Gas and Electric Company is described in *Fresno Daily Evening Expositor*, March 7, 1896.

52. See previously referenced articles in the May 30, 1896, *Electrical World*, pp. 661–62; and the July 23, 1897, *Electrical Review*, pp. 105–8. See also "A 35-Mile Power Transmission," *Electrical World* 28 (June 27, 1896): 786–87; and "Electric Power Transmission at Fresno, Cal.," *Electrical Review* 41 (July 16, 1897): 76–79. Eastwood experienced problems with "water hammer"—a phenomenon affecting high-pressure penstocks—that were virtually unprecedented. The highest-head siphon then in use in the American West was part of the 1873 water supply system built to serve Nevada's Comstock mining district. This siphon operated under a head of 1,887 feet. See Hugh A. Shamberger, *Water Supply for the Comstock* (Washington, D.C.: Government Printing Office, 1972) pp. 16–22.

53. *Journal of Electricity* 4 (April 1897): 16.

54. George P. Low was born in 1863 and came to the West Coast in 1883. He became involved in electrical work in 1888 and later worked for the Pacific Insurance Union. In 1895, he founded the *Journal of Electricity* and became its first publisher. He also served as secretary of the Pacific Coast Electric Transmission Association. He died in 1909 of unknown causes. See "In Memoriam: George Perley Low," *Journal of Electricity Power and Gas* 23 (October 2, 1909): 311. Low's publication began as the *Electrical Journal* in July 1895 and became the *Journal of Electricity* two months later. In July 1899, its name was changed to the *Journal of Electricity Power and Gas*. In 1917, it reverted to the *Journal of Electricity*.

55. Between 1897 and 1904, the PCETA held annual meetings in the San Francisco area, and the *Journal of Electricity* published transactions reporting on these meetings. By 1902, the association had 24 full members, 6 honorary members, and 35 associate members. For data on membership requirements, see the PCETA's Constitution and Bylaws in *Transactions of the 6th Annual Conference* (1902), pp. 205–11. The PCETA's membership policy was more focused than was that of the Technical Society of the Pacific Coast, described by Carroll Pursell in his article, "The Technical Society of the Pacific Coast (1884–1914)," *Technology and Culture* 17 (October 1976): 702–17. After 1903, the PCETA evolved into the Pacific Coast Electrical Association, which functioned as a utilities trade association.

56. John S. Eastwood, "The Construction of Transmission Lines," *Journal of Electricity* 4 (September 1897): 115–17. In his paper, Eastwood provided a practical discourse on various technical and economic factors associated with the layout and erection of transmission lines. To him, it was a logical subject for discussion because "the hydraulic [that is, turbines and penstocks] and electrical equipment are accompanied by the plans and specifications of the engineers of the manufacturing companies." In contrast, "the pole line material, being usually furnished by a number of different parties, is usually thrown together under the direction of a lineman and a carpenter."

57. In 1897, the Central California Electric Company began transmitting three-phase current to Sacramento at "a little under" 16,000 volts. In 1898, the Pioneer Electric Power Company of Ogden, Utah, began transmitting three-phase current 37 miles at 16,000 volts. See C. H. Van Norden, "The Line Insulation of 16,000 Volts," *Journal of Electricity* 4 (September 1897): 113–14; and "The Pioneer Electric Power Transmission," *Journal of Electricity* 5 (March 1898): 109–13.

58. The H. G. Lacey Company began providing steam-generated, direct current service to Hanford in 1891; see Kathleen Edwards Small and J. Larry Smith, *History of Tulare County, California and Kings County, California* (Chicago: S. J. Clarke Publishing, 1926), p. 554. On November 27, 1897, the Lacey Company agreed to purchase a minimum of 150 HP constant power per year from the SJEC at a rate not exceeding "$48 per HP per annum," starting by June 1, 1898; See Box 51, Drawer 13, Doc. 17, H. W. O'Melveny Papers, the Huntington Library, San Marino, Calif. [hereafter, O'Melveny Papers, HEH]. See also John S. Eastwood, "The Hanford Extension," *Transactions of the Pacific Coast Electric Transmission Association* (San Francisco; PCETA, 1898): 37–39.

59. The *Fresno Daily Evening Expositor*, May 4, 1896, stated that: "a report had gained currency a few days ago that considerable difficulty had been experienced at the river powerhouse on account of sawdust in the stream having in a measure clogged the meshes of the screen. On further examination this was found not to be the case."

60. The diversion of water by the gas company is noted in Whitney, "Life and Times," chapter 3, pp. 34–35. Wishon, "Reminiscences of Power Development on the San Joaquin," pp. 267–68; and Coleman, *P. G. and E. of California*, p. 187. Legal action by the SJEC against "Joseph N. Goode and others designated by fictitious names" to prevent the diversion of water upstream from the power plant is documented in the *Fresno Daily Evening Expositor*, July 22, 1898.

61. Whitney, "Life and Times," chapter 3, pp. 25–48, describes problems with the gas company.

62. For confirmation of the extreme aridity of the late 1890s, see C. E. Grunsky, "Some Notes on California Rainfall," *Journal of Electricity* 44 (March 1, 1920): 204–6; and Andrew H. Palmer,

"California Precipitation," *Journal of Electricity* 44 (June 15, 1920): 607–10.

63. J. B. Lippincott to V. D. Clotfelter, December 13, 1927, in "Lake Pleasant Dam, Aqua Fria River," File #5, J. B. Lippincott Collection, Water Resources Center Archives, University of California, Berkeley.

64. Pisani, *Family Farm to Agribusiness,* p. 290.

65. "Statistical Highlights: Big Creek–San Joaquin River Hydro-Electric Development," pamphlet published by Southern California Edison Company (1971), p. 1.

66. "Notice of Reservoir Location" filed by John S. Eastwood and John J. Seymour, dated April 21, 1898, Madera County Water Rights Book No. 1, p. 122. Efforts to increase water supply for the SJEC by building a small reservoir in the mountains are also noted in the *Fresno Morning Republican,* December 13, 1898.

67. The bankruptcy is described in the *Fresno Morning Republican,* August 23, 1899. General Electric had accepted the company's bonds as payment for the electrical equipment and, when GE did not receive interest payments, it initiated legal action. A copy of General Electric's contract with the SJEC is available in Box 5, Drawer 13, Doc. 32, O'Melveny Papers, HEH. The bankruptcy is also discussed in Fowler, *Hydroelectric Power Systems of California,* pp. 454–58.

68. Evidence that Eastwood surveyed the site of the Crane Valley Dam can be found in W. E. Durfey to J. F. [*sic*] Eastwood, September 30, 1913, San Joaquin Light and Power Co. Folder (#50), JSE, WRCA. Maps documenting his surveys for both the dam site (undertaken February 23 to March 2, 1900) and the ditch line for the hydraulic fill (undertaken June 24 to 26, 1901) are available in Records of the U.S. Forest Service, Record Group 95, Entry 86, Folder 119 National Archives, College Park, Maryland, [hereafter Forest Service, RG 95, Entry ___, Folder ___].

69. James D. Schuyler, "Recent Practice in Hydraulic-Fill Dam Construction," *Transactions of the American Society of Civil Engineers* 57 (1907): 196–277. This article includes photos of the Crane Valley Dam's construction and a lengthy description of its near failure, written by Seymour.

70. Whitney, "Life and Times," chapter 3, p. 50.

71. An extensive file of correspondence and records related to the takeover of the SJEC by Kerckhoff and Balch is provided in Box 51, Drawer 13, of the O'Melveny Papers, HEH. Document No. 11 in this drawer includes notice of the foreclosure sale scheduled to take place on September 16, 1902, and indicates that no bid less than $350,000 would be accepted for the entire

system. By February 1903, all financial details related to the bankruptcy sale had been resolved, and the San Joaquin Power Company took full control of the property. The SJPC reorganized as the San Joaquin Light and Power Company in 1905, and in 1910 it became the San Joaquin Light and Power Corporation. See Fowler, *Hydroelectric Power Systems of California,* pp. 454–58; and Coleman, *P. G. and E. of California,* pp. 190–91.

72. Coleman, *P. G. and E. of California,* pp. 190–91.

Chapter Four

1. George P. Low, "Edison Electric Company of Los Angeles," *Journal of Electricity Power and Gas* 13 (January 1904): 16–21, 38–41, describes the 1899 Santa Ana power system built by the Southern California Power Company under the direction of H. H. Sinclair. The system was soon sold to the Edison Electric Company of Los Angeles, and the combined operations were named the Southern California Edison Company in 1909. See William Myers, *Iron Men and Copper Wires: A Centennial History of the Southern California Edison Company* (Glendale, Calif.: Trans-Anglo Press, 1983), pp. 38–39.

2. Charles M. Coleman, *P. G. and E. of California: The Centennial Story of Pacific Gas and Electric Company, 1852–1952* (New York: McGraw-Hill, 1952), pp. 144–52; and George Low, "The World's Longest Electric Power Transmission," *Journal of Electricity Power and Gas* 11 (July 1901): 151–67.

3. "Mammoth Power Company: Articles of Incorporation," October 19, 1900, California State Archives. Except for Eastwood, all members of the company's board of directors resided in Hanford. A complete listing of water rights claims along the upper San Joaquin made by Eastwood and Richard Lacey (and witnessed by photographer A. W. Peters) for the Mammoth Power Company in 1900–1901 is recorded in File #15455, Southern California Edison Company Corporate Records, Rosemead, California (hereafter referenced as SCEC File #___).

4. John S. Eastwood, "Engineers Report to the Board of Directors of the Mammoth Power Company," Mammoth Power Company Folder (#64), JSE, WRCA. Under the heading "Water Storage," he briefly described plans to erect several earth, rockfill, or timber dams; he also proposed a design based on the "arch principle" at Thousand Island Lake and another based on the "arch principle"

with buttresses resting on solid dikes, at Badger Lake.

5. Entry for November 1901, H. H. Sinclair Diary, Sinclair Papers, the Huntington Library, San Marino, California [hereafter, Sinclair Papers, HEH].

6. Any 20-mile-long tunnel represents a major engineering project. However, Eastwood's plan would have been relatively easy to build because the entire length of the tunnel was to be near the ground surface and thus reachable by numerous adits that would provide access to "working faces" for drilling and excavation.

7. The Henry E. Huntington Collection at the Huntington Library, San Marino, California, contains a limited number of letters and reports that shed light on the history of Big Creek and the Pacific Light and Power Company. References to the Henry E. Huntington Collection are listed as HEH, followed by the archival file number. For more on Huntington's general business career, see William B. Friedricks, *Henry E. Huntington and the Creation of Southern California* (Columbus: Ohio State University Press, 1992). James Thorpe, *Henry Edwards Huntington: A Biography* (Berkeley: University of California Press, 1994), concentrates on his personal life and on his activities as a book collector.

8. Friedricks, *Henry E. Huntington*, p. 1. Perhaps best remembered for its "Big Red Cars," Huntington's Pacific Electric Railway (as well as his Los Angeles Railway) is legendary among railroad historians. George W. Hilton and John F. Due, *The Electric Interurban Railways in America* (Stanford, Calif.: Stanford University Press, 1960), pp. 406-13, indicate that the Pacific Electric represented America's largest interurban system.

9. Friedricks, *Henry E. Huntington*, p. 6, also observes that "the inability to emulate his uncle and mentor by following him as the head of the SP [Southern Pacific] had a profound effect on Huntington. Unable to match Collis's achievements, Huntington apparently sought to build a business empire that would rival or even surpass that of his famous relative. To carry out this vision, he had to maintain a free hand and avoid future situations where his plans might be thwarted."

10. The most detailed source of data on Kerckhoff's career is Henry W. O'Melveny, *William G. Kerckhoff: A Memorial* (Los Angeles: privately printed, 1935). Material is also provided in Rudolph W. Van Norden, "San Joaquin Light and Power Corporation," *Journal of Electricity Power and Gas* 28 (May 11, 1912): 416.

11. Friedricks, *Henry E. Huntington*, pp. 61-62; W. G. Kerckhoff to I. W. Hellman, June 1, 1901, HEH 8439; W. G. Kerckhoff to H. E. Huntington and I. W. Hellman, February 8, 1902,

HEH 11/5/(2); and W. G. Kerckhoff to H. E. Huntington, March 13, 1902, HEH 9583.

12. John S. Eastwood, "The Hydraulic End of Power Transmission," *Transactions of the Sixth Annual Conference of the Pacific Coast Electric Transmission Association* (San Francisco: PCETA, 1902), pp. 145-60. These *Transactions* (pp. 213-14) note that Masson and the Pacific Light & Power Company joined the PCETA at this meeting.

13. Masson's involvement with electrical designs for the Mammoth Power Company are described in testimony given by H. A. Barre in 1925 in the case of *Herminghaus v. Southern California Edison Company*. In 1902, Barre served as an assistant in Masson's office; see "Reporter's Transcript on Appeal," pp. 547-48, Records of the California Supreme Court, California State Archives, Sacramento. The Eastwood/Masson/Balch negotiations are also noted in Whitney, "Life and Times," chapter 4, pp. 20-23. For a short time, Masson remained involved with Big Creek; and in 1903, he submitted a report to Kerckhoff entitled "Comparative Estimate of Cost of Water Power Transmission Plant, Big Creek–Los Angeles, Distance 250 Miles, Delivered at Los Angeles 40,000 H.P. Vs. Steam Plant Located in Los Angeles County." SCEC #12781; reference to this report is made in William G. Kerckhoff to Henry E. Huntington, August 10, 1903 (HEH 11/7/(2)).

14. "Agreement" between John S. Eastwood and Allan C. Balch, July 15, 1902; and "Agreement" between John S. Eastwood and R. S. Masson, July 15, 1902; SCEC #15455.

15. The amount of Eastwood's stipend is not stipulated in the July 15 agreement. Based on claims that Eastwood made for his work for the Mammoth Power Company (also documented in SCEC #15455), however, it could have been as low as $10 per day. For some other short-term surveying work that Eastwood took on during the summer of 1902, he was paid $25 per day; see unnumbered field notebook, survey notes for Dog Creek and Copper King Ranch, August–September 1902, JSE 11, WRCA.

16. W. G. Kerckhoff to H. E. Huntington, December 5, 1902, HEH 8446. Meaningful financial records related to Big Creek prior to 1910 do not exist. At the time the PL&P Corporation was organized (in early 1910), Henry Huntington's personal "Balance Sheet" dated January 31, 1910, indicates an expenditure of $63,634.86 under the heading "Big Creek and Mammoth Power Company," while his "Balance Sheet" for March 1, 1907, lists expenditures of $29,036.63 under this same account; both in HEH 11/2/(1). While the potential marketing of electric power in San Francisco and/or

Los Angeles justified support for Eastwood's work, Huntington's interest in Big Creek also related to hopes for building an electric-powered railroad up through California's Central Valley. The April 24, 1903, *Los Angeles Times* reported: "[Huntington] said that he might ultimately build a big electric railroad system in the San Joaquin electric power plant in the mountains east of Fresno, which can furnish power enough for a network of electric lines. . . . [Huntington said] 'Mr. Harriman is preparing to fight [my] electric roads in southern California . . . [he and I cannot] be associated in a business way any longer.'" Huntington's dreams for a Central Valley railroad survived for a few years (at one point he discussed building an electric railroad up to Yosemite), but such schemes ultimately proved fruitless; see "Huntington Plans to Build Road to Yosemite Valley," *Los Angeles Times*, January 21, 1905.

17. JSE to William Kerckhoff, October 7, 1902; quoted in David Redinger, *The Story of Big Creek* (Los Angeles: Angeles Press, 1949), p. 19 [updated with new material by Edith I. Redinger and William A. Myers (Glendale, Calif.: Trans-Anglo Press, 1986); references to Redinger's text are from the 1986 edition]. This letter refers either to the penstock tunnel feeding into powerhouse No. 1 or to the tunnel between powerhouses No. 1 and No. 2.

18. Quotation from John S. Eastwood, "Progress Report for 1903-04 of Right of Way Surveys and Outline Plan for Power Plant No. 1," March 10, 1904, pp. 3-4, SCEC #12778. Complete documentation of Eastwood's water rights and right-of-way filings for Big Creek (including work done for the Mammoth Power Company in 1900-1901) is provided in SCEC #15455, SCEC #15456, and SCEC #8114. Eastwood's filings for water rights on Big Creek are noted in *Herminghaus v. Southern California Edison Company,* "Reporter's Transcript on Appeal," pp. 754-56, and in numerous newspaper reports including the *Fresno Morning Republican*, December 10, 1902, and the *Fresno Morning Republican*, August 3, 1903; copies of the latter in Marguerite Eastwood Welch Notebook, Folder (#62), JSE, WRCA. Regulations for obtaining rights-of-way over public land are discussed in A. E. Chandler, "Western Laws of Electricity and Water: Rights of Way over Public Lands, for Ditches and Reservoirs," *Journal of Electricity Power and Gas* 28 (June 22, 1912): 618-21. In the 1920s, a major water rights dispute concerning the Big Creek project's storage of water broke out between the SCEC and a holder of riparian rights on the lower San Joaquin River; for more on this, see M. Catherine Miller, "Water Rights and the Bankruptcy of Judicial Action: The Case of *Herminghaus v. Southern California Edi-*

son," *Pacific Historical Review* 58 (February 1989): 83-107.

19. The complete record of Eastwood's water rights filings for Big Creek is documented in the Fresno County Recorder's Office, Fresno, and the Madera County Recorder's Office, Madera; original copies of all these filings are also retained within SCEC #15455.

20. "An Act Relating to rights of way through certain parks, reservations, and other public lands," February 15, 1901, 56th Cong., 2d sess., chap. 372. This law largely supplanted earlier provisions governing the use of the public domain for water projects included in the March 3, 1891, "Act to repeal timber culture laws" and the May 11, 1898, "Act to amend an Act to permit the use of the right of way through public lands for tramroads, canals, and reservoirs, and other purposes." The Act of February 15, 1901, was the first federal law specifically authorizing use of the public domain for power production that was not associated with agricultural development.

21. Evidence of right-of-way, reservoir, and powerhouse filings for the overall Big Creek project (including transmission lines to both San Francisco and Los Angeles) made by Eastwood with the General Land Office are available in Records of the Forest Service, RG 95, Entry 86, Box 119, NA.

22. John S. Eastwood, "Engineer's Report. Big Creek Power Plants," circa March 1903; reference to this report is made in a letter from W. G. Kerckhoff to H. E. Huntington, August 10, 1903; both in HEH 11/7/(2). Also, John S. Eastwood, "Progress Report for 1903-04," SCEC #12778; the latter report notes an earlier "outline preliminary report" dated March 1903 that almost certainly refers to the document in HEH 11/7/(2).

23. Eastwood, "Hydraulic End of Power Transmission," pp. 147-48.

24. Eastwood, "Progress Report for 1903-04," SCEC #12778.

25. Several final design drawings for Big Creek dating to 1906 are retained in the SCEC archives. An excellent cross-section elevation of powerhouse No. 1 signed by Eastwood is reproduced in Redinger, *Story of Big Creek*, p. 19.

26. JSE to Luigi Luiggi, January 6, 1921, JSE 62, WRCA.

27. John S. Eastwood, "Dams," n.d., ca. 1907, pp. 1-19, Big Creek Folder (#21), JSE, WRCA.

28. Ibid., pp. 1-2.

29. In this initial design, the upper 10 feet of the arches were to be 2 feet thick; below this depth, the arches were to become thicker at a rate of 6 inches for every 15 feet of vertical drop; at a depth of 170 feet below the crest, the arches would reach their maximum thickness of 7.5 feet. At the

top, the buttresses were to have a thickness of 2 feet; they were to increase gradually in thickness to a maximum of 7 feet. The arch rings were "to be reinforced with steel rods near both faces to prevent shrinkage," and the buttresses were to be supported laterally by "strut arches" designed to make them "amply stiff against any tendency to buckle." The design described in "Dams" closely adheres to the basic form of structures Eastwood began building after 1908. In fact, the only substantive difference involved plans to use 20-foot-span arches (instead of 40-foot spans) for shallow sections of the Big Creek structures that were less than 22 feet tall. His later designs dropped the use of arches with two different widths, in favor of one constant arch width for the entire structure. Nonetheless, by 1906, his conceptualization of the multiple-arch dam had reached a remarkably mature stage of development.

30. Eastwood, "Dams," pp. 3–5.

31. Ibid., p. 16.

32. H. Hawgood and J. S. Eastwood, "Earth Fill Dam with Concrete Corewall," 1906; H. Hawgood and J. S. Eastwood, "Cross Section of Concrete Buttressed Dam," 1906; and "Croton Profile" gravity dam design for Big Creek, ca. 1906; all in HEH 11/7/(2). The reference to Harry Hawgood on two of these drawings is somewhat mysterious since Hawgood's name hardly ever appears in any other material related to Eastwood. Hawgood was a consulting engineer who had helped design the PL&P Company's Borel hydroelectric plant on the Kern River. This prior association with the company is almost certainly the basis for his involvement with Eastwood in 1906. See Myers, *Iron Men and Copper Wires*, p. 55; and "Harry Hawgood," *Transactions of the American Society of Civil Engineers* 95 (1931): 1497–1500.

33. "Comparative Cost of Plant Showing the Advantages of the Use of Buttressed Dams," August 3, 1906, HEH 11/7/(2); This typewritten sheet (labeled "Mr. Eastwood") estimated the entire Big Creek system to cost $9,431,400 if concrete gravity dams were built; $7,053,750 if earth dams with concrete corewalls were erected; and $6,448,646 if concrete buttressed dams were built. In "Dams," p. 16, JSE 21, WRCA, Eastwood estimated that, depending on the cost of cement, the multiple-arch dams would be $2.5 million to $3 million cheaper than concrete gravity dams and $650,000 cheaper than earthfill dams. Some of the estimated savings involved reduced financing costs, derived from an assumption that the multiple arch dams could be built in two years while the other designs would take three years to build.

34. See Mammoth Power Company Stock Journal and Stock Ledger (SCEC #35272 and #35273);

and Articles of Incorporation file, California State Archives.

35. "Agreement Between Miller & Lux, Incorporated and Another of the First Part, and John S. Eastwood and Others of the Second Part," August 17, 1906, SCEC #8114. This agreement is briefly described in Edward F. Treadwell, *The Cattle King: The Biography of Henry Miller, Founder of the Miller & Lux Cattle Empire* (Santa Cruz, Calif.: Western Tanager Press, 1981), pp. 335–39; Treadwell's account makes some ill-informed and unfounded statements about Huntington's desire to use the Big Creek reservoir to support agricultural development. For a detailed legal analysis of Miller & Lux's efforts to protect its hold over riparian water rights on the San Joaquin River, see M. Catherine Miller, *Flooding the Courtrooms: Law and Water in the Far West* (Lincoln: University of Nebraska Press, 1993). Eastwood's signing of a "declaration of trust" is noted in entry for August 17, 1906, H. W. O'Melveny Journals, O'Melveny Papers, HEH.

36. The corporate records of the Sierra Nevada Electric Company are available in SCEC #29429.

37. Extensive correspondence on Pinchot's battles with hydroelectric power companies, including the Pacific Light and Power Company, in the period 1906–1908 is available in Forest Service Records, RG 95, Entry 10, Box 10; and Entry 22, Box 2; NA.

38. Charles Shinn to Gifford Pinchot, April 3, 1907, copy of letter in June English Collection, Box I, "Power–Hydro–Policy Decisions," Special Collections, California State University, Fresno.

39. Details of this agreement and subsequent modifications of it can be found in Forest Service Records, RG 95, Entry 86, Box 119, NA; further documentation is provided in SCEC #15456.

40. Whitney, "Dollars and Genius Built Southern California: The Story of Henry Huntington and John Eastwood" (unpublished ms., ca. 1970, at Water Resources Center Archives, Berkeley, California), p. 13, refers to a final "Synopsis of Report on the San Joaquin Big Creek Project" submitted by Eastwood in May 1907. Although copies of this report evidently existed into the late 1960s, they are currently unavailable. Given that Eastwood had prepared annual reports on his work in 1903 and 1904, it seems extremely unlikely that he would not have prepared a final report after completing his design work for Big Creek. However, William Myers—the historian who possesses the best contemporary knowledge of archival material in the Southern California Edison Company's files—indicates that he has never seen this report and that, to the best of his knowledge, it no longer exists. The SCEC archives contain several drawings dating to 1906–1907 that confirm the completion

of Eastwood's design work for Big Creek by the spring of 1907.

41. G. S. Hewes, "Power Development of the North Fork of the San Joaquin River," *Engineering Record* 63 (February 4, 1911): 124–28.

42. "Prospectus of a proposed corporation to be formed for the purpose of consolidating certain gas, electric light and power companies in Southern California; The acquisition of various water rights and real estate and the construction of hydroelectric generating plants thereon," n.d. (ca. June 1909), HEH 8220. Further financial arrangements related to this proposal are outlined in "Agreement between Henry E. Huntington and William G. Kerckhoff and N. W. Halsey & Co." February 19, 1909, HEH 8219.

43. See William G. Kerckhoff to Henry E. Huntington, August 10, 1903, HEH 11/7/(2), for reference to Eastwood as "our engineer." See William G. Kerckhoff to Henry E. Huntington, September 13, 1910, HEH 9602, for reference to J. G. White and Company as "our engineers."

44. See "John Gilbert White," *Transactions of the American Society of Civil Engineers* 109 (1944): 1548–49. The firm's early work in electric railroads is noted in George W. Hilton and John F. Due, *The Electric Interurban Railways in America* (Stanford, Calif.: Stanford University Press, 1960), pp. 21, 237, 337. T. W. Mermel, comp. and ed., *Register of Dams in the United States (as of January 1, 1963)* (United States Committee on Large Dams, 1963), pp. 16, 19, references early masonry gravity dams built by the J. G. White organization, including Ocoee No. 1 in Tennessee (1911) and the Lacrosse Dam in Wisconsin (1908).

45. The PL&P Corporation was officially organized on January 12, 1910; see Articles of Incorporation, California State Archives.

46. "Settlement Between John S. Eastwood and A. C. Balch," February 23, 1910, SCEC #15455, documents more than twenty "filings" that were transferred to the PL&P by Eastwood and the Mammoth Power Company. John S. Eastwood, "Memorandum of Trust," August 17, 1906, SCEC #8114, committed him to transfer his Big Creek holdings to the Huntington interests when construction of the project was ready to proceed. Had he balked at the terms presented to him in early 1910 by the PL&P, this memorandum would have limited his options severely. During early planning for Big Creek, Eastwood had raised the issue of his future stock holdings. On September 5, 1905, H. W. O'Melveny recorded in his journal: "Matter of Eastwood's compensation came up. He desired part of his stock to be interest bearing." In the end, Eastwood's $600,000 worth of common stock was interest bearing, but *only* if sufficient profits remained after paying dividends due on first pre-

ferred and second preferred stock. See H. W. O'Melveny Journals, O'Melveny Papers, HEH.

47. See Samuel Storrow to William G. Kerckhoff, August 31, 1910, HEH 9602. In 1903, Storrow had provided Balch with a preliminary report assessing Eastwood's work developing the Big Creek project (see SCEC #52485); and during 1909–1910, he was helping J. G. White collect hydrological data. S. W. Curtis to W. H. Hood, October 1, 1909, HEH 9602, indicates that an earlier report on Big Creek's water supply was prepared by Storrow and J. G. White in May 1909. The decision to proceed with Big Creek reflected fears that other groups might grab water power rights in the upper San Joaquin. As Kerckhoff explained to Huntington in September 1910: "Our rights [to Big Creek] . . . are well secured . . . in order to preserve our rights, however, we must begin work this fall and prosecute the work in good faith . . . [this work] need not be very much, but it must be such that it cannot be questioned by anyone." See William G. Kerckhoff to Henry E. Huntington, September 13, 1910, HEH 9602. Filings with the U.S. Forest Service for a power plant to be built along the upper San Joaquin River by the Sierra Park Power Company were preliminarily recorded in November 1909; see W. L. Huber, "District Engineer's Report on Application for Final Water Power Permit" November 7, 1911, Walter L. Huber Papers, Folder 73, WRCA, Berkeley, California.

48. Friedricks, *Henry E. Huntington*, pp. 99–103, describes events leading up to the Southern Pacific takeover of the Pacific Electric; Harriman died in 1909, but the rivalry between Huntington and the Southern Pacific continued after his death.

49. A. C. Balch to JSE, November 28, 1910, as quoted in Whitney, "Life and Times," preface, p. 1. This source quotes Eastwood's dismissal letter in full.

50. JSE to Pacific Light and Power Corporation, November 30, 1910 (plus attachments), SCEC #15455. In this document, Eastwood agreed to "turn over to A. G. Wishon, or such person as the [PL&P] Corporation may direct, all engineering data and maps and property secured for prosecution of the work on the Big Creek or Mammoth Power propositions." By this time, Masson was uninvolved in the affairs of the PL&P. See R. S. Masson "Hydroelectric Development of the Arizona Power Company," *Engineering Record* 62 (August 20, 1910): 214–17.

51. See J. G. White & Company, "Memorandum on Big Creek Power Project," May 29, 1911, HEH 11/7/(2). Stone & Webster still exists as a thriving engineering conglomerate. Several interrelated operations have shared the same appella-

tion, including the Stone & Webster Engineering Corporation, the Stone & Webster Management Association, and the Stone & Webster Construction Company. In 1985, Ms. Nancy Pellini, Manager of Stone & Webster's Technical Information Center, kindly reviewed company files for any primary source documentation on the firm's involvement in the initial construction of Big Creek. Her search did not reveal any original correspondence, memos, or other material. Only previously published articles on Big Creek's construction are available. For example, see *Stone & Webster Public Service Journal* 11 (September 1912): 170-75.

52. For background on Stone & Webster's history, see Sam Bass Warner, Jr., "Technology and Its Impact on Urban Culture, 1889-1937," in Robert Weible, ed., *Essays from the Lowell Conference on Industrial History, 1982 and 1983*, (North Andover, Mass.: Museum of American Textile History, 1985), pp. 312-22; and Hughes, *Networks of Power: The Electrification of Western Society, 1880-1930* (Baltimore: Johns Hopkins University Press, 1984), pp. 386-90. A corporate history is available in David Neal Keeler, *Stone & Webster, 1889-1989: A Century of Integrity and Service* (New York: Stone & Webster, 1989).

53. Huntington's reliance on a financial syndicate formed by the investment house of William Salomon and Company is noted in Friedricks, *Henry E. Huntington*, pp. 112-13. William Myers's review of archival records in the Southern California Edison Company files uncovered no correspondence relating to why Stone & Webster received the initial Big Creek construction contract from the PL&P. Perhaps the directors of the PL&P considered construction of Big Creek too big a job for Eastwood to undertake as chief engineer, and they may have determined that a large firm was better prepared for the task. This supposition is plausible, but given Eastwood's previous experience with the SJEC in high-head hydroelectric plant construction (experience that Stone & Webster could not match) and his knowledge of the Sierra Nevada, he was hardly unqualified to supervise Big Creek's construction.

54. Hank Johnston, *The Railroad that Lighted Southern California* (Glendale, Calif.: Trans-Anglo Books, 1966), pp. 16-17.

55. The construction of Big Creek is described in Redinger, *The Story of Big Creek;* in Johnston, *The Railroad That Lighted Southern California;* and in "Progress of the Big Creek Initial Development: Report to Pacific Light and Power Corporation, January 1, 1913," Stone & Webster Construction Company, Boston. This published report is available at the Water Resources Center Archives, Berkeley. Profusely illustrated, it makes no mention of Eastwood.

56. "Big Creek Dams, Comparative Estimates and Quantities," n.d., and "Estimate of Cost of Gravity Dams of Cyclopean Concrete for the Big Creek Power Development," February 24, 1912; both in Big Creek Dams Folder (#21), JSE, WRCA.

57. E. H. Rollins to Stone & Webster, May 7, 1912; and JSE to E. H. Rollins, May 3, 1912; both in Big Meadows Dam Folder (#18), JSE, WRCA. Rollins's important role as an investor in the PL&P is noted in Friedricks, *Henry E. Huntington*, p. 114.

58. JSE to E. H. Rollins, May 22, 1912, JSE 18, WRCA, reports that "Mr. Shuffleton has already returned to the Coast [from Boston], and has gone to Fresno. I have had no further word [on] this matter since the date of your communication."

59. "Minutes," PL&P Board of Directors Meeting, July 5, 1912, SCEC #21167; Huntington presided as PL&P president at this meeting, and the board unanimously resolved that "an assessment (No. 1) of five dollars per share be and the same is hereby levied upon each and every share of the capital stock of this corporation," for the purpose of paying "a portion of its outstanding indebtedness, interest charges, and the expenses of conducting its business." The resolution indicated a due date of August 30 and set September 27, 1912, as the date for auctioning delinquent stock. The company intended to raise $1,169,800 from the 233,960 outstanding shares of first preferred, second preferred, and common stock. The assessment is noted in *Commercial and Financial Chronicle* 95 (August 3, 1912): 298; and in Whitney, "Dollars and Genius," pp. 18-19.

60. Under common law, it is not possible to assess "full paid stock"; but this can be changed by state law. Stock can be issued as "nonassessable" but no PL&P stock fell into this category. See William M. Fletcher, *Cyclopedia of the Law of Private Corporations* vol. 7 (Chicago: Callaghan, 1919), pp. 7517-40; and M. U. Overland, *Classified Corporation Laws of All the States* (New York: Ronald Press, 1908), pp. 41-52. Stock assessment default procedures are covered in sections #334-49 of the California Corporation Code.

61. Henry E. Huntington, "Balance Sheet," May 31, 1913, HEH 11/2/(2). The fact that the $5 per share assessment was applied equally against the first preferred, second preferred, and common stock placed the greatest hardship on owners of stock that fell in the last category, because the assessment constituted a greater proportion of that stock's actual value. Huntington's personal "Cash Abstracts" for August 14, August 31, and September 7, 1912, indicate disbursements of over $578,000 to pay for the PL&P assessment; HEH 11/8/(3).

62. Public notice of the delinquent shareholders appears in the *Los Angeles Evening Herald*, September 11, 1912; "Minutes," PL&P Board of Directors Meeting, October 5, 1912, SCEC #21167, does not list the specific names of persons whose stock was sold.

63. Redinger, *Story of Big Creek*, p. 20. Whitney, "Dollars and Genius," p. 19, reports that Eastwood was allowed a year (that is, until August 1913) to raise the money, including 6 percent interest, necessary to pay off the assessment. Supposedly, he hoped to sell part of his stock; but because the assessment drastically reduced the stock's value, he could not arrange for its sale. Whitney indicates that Eastwood's failure to pay the debt by the summer of 1913 resulted in forfeiture of the stock at that time. This account is difficult to reconcile with legally established measures for handling delinquent assessment payments. In any case, however, the result is the same: Eastwood lost all his PL&P holdings and received no financial compensation.

64. A list of stockholders as of six weeks before the assessment is available in "Stockholders in PL&P Corporation," May 22, 1912, HEH 9603. This list contains exactly the same number of shares as were assessed on July 5, 1912; and except for a few possible minor changes, it almost certainly notes the same stockholders affected by the assessment. Eastwood is listed as owning 5,400 shares of common stock, and Masson is credited with having 600 shares. Many of Kerckhoff's holdings are listed under the name of Henry P. Baumgaertner, a Pasadena businessman who frequently acted as his "attorney-in-fact"; this status is noted in the "Minutes" of the PL&P Board of Directors, June 27, 1912, SCEC #21167. Huntington and Kerckhoff had long understood the possibility of utilizing assessments as a business tactic. In 1904 they had employed this method to pressure minority shareholders when financing the PL&P's Kern River power plant; as Kerckhoff acknowledged: "Some of our people . . . think it is a hardship to pay an assessment on the stock, but I have no doubt they all will pay. There are a number who have not been willing to take bonds; will not be willing to take any bonds now; and it is impossible to reach them in any other way [other than a stock assessment]." See W. G. Kerckhoff to H. E. Huntington, July 23, 1904, HEH 9587; and Friedricks, *Henry E. Huntington*, pp. 93–94.

65. Dissolution of the partnership is discussed in Friedricks, *Henry E. Huntington*, pp. 114–15, and is documented in "Gas and Power Deal," Box 4, Huntington Vault Material, HEH. See also *Herminghaus v. Southern California Edison Company*, Reporter's Transcript on Appeal, p. 760. The "PL&P Corporation List of Stockholders,"

October 4, 1913, HEH 11/7/(2), reveals that Huntington controlled 29,312 shares of first preferred (out of 30,570), 94,485 shares of second preferred (out of 99,750), and 104,575 shares of common stock (out of 105,595). The principal parties in the organization of the PL&P (Huntington, Kerckhoff, Balch, and their attorney H. W. O'Melveny) always retained a very possessive attitude toward the Big Creek project; for example, on May 6, 1904, O'Melveny recorded in his journal that "Balch showed me a letter from [A. G.] Wishon in which the latter claims an interest in the upper San Joaquin filings [Big Creek]. It tends to destroy confidence in Wishon." O'Melveny Papers, Huntington Library. Another factor may relate to the de facto disenfranchisement of Eastwood. During early 1912, he had unsuccessfully tried to convince Stone & Webster—and particularly the firm's California manager S. L. Shuffleton—to adopt multiple arch dams for Big Creek. Clearly, Stone & Webster understood the extent of Eastwood's involvement in planning Big Creek; their task was simply to build a system that Eastwood could reasonably take full credit for conceiving. Eleven days after the July 5 assessment, the PL&P board appointed Shuffleton to the newly authorized position of "Engineer" (see "Minutes," PL&P Board of Directors Meeting, July 16, 1912, SCEC #21167). Shuffleton held this post for a year and half; after his resignation, it was never occupied again. Stone & Webster and Shuffleton had reason to minimize Eastwood's relationship to the project, and (although it remains a matter of speculation) they may have lobbied for actions that would pressure him to abandon his financial stake in the PL&P. During the latter part of his career, Huntington relied upon George Ward, who had worked for Collis P. Huntington on railroads in New York State, as his personal engineer and technical adviser. Ward eventually played a significant role in the PL&P and the Southern California Edison Company, but prior to 1912 he was uninvolved in the design and conception of Big Creek. See "George Clinton Ward," *Transactions of the American Society of Civil Engineers* 101 (1936): 1664–67.

66. See "Revised Estimate, Stone & Webster, April 1st, 1913," and "Revised Memorandum re Big Creek Requirements (April 8, 1913)" HEH 11/6/(2). The ultimate cost of $13,886,250 for the initial development (with a generating capacity of 60,000 kw) is documented in a final estimate sheet dated January 24, 1914, HEH 11/7/(2).

67. Friedricks, *Henry E. Huntington*, pp. 113–14; Huntington's assistant C. E. Graham reported in July 1913 that: "We shall be obligated to stop work on Big Creek unless we get additional large sums of money."

68. E. R. Davis [PL&P general manager] to

Secretary of Agriculture, June 26, 1913; SCEC #8114. Although all the dams used to impound Huntington Lake were gravity structures, Stone & Webster did use a thin arch design for the small dam that directed water into the tunnel leading to Powerhouse No. 2.

69. The first transmission of power from Big Creek to Los Angeles is described in "Big Creek Power Put to Work in This City," *Los Angeles Sunday Times* (November 9, 1913).

70. The relationship of Balch and Kerckhoff to Cal Tech is noted in Judith R. Goodstein, *Millikan's School: A History of the California Institute of Technology* (New York: W. W. Norton, 1991), pp. 120-24. The Cal Tech Archives retains a file on Balch that holds his 1889 B.S. thesis for Cornell University and a small amount of material on his activities as president of the Cal Tech board of trustees; the Millikan papers also contain material documenting Balch's relationship to Cal Tech. The archives' only material on Kerckhoff is a copy of the memorial biography written by O'Melveny and published in 1935. The UCLA archives contains nothing related to Kerckhoff except for a few minor letters dating to circa 1900.

71. Redinger, *Story of Big Creek*, p. 18.

72. John S. Eastwood, "Report on Shaver Project," June 22, 1918, SCEC #10723.

73. Redinger, *Story of Big Creek*, p. 247; personal communications with William Myers, March 1993. The Huntington Lake dams were raised to their full height in 1916-1917, and in 1920 blasting began for the 14-mile-long tunnel under Kaiser Ridge that was to divert water from the upper reaches of the San Joaquin River into Big Creek Basin. Acting on plans that Eastwood had first outlined in his 1904 report to Balch, Edison purchased Shaver Lake from the Fresno Flume and Lumber Company in 1919 and integrated it into the Big Creek system. In 1960, the Mammoth Pool dam and power plant that Eastwood proposed back in 1901 were finally put into operation.

74. It appears that Huntington made this trip in 1914 and was accompanied by E. H. Rollins and George Ward. A photo of the three men visiting Big Creek appears in Myers, *Iron Men and Copper Wires*, p. 109.

75. William G. Robbins, *Colony and Empire: The Capitalist Transformation of the American West* (Lawrence: University Press of Kansas, 1994), pp. 103-5.

Chapter Five

1. Hank Johnston, *They Felled the Redwoods* (Glendale, Calif.: Trans-Anglo Books, 1966) pp. 39-81. In 1894, Moore and Smith's King's River Lumber Company failed, but it was then reorganized as the Sanger Lumber Company. The latter firm went bankrupt in 1897 and came under the control of the Canadian Bank of Commerce in San Francisco. This bank ultimately sold its holdings to the Hume interests.

2. Richard Harms, "Life After Lumbering: Charles Henry Hackley and the Emergence of Muskegon, Michigan" (unpublished Ph.D. dissertation, Michigan State University, 1984), describes the history of the Hackley-Hume partnership.

3. Frederick L. Honhart, "Sources of Forest History: The Hackley and Hume Papers," *Journal of Forest History* 23 (July 1979): 136-43, provides context for the Hackley and Hume Papers in the Michigan State University Archives and Historical Collections, East Lansing, Michigan (hereafter referenced as Hackley-Hume Papers, MSU).

4. Eastwood surveyed the Long Meadow dam site on December 23, 1886; see Fieldbook No. 5/20, JSE 11, WRCA. Joseph B. Lippincott, *Water Storage on the Kings River, California* (Washington, D.C.: Government Printing Office, 1902) [USGS Water Supply and Irrigation Paper No. 58], pp. 44-46, includes a description of the Long Meadow location.

5. Thomas Hume to Ira Bennett, August 1, 1907, and Thomas Hume to Ira Bennett, August 21, 1907. George A. Hume to Ira Bennett, September 3, 1907, refers to "Mr. John B. Rogers" and a "Mr. Arnold" as proposed engineers for the Hume Lake Dam. George A. Hume to Ira Bennett, September 18, 1907, states that "we hope that the new man, Mr. Eastwood, will be able to do the work in good shape." All letters in the Hackley-Hume Papers, MSU.

6. Eastwood's 1906-1907 filings on power sites along the Kings River's North Fork are documented in "Water Rights," Fresno County Recorder's Office; for example, see Book D, p. 113, for a filing dated July 13, 1907. In addition, the *Fresno Morning Republican*, July 7, 1905, describes a trip led by Eastwood into the upper Kings River Canyon to help determine whether the state government would help build a road into the region.

7. In John S. Eastwood to Hume-Bennett Lumber Company, October 1, 1907, Hume Lake Dam Folder (#12), JSE, WRCA, he estimated that the rockfill dam would cost more than $72,000 and that his own multiple arch design would cost $25,862. The nearby Millwood logging pond and the Fresno Lumber and Irrigation Company's Shaver Lake were impounded by rockfill dams.

8. A multiwidth arch design is described in John S. Eastwood to Hume-Bennett Lumber Company, October 1, 1907, and in the 15-page "Speci-

fications for a Buttressed Arched Concrete Dam for Ten-Mile Creek" (ca. October 1907), JSE 12, WRCA.

9. Thomas Hume to Ira Bennett, October 31, 1907. Only outgoing correspondence related to the company's operations survives for the latter part of 1907, making it difficult to piece together a complete picture of how the company reacted to Eastwood's proposal. In Hume, Hefferan and Company to William C. Fargo, October 9, 1907, the Hume-Bennett interests requested an independent appraisal of Eastwood's design; and as reflected in Hume's October 31 letter, Fargo evidently offered a negative assessment of the new design. Fargo's specific comments are unknown, but they may have prompted the change to a design with constant-width arches. Both letters in Hackley-Hume Papers, MSU.

10. The Hackley-Hume letter books covering the first half of 1908 are missing and presumed destroyed. Eastwood's papers do not document negotiations with the lumber company in early 1908.

11. Johnston, *They Felled the Redwoods,* p. 110, reports that the Hume interests had expended $1.6 million on their California properties as of late 1910; most of this was incurred in moving their sawmill operations to Long Meadow/Hume Lake.

12. "Construction of Dam at Hume," (n.d., ca. December 1908), Hackley-Hume Papers, MSU, indicates a total expenditure of $46,326.76 through November 30, 1908.

13. Design and dimension data are included in John S. Eastwood "Hume Lake Dam," *Journal of Electricity Power and Gas* 23 (October 30, 1909): 398–404; and a manuscript entitled "Hume Lake Dam," (n.d, ca. 1909) JSE 12, WRCA.

14. Johnston, *They Felled the Redwoods,* pp. 130–31, notes that a 320-acre tract at the edge of Long Meadow was controlled separately from other holdings in the region. In his letter of October 1, 1907, Eastwood urged that the dam's height be determined by "the property lines of this company," JSE 12, WRCA.

15. See Howard Newlon, ed., *A Selection of Historic American Papers on Concrete, 1876–1976* (Detroit: American Concrete Institute, 1976) for more on Ransome and other early innovators in reinforced concrete. John W. Snyder, "Buildings and Bridges for the 20th Century," *California History* 63 (Fall 1984): 280–92, 338–39, describes the career of John B. Leonard, an early editor of *Architect and Engineer of California,* who designed many reinforced concrete structures and participated in rebuilding San Francisco after the 1906 earthquake.

16. Homer A. Reid, *Concrete and Reinforced Concrete Construction* (New York: Myron C. Clark Publishing, 1907); Frederick W. Taylor and Sanford E. Thompson, *A Treatise on Concrete Plain and Reinforced* (New York: John Wiley & Sons, 1905); and Albert W. Buel and Charles S. Hill, *Reinforced Concrete* (New York: Engineering News Publishing, 1904). It is not known which references on reinforced concrete construction Eastwood actually used, but the preceding books were widely available. The growth of reinforced concrete technology during the first decade of the twentieth century is also reflected in numerous trade catalogs, including the 72-page *National Bridge Company* (Indianapolis: National Bridge Company, 1907); the 160-page *Tests and Other Facts Concerning the Kahn Trussed Bar* (Detroit: Trussed Concrete Steel Company, 1906); and the 232-page *Corrugated Bars for Reinforced Concrete* (St. Louis: Expanded Metal and Corrugated Bar Company, 1906).

17. Eastwood, "Hume Lake Dam," p. 403. A fieldbook in the JSE 11, WRCA, documents that layout work started on June 20.

18. John S. Eastwood, "Hume Lake Multiple Arch Dam," *Journal of Electricity Power and Gas* 24 (February 12, 1910): 137.

19. Eastwood, "Hume Lake Dam," p. 400.

20. Ibid., p. 401, reported that the arches were provided with "a cable for each square foot area of the end section."

21. Ibid., pp. 403–4, indicates the "last concrete was laid on the 27th of November," with the "working time being 114 days." Apparently, the crew did not toil seven days a week, and rain probably interfered with work on occasion.

22. Johnston, *They Felled the Redwoods,* pp. 131–36.

23. The Hume Lake Dam briefly came under the control of the State of California in the late 1950s; at that time, the upstream face was coated with a 6-inch layer of concrete and the original spillway openings were filled in. State regulation of the structure is chronicled in File #692, Dam Safety Division, Department of Water Resources, Sacramento, California. Some minor remedial work on the upstream face was completed by the Forest Service in the early 1940s; this is documented in Folder #80, Walter L. Huber Papers, WRCA.

24. George Hefferan to JSE, August 5, 1909, JSE 12, WRCA.

25. Eastwood, "Hume Lake Dam." Prior to this, Eastwood's last publication had been in the 1902 *Transactions* of the Pacific Coast Electric Transmission Association. The article "A Multiple Arch Dam," *Engineering Record* 61 (January 15, 1910): 71, was drawn from data appearing in Eastwood's original article. A slightly edited version also appeared in the *California Journal of Technology* 15 (March 1910): 17–39.

26. Eastwood, "Hume Lake Dam," p. 403; Eastwood reported the maximum compressive stress in the arch rings as being 13.5 tons per square foot (187 psi). Calculations confirm that he employed the cylinder formula as the basis of the arch design, but the article does not mention this method.

27. C. E. Grunsky, "The Multiple Arch Dam," *Journal of Electricity Power and Gas* 23 (December 25, 1909): 582-83. For more on his career see "Grunsky, Carl Ewald," *Transactions of the American Society of Civil Engineers* 100 (1935): 1591-95.

28. *Journal of Electricity Power and Gas* 24 (January 1, 1910): 19.

29. "Hume Lake Multiple Arch Dam," *Journal of Electricity Power and Gas* 24 (February 12, 1910): 135-39. In responding to critiques of his original article, Eastwood also noted comments from two engineers, Hugh L. Cooper and F. O. Blackwell, whose letters were not published (and do not survive).

30. JSE to *Engineering News*, April 28, 1910, Big Bear Valley Dam Folder (#1), JSE, WRCA. Referring to the preparation of new dam designs, Eastwood said he wanted "to do this kind of work very carefully."

31. John Brown and James Boyd, *History of San Bernardino and Riverside Counties* (Los Angeles: Western Historical Association, 1922), pp. 81-89; and George William Beattie, "Origin and Early Development of Water Rights in the East San Bernardino Valley," *San Bernardino Valley Water District Bulletin No. 4* (November 1951). Mormon abandonment of San Bernardino came in 1856-1857, when Utah Territory was occupied by federal troops. See Leonard Arrington, *Great Basin Kingdom: An Economic History of the Latter-Day Saints, 1830-1900* (Cambridge, Mass.: Harvard University Press, 1958), pp. 87-88, 177-78.

32. William H. Hall, *Irrigation in California (Southern)* (Sacramento: J. D. Young, 1888), p. 187. Assistant state engineer Fred Perris's survey of the reservoir site is described in John W. Robinson, *The San Bernardinos* (San Bernardino, Calif.: Big Santa Anita Historical Society, 1989), p. 169.

33. Robinson, *The San Bernardinos*, p. 169. Photos of Brown and the Bear Valley Dam are included in William G. Moore, *Redlands Yesterdays* (Redlands, Calif.: Moore Historical Foundation, 1983), pp. 6-7, 82. Further material on Brown is available in the A. K. Smiley Library, Redlands, California.

34. Hall, *Irrigation in California (Southern)*, pp. 183-95; and Beattie, "Origin and Early Development of Water Rights," pp. 56-57.

35. Horace Hinckley, "The Four Dams at Big Bear and the Damkeepers House," *San Bernardino County Museum Association Quarterly* 22 (Fall 1974): 42-43.

36. Horace Hinckley, "An History of Bear Valley Mutual Water Company," unpublished manuscript, Bear Valley Mutual Water Company, Redlands, California, ca. 1984, p. 1. The bankruptcy proceedings that engulfed the Bear Valley Irrigation Company and associated enterprises are described in Clary, *History of the Law Firm of O'Melveny & Myers: 1885-1965*, pp. 128-31.

37. James D. Schuyler to H. H. Garstin, October 5, 1909 ("Report on Plans for a New Dam at Bear Valley"), Folder 51.3, James D. Schuyler Papers, WRCA.

38. JSE to H. H. Garstin, April 6, 1910, JSE 1, WRCA. Garstin was president of the Bear Valley Mutual Water Company. Hinckley, "An History of Bear Valley Mutual Water Company," p. 10, indicates that Eastwood's proposal was accepted on April 7, 1910.

39. Hinckley, "An History of Bear Valley Mutual Water Company," pp. 10-11, describes the raising of the dam from the 65-foot contour to the 72.4-foot contour (in this context, "contour" measurements relate to the elevation of the outlet pipe from Brown's arch dam: the crest of the arch dam was at the 51.25-foot contour) as being an informal decision made by Garstin and Eastwood. According to Hinckley, the higher dam "later proved embarrassing to the Company because [it] flooded land [the company] did not own." Both Hinckley and an accounting sheet in JSE 1, WRCA, report the cost of the larger dam at $137,654 with Eastwood receiving a fee of $6,000.

40. John S. Eastwood, "New Big Bear Valley Dam," *Western Engineering* 3 (December 1913): 458-70, is the source for most data related to design and construction. See also "Big Bear Valley Dam, Outline Specifications" (n.d., ca. 1910-1911); and John S. Eastwood and H. H. Garstin, "Building the New Big Bear Valley Dam for the Bear Valley Mutual Water Company, Redlands, San Bernardino County, California, 1910-1911," JSE 1, WRCA. This last source is a script for a lantern slide lecture (none of the lantern slides referred to are known to survive); see p. 12 for reference to "Lucky Bob." Unfortunately, no prints of the film are available. The Bison Moving Picture Company was an independent company that worked in remote locations in order to avoid agents of Thomas Edison's motion picture trust.

41. Eastwood, "New Big Bear Valley Dam," p. 459.

42. The ferro-inclave method of construction is discussed in Frederick W. Taylor and Sanford E. Thompson, *A Treatise on Concrete Plain and Re-*

inforced, 2d ed. (New York: John Wiley & Sons, 1909), p. 507.

43. "Outline Specifications," p. 3; and Eastwood and Garstin, "Building the New Big Bear Valley Dam," p. 10; both in JSE 1, WRCA. In 1930, some remedial work was completed on parts of a few arches; photographs taken during this work clearly document the use of both ferro-inclave sheeting and more traditional steel bars to reinforce the arches. See Folder #61, Hiram N. Savage Papers, WRCA, Berkeley, California.

44. Eastwood and Garstin, "Building the New Big Bear Valley Dam," p. 8; JSE 1, WRCA.

45. Eastwood, "The New Big Bear Valley Dam," p. 463.

46. "Bear Valley Multiple Arch Dam Overflows for First Time," Engineering News 75 (May 18, 1916): 961.

47. Jerry L. Coffman and Carl A. von Hake, eds., Earthquake History of the United States, Revised Edition (Through 1970) (Washington, D.C.: Government Printing Office, 1973), pp. 4, 141, 164–65.

48. B. T. Weed to JSE, January 11, 1921, Bear Valley Mutual Water Company files, Redlands, California.

49. In JSE to H. H. Garstin, September 1, 1923, Eastwood took a protective view of the dam and his client, counseling that: "it is first necessary that the bridge be designed as not to make the property inoperative for the service of the B. V. Co., namely the storage, control and distribution of water. It is also necessary that it be so designed as to not be a detriment to the safety of the dam. . . . [I]f the plans for the [bridge] must conform to the preconceived standards of the Bureau of Public Roads, and they are to approve the plans, it seems that they will be under the necessity of locating the structure elsewhere than on the dam belonging to the B.V.M.W.Co." A drawing for the bridge design (prepared by the Bureau of Public Roads) received Eastwood's approval as "Consulting Engineer, Bear Valley Mutual Water Company" on March 7, 1924; later, an illustrated report was sent to Eastwood's widow, documenting the bridge's construction from July through November 1924; JSE 1, WRCA.

50. Eastwood and Garstin, "Building the New Big Bear Valley Dam," pp. 2–3, JSE 1, WRCA.

Chapter Six

1. Major sources documenting the history of the Big Meadows Dam include the Eastwood Papers, JSE 18, WRCA; the Freeman Papers, MIT; the Henry H. Sinclair Papers at the Huntington Library, San Marino, California (hereafter Sinclair Papers, HEH); and the records of the State Railroad Commission of California (now the Public Utilities Commission) in the California State Archives, Sacramento, California. The most relevant Railroad Commission records are filed under Application No. 357, Box 68, Bin 6090, F3725: 1896–1900 (hereafter PUC, App. No. 357).

2. H. H. Sinclair to H. P. Wilson, April 8, 1909, Box 4, Sinclair Papers, HEH; William Myers, Iron Men and Copper Wires: A Centennial History of the Southern California Edison Company (Glendale, Calif.: Trans-Anglo Books, 1983) p. 178, notes Sinclair's involvement in 1902 studies for a hydroelectric power plant in Boulder Canyon on the Colorado River.

3. A group photograph published in the 1900 Transactions of the Pacific Coast Electric Transmission Association shows Sinclair and Eastwood within arm's length of one another. See also H. H. Sinclair diary entry for November 12, 1901, Box 1, Sinclair Papers, HEH.

4. Photo Album #192 in the Huntington Library includes a view of the original Bear Valley Dam, with an inscription indicating that Sinclair gave the photograph to F. E. Brown in December 1898.

5. J. S. Holliday, The World Rushed In: The California Gold Rush Experience (New York: Simon & Schuster, 1981), pp. 283–84, describes Big Meadows (called the Feather River Meadows) as perceived by "49ers."

6. Charles M. Coleman, P. G. and E. of California: The Centennial Story of Pacific Gas and Electric Company, 1852–1952 (New York: McGraw-Hill, 1952) pp. 211–24, 267–76, describes the basic history of the Great Western Power Company and its parent corporation the Western Power Company.

7. Ibid., pp. 213–18.

8. Reports written by Howells and James D. Schuyler between 1902 and 1905 relating to the Feather River power development are retained in Folder #44, Schuyler Papers, WRCA.

9. "John Ripley Freeman," Transactions of the American Society of Civil Engineers 98 (1933): 1471–1676; Catskill Water Supply: A General Description and Brief History (New York: Board of Water Supply, 1917), pp. 7, 15, reports that Freeman served on the Commission on Additional Water Supply in 1902–1904; in 1905, he became consulting engineer to the Board of Water Supply, a position he held for many years. He was born in 1855 and died in 1932.

10. Data related to his work on the Owens Valley/Los Angeles aqueduct is available in Box 54, Freeman Papers, MIT. A copy of the December 1906 report prepared by Freeman, Schuyler, and Frederic Stearns regarding the proposed aqueduct is available in Folder #29, Schuyler Papers, WRCA.

11. Records documenting Freeman's extensive involvement in the GWPC's corporate and financial affairs from 1905 through 1926 are available in Box 65, Freeman Papers, MIT.

12. Coleman, *P. G. and E. of California,* pp. 217–24. Sinclair's appointment to replace E. P. Bryan is documented in H. P. Wilson to E. P. Bryan, May 8, 1909; and Edwin Hawley to H. H. Sinclair, May 6, 1909, Box 4, Sinclair Papers, HEH.

13. H. P. Wilson [secretary of the GWPC] to John R. Freeman, September 2, 1909; H. P. Wilson to John R. Freeman, September 8, 1909; and John R. Freeman to A. P. Davis, September 10, 1909, Box 62, Freeman Papers, MIT.

14. John R. Freeman to H. P. Wilson, September 10, 1909, indicates the contractors were Thomas F. Richardson (then general superintendent of construction for J. G. White & Company) and Jules Breachaud (a former engineer with the Boston Water Works and a contractor on the Croton Dam). Reference to the Croton Dam spillways is made in John R. Freeman to A. P. Davis, September 10, 1909; Box 62, Freeman Papers, MIT.

15. John R. Freeman to William Mulholland, September 16, 1909, and A. P. Davis to John R. Freeman, September 21, 1909, Box 62; and John R. Freeman, William Mulholland, and A. P. Davis, "Big Bend Dam Report, October 26, 1909," Box 63, Freeman Papers, MIT.

16. H. P. Wilson to John R. Freeman, December 11, 1909, Freeman Papers, MIT. Noble's approval of Freeman's design is noted in this letter, but no copy of the "Noble Report" on Big Bend survives. Noble's career is described in "Alfred Noble, Past-President, Am. Soc. C.E.," *Transactions of the American Society of Civil Engineers* 69 (1915): 1352–1415.

17. H. H. Sinclair to Edwin Hawley, October 8, 1909, Box 4, Sinclair Papers, HEH.

18. See H. H. Sinclair to John R. Freeman, February 21, 1910, and F. H. Tompkins to John R. Freeman, February 21, 1910, Box 62, Freeman Papers, MIT; H. H. Sinclair to H. P. Wilson, March 12, 1910, and "Memorandum of Discussions at Intake Dam, April 9th to 11th, 1910," prepared "by Mr. Freeman [and sent] to Messrs. Earl, Sinclair, Cone and Field," Box 4, Sinclair Papers, HEH.

19. "Minutes of a Special Meeting of the Executive Committee of the Great Western Power Co.," May 20, 1910, reveals that the committee "resolved that the recommendation of Vice President and General Manager H. H. Sinclair, dated May 20th, 1910 . . . is hereby accepted, adopted and approved." Originally, the firm intended to truncate the Freeman design in order to create the smaller

Big Bend Dam. Later, Sinclair reported that the structure was "built upon entirely new and distinct plans, made by our own force at an expenditure of less than $600." Sinclair indicated that the GWPC "paid to Messrs. Freeman, Davis, Mulholland, Crosby and Noble the sum of $41,453.17 for engineering services" at Big Bend; see H. H. Sinclair to H. P. Wilson, September 13, 1910, Box 4, Sinclair Papers, HEH. See also John R. Freeman to Julian Thornley, May 27, 1910; John R. Freeman to Edwin Hawley, July 2, 1910 [draft letter marked "not sent"]; and John R. Freeman to Julian Thornley, September 3, 1910; Box 62, Freeman Papers, MIT. Thornley acted as Freeman's resident engineer at Big Bend prior to June 1910.

20. "Edwin Hawley," *Railway Age Gazette* 52 (February 9, 1912): 237. Hawley's and Henry E. Huntington's shared participation in a Colorado and Southern Railroad syndicate is documented in HEH 11/1/(2) and HEH 11/6/(3); Edwin Hawley to Henry E. Huntington, June 7, 1901, HEH 2533, provides evidence of their personal relationship. See also "Hawley Roads of 8600 Miles Merge," *Los Angeles Examiner* (November 16, 1909), HEH 7/4/(24). Coleman, *P. G. and E. of California,* p. 218, reports that "through his connection with the Western Pacific Railroad [Hawley] knew something of the wealth of water power hidden in the Feather River Canyon." The main line of the Western Pacific extends up Feather River Canyon and passes near Big Meadows.

21. R. C. Clifford, "Canon Dam Explorations," October 23, 1910, Big Meadows Dam Folder (#18), JSE, WRCA. These studies included several "drill holes," each between 30 feet and 150 feet deep, that revealed a foundation of hardened "lava flow" with a few "clay streaks."

22. "James Dix Schuyler," *Transactions of the American Society of Civil Engineers* 76 (1913): 2243–45.

23. James D. Schuyler, "Report on the Design of Dams Suitable for the Impounding Reservoir of Great Western Power Company, at Big Meadows, Plumas County, California, March 4, 1911," Folder #44, Schuyler Papers, WRCA; this report refers to Sinclair's February 24, 1911, letter to Schuyler. The design submitted to Schuyler featured 21 arches with 28-foot spans.

24. The April 27, 1911, letter from the GWPC requesting Noble's assistance is referred to in Alfred Noble to Great Western Power Company, May 12, 1911, JSE 18, WRCA; this letter also notes Eastwood's conferences with Noble.

25. Ibid.

26. "The Big Meadows Dam," *Journal of Electricity Power and Gas* 27 (September 30, 1911): 287–89.

27. John S. Eastwood, "Description and General Specifications of the Big Meadows Dam, Great Western Power Company," (undated, ca. September 1912), noted that a "natural site" for the dam would have been about 3,000 feet "downstream from the selected site." Because this site was "located partly on Forest Reserve and partly on Indian allotment lands," the GWPC used "the most favorable site remaining."

28. Sinclair's temporary resignation from the company as of July 1, 1911, is noted in a corporate "Resolution" dated April 8, 1911, and confirmed in a letter from Sinclair to Edwin F. Robbins, June 13, 1911, Box 4, Sinclair Papers, HEH. The "Resolution" notes the GWPC's "high appreciation" of Sinclair's work. Despite his resignation, Sinclair retained active interest in the Big Meadows Dam, and the *Journal of Electricity Power and Gas* 27 (August 19, 1911): 172, described him as being responsible for "general supervision" of the company's "extension work" while indicating that he had recently "visited the scene of operations" at Big Meadows.

29. *Journal of Electricity Power and Gas* 28 (February 8, 1912): 125, and the *Sacramento Bee*, February 8, 1912.

30. Coleman, *P. G. and E. of California*, pp. 267–68.

31. Biographical data on Mortimer Fleishhacker is provided in *Makers of Northern California: Press Reference* (Sacramento: Sacramento Union, 1917), n.p.; Herbert Fleishhacker's business affairs are described in *Press Reference Library: Southwest Edition* (Los Angeles: *Los Angeles Examiner*, 1912), p. 159.

32. A. W. Bullard to John R. Freeman, Feb. 15, 1912, Box 63, Freeman Papers, MIT.

33. Freeman's involvement with San Francisco's water supply situation intensified in the summer of 1912 when he submitted a lengthy report recommending the flooding of Hetch Hetchy Valley in the Yosemite National Park. During this period, he was also a consultant on the construction of the concrete gravity Holter and Hauser dams in Montana and on the hydraulic fill Coquitlam Dam near Vancouver in British Columbia; see Boxes 97–99, Freeman Papers, MIT, and Charles A. Lee, "Enlargement of the Coquitlam-Buntzen Hydroelectric Power Development," *Engineering Record* 66 (September 21, 1912): 312–17.

34. John R. Freeman to Guy C. Earl, October 11, 1911; and John R. Freeman to A. W. Bullard, February 23, 1912, Box 63, Freeman Papers, MIT. In this context it is important to point out that all of the Great Western Power Company's stock (except for a nominal quantity held by board members to meet the requirements of California's incor-poration law) was held in trust by the Western Power Company (incorporated in New Jersey). Investors who wished to participate in the ownership and profits of the GWPC bought the stocks and bonds of this latter company.

35. "The Failure of a Concrete Dam at Austin, Pa., on September 30, 1911," *Engineering News* 66 (October 5, 1911): 419–22.

36. Bruce Sinclair, "Inventing a Genteel Tradition: MIT Crosses the River," p. 13, in *New Perspectives on Technology and American Culture* (Philadelphia: American Philosophical Society, 1986). The quotation is taken from John R. Freeman, "Study #7," Freeman Papers, MIT.

37. H. H. Sinclair, "Description of Big Meadows Reservoir and Dam Now Being Built by Great Western Power Company," April 11, 1912. JSE 18, WRCA.

38. A. W. Bullard to John R. Freeman, April 18, 1912, Box 63, Freeman Papers, MIT. Fleishhacker's support for multiple arch dams in the spring of 1912 is also reflected in his request that Eastwood prepare a multiple arch design for the White Salmon power project in Washington State. This request came to naught, as Stone & Webster soon built a concrete gravity dam at the site. See JSE to E. H. Rollins, May 3, 1912, JSE 18, WRCA; the White Salmon Dam Folder (#19), JSE, WRCA; and Wilbur B. Foshay, "The White Salmon River Development," *Journal of Electricity Power and Gas* 30 (June 28, 1913): 599–601.

39. JSE to John R. Freeman, May 21, 1912, JSE 18, WRCA.

40. "Specifications for Cantilever for Concrete Distribution. Big Meadows Dam," (no date, ca. May 1912); JSE to H. H. Sinclair, May 18, 1912; H. H. Sinclair to Mortimer Fleishhacker, June 30, 1912, reported that the first concrete was poured on June 13; JSE 18, WRCA.

41. H. H. Sinclair to George A. Batchelder, September 16, 1912; Box 4, Sinclair Papers, HEH.

42. Freeman's arrival on the Pacific coast is noted in the *Journal of Electricity Power and Gas* 28 (June 15, 1912): 606. His report "On the Proposed Use of a Portion of the Hetch Hetchy, Eleanor and Cherry Valleys . . . for the Water Supply of San Francisco, California, and Neighboring Cities" was formally submitted on July 15, 1912. This document, with its recommendations to flood the Hetch Hetchy Valley in Yosemite National Park, is synopsized in "A Notable Water-Supply Report," *Engineering News* 68 (December 26, 1912): 1207–14.

43. Freeman's visit to Big Meadows on August 5 and subsequent meetings on August 12 and August 26 are noted in John R. Freeman to H. P. Wilson, September 30, 1912, JSE 18, WRCA.

44. JSE to H. H. Sinclair, September 4, 1912, JSE 18, WRCA.

45. The State Railroad Commission's general file on the Big Meadows Dam (PUC, App. No. 357) does not contain material relevant to Eastwood's design earlier than the latter part of 1912. The PUC records also contain files from the Railroad Commission's "Hydraulic Division" that relate to dam construction. Among this division's files is a folder labeled "Big Meadows Dam" that contains several drawings of Eastwood's design, some dating to March, 1912; however, the file lacks any written material or correspondence.

46. Early designs for the outlet gates are discussed in JSE to Ralph Bennett, May 9, 1912, and in Ralph Bennett to JSE, August 6, 1912; both letters in JSE 18, WRCA.

47. A spillway's purpose is to provide a safe means of releasing water from a reservoir that is filling up too quickly with storm runoff. Siphon spillways utilize "suction action" to draw water out of a reservoir and disperse it more rapidly than a simple overflow spillway can. The major advantage of siphon spillways compared with overflow spillways is that they increase a dam's safe storage capacity. A memorandum from Ralph Bennett to H. H. Sinclair, July 24, 1912, explains that "the siphon spillway, with greater security and a cost less than half of that of a plain open weir adds 75,000 acre feet to the effective storage of the reservoir." This memo lists references to recent European installations, including Adolf Ludin, "Siphon Spillways in Europe," *Engineering News* 65 (April 20, 1911): 497-99. In JSE to P. E. Harroun, September 26, 1912, Eastwood acknowledged that siphon spillways were not an element of "general practice" in America and that some engineers considered them "too much of a novelty." Nonetheless, Eastwood considered the technology to be "highly recommended by the best posted hydraulic engineers." JSE 18, WRCA.

48. John R. Freeman, "Some Thoughts Suggested by the Austin Dam Failures Regarding Text Books on Hydraulic Engineering and Dam Design in General," *Engineering News* 66 (October 19, 1911): 462-63, acknowledges the susceptibility of gravity dams to weaken by "uplift" pressures. The article discusses the failure of gravity dams in Austin, Texas, and Austin, Pennsylvania, concentrating on the latter design.

49. Freeman's motive in writing the article is problematic because the article is inherently critical of gravity dam technology. After Eastwood and Sinclair began to draw attention to its contents, Freeman seems to have pretended that it did not exist; he never responded to Eastwood's assertions that the article bolstered arguments against using a gravity dam at Big Meadows.

50. H. H. Sinclair to H. H. Garstin, September 11, 1912; and H. H. Garstin to H. H. Sinclair, September 16, 1912; both letters in files of Bear Valley Mutual Water Company, Redlands, California. See also T. W. Decker to H. H. Sinclair, JSE 18, WRCA.

51. John S. Eastwood, "Statement Regarding the Stability and Safety of the Eastwood Multiple Arch Dam and Three Reasons for the Use of This Design at the Big Meadows Site of the Great Western Power Company" (undated, ca. September 1912), JSE 18, WRCA.

52. John S. Eastwood, "The Eastwood Multiple Arched Dam: An Outline and Description of the Structure, Methods and Purposes of Design," September 20, 1912, JSE 18, WRCA.

53. John R. Freeman to Arthur P. Davis, September 26, 1912, Box 63, Freeman Papers, MIT.

54. The October 3 *Sacramento Bee* noted a recent cave-in at the dam site but indicated that no one had been injured. This minor cave-in occurred near the east end of the dam and covered up some foundation excavations. The only article that reflected public interest in the dam design appeared on October 18 and focused on the concerns of the Indian Valley Light and Power Company that water for its small hydroelectric plant on the lower Feather River would be cut off when the Big Meadows Dam reached completion. The article also described "fears" among residents of Oroville, Chico, and Marysville over the safety of the dam and noted that GWPC stock was falling in price, supposedly because of these fears; however, the "fears" of Marysville residents went unreported by the *Marysville Appeal*.

55. JSE to H. H. Sinclair, September 4, 1912, JSE 18, WRCA. Significantly, Big Meadows did not represent the first time that Freeman had interjected the concept of "psychology" into a dam design process; in his July 1912 Hetch Hetchy report, he justified a massive earthen and rockfill design for the San Leandro Dam near Oakland with the disclaimer: "I have included the depositing of an immense amount of [rock] on top of the downstream slope of the proposed dam, more for its psychological effect on the public than for any sound engineering reason." See Freeman, "On the Proposed Use of a Portion of the Hetch Hetchy, Eleanor and Cherry Valleys . . . ," p. 134.

56. John R. Freeman to H. P. Wilson, September 30, 1912, JSE 18, WRCA, and Box 64, Freeman Papers, MIT. The letter appeared with the heading "Concerning the Tightness of Foundations of Proposed Big Meadows Dam, Great Western Power Company."

57. "Outline and Description of the Structure, Methods and Purposes of Design," September 20, 1912, p. 7, JSE 18, WRCA. In his September 30

letter to Wilson, Freeman estimated that placing the upstream fill would require a crew of five to ten men working two to three years.

58. Anson B. Burchard to John R. Freeman, October 5, 1912, Box 63, Freeman Papers, MIT.

59. James D. Schuyler to R. H. Perling ("Report on Construction of the Coquitlam Dam"), April 21, 1911. This letter also makes a veiled reference to Freeman in complaining about "the caprice, poor judgement, and inexperience of men in authority." Folder #310, Schuyler Papers, WRCA. Schuyler reportedly still held a favorable view of Eastwood's designs, at least as indicated in a letter to Eastwood in early 1914 from a prospective client who reported that "about a year ago Mr. Schuyler strongly advocated the Eastwood Multiple Arch Type." See James Lindsey to JSE, February 26, 1914, Smith Ferry Folder (#14), JSE, WRCA.

60. Noble and Woodward, "Memorandum on Big Meadows Dam," October 10, 1917, Box 63, Freeman Papers, MIT. Although this memo officially came from the office of Noble and Woodward, Noble evidently prepared it without any participation by his partner. It refers to a letter from Freeman to Wilson dated October 7 that does not survive.

61. John R. Freeman and Alfred Noble to H. P. Wilson, October 17, 1912; Box 63, Freeman Papers, MIT.

62. Efforts to assuage company concerns about the spillway, outlet gate, and temperature stresses in the arches are evident in JSE to P. E. Harroun, October 9, 1912 and JSE to P. E. Harroun (undated, ca. late October 1912), JSE 18, WRCA. In a "Discussion of the Temperature Stresses in the Multiple Arch Dam" that accompanied the latter letter, Eastwood undertook a sophisticated analysis based on the latest developments in elastic arch theory. His analysis is directly based on methods outlined in Ira O. Baker, *A Treatise on Masonry Construction,* 10th ed. (New York: John Wiley & Sons, 1909) pp. 691–701, to determine the magnitude of stresses due to temperature change and "rib-shortening." His analysis indicated that the reinforcing steel in the arches was capable of withstanding temperature changes of up to 250 Fahrenheit degrees without cracking. Eastwood's concern about temperature stresses and his thoughts on the validity of the elastic theory are discussed in Chapter 8. Clearly, however, he was adept at responding to technical questions related to the Big Meadows design and capable of drawing on the latest developments in structural analysis. The tenth edition of Baker's treatise was the first to include a section on elastic theory.

63. JSE to A. W. Burchard, October 29, 1912, JSE 18, WRCA. This letter was prompted by a sketch prepared by Burchard that undertook to show a "method of putting in stiffeners" in the Big Meadows Dam.

64. Along with "Description and General Specifications of the Big Meadows Dam," other general descriptions of Eastwood's design appear in JSE 18, WRCA. These include "Big Meadows Reservoir and Dam" (undated, fall 1912) and "Non-Technical Description of the Big Meadows Dam" (undated, fall 1912).

65. "Big Meadows Dam, Monthly Progress Statements," November 2, 1912, JSE 18, WRCA, provides statistics on work undertaken at the site between April and October 1912. These statements include data on quarry work, crushing plant operations, concrete production, excavation, and sawmill operations. The fact that concrete was placed in the arches in the deepest section of the dam is verified in several October 1912 photographs, Box 63, Freeman Papers, MIT.

66. H. H. Sinclair to Mortimer Fleishhacker, February 22, 1913, JSE 18, WRCA, confirms that "further work on the dam was stopped under your [Fleishhacker's] instructions." The "Monthly Progress Reports" indicate that all work at the site stopped as of October 22, 1912.

67. "Total Expenditure for Construction of Eastwood Multiple Arched Dam to December 1st, 1912," December 20, 1912, JSE 18, WRCA. Estimates of construction costs are difficult to interpret because they often included such things as (in this case) the construction of the Butt Creek hydroelectric plant and various roads, flumes, and buildings that were distinct from the dam proper.

68. A. W. Bullard to Executive Committee of the GWPC, November 27, 1912. This letter included corporate earnings data for the previous ten months and was printed in a form suitable for public distribution; Box 65, Freeman Papers, MIT. As evident in Great Western Power Company, "Application," January 11, 1913, PUC, App. No. 357, the company still officially planned to build a multiple arch dam as of this date.

69. Alfred Noble to H. P. Wilson, January 25, 1913, JSE 18, WRCA.

70. JSE to Mortimer Fleishhacker, February 14, 1913, JSE 18, WRCA.

71. H. H. Sinclair to Mortimer Fleishhacker, February 22, 1913, JSE 18, WRCA.

72. R. A. Thompson to Railroad Commission, February 7, 1913, PUC, App. No. 357. This letter indicates that P. E. Harroun, (hydraulic engineer for the Railroad Commission) and Thompson had visited the dam site on September 10, 1912.

73. According to "Reporter's Transcript," February 8, 1913, PUC, App. No. 357, Sinclair provided verbal estimates of the cost of completing Eastwood's design and also indicated a belief that

the company had "adopted final plans in all respects." In private correspondence with his nephew only a week later, however, Sinclair stated that "in all probability Stone and Webster will probably take my place in direct charge of construction [at Big Meadows]." This is the only time that Stone & Webster is mentioned in surviving material related to the Big Meadows controversy, and it reveals that Sinclair anticipated Eastwood's impending dismissal. H. H. Sinclair to H. S. Hall, February 15, 1913, Box 5, Sinclair Papers, HEH. The cost estimates for a gravity dam are given in "Big Meadows Dam, Amended Estimate," February 19, 1913, PUC, App. No. 357; and JSE 18, WRCA.

74. Railroad Commission of California, "Order," March 11, 1913, PUC, App. No. 357.

75. Railroad Commission of California to JSE, March 25, 1913, PUC, App. No. 357.

76. H. P. Wilson to John R. Freeman, March 5, 1913, Box 63, Freeman Papers, MIT.

77. Memorandum from John R. Freeman (with Alfred Noble's concurrence) to Railroad Commission of California, April 25, 1913, PUC, App. No. 357, and Box 64, Freeman Papers, MIT.

78. In James D. Schuyler to Don Eduardo Giorgetti ("Report on a System of Irrigation for the Sugar Cane Lands, Near Barceloneta, P.R., owned or leased by the Plazuela Sugar Company,"), October 31, 1911, Schuyler indicated that he had "engaged the services of Mr. Julius Howells, of San Francisco, as my assistant to make the necessary studies in the field." See also Julius Howells to James D. Schuyler, August 1, 1911, Folder #351. In James D. Schuyler to B. F. Johnston, September 20, 1904, Schuyler offered to "send my associate, Mr. J. M. Howells . . . to make preliminary studies on the ground" for an irrigation project in Mexico. Folder #335; Schuyler Papers, WRCA. In Julius Howells to John R. Freeman, April 11, 1913, Howells commented that "after years of wandering I find myself back with a house at my old home and that is quite as much to my pleasure. I am again working at the problems of the Great Western Power Company." Box 63, Freeman Papers, MIT.

79. Freeman left for Europe in early June and did not return to America until the end of August. He indicated displeasure with Howells's design (for example, that it wasn't thick enough) in John R. Freeman to Mortimer Fleishhacker, October 7, 1913, and John R. Freeman to Mortimer Fleishhacker, October 30, 1913; Box 63, Freeman Papers, MIT.

80. No articles appeared in the technical or popular press describing the hydraulic fill dam's initial construction. The best description of both the 1913 construction and the enlargement undertaken in the mid-1920s is in R. F. Krafft, "Big Meadows Dam Enlargement, 1925-1926: A De-

scription," Folder #40, John D. Galloway Papers, WRCA. See also D. R. Warren, "Raising of the Big Meadows Dam, Plumas Co., Cal.," *Modern Irrigation* 3 (June 1927): 42-44, and Coleman, *P. G. and E. of California*, pp. 270-72. Soon after the structure was raised in 1925-1926 it began to spring muddy leaks. These leaks greatly concerned the company's engineers but were never given any public notice; for more on this persistent but not catastrophic problem, see "Report of Unusual Conditions at Big Meadows Dam, June 18th, 1929," Folder #39, and extensive correspondence among A. H. Markwart, D. C. Henny, and John D. Galloway in Folder #41, John D. Galloway Papers, WRCA. Development of the earth dam's profile from 1914 through 1963 is illustrated in State of California, Department of Water Resources, "Environmental Impact Report: Lake Almanor Project," February 1976, p. 16. The name *Almanor* given to the Big Meadows reservoir was derived from the names of Guy Earl's three daughters: Alice, Mary, and Eleanor.

81. See W. O. Crosby, "Report on the Big Meadows and Butt Valley Dam Sites of the Great Western Power Company on the North Fork of the Feather River and on Butt Creek, Plumas County, California," April-June, 1913, Box 64; and John R. Freeman to H. A. Rands, September 17, 1913, Box 63; Freeman Papers, MIT.

82. J. A. Bumgarner to H. H. Sinclair, September 15, 1913, provides evidence that Sinclair kept abreast of activities at Big Meadows. His records also detail numerous GWPC stock transactions during 1913-1914; Box 4, Sinclair Papers, HEH. The *Journal of Electricity Power and Gas* 33 (September 12, 1914): 256, and *The Pasadena Star,* September 2, 1914, include obituaries for Sinclair.

83. See Dan Van Wagenen to H. H. Sinclair, March 21, 1913, and Dan Van Wagenen to H. H. Sinclair, March 30, 1913, Box 5, Sinclair Papers, HEH; and JSE to H. H. Sinclair, April 8, 1913, Twin States Irrigation and Power Co. Folder (#5), JSE, WRCA. Eastwood investigated the investment potential of a power and irrigation project along the north slope of the Uintah Mountains on the Utah/Wyoming border and advised Sinclair that the proposed undertaking was infeasible.

84. Freeman's ascension to the Western Power Company's board of directors is noted in John R. Freeman to H. P. Wilson, June 18, 1915, Box 65, and his impending resignation is documented in F. L. Dame to John R. Freeman, January 9, 1926, Box 67. A note at the bottom of the latter letter indicates that, at the start of 1926, Freeman controlled more than $375,000 worth of the firm's securities. The North American Company sold the GWPC system to PG&E in 1930.

85. Quotation from Bruce Sinclair, "Inventing a Genteel Tradition," p. 8. Freeman's initiative to build the enlarged Big Meadows Dam (including a lengthy legal dispute regarding compensation for design work) is documented in Boxes 64–67, Freeman Papers, MIT.

86. In the only previously published account mentioning Eastwood's dam at Big Meadows, Coleman, *P. G. and E. of California*, p. 270, reported that a "thick seam of clay lay beneath the stratum of lava on which the buttresses were to rest" and implied that technical considerations were responsible for the abandonment of Eastwood's design. This is false. Freeman did his best to heighten concern over the thin clay streaks found in some of the buttress excavations, but uneasiness about these streaks did not constitute the official reason why the design was abandoned.

87. John R. Freeman to Arthur P. Davis, September 26, 1912, Box 63, Freeman Papers, MIT. He also "confessed to sharing the feeling of wise Old Mr. Francis," who apparently once stated that he "somehow liked that type of dam best which would be as tall after it had been tipped over as it was before."

88. John R. Freeman to Arthur P. Davis, September 26, 1912, and Noble and Woodward, "Memorandum on Big Meadows Dam," October 10, 1912, Box 63, Freeman Papers, MIT.

89. Railroad Commission of California to JSE, March 25, 1913, PUC, App. No. 357.

90. JSE to Railroad Commission of California, March 17, 1913, PUC, App. No. 357; and JSE 18, WRCA. In this letter, Eastwood also complained that "if all things were to be condemned because they were new, there could be no advancement."

91. "Report on the Construction of Big Meadows Dam, Great Western Power Company," February 27, 1913, PUC, App. No. 357, includes data on payments made to Eastwood.

92. The "force account" method for compensating Eastwood was initially recommended by Noble. See Alfred Noble to GWPC, May 12, 1911, JSE 18, WRCA. "Force account work" is defined in Daniel J. Hauer, *The Economics of Contracting* (Chicago: E. H. Baumgartner, 1911), p. 29.

93. See John R. Freeman to A. W. Bullard, February 23, 1912, Box 63, Freeman Papers, MIT, for evidence of what Freeman intended to charge the GWPC for his services during 1912.

94. In the pre–World War I era, three major hydroelectric projects were developed in California: the Pacific Light and Power Corporation's Big Creek project; the Great Western Power Company's Feather River project; and the Pacific Gas and Electric Company's Bear River development. Eastwood played a prominent role in two of these projects.

95. Extended calculations and notes for this 300-foot-high design are included in JSE 21, WRCA.

96. "Eastwood Bulletin," *Western Engineering* 5 (March 1915).

Chapter Seven

1. *Journal of Electricity Power and Gas* 27 (November 11, 1911): 466, reports Eastwood's establishment of an office in the Hearst Building.

2. See Carroll Purcell, "The Technical Society of the Pacific Coast (1884–1914)," *Technology and Culture* 17 (October 1976): 707–17.

3. For an uncritical history of the ASCE, see William H. Wisely, *The American Civil Engineer (1852–1974)* (New York: American Society of Civil Engineers, 1974). Events in the early nineteenth century are chronicled in Daniel B. Calhoun, *The American Civil Engineer* (Cambridge, Mass.: MIT Press, 1960).

4. Eastwood's June 12 talk to the ASCE in San Francisco is noted in "The New Bear Valley Dam in California," *Engineering Record* 66 (August 31, 1912): 239.

5. *Proceedings of the American Society of Civil Engineers* 39 (October 1913): 658, lists Eastwood's "Date of Membership" as September 3, 1913. No record documents his departure from the ASCE.

6. Discussion by John S. Eastwood on Arthur P. Davis and D. C. Henny, "Dams," *Transactions of the International Engineering Conference, 1915: Waterways and Irrigation* (San Francisco: Neal Publishing, 1916), p. 714. In a private letter, Eastwood further criticized Davis and Henny's paper as being "a tame and inane resume of what the [Reclamation] Service has done in trying to build dams on the wrong principles." See JSE to Gardiner Williams, September 9, 1915. Multiple Arch Dam Folder (#4), JSE, WRCA.

7. JSE to I. C. Steel[e], February 9, 1921, JSE #4, WRCA.

8. John S. Eastwood, "The Railroad Commission and the Public," *Journal of Electricity Power and Gas* 32 (January 17, 1914): 51–54; and John S. Eastwood, "Thinks Favorably of the New Water Power Bill," *Journal of Electricity Power and Gas* 32 (March 7, 1914): 208. The proposed "Jones Bill" (a distant forerunner of the 1920 Federal Water Power Act) discussed in the latter article is described in the *Journal of Electricity Power and Gas* 32 (February 28, 1914): 181–82.

9. Donald J. Pisani, *From Family Farm to Agribusiness: The Irrigation Crusade in California, 1850–1930*, (Berkeley: University of California

Press, 1984), pp. 303-4, 327-33, 386-87, discusses the Sacramento River navigation controversy.

10. John S. Eastwood, "Syllabus of an Illustrated Lecture Proposed for the Internal Water Ways Congress, January 15-18, 1914" JSE 3, WRCA.

11. George Holmes Moore, "Neglected First Principles of Masonry Dam Design," *Engineering News* 70 (September 4, 1913): 442-45. Moore is identified as a member of the "City Engineer's Office, Seattle, Washington." Eastwood's response appeared in *Engineering News* 70 (October 23, 1913): 832-33. Other responses (by Robert Fletcher, Lars Jorgensen, and Edward Wegmann) appeared in *Engineering News* 70 (September 25, 1913): 623-26.

12. John S. Eastwood, "The Ultimate Dam," *Western Engineering* 3 (September 1913): 175-79.

13. "The Ultimate Dam" does not ignore economic issues, but it primarily describes the structural merits of multiple-arch designs.

14. George L. Dillman, "The Great Hydraulic Principle: Or How to Make Engineering Structures Hold Water," *Engineering News* 69 (June 12, 1913): 1225.

15. John S. Eastwood, "The New Big Bear Valley Dam," *Western Engineering* 3 (December 1913): 458-70.

16. The "Eastwood Bulletin" was distributed with the March 1915 issue of *Western Engineering* but was also intended to serve as an independent promotional leaflet for prospective clients.

17. "Eastwood Bulletin," p. 4.

18. In the period 1913-1917, Eastwood employed E. M. Whitlock as an office helper and survey assistant. He later engaged George E. Holyoke to help prepare drawings; Holyoke also served for several months as his on-site representative during construction of the Anyox Dam.

19. "Eastwood Bulletin," p. 4.

20. John S. Eastwood, "Los Verjels Dam, A Multiple Arched Structure," *Western Engineering* 5 (July 1914): 7-9.

21. V. T. McGillicuddy to H. M. Wells, December 9, 1915, JSE 16, WRCA. See also JSE to Chico Construction Company, September 11, 1913; and JSE to Chico Construction Company, September 12, 1913; both in JSE 23, WRCA.

22. JSE to V. T. McGillicuddy, September 1, 1914, JSE 23, WRCA.

23. In JSE to C. Gulling, July 25, 1914, he requests an opportunity to "make you then a new figure below the $10,000 mark for building this dam." This project involved an ice company near Reno, Nevada. Grizzly Creek Dam Folder (#25), JSE, WRCA.

24. Eastwood, "Los Verjels Dam." The maximum arch thickness of 13 inches and the minimum arch thickness of 6 inches is noted in V. T. McGillicuddy to H. M. Wells, December 9, 1915, JSE 16, WRCA. Eastwood later stated that the top 36 feet of the arches as built were only 6 inches thick (see JSE to George L. Davenport, August 16, 1921, Cave Creek Dam Folder #45, JSE, WRCA) but this was almost certainly an exaggeration. In Edward Wegmann and Fred Noetzli, *The Design and Construction of Dams*, 8th ed. (New York: John Wiley & Sons, 1927), p. 472, the dam's arches are described as being 6 inches thick for the top 26 feet. This dimension corresponds to what the cylinder formula would stipulate.

25. Quotations taken from "Description and General Specifications of the Los Verjels Dam" and JSE to Chico Construction Company, November 16, 1913, both in JSE 23, WRCA. Eastwood "selected and staked out" the dam site on September 2, 1913. Dates of construction are from "Eastwood Bulletin," p. 3.

26. Eastwood, "Los Verjels Dam," p. 8; and "Description and General Specifications," pp. 7-8, JSE 23, WRCA.

27. By late 1913, R. A. Thompson, the engineer who expressed so little confidence in Eastwood during the Big Meadows controversy, was no longer with the State Railroad Commission. Robinson Wilber Hawley's appointment as hydraulic engineer for the commission was reported in *Engineering News* 70 (November 20, 1913): 1057. Hawley graduated from Colorado State College in 1896 with a degree in irrigation engineering. He worked for the U.S. Reclamation Service before joining the Railroad Commission in 1913 at the age of 37. Information about his early career is outlined in F. H. Newell, comp., *Proceedings of the First Conference of Engineers of the Reclamation Service* (Washington, D.C.: Government Printing Office, 1904), p. 328.

28. Railroad Commission of the State of California to J. H. Wood, March 25, 1914. PUC File #630.1. See also Charles R. Detrick to JSE, February 19, 1914, and JSE to Charles R. Detrick, February 20, 1914; both in JSE 23, WRCA.

29. Railroad Commission of the State of California to J. H. Wood, March 25, 1914. In Railroad Commission of the State of California to Ralph W. McCormick (Secretary, Merchants Association of Marysville and Yuba City), March 25, 1914, the commission offered reassurance that "the type of dam and the method of construction are of such a character that the life and property of individuals below the reservoir will not be endangered" and that reports of "dirt in the mixture of concrete" were "entirely without foundation." PUC File 630.1. See also Railroad Commission of the State of California to JSE, March 26, 1914, JSE 23, WRCA.

30. JSE to V. T. McGillicuddy, September 1, 1914, JSE 23, WRCA.

31. Ibid.; and V. T. McGillicuddy to H. M. Wells, December 9, 1915, JSE 16, WRCA.

32. Eastwood, "Los Verjels Dam," p. 9.

33. Robert Kelley, *Gold vs. Grain: The Mining Debris Controversy* (Glendale, Calif.: Arthur H. Clark, 1959); and Joseph J. Hawgood, Jr., *The California Debris Commission: A History* (Sacramento: Army Corps of Engineers, 1981).

34. Major S. A. Cheney to JSE, February 26, 1914, JSE 4, WRCA; Reference to Colonel Heuer's approval appears in John S. Eastwood, "The Kennedy Dam," *Western Engineering* 5 (April 1915): 407-9. Eastwood's first plans for a debris dam were developed in the fall of 1913 for the Brandy City Mining Company's operation on the North Fork of the Yuba River (not far from the Los Verjels Dam); see Yuba Dam Folder (#8), JSE, WRCA.

35. "Outline Statement of General Dimensions of the Kennedy Dam," n.d. (ca. May 1914), and "Description and Specifications of the Kennedy Debris Dam Extension," (1916), both in Kennedy Dam Folder #14, JSE, WRCA. The completed structure is described in "Two Eastwood-Dam Installations in California," *Engineering and Mining Journal* 103 (February 24, 1917): 334-35.

36. "The Kennedy Dam," pp. 407-8.

37. One of the earliest references to three-hinged construction in the American technical press is "A Three-Hinged Concrete Arch Bridge Over the Danube at Eringen," *Engineering News* 47 (January 9, 1902): 35-36. An excellent description of William Thomas's three-hinged arch bridges built in the period 1908-17 is available in Bonnie Wehle Parks, "Parks Bar Bridge (Yuba River Bridge)," HAER File CA-#132, 1993. Prints and Photographs Division, Library of Congress, Washington, D.C.

38. "The Kennedy Dam," p. 409; The "Eastwood Bulletin," p. 3, identifies the total cost of the dam. In "Two Eastwood-Dam Installations in California," p. 334, the cost of the extension is given as $26,367.

39. Argonaut Dam Folder (#13), JSE, WRCA; "Two Eastwood-Dam Installations in California;" and Lewis H. Eddy, "The Argonaut Mine, California," *Engineering and Mining Journal* 102 (August 5, 1916): 265-67.

40. Cannon's April 6, 1915, letter to Eastwood is referenced in JSE to Sylvester Q. Cannon, April 16, 1915, JSE 4, WRCA. The Twin Lakes Dam was designed to expand the capacity of a natural lake in the headwaters of Big Cottonwood Creek. For more on Salt Lake City's water supply system during this era, see Sylvester Muir and Gilbert Wheelwright, "Municipal Water Supply of Salt Lake City, Utah" (B.S. thesis, University of Utah, 1932).

41. Eastwood Construction Company to Board of Commissioners, Salt Lake City Corporation, April 17, 1915; and "Data Sheet for an Eastwood Multiple-Arched Dam" n.d. (ca. April 1915) in Twin Lakes Dam Folder #35, JSE, WRCA.

42. "New Dam Increases Salt Lake City Water Supply," *Engineering Record* 74 (September 9, 1916): 314-15, describes the concrete gravity dam built at Twin Lakes. Construction began on June 9, 1915, so Eastwood's overtures came at a late date in the contracting process. Cannon first approached Eastwood about the proposed Mountain Dell Dam in Sylvester Q. Cannon to JSE, [July] 10, 1915, Mountain Dell Dam Folder (#16), JSE, WRCA. [A stenographer misdated the letter sent to Eastwood and erroneously typed June instead of July.]

43. "Memorandum Relative to Mountain Dell Dam in Parleys Canyon," July 8, 1915, JSE 16, WRCA. Eastwood's procedure in developing the Mountain Dell design is described more fully in Chapter 8.

44. JSE to Sylvester Q. Cannon, July 26, 1915, JSE 16, WRCA.

45. Sylvester Q. Cannon to JSE, September 17, 1915, JSE 16, WRCA. Lack of interest in an earthfill dam may have been fueled by the failure of a large structure of this type in southern Utah during the previous year. See Guy Sterling, "Failure of the Dam of the Hatchtown Reservoir, Utah," *Engineering News* 71 (June 4, 1914): 1274-75.

46. "Summary of Bids, Mountain Dell Dam," November 24, 1915; and an "Abstract of Bids," JSE 16, WRCA.

47. JSE to Sylvester Q. Cannon, December 7, 1915, JSE 16, WRCA, notes Eastwood's recent trip to Salt Lake City. "Proceedings of the Board of Commissioners," *Salt Lake City Municipal Record* 5 (February 10, 1916): 9, documents the state engineer's approval of the design and the formal acceptance of Parrott Brothers' bid.

48. "High Multiple-Arch Concrete Dam for Salt Lake City Water Supply," *Engineering News-Record* 80 (March 7, 1918): 455-57; and Sylvester Q. Cannon, "The Mountain Dell Dam," *Monthly Journal Utah Society of Engineers* 3 (September 1917): 223-30; Salt Lake City Engineering Dept., *Annual Report of the City Engineer, 1916*, p. 99; and Salt Lake City Engineering Dept., *Annual Report of the City Engineer, 1917*, p. 44.

49. For contemporaneous discussion of this technology, see "Concrete Chuting Predominant," *Engineering News* 74 (August 12, 1915): 321; "Opposition to Concrete Chutes," *Engineering News* 74 (September 2, 1915): 468; and "Improved

Chuting of Concrete," *Engineering News* 74 (September 23, 1915): 612.

50. "Excess Water in Spouted Concrete," *Engineering News* 69 (March 27, 1913): 631; and "Effect of Too Much Water in Mixing Concrete," *Engineering News* 69 (May 22, 1913): 1063.

51. Cannon, "The Mountain Dell Dam," p. 229, noted that the "28 day" strength of the buttress concrete was 1,500 psi, while for the arch concrete it was 2,000 psi. This was less than the 3,000 psi that Eastwood claimed provided his designs with a "safety factor" of 10 in crushing. Cannon expressed satisfaction with the concrete, however, and claimed that it allowed a "safety factor" of 7.

52. "High Multiple-Arch Dam for Salt Lake City Water Supply," p. 457.

53. Fred Noetzli served as consultant to Salt Lake City when the dam was raised after Eastwood's death (see *Engineering News-Record* 93 (October 20, 1924): 563). Noetzli apparently counseled the city to build the enlarged dam without a vertical head.

54. Eastwood's payment is noted in "Special Engineer for Mountain Dell Dam," *Salt Lake City Municipal Record* 5 (February 10, 1916): 7. He was to receive "$2,672 additional" if the dam were extended to its full height.

55. "The Mountain Dell Dam," p. 226.

56. Sylvester Q. Cannon to JSE, [July] 10, 1915, JSE 16, WRCA.

57. George Q. Cannon was a prominent leader in the church hierarchy and played a role in the "Americanization" of Utah in the 1890s. Leonard Arrington, *Great Basin Kingdom: An Economic History of the Latter-Day Saints, 1830–1900* (Lincoln: University of Nebraska Press, 1958), p. 395, notes that he served as president of the church-controlled Pioneer Electric Power Company (which was to have built the multiple arch dam proposed by Henry Goldmark in 1897) when it was organized in 1895. Biographical information on his son, Sylvester Quayle Cannon, is available in *Transactions of the American Society of Civil Engineers* 109 (1944): 1472-74. See also Sylvester Q. Cannon, "An Unusual Dam," *Engineering News* 73 (May 6, 1915): 860, which provides an account of the diversion structure at the Jordan Narrows between Utah Lake and the Great Salt Lake; and Sylvester Q. Cannon, "Concrete-Lined Reservoir at Salt Lake City, Utah," *Engineering News* 74 (December 30, 1915): 1249, which describes the holding basin built in the upper reaches of City Creek.

58. "Special Engineer for Mountain Dell Dam," pp. 7-8.

59. Malad Dam Folder (#7), JSE, WRCA. The Malad River flows southward out of Idaho

into the Great Salt Lake. Historically, the river basin was closely tied to the economy of northern Utah.

60. Carey Valley [Fish Creek] Dam Folder (#15), JSE, WRCA. The Fish Creek Dam is noted in George A. McLeod, *History of Alturas and Blaine Counties, Idaho* (Hailey, Idaho: *Hailey Times*, 1946): 118.

61. J. H. Smith to JSE, August 19, 1915; JSE to J. H. Smith, December 14, 1916; and J. H. Smith to JSE, December 23, 1916; JSE 7, WRCA.

62. Eastwood made trips to visit both the Malad and the Fish Creek dam sites, but both projects required relatively little effort once a design had been accepted. Eastwood's fee for the two dams is unknown, but it was probably around 5 percent of the total construction cost.

63. JSE to C. H. Thompson, October 16, 1915, JSE 7, WRCA.

64. The career of this important San Diego developer is described in his autobiography, *Memoirs of Ed Fletcher* (San Diego: privately printed, 1952). Although historians must treat Fletcher's memoirs with the degree of skepticism appropriate for all autobiographies, they constitute a valuable source of information on San Diego County history and on several projects involving Eastwood.

65. See "Agreement" between C. W. Gates and W. G. Kerckhoff [parties of the first part] and Frank Salmons and Ed Fletcher [parties of the second part], November 1905, Box 35, Drawer 1; O'Melveny Papers, HEH.

66. "The Five Dams and Wood Stave Conduit of the Southern California Water Co." *Engineering News* 51 (April 7, 1904): 335-337; and Robert Fletcher, "Noteworthy Water Storage and Irrigation Works of Southern California," *Engineering News* 46 (August 22, 1901): 124-27. H. Austin Adams, *The Story of Water in San Diego and What the Southern California Mountain Water Company Has Done to Solve the Problem* (Chula Vista, Calif.: Denrich Press, n.d. [ca. 1910]) describes how the Spreckels interests controlled San Diego's water supply. See also Fletcher, *Memoirs*, pp. 205-10.

67. Fletcher, *Memoirs*, pp. 71-116. Impetus for the project came from Henry Huntington and William Kerckhoff, who were interested in developing power for an electric railroad line from Los Angeles to San Diego. More data is available in the H. W. O'Melveny Papers and the Henry E. Huntington Papers, at the Huntington Library, San Marino, California.

68. Fletcher, *Memoirs*, pp. 231-54. Eastwood's preliminary proposals for the Fletcher/Henshaw interests in 1914 are documented in Warner Dam Folder (#56), JSE, WRCA.

69. Fletcher, *Memoirs*, pp. 211-30, describes

his association with the Santa Fe Railway. The railroad's troubles with its tree farm may have had less to do with its tending techniques than with its choice of tree to grow. In the early 1900s, enterprising Australians had introduced American entrepreneurs to the eucalyptus—showing them stands of fine tall blue gum eucalyptus trees, presenting examples of hardwood eucalyptus building materials, assuring them of the trees' rapid growth rate in California-like conditions of temperature and rainfall, and selling them millions of blue gum eucalyptus seedlings. A boom in eucalyptus-growing ventures ensued in California, which collapsed only when the Californians belatedly discovered that the blue gum eucalyptus they had planted was a commercially worthless species entirely different from the hardwood eucalyptus that was used for lumber in Australia. Fletcher appears to have taken over the reins of Santa Fe's tree farm just as the eucalyptus bubble was bursting. See Malcolm Margolin, *The East Bay Out* (Berkeley, Calif.: Heyday Books, 1974), pp. 28, 36-37. This reference courtesy of Steven Gray.

70. Fletcher, *Memoirs,* pp. 179-86.

71. Ibid., pp. 151-79, describes the history of the San Diego Flume Company and its subsequent reorganization as the Cuyamaca Water Company. See also Hiram N. Savage Papers, Folder #36, WRCA.

72. Julius Howells designed and built the La Mesa Dam in 1895. For a description, see James D. Schuyler, *Reservoirs for Irrigation, Water Power and Domestic Water Supply,* 2d ed. (New York: John Wiley & Sons, 1909), pp. 95-105.

73. This near disaster is described in John S. Eastwood, "Recent Multiple Arch Dams," *Journal of Electricity* 42 (March 15, 1919): 263-64.

74. JSE to W. S. Post, March 12, 1917, Box 8, Fletcher Papers, UCSD, indicates that, in the spring of 1916, Eastwood made "two estimates" to replace the La Mesa Dam; however, no correspondence related to this work survives. Fletcher explored the idea of building a multiple-arch dam at the Carroll site in 1914-1915, using designs prepared by W. S. Post. See drawings by Post in Box 8, Ed Fletcher Papers, UCSD. The first evidence of Eastwood's work on the Carroll site is in JSE to W. G. Henshaw, June 2, 1916, Lake Hodges (Carroll) Dam Folder (#31), JSE, WRCA.

75. JSE to Ed Fletcher, March 15, 1917; and "Descriptive and Detail Specifications of the Murray Dam," (ca. March 1917); San Diego Dams Folder (#54), JSE, WRCA.

76. Ed Fletcher to Railroad Commission, March 29, 1917; R. W. Hawley to Max Thelan, April 24, 1917; and Railroad Commission to Cuyamaca Water Company, April 28, 1917; File #630.1, PUC. See also memo from H. F. Clark to

R. W. Hawley, June 1917, Hydraulic Division File #D1383-85 F3439-36, PUC.

77. Eastwood, "Recent Multiple Arch Dams," p. 264.

78. "Contract" between Ed Fletcher, James Murray, and William Henshaw [parties of the first part] and John S. Eastwood [party of the second part], March 28, 1917, stipulates Eastwood's design fee at $5,000; Eastwood's offer to act as contractor for a fee of $9,500 is made in JSE to Ed Fletcher, March 15, 1917; JSE 54, WRCA. Faude's role is noted in Eastwood, "Recent Multiple Arch Dams."

79. Railroad Commission to JSE, August 17, 1917, JSE 54, WRCA. Concrete quantities for the completed Murray Dam are listed in Ed Fletcher to A. P. Davis, April 25, 1919; NA, RG 115, Entry 3, Box 287. In a memo from R. W. Hawley to Max Thelan, September 20, 1917 (File #D1383-85 F3439-36, PUC), Hawley mentioned that "there has been a great deal of energetic opposition to Mr. Eastwood and the building of this type of dam," but he remained untroubled by the controversy over the integrity of the multiple arch structure. Hawley also alluded to W. S. Post's involvement with Lippincott in an alternative design for the site. For more, see Sharp and Fellows Company File #90, J. B. Lippincott Papers, WRCA.

80. Eastwood's visit to the Carroll Dam site in May 1916 is described in JSE to W. G. Henshaw, February 5, 1917, JSE 31, WRCA.

81. JSE to W. G. Henshaw, June 2, 1916, JSE 31, WRCA.

82. JSE to W. G. Henshaw, February 5, 1917, JSE 31, WRCA.

83. Lars Jorgensen, "Estimate of Cost of Constant Angle Arch on Carroll Dam Site 'C'," (ca. February 1917); and "Estimate of Cost of Multiple Arch Dam on Carroll Dam Site 'C'," (ca. February 1917); Box 8, Ed Fletcher Papers, UCSD. Jorgensen considered a single arch dam for the site to be cheaper than a multiple arch dam. He later expressed dissatisfaction with Eastwood's design for the Carroll site, claiming that its concrete members were too thin. See Lars Jorgensen, "Safety Factors in Multiple Arch Dam," *Journal of Electricity* 42 (April 1, 1919): 327-28.

84. W. S. Post to E. O. Faulkner, March 26, 1917; JSE to W. S. Post, March 27, 1917; and George L. Davenport to G. C. Millett, April 7, 1917; Box 8, Fletcher Papers, UCSD.

85. Agreement between "Arthur S. Bent and H. Stanley Bent, doing business as a co-partnership under the firm name of Bent Brothers and the San Dieguito Mutual Water Company," dated May 15, 1917, Box 8, Fletcher Papers, UCSD. Bent Brothers became one of the premier dam-building contractors in the West during the 1920s.

See Arthur S. Bent, "Problems in Concrete Dam Construction on the Pacific Coast," *Transactions of the American Society of Civil Engineers* 92 (1928): 1400-1403.

86. Concrete quantities from Ed Fletcher to A. P. Davis, April 25, 1919, NA, RG 115, Entry 3, Box 287.

87. Eastwood's original Lake Hodges Dam spillway design is described in "Detailed Specifications for Multiple Arch Dam at Carroll Reservoir for the San Dieguito Mutual Water Co." (ca. April 1917), JSE, WRCA.

88. Eastwood declared that "the spillway is McClure's and Huber's" and indicated that the new spillway increased costs by more than $50,000 in JSE to Mr. Bowers, February 25, 1919, JSE 31, WRCA. Bowers served as Pacific Coast representative for *Engineering-News Record*.

89. JSE to Mr. Bowers, February 25, 1919, JSE 31, WRCA. In his *Memoirs*, p. 598, Ed Fletcher also bemoaned the huge amount of water wasted over the Lake Hodges spillway. He reported that long-time San Diego city manager F. A. Rhodes believed that "more water has run over the Lake Hodges spillway [between 1925 and 1950] than the entire City of San Diego used during that same twenty-five year period."

90. Excavation data are given in E. O. Faulkner to JSE, November 13, 1917, and in W. A. Sumner to E. O. Faulkner, November 11, 1917, both letters in JSE 31, WRCA. Beyond the work required by the altered spillway, excavation for the arch and buttress foundations exceeded the original estimates.

91. JSE to Mr. Bowers, February 25, 1919, JSE 31, WRCA. Referring to "clogging" within the "cable suspended" chutes, Eastwood observed that "the wad of concrete coming through destroys the nicely planned gradient in the spout and it sags where you want the grade the most."

92. H. L. Tilley, "Multiple Arch Dam Withstands Overtopping During Construction," *Western Engineering* 9 (May 1918): 177-78. This article provides a detailed description of the flood that passed through the partially completed structure. The flood is also noted in "Record Height Concrete Multiple-Arch Dam Completed," *Engineering News* 82 (April 10, 1919): 720-21. This article reported that "the low arch was overtopped to a depth of about 20 feet, the flow falling between the two buttresses for several days without damage."

93. In planning for the Big Meadows Dam, Eastwood had first encountered the suggestion that a multiple-arch dam might collapse like a row of dominoes if one arch were suddenly damaged; responding to comments made by James D. Schuyler, he referred to this hypothesis as "nonsensical" and "an impossible occurrence," explaining that— even if one arch did suddenly give way—the water from the reservoir would merely drain through the opening left by the missing arch. The experience at Lake Hodges served to validate his prognostication. See John S. Eastwood, "Notes on the Schuyler Report and on the Chodzko Report" (undated), JSE 18, WRCA. These comments were apparently not written until 1912; but with regard to the sections quoted, they almost certainly reflect his beliefs as of early 1911. Chodzko's report (p. 5) indicates that Eastwood had said that destruction of an arch would do nothing other than cause the reservoir to empty quickly.

94. As at Lake Hodges, Eastwood expressed some dissatisfaction with the quality of construction at San Dieguito. In particular, he complained that the buttress foundations were not properly cleaned, arguing that this would have involved "washing [them] . . . with a hose under pressure." He also criticized the contractors' practice of pouring arch concrete "on a slope" (instead of completing each lift so that it was horizontally level) because this "[precipitates] sagging in the concrete after the initial set has taken place [and] opens up numerous cracks across the wall." In his specifications, Eastwood stipulated that concrete was to be poured in "longitudinal lifts" to prevent sagging and later cracking. JSE to E. W. Case, May 13, 1918, San Dieguito Dam Folder (#51), JSE, WRCA.

95. A brief description of the San Dieguito Dam (including photograph) is contained in Eastwood's article "Some Recent Multiple Arch Dams."

96. Structural dimensions are listed in "Detailed Specifications for the Multiple Arched Dam on San Dieguito Ranch for the San Dieguito Mutual Water Co.," no date (ca. February 1918), JSE #51, WRCA.

97. Eastwood's frustration with McClure over the minimum thickness of the arches is expressed in JSE to E. O. Faulkner, February 5, 1918; See also Wilbur F. McClure to San Diego [*sic*] Mutual Water Company, February 15, 1918, where McClure "approved the revised plans . . . prepared by Mr. Eastman [*sic*]." Both letters in JSE 51, WRCA.

98. Fletcher describes the family retreat near Warner Springs as "our Massachusetts where your Mother and I came from. I am sure there is no other place more beloved in San Diego County by you children. The property was not bought for profit. It represents the state where your mother and I were born." The lake formed by the Eagles Nest Dam is an integral part of the Fletcher estate. See Fletcher, *Memoirs*, p. 98.

99. Little material related to the Eagles Nest Dam survives in either Eastwood's or Fletcher's papers. The best description is in "Eagles Nest Dam,

General Specifications," October 31, 1917, Miscellaneous Dams Folder (#43), JSE, WRCA. In "Recent Multiple Arch Dams," Eastwood described the Eagles Nest structure as being reinforced with "old cables." In this article he referred to his small, three-arch designs as "Butterfly" or "Matilja" dams. Eastwood's use of completely vertical arches in small designs is similar to his use of vertical "heads" at the top of his larger dams. Unfortunately, I have not been able to locate any good photograph of the Eagles Nest Dam; it is now surrounded by trees and plant growth and does not present any easy camera angles.

100. Eastwood, "Recent Multiple Arch Dams," p. 264.

101. A complete breakdown of construction costs for the Murray and Lake Hodges dams is provided in Ed Fletcher to A. P. Davis, April 25, 1919, NA, RG 115, Entry 3, Box 287.

Chapter Eight

1. David Billington, *The Tower and the Bridge: The New Art of Structural Engineering* (New York: Basic Books, 1983), pp. 213–14.

2. Ibid., pp. 214–15.

3. Ibid., p. 215, reports that the conflict between mathematical complexity and the development of structural forms "would engage [Robert] Maillart over his entire career, and the power of his designs both scientifically and visually would grow as he went further and further from the mathematical tradition which was increasingly dominating the profession [in the twentieth century]."

4. "Eastwood Bulletin," *Western Engineering* 5 (March 1915): 4.

5. Ladshaw's "Complaint" against Eastwood and the Hume-Bennett Lumber Company dated August 16, 1911, is in the Hackley-Hume Papers, MSU. Ladshaw received his patent for what he called a "multi-differential" dam on August 14, 1906 (#828,752). Ladshaw was not a major figure in the field of American dam engineering, and his name appears infrequently in material related to dam technology. Apparently, however, he was active in advising clients on legal issues related to waterways, marshes, property lines, and the like. For example, see his letter on "The Effect on Meadow Lands of Back Water from Dams," *Engineering News* 48 (October 16, 1902): 316–17, where he describes a court case related to water backing up behind a dam on Lawsons Fork Creek in South Carolina. For examples of how Ladshaw described his design after Eastwood had already published his 1909 article on the Hume Lake Dam, see *Journal of Electricity Power and Gas* 27 (December 23, 1911): 603–4; and *Journal of Electricity Power and Gas* 28 (January 6, 1912): 5.

6. Ladshaw also attempted to enjoin Gardiner Williams from building multiple arch dams in Michigan in 1912. The Ambursen Hydraulic Construction Company tried to stop other engineers from building reinforced concrete flat-slab dams by claiming that its patents gave it complete proprietary control of this technology. However, the company's claims were generally struck down in court. For example, see "A Lower Court Decision on a Concrete Dam Patent," *Engineering News* 69 (June 5, 1913): 1201, in which the judge observed that "[Ambursen's] concrete dam is substantially a reproduction in concrete of an old and familiar style of timber dam." Interestingly, the Ambursen Hydraulic Construction Company never claimed that Eastwood infringed on their rights. During the early twentieth century, numerous other patent disputes arose over reinforced concrete patents, many of which involved arch bridges. For example, see "Six Concrete-Bridge Patents Void on Broad Grounds," *Engineering News* 74 (December 2, 1915): 1094–95; and "Decision Against Luten Spandrel and Bar Patents Upheld," *Engineering News-Record* 80 (June 6, 1918): 1108. For an interesting exchange of views on the value of patents in the field of structural engineering, see "Protecting Towns and Cities from Blackmailing Patent Litigation," *Engineering News* 70 (September 25, 1913): 617; and Daniel B. Luten, "The Collection of Patent Royalties from Towns and Cities," *Engineering News* 70 (October 30, 1913): 883–85. C. A. P. Turner and Henry T. Eddy, *Concrete Steel Construction* (Minneapolis: privately printed, 1914), pp. 418–31, offer a strong denunciation of the patent system's effect on reinforced concrete design.

7. See Thomas Hume to JSE, April 19, 1911; Hume, Hefferan & Co. to F. E. Cook, January 27, 1912; Thomas Hume to George Hume, May 4, 1912; and Thomas Hume to George Hume, November 23, 1912, for references to Ladshaw's action against Eastwood and the Hume-Bennett Lumber Company. Eastwood agreed to absorb many of the expenses he incurred in the case, but the Hume interests also paid for legal representation, court costs, and so on. Ladshaw's case never proceeded beyond the Northern Division of the Southern District of California Circuit Court. Thomas Hume to George Hume, November 23, 1912, reports that the "[Hume-Bennett Lumber Company] demurrer in the Ladshaw case had been sustained and his bill dismissed." All in Hackley-Hume Papers, MSU.

8. John S. Eastwood, "Multiple Arched Con-

crete Dams," n.d. (ca. 1913-1914), Multiple Arch Dam Folder (#3), JSE, WRCA.

9. Eastwood's thoughts on the unpatentability of the multiple arch dam were first expressed in John S. Eastwood, "Hume Lake Multiple Arched Dam," *Journal of Electricity Power and Gas* 24 (February 12, 1910): 135-39.

10. John S. Eastwood, "The Eastwood Multiple-Arched Dam," 33 *Western Engineering* (July 18, 1914): 49-52. Eastwood's interest in highlighting the special skills required in designing multiple arch dams probably related to some contemporaneous publications by other engineers describing the technology. For example, see C. E. Grunsky, "The Multiple Arch Dam of Reinforced Concrete," *Journal of Electricity Power and Gas* 32 (June 20, 1914): 531-37: and Gale S. Strout, "Multiple Arch Dam Stresses," *Journal of Electricity Power and Gas* 33 (July 4, 1914): 4-5. Neither Grunsky or Strout ever designed a multiple arch dam that was actually built.

11. "Gardiner Stewart Williams," *Transactions of the American Society of Civil Engineers* 98 (1933): 1659-62.

12. Brief notice of this design appears in Williams's discussion of an article by Charles L. Harrison and Silas H. Woodward, "Lake Cheeseman Dam and Reservoir," *Transactions of the American Society of Civil Engineers* 53 (1904): 89-209. Most of Williams's comments (which appear on pp. 182-202) relate to the main dome-shaped section of his proposed Six Mile Creek Dam, but he also notes plans for a small multiple arch structure to close the opening at "the west abutment, where . . . the rock did not rise to the height of the crest."

13. Gardiner S. Williams and Lewis Ayres, "A Municipal Hydroelectric Plant," *Engineering Record* 65 (March 2, 1912): 230-31.

14. A detailed table providing design data on all of Williams's multiple arch dams as of March 17, 1928, is available within the Gardiner S. Williams Papers, at Ayres, Lewis, Norris & May, Inc., Ann Arbor, Michigan. This engineering firm was established by former students of Williams at the University of Michigan, and he maintained close ties with it. Ms. Adrienne Malley, a planner with the firm in 1980, provided generous assistance in accessing its historical records.

15. An extensive memo on "The Magnitogorsky Dam," dated May 10, 1930, is available in the Williams Papers; his papers also include copies of drawings for the structure. It appears that he received the commission through the involvement of former students in the larger Magnitogorsk industrial project. A photo of the Magnitogorsky Dam appears in *Twentieth Century Engineering* (New York: Museum of Modern Art, 1964).

16. Gardiner S. Williams to George Ladshaw, April 22, 1912, notes that "the multiple arch dam upon which you have a patent has been designed a number of times in the past century . . . [and] I feel sure that the design was not strictly patentable"; the letter also directly refers to Goldmark's 1897 ASCE article. See also George E. Ladshaw to Gardiner S. Williams, May 22, 1912; both letters in Williams Papers, Ann Arbor, Michigan.

17. JSE to Gardiner S. Williams, September 9, 1915, JSE 4, WRCA.

18. Gardiner S. Williams and Albert A. Greene, *Engineering News-Record* 89 (July 13, 1922): 79. Greene was an associate in Williams's consulting practice.

19. JSE to Thomas Maddock, August 9, 1922, Cave Creek Dam Folder #45, JSE, WRCA.

20. See "William Barclay Parsons," *Transactions of the American Society of Civil Engineers* 98 (1933): 1485-92; "Harry de Berkeley Parsons," *Transactions of the American Society of Civil Engineers* 101 (1936): 1617-20; and "Walter Jules Douglas," *Transactions of the American Society of Civil Engineers* 107 (1942): 1740-46. Descriptions of their multiple arch dams appear in Edward Wegmann and Fred Noetzli, *The Design and Construction of Dams*, 8th ed. (New York: John Wiley & Sons, 1927), pp. 471-72, 490-92.

21. Harry de B. Parsons, "Sherman Island Dam and Powerhouse," *Transactions of the American Society of Civil Engineers* 88 (1925): 1257-1328.

22. JSE to Ed Fletcher, April 25, 1924, JSE 62, WRCA. The original of this letter may be found in Box 8, Ed Fletcher Papers, University of California, San Diego, Library and Special Collections, San Diego, California.

23. JSE to Adolf A. Meyer, January 26, 1924, JSE 62, WRCA. In JSE to Luigi Luiggi, January 6, 1921, JSE 62, WRCA, he also refers to "imitations of my work, particularly by Jorgensen and [R. P.] McIntosh, wherein . . . they fall into the error of having put out matter that has not been the result of exhaustive and complete study and is therefore in error, often the reverse being true."

24. "Jorgensen, Lars R.," in Winfield Scott Downs, ed., *Who's Who in Engineering* (New York: Lewis Historical Publishing, 1937) p. 727. No obituary for him appears in the ASCE *Transactions*. He became professionally inactive in the late 1930s and is not listed in subsequent editions of *Who's Who in Engineering*. See also Nancy Farm Mannikko, "Seattle City Light's Constant Angle Arch Dam at Diablo Canyon," *IA: The Journal of the Society for Industrial Archeology* 17 (1991): 17-31.

25. A description of Jorgensen's and Baum's patent #986,718 appears in the *Journal of Electricity Power*

and Gas 26 (March 25, 1911): 275. Jorgensen correctly reported the arc of economic quantity to be 133 degrees 34 minutes in *Journal of Electricity Power and Gas* 24 (January 1, 1910): 19. See also "Frank George Baum," *Transactions of the American Society of Civil Engineers* 99 (1934): 1407–9; Lars Jorgensen, "The Constant-Angle Arch Dam," *Transactions of the American Society of Civil Engineers* 78 (1915): 685–733; Lars Jorgensen, "The Constant Angle Arch Dam," *Journal of Electricity* 38 (January 15, 1917): 33–37. The patented design is described in a ca. 1913 pamphlet entitled "New Type of Dam," published by F. G. Baum & Company. Eastwood's description of a variable-radius design appears in John S. Eastwood, "An Arch Dam Design for the Site of the Shoshone Dam," *Engineering News* 63 (June 9, 1910): 678–80.

26. Lars Jorgensen, "Multiple-Arch Dams on Rush Creek, California," *Transactions of the American Society of Civil Engineers* 81 (1917): 850–906. Jorgensen differed from Eastwood in that he did not use a "vertical head" for the top of the arches. He also described his approach to multiple arch dam design in "Advances in Multiple Arch Design," *Journal of Electricity* 40 (March 15, 1918): 286–87; "Advances in Multiple Arch Dam Construction," *Journal of Electricity* 40 (May 1, 1918): 448–49; and "The Stability Factor in Multiple Arch Design," *Journal of Electricity* 41 (August 15, 1918): 170–71. His later work on single arch dams is documented in Lars Jorgensen, "Improving Arch Action in Arch Dams," *Transactions of the American Society of Civil Engineers* 83 (1919–1920): 316–36; and Lars Jorgensen, "Memorandum on Arch Dam Developments," *Journal of the American Concrete Institute* 27 (September 1930): 1–64.

27. See "Jakobsen, Bernhard Faaborg," in John William Leonard, ed., *Who's Who in Engineering* (New York: Who's Who Publications, 1925), p. 1076; and "Fred Adolph Noetzli," *Transactions of the American Society of Civil Engineers* 99 (1934): 1496–97.

28. B. F. Jakobsen, "Stresses in Multiple-Arch Dams," *Transactions of the American Society of Civil Engineers* 87 (1924): 276–341; and Fred Noetzli, "Improved Type of Multiple Arch Dam," *Transactions of the American Society of Civil Engineers* 87 (1924): 342–413.

29. Their other publications include B. F. Jakobsen, "Stresses in Thick Arches of Dams," *Transactions of the American Society of Civil Engineers* 90 (1927): 475–601; Fred Noetzli, "Gravity and Arch Action in Curved Dams," *Transactions of the American Society of Civil Engineers* 84 (1921): 1–135; Fred Noetzli, "The Relation Between Deflections and Stresses in Arch Dams," *Transactions of the American Society of Civil Engineers* 85 (1922): 284–353; and Fred Noetzli, "Laminated Arch Dams with Forked Abutments," *Transactions of the American Society of Civil Engineers* 95 (1931): 533–96. Jakobsen consulted on the Hamilton Dam in Texas. See "Building Hamilton Dam

on Colorado River in Texas," *Engineering News-Record* 110 (January 12, 1933): 58–62.

30. R. A. Munroe, "Rock Creek Multiple Arch Dam," *Journal of Electricity* 38 (June 1, 1917): 421–23, states that the structure was designed "under the direction of H. C. Vensano." However, JSE to P. M. Downing, September 27, 1916, JSE 4, WRCA, documents that Eastwood also provided consultation to PG&E on the Rock Creek Dam. See also "Harry Chittenden Vensano," *Transactions of the American Society of Civil Engineers* 127 (1962, part five): 76–77. Lake Eleanor Dam is described in R. P. McIntosh, "Fundamentals in the Design of a Multiple-Arch Dam," *Engineering News-Record* 83 (September 4, 1919): 464–68. This unusual structure did not use circular arches perpendicular to the water pressure; instead the arches were elliptical. This was the only multiple arch dam ever built in this fashion. McIntosh also reported his intention that "this dam will form part of the upstream toe of a rock-fill dam." The Reclamation Service's multiple arch dams are described in W. W. Patch, "The Lost River Multiple-Arch Curved Dam," *Engineering News* 71 (April 30, 1914): 962–68; and H. D. Newell, "Multiple Arch Diversion Dam at Three Miles Falls, Oregon," *Engineering News* 73 (May 27, 1915): 1009–12. It appears that E. G. Hopson played a role in designing these two dams.

31. John S. Eastwood, "The Eastwood Multiple Arched Dam," *Western Engineering* (July 18, 1914).

32. In JSE to I. C. Steel[e], February 9, 1921, JSE 4, WRCA, Eastwood opined that "it is a difficult matter to get the best practice in any branch of engineering into concrete [published] form for the reason that so many of the works built are the work of busy men who have not the spare time to write about them." In the same letter, he acknowledged that "much of the data on the design of specialties is in its nature the 'stock in trade' of the engineer that has perfected it . . . It is his means of making his services salable, and therefore, cannot be spread broadcast."

33. Of course, Eastwood could have abandoned the use of arches altogether and, following the lead of the Ambursen Hydraulic Construction Company, adopted a flat-slab design for the upstream face of his designs. In his ca. 1906 discourse entitled "Dams," he discussed the possibility of recommending flat-slab designs for the Big Creek dams but then rejected the idea because tensile stresses in the slabs would necessitate more closely spaced buttresses and, consequently, would require more concrete than a comparable multiple arch structure. In responding to a question by Sylvester Cannon about "the permanency of the life of steel in concrete under the conditions of a dam," Eastwood expanded on these comments and revealed that his "reasons for perfecting" the multiple arch dam were largely based on this issue. Eastwood valued the use of good-

quality concrete in protecting the steel reinforcement placed within the upstream face of a buttress dam, but he also believed that "the character of the loading has more to do with the safety and permanence of the steel than the [construction] quality and workmanship." To his mind, an entirely compressive loading (as in an arch) protected the steel better than did a loading that created tensile stresses (as in a flat slab). If cracks occur in a water face, reinforcement can deteriorate through contact with the moisture that seeps through the structure. When steel rusts, the chemical reaction causes the oxidized metal to expand, and this encourages further cracking. Eastwood explained that, in a flat-slab dam, the upstream face must resist some tensile stresses and that, "to permanently protect the steel," the concrete "must be lightly loaded." Only low stresses could eliminate the possibility of harmful cracking, but this required using large amounts of concrete. Consequently, he advised Cannon that flat-slab designs would be uneconomical "for any but low structures." See JSE to Sylvester Q. Cannon, July 26, 1915, JSE 16, WRCA.

34. The two exceptions to this were the Los Verjels Dam (minimum arch thickness of 6 inches) and the Murray Dam (minimum arch thickness of 9 inches).

35. "Parleys Canyon, Mountain Dell Dam," July 15, 1915, JSE 16, WRCA.

36. During this period, Eastwood supplied many of his designs with arches encompassing 133 degrees 34 minutes. For example, his Twin Lakes Dam design used this dimension, as did a design for a proposed dam in Oregon in 1914. Both of these designs also stipulated three-hinged arches. See JSE 14 and JSE 35, WRCA.

37. JSE to Sylvester Q. Cannon, July 26, 1915, JSE 16, WRCA.

38. Sylvester Q. Cannon to JSE, September 17, 1915, JSE 16, WRCA.

39. $\text{Radius } R = \dfrac{\text{arch span}/\,2}{\sin\,(\text{arc of the angle})}$

$= \dfrac{35 \text{ feet}/\,2}{\sin\,(120 \text{ degrees}/\,2)}$

$= \dfrac{17.5}{\sin\,(60 \text{ degrees})}$

$= \dfrac{17.5}{.88803}$

$= 20.20 \text{ feet}$

40. JSE to Sylvester Q. Cannon, December 7, 1915, JSE 16, WRCA.

41. In JSE to Sylvester Q. Cannon, December 7, 1915, JSE 16, WRCA, Eastwood described finding the horizontal surface area of an arch section by adding the crown thickness plus two times the thickness at the spring line and then dividing by three. Then he multiplied this average thickness by the length of the arch along a horizontal plane.

Because the arch was inclined, it had the shape of an ellipse (not a circle) along its horizontal section.

42. For evidence that Eastwood had a good grasp of the "shear" forces acting on his dams, see John S. Eastwood to Mr. Ready, July 30, 1921, PUC, File #630.1, Gibraltar Dam and Palermo and Water Company Folder. In this letter, Eastwood noted that " 'shear' occurring along the base of a [multiple arch] dam is what is also termed 'detrusion' or single shear, or of one side only. It is described in Turneaure and Maurer, page 17, Edition 1911, where the tests of Professor C. M. Spofford are described." The citation referred to F. E. Turneaure and E. R. Maurer, *Principles of Reinforced Concrete Construction* (New York: John Wiley & Sons, 1911), pp. 17–19, where the "shearing strength" of concrete was discussed; this volume acknowledged "a lack of uniformity among writers as to just what is meant by the term 'shearing strength'." In particular the authors noted that much confusion resulted from referring to the "complex action which occurs in the web of a beam" as "shearing stress" when this was actually quite different than the "sliding" shear that acted on such things as the buttresses of multiple arch dams. In the later years of his career, Eastwood explicitly observed that his method of calculating "shear stresses" was extremely conservative and not entirely accurate. He subsequently referred to the total horizontal thrust of water pressure divided by the horizontal surface area as being the "shear ratio." He then described the actual shearing stresses as being the "shear ratio" minus the "friction resistance" of the concrete acting under the vertical weight component of the water and the concrete. See JSE to Thomas Maddock, August 9, 1922, JSE 45, WRCA.

43. Cannon's October 30, 1915, telegram to Eastwood mandating the change from 350 psi to 300 psi does not survive. However, the instruction is directly referred to in JSE to Sylvester Q. Cannon, November 5, 1915, JSE 16, WRCA.

44. In JSE to Sylvester Q. Cannon, November 5, 1915, JSE 16, WRCA, Eastwood stated that he had used the 10:12 ratio for the Kennedy Dam. He also commented that he would have stipulated the 10:12 ratio earlier "had I known before that there was to be a loading of but 300#[psi] allowed."

45. In JSE to Sylvester Q. Cannon, November 5, 1915, JSE 16, WRCA, Eastwood reported that, by his calculations his design had "the resultant thrust line fall in front of the buttress at the 140 foot level 4.9 feet in front and at the 80 foot level, 3.5 feet in front of the center of the buttress." He called this a "practically even base loading." Although Eastwood did not specifically describe how he calculated the magnitude and placement of the resultant force at Mountain Dell, on other occa-

sions he indicated his basic approach to the problem. Assuming that water weighed 62.5 pounds per cubic foot and that concrete weighed 150 pounds per cubic foot, he divided the forces acting on a multiple arch dam into four components: (A) the horizontal thrust of water pressure; (B) the vertical weight of water above arches; (C) the vertical weight of concrete arches; and (D) the vertical weight of concrete buttresses.

The horizontal force of water pressure (A) acts at an elevation one-third of the distance between the base and the surface of the reservoir. The vertical weight of water (B) is determined by calculating the volume of water above the arch in cubic feet and then multiplying this by 62.5 pounds. Because of the curvature of the arch, Eastwood considered the vertical weight of water to act not at the upstream face, but instead at the arch's center of gravity, located a short distance downstream from the arch surface. Similarly, he calculated the weight of the concrete arch (C), and the weight of the concrete buttress (D) by multiplying their volumes by 150 pounds per cubic foot; he then assumed that both of these forces acted at the component's center of gravity. Using this approach, Eastwood could determine the magnitude and location of the four component forces (or vectors) that formed the resultant force. Along any horizontal cross section of the buttress, he could calculate the resultant force by adding together these four components (A, B, C, and D), using simple techniques of vector analysis. Thus, Eastwood had no compelling reason to attempt to make a precise calculation of the magnitude or location of the resultant force once he had satisfied himself that the resultant fell close to the center of the buttress. See "Method Employed for Finding the Center of Gravity of the Superimposed Water Load on the Inclined Arch for Dam at Big Meadows and the Application of Resultant Water Load," n.d. (ca. 1912); and "Method Employed for Finding the Center of Gravity of the Superimposed Water Load," JSE 18, WRCA.

46. JSE to Sylvester Q. Cannon, November 5, 1915, JSE 16, WRCA.

47. During the early twentieth century, structural engineers were aware of the dangers posed by earthquakes, but little analysis of the performance of structures under seismic loads had been conducted. In the attention he gave to calculating the effect of earthquakes on multiple arch dams, Eastwood was not negligent; he merely conformed to the approach taken by the rest of the profession. After the Big Bear Valley Dam safely withstood the San Jacinto earthquake of April 1918, he boasted that "the attendant who was on it at the time says it 'writhed like a snake' but there is not a crack of any kind or size in it so [the idea that multiple arch dams cannot resist earthquakes] is bunk, pure bunk, these dams are earthquake proof." Despite this bravado, his views were much more grounded on intuition than on any use of mathematical theory or structural analysis. Quote taken from JSE to J. T. Crabbs, February 12, 1922, JSE 9, WRCA.

48. "High Multiple-Arch Concrete Dam for Salt Lake City Water Supply," *Engineering News-Record* 80 (March 7, 1918): 456.

49. Telegram from JSE to Sylvester Q. Cannon, December 21, 1915, JSE 16, WRCA.

50. Eastwood's fundamental approach to form making only considered the structure in terms of what engineers call "static equilibrium." In transforming the external loads of water pressure into internal forces acting within the concrete, his calculations did not attempt to quantify the effect of structural deformations on stress distribution. He understood that such deformations occurred, but he did not attempt to represent them within the mathematical formula used to proportion the dimensions of his dams.

51. John S. Eastwood, "Limitations to Formulae," n.d. (ca. 1922), JSE 45, WRCA. This handwritten memo was written during a period of time when other engineers were challenging Eastwood's designs after subjecting them to "advanced" mathematical analysis. The memo was apparently never typed up for more general distribution.

52. "Limitations to Formulae," JSE 45, WRCA. Kutter's formula and the coefficient "N" of roughness relate to analytical means of calculating the flow of water in canals and conduits. Both are based on data derived empirically and are not absolutely correct under all conditions. They are most useful when applied to man-made channels or canals. Eastwood's point, of course, is to emphasize the unreliability of taking values and formulas applicable in one set of circumstances and assuming that they will be accurate for a much larger and more complex set of conditions. For more on Kutter's Formula and coefficient "N," see Mansfield Merriman, *Treatise on Hydraulics*, 10th ed. (New York: John Wiley & Sons, 1916), pp. 272–317.

53. JSE to E. A. Cleveland, June 4, 1922, Anyox Dam Folder (#9), JSE, WRCA.

54. Cotten's criticism appears under the pseudonym "Enquirer" in the *Engineering-News Record* 88 (April 13, 1922): 623–24. Williams's response appears in a letter signed by him and his associate Albert A. Greene published in *Engineering News-Record* 89 (July 13, 1922): 79. Williams stated the problem as being "whether the footings under the arches of a multiple arch dam should be included with the buttress footings [in] computing foundation pressures" and opined that the ques-

tion "in its general form cannot be answered as each case must be considered on it own merits." After observing that "it is quite out of the question to compute the distribution of pressure on a [multiple arch dam] foundation with any such accuracy as we can compute the stresses on a cross-section of a steel beam," he concludes that "the best we can do . . . is make reasonable assumptions and find approximate stresses." In grappling with the conundrum posed by Cotten, Eastwood came to appreciate that any method in which the resultant was considered to be a "concentrated load" acting on a "rigid body" (namely, the buttresses) represented an ideal case not reflected by conditions in real structures. His method of calculating buttress stresses assumed that the stresses would be evenly distributed along the buttress's entire length. He readily acknowledged, however, that this was not absolutely correct "due to the elasticity of both the structure and the foundations." In perceiving the elasticity of rock foundations, Eastwood focused on a problem that would continually bedevil engineers who attempted to develop mathematically rigorous methods of analyzing large dams.

55. These structures are described in L. A. B. Wade, "Concrete and Masonry Dam Construction in New South Wales," *Minutes of the Proceedings of the Institution of Civil Engineers* 178 (1909): 1–110.

56. For more on the elastic theory of arches as it applies to dams, see William Cain, "The Circular Arch Under Normal Loads," *Transactions of the American Society of Civil Engineers* 85 (1922). A professor of mathematics at the University of North Carolina, Cain was a leading academic theorist interested in developing the structural mechanics of elastic arches. Among his important books are *Theory of Steel-Concrete Arches and of Vaulted Structures*, 4th ed. (New York: D. Van Nostrand, 1906), and *Theory of Solid and Braced Elastic Arches*, 2d ed. (New York: D. Van Nostrand, 1909).

57. Ira O. Baker, *A Treatise on Masonry Construction*, 10th ed. (New York: John Wiley & Sons, 1909). Chapter 23 ("Elastic Arch"), pp. 670–703, extensively discusses analyzing arches that are considered to support their load "by virtue of the internal stresses developed in the material." In a section on the "Reliability of Elastic Theory" (pp. 700–701), Baker acknowledges problems associated with the accuracy of the theory as it applies to actual conditions. Baker is primarily concerned with analyzing concrete arch bridges.

58. JSE to Paul M. Downing, September 27, 1916, JSE 4, WRCA; and JSE to W. S. Post, March 27, 1917, Carroll Dam Folder, Box 8, Ed Fletcher Collection, Special Collections, University of California, San Diego.

59. Wegmann and Noetzli, *The Design and Construction of Dams*, p. 482. Noetzli's unsolicited observation provides compelling evidence that the arches in Eastwood's designs were not affected by temperature and rib-shortening stresses to any noticeable degree.

60. JSE to Paul M. Downing, September 27, 1916, JSE 4, WRCA. Variances between theoretical assumptions and physical realities arose in at least two respects: first, rather than being uniform, the hydrostatic loadings on the arch varied because the arch was built on a slope; and second, the supports for the arches (that is, the buttresses) were not "rigid and inelastic" but were similar in elasticity to the arches themselves. In addition, with the reservoir filled, the upstream side of the arches was saturated with water, and the resulting expansion in volume tended to relieve any rib-shortening stresses caused by the hydrostatic loading. Finally, Eastwood argued that the range of temperatures experienced by a multiple arch dam during construction and operation were not as great as many engineers imagined. One reason was that the thin arches quickly released the heat produced by the hardening concrete. He even went so far as to claim that "the water used [in construction] and the water stored [in the reservoir] will not vary much in temperature from each other." Consequently, "the temperature range cannot exceed a few degrees from temperature of setting to temperature of service." Other factors vitiating the reliability of the elastic theory include variation in the modulus of elasticity for concrete, the expansive effect of water-soaking on the concrete in the arches' upstream face, and the effect of Poisson's ratio on the form of the arch. The latter two factors were noted in Eastwood's 1914 article "The Eastwood Multiple-Arched Dam," p. 52. [Poisson's ratio relates to a structural material's tendency to expand at right angles to the direction of an applied compressive force.]

61. For a discussion of analyzing principal stresses in the buttresses of multiple arch dams, see B. F. Jakobsen, "Stresses in Multiple-Arch Dams," *Transactions of the American Society of Civil Engineers* 87 (1924): 276–341; and Wegmann and Noetzli, *The Design and Construction of Dams*, pp. 453–69.

62. These small cracks are described and illustrated in Jakobsen, "Stresses in Multiple-Arch Dams," pp. 311–12.

63. Wegmann and Noetzli, *The Design and Construction of Dams*, p. 475. Noetzli noted that "the contraction of the concrete due to shrinkage and changes in temperature has produced cracks in the unreinforced concrete . . . [and] the cracks

have been under observation for a number of years. The width is measured periodically with a strain gage. It has been found that there exists no definite relation between width of crack and height of water in the reservoir. The width of the cracks generally increases with a decrease in temperature . . . [and they] almost close up when the temperature rises to a seasonal maximum in summer. This seems to indicate that these cracks merely facilitate 'breathing' of the concrete with changes of temperature."

64. JSE to Sylvester Q. Cannon, November 5, 1915, JSE 16, WRCA.

65. The use of expansion joints in buttresses is described in E. C. Eaton, "Design and Construction of Big Dalton Multiple-Arch Dam," *Engineering News-Record* 103 (December 26, 1929): 994–97. The Coolidge Dam in Arizona (completed in 1929) was a multiple dome structure in which the buttresses also featured expansion joints.

66. Notes 32–36 in this chapter list references to these myriad sources.

67. Billington, *The Tower and the Bridge*, pp. 213–14.

68. See Lars Jorgensen, "Memoranda on Arch Dam Development," *Journal of the American Concrete Institute* 27 (September 1929): 1–64, for descriptions and drawings of several constant-angle arch dams he designed during the 1920s that bear a remarkable similarity to his Salmon Creek design.

69. See Box No. 219–38 in the Salt River Project Archives, Tempe, Arizona, for documentation concerning the Constant Angle Arch Dam Company's claims of patent infringement against the Salt River Valley Water Users' Association.

70. Eaton, "Design and Construction of Big Dalton Multiple-Arch Dam," pp. 994–97.

71. Among Noetzli's more interesting theoretical experiments involved his construction of a thin arch "test dam" on Stevenson Creek near the Southern California Edison's Big Creek system that contained devices to measure the stresses and deflections within the structure under various hydrostatic loads; see Wegmann and Noetzli, *The Design and Construction of Dams*, pp. 528–36, for more on this project. Why Noetzli would have been more interested in testing the physical properties of this large-scale model than in drawing conclusions from the actual performance of the Mountain Dell arches remains a mystery.

72. This incident is described in Edwin Layton, *The Revolt of the Engineers: Social Responsibility and the American Engineering Profession* (Baltimore: Johns Hopkins University Press, 1971), p. 17. For more on the controversy, see B. F. Jakobsen, "Ethics and the American Society of Civil Engineers" (privately published pamphlet, 1955),

available in the Andrae Nordskog Papers, Water Resources Center Archives, Berkeley.

73. A good source of biographical information on Newell is his professional obituary: "Frederick Haynes Newell," *Transactions of the American Society of Civil Engineers* 98 (1933): 1597–1600.

74. Quotes from *First Annual Report of Reclamation Service* (Washington, D.C.: Government Printing Office, 1903), p. 60; and *Third Annual Report of Reclamation Service* (Washington, D.C.: Government Printing Office, 1905), p. 43.

75. Lawrence Lee, *Reclaiming the American West: An Historiography and Guide*, (Santa Barbara, Calif.: ABC-Clio, 1980), p. 17.

76. The records of the Reclamation Service contain little evidence that Newell participated in the technological work of the agency. For example, in 1903 Newell directed Davis to: "Concentrate your energies as far as practicable on the pushing forward of the Salt River Project . . . and laying out a scheme of further work, involving the purchase of lands, rights of way, etc., also [on] action which may be taken regarding the Arizona Canal and the construction of the new dam in the river. I should like to have, in brief, a consistent plan for future operations covering these important matters." Such delegation could be a sign of an administrator leaving details to a trusted subordinate, but it also reflects that Newell remained uninvolved in the agency's engineering work. See F. H. Newell to A. P. Davis, June 23, 1903, NA RG 115, Entry 3, Box 490.

77. Davis's career is described in his professional obituary: "Arthur Powell Davis," *Transactions of the American Society of Civil Engineers* 100 (1935): 1582–91. At the time he graduated, George Washington University was known as Columbian University.

78. The "engineering board" system of project review is described in the *Third Annual Report of the Reclamation Service, 1903–4*, p. 41.

79. For unknown reasons, no obituary for Wisner was published in the *Transactions of the American Society of Civil Engineers* after his sudden death in 1906. His career is synopsized in F. H. Newell, comp. *Proceedings of the First Conference of Engineers of the Reclamation Service* (Washington, D.C.: Government Printing Office, 1904), p. 350. He graduated as a civil engineer from the University of Michigan in 1865 and spent most of his professional life working on harbor and transportation projects involving the Great Lakes, the Illinois River, the Mississippi River, and ports on the Gulf of Mexico. He also served with the Lighthouse Service and the International Waterways Commission.

80. Wisner's role in designing and analyzing designs for Shoshone Dam and Pathfinder Dam is

documented in the file labeled "Discussion Related to Dams," NA RG 115, Entry 3, Box 287.

81. See Wegmann and Noetzli, *The Design and Construction of Dams*, pp. 547-53, for descriptions of the Pathfinder and Shoshone dams.

82. See Harrison and Woodward, "Lake Cheeseman Dam and Reservoir," including methods presented in discussion by R. Sherieff. The specific design method used for the Pathfinder and Shoshone dams is documented in "Discussion Related to Dams," NA RG 115, Box 287; and in George T. Wisner and Edgar T. Wheeler, "Investigations of Stresses in High Masonry Dams of Short Spans," *Engineering News* 54 (August 10, 1905): 141-44.

83. John S. Eastwood, "An Arch Dam Design for the Site of the Shoshone Dam," *Engineering News* 63 (June 9, 1910): 678-80.

84. In the letter officially recommending selection of the Salt River Project (which featured the Roosevelt Dam) for construction by the Reclamation Service, the director of the U.S. Geological Survey made explicit reference to recent work on the New York and Boston water supply systems. The Salt River Project was the service's only initial project intended to serve the region surrounding a burgeoning city. It is not surprising, therefore, that the Roosevelt Dam adopted a technology similar to that employed for prominent eastern dams. See Charles Walcott to E. A. Hitchcock [Secretary of the Interior], March 7, 1903, NA RG 115, Entry 3, Box 492. Specific comparison of the proposed Salt River dam with the Croton and Wachusett dams is made in Arthur P. Davis, "Investigations in Arizona," in *Proceedings of the First Conference of Engineers of the Reclamation Service*, p. 129. The first design description of Roosevelt Dam appeared in Arthur Powell Davis, *Water Storage on Salt River, Arizona* (Washington, D.C.: Government Printing Office, 1903).

85. F. H. Newell to A. H. Dimock, April 16, 1912; NA RG 115, Entry 3, Box 287, "Discussion Related to Dams."

86. Quotation from F. H. Newell, "Irrigation: An Informal Discussion," *Transactions of the American Society of Civil Engineers* 62 (1909): 13.

87. Evidence of their correspondence can be found in NA RG 115, Box 287, "Discussion Related to Dams." Freeman's friendship with Davis is also documented in Box 33, Freeman Papers, MIT.

88. John R. Freeman to Arthur P. Davis, September 30, 1912, Box 63, Freeman Papers, MIT.

89. Specifically, it referred to a flat-slab buttress dam being planned for the Clackamas River in Oregon.

90. The financial problems of the Reclamation Service/Bureau are discussed in many sources including Ray P. Teele, *The Economics of Land Reclamation in the United States* (Chicago: A. W. Shaw, 1927).

91. The "trial load" method used by the Bureau of Reclamation in the 1920s is described in C. H. Howell and A. C. Jacquith, "Analysis of Arch Dams by the Trial Load Method," *Transactions of the American Society of Civil Engineers* 93 (1929): 1191-1316.

92. As engineering historian Nicholas J. Schnitter has stated, the interdependence of these two systems in the "trial-load" method is taken into account by considering "the median vertical section of the dam [to be] a cantilever fixed at the base. The water and other external loads [are] then divided [into] vertically and horizontally carried parts by adjusting the horizontal deformations of the median cantilever to the radial deflections of the arch crown." See Schnitter, "The Evolution of the Arch Dam," *International Water Power and Dam Construction* 28 (October and November 1976): 34-40, 19-21. Arch deflections are determined according to elastic arch theory, while the cantilever deflections are calculated according to a similar method that engineers term "beam theory."

93. Herbert Vischer and Luther Wagoner, "On the Strains in Curved Masonry Dams," *Transactions of the Technical Society of the Pacific Coast* 6 (December 1889): 75-86. Prior to the early twentieth century engineers often used the term "strain" synonymously with what is now termed "stress." See Harrison and Woodward, "Lake Cheeseman Dam and Reservoir."

94. Descriptions of the Gibson and Owyhee dams are provided in Bureau of Reclamation, *Dams and Control Works* (Washington, D.C.: Government Printing Office, 1929).

95. As David Introcaso documents in his "History of Bartlett Dam," HAER AZ-#25, Library of Congress, Bartlett Dam represented one of the few Bureau of Reclamation projects of the 1930s in which construction costs had to be kept low. The reasons for this relate to the Salt River Valley Water Users' Association's existing debt on other dams and its battles with the Paradise Valley Irrigation District over which group should control the Bartlett site.

Chapter Nine

1. Robert Maillart created his masterful reinforced concrete arch bridge at Salginatobel, Switzerland, when he was 56 years old. Similarly, Thomas Telford designed his first cast-iron arch bridge in Great Britain at age 53, and John Roe-

bling was 67 years old when he designed the Brooklyn Bridge.

2. JSE to Ed Fletcher, April 25, 1924, JSE 62, WRCA.

3. David F. Billington, *The Tower and the Bridge: The New Art of Structural Engineering* (New York: Basic Books, 1983), p. 273.

4. For more on these various water supply systems, see Norris Hundley, *The Great Thirst: Californians and Water, 1770–1990* (Berkeley: University of California Press, 1992), pp. 161–254. See also Donald J. Pisani, *From Family Farm to Agribusiness: The Irrigation Crusade in California and the West, 1850–1931* (Berkeley: University of California Press, 1984), pp. 381–452; and James R. Kluger, *Turning on Water with a Shovel: The Career of Eldwood Mead* (Albuquerque: University of New Mexico Press, 1992), pp. 85–101.

5. See "A New Phase of State Supervision of Dams," *Engineering News* 68 (November 21, 1912): 973–74; "The Desirability of State Supervision of Design, Construction and Operation of Dams and Reservoirs," *Engineering and Contracting* 38 (October 23, 1912): 450–51; "A Symposium on Engineering Opinion on State Supervision of Engineering Construction," *Engineering and Contracting* 38 (December 4, 1912): 619–20. For evidence of this, see "A Study of the Failures and Partial Failures of Dams in Pennsylvania," *Engineering and Contracting* 43 (January 27, 1915): 75; and "The Growth of the Doctrine of State Supervision of Engineering Construction," *Engineering and Contracting* 38 (October 30, 1912): 475–76. The latter article reported that "the Austin Dam failure stirred into activity a number of states by its disastrous consequences a sentiment for state supervision of dam construction which otherwise would have longer remained dormant."

6. Eastwood received approval for his two mining debris dams in a relatively informal way. For example, in his article on the Kennedy Dam in *Western Engineering* 5 (April 1915): 407–9), Eastwood reported that "plans for the dam were approved by Col. W. H. Heuer, U.S.A., engineer, retired." Heuer served with the U.S. Army as an engineer from 1865 until 1907, when he entered private practice. During this time he became a member of the California Debris Commission and worked on problems related to hydraulic debris. Presumably this led to his becoming involved in reviewing the Kennedy Dam plans for the Debris Commission. See "William Henry Heuer," *Transactions of the American Society of Civil Engineers* 90 (1926): 1562–64.

7. Hawley's early career is briefly described in *Engineering News* 70 (November 20, 1913): 1057.

8. Evidence of the state engineer's efforts to assemble design data on California dams can be found in the files of the Bear Valley Mutual Water Company Archives, Redlands, California. See W. F. McClure to Bear Valley Mutual Water Company, March 28, 1916. The state engineer's limited role in dam supervision is also noted in "California Board Urges State Control of Dams," *Engineering News* 76 (August 10, 1916): 259.

9. "The Otay Dam Failure," *Western Engineering* 7 (March, 1916): 86. See also Charles Whiting Baker, "Otay Rock-Fill Dam Failure," *Engineering News* 75 (February 3, 1916): 236–39; and Roy A. Silent, "Failure of the Lower Otay Dam," *Engineering News* 75 (February 17, 1916): 334–36. Construction of the dam was originally described in W. S. Russell, "A Rock-Filled Dam with a Steel Heartwall at Otay, Cal.," *Engineering News* 39 (March 10, 1898): 157–58.

10. See Ralph Bennett, "More Proof of Need for Supervision of Dams," *Engineering Record* 74 (September 16, 1916): 357–58.

11. Notice of this law is given in *Sixth Biennial Report of the State Department of Engineering* (Sacramento: California State Printing Office, 1918), pp. 77–78. It was formally known as "Assembly Bill No. 1027, Chapter 377, State of California, approved May 14, 1917."

12. His career development is described in "Wilbur Fisk McClure," *Transactions of the American Society of Civil Engineers* 91 (1927): 1106–9.

13. Quoted from M. M. O'Shaughnessy to Edward Hyatt, October 3, 1928, File on "Supervision of Dams, 1928," Records of the Hydraulic Division of the State Railroad Commission, Public Utility Commission Records, California State Archives, Sacramento, California. [Hereafter Public Utility Commission Records are listed as PUC.] Biographical data on the longtime city engineer for San Francisco can be found in "Michael Maurice O'Shaughnessy," *Transactions of the American Society of Civil Engineers* 100 (1935): 1710–13.

14. This delay is evident in "Urges Better State Supervision of Dams," *Engineering News-Record* 79 (October 4, 1917): 637.

15. Biographical data are taken from "Walter Leroy Huber," *Transactions of the American Society of Civil Engineers* 126 (1961, part five): 27–28.

16. For more on his career, see "John Debo Galloway," *Transactions of the American Society of Civil Engineers* 109 (1944): 1451–56.

17. John R. Freeman to H. P. Wilson, September 4, 1925, Box 64, Freeman Papers, MIT.

18. A succinct accounting of his career is given in "Joseph Barlow Lippincott," *Transactions of the American Society of Civil Engineers* 108 (1943): 1543–50. His first public acknowledgment of multiple arch dams came in J. B. Lippincott,

"Old and New Bear Valley Dams and Crags Dams in Service," *Engineering News* 74 (October 28, 1915): 854–55.

19. "Bear Valley Multiple-Arch Dam Overflows for First Time," *Engineering News* 75 (May 18, 1916): 961.

20. Lars Jorgensen, "The Record of 100 Dam Failures," *Journal of Electricity* 44 (March 15 and April 1, 1920): 274–76, 320–21, documents that the great majority of late nineteenth- and early twentieth-century dam failures concerned earthfill and rockfill embankment structures. Two prominent earth dam failures are described in "The Slide of the Necaxa Hydraulic-Fill Dam, *Engineering News* 62 (July 15, 1909): 72–74; and "Failure of Part of the Calaveras Dam," *Western Engineering* 9 (May 1918): 173–74.

21. Early irrigation along Little Rock Creek is discussed in Harry R. Johnson, *The Resources of Antelope Valley, California* (Washington, D.C.: Government Printing Office, 1911), pp. 33–35; and Frank Adams, *Irrigation Districts in California, 1887–1915* (Sacramento: California State Printing Office, 1916), pp. 38–39, 91–92. The drought of the late 1890s wreaked havoc with irrigation projects in the Antelope Valley (just as it had with Eastwood's San Joaquin Electric Company); Adams indicates that the colony at Littlerock began to grow after 1910 and by 1915 "between 1,400 and 1,500 acres, mostly in Bartlett pears, [were] under cultivation." He also reports that "about forty voters voted at the district election in 1913."

22. Plans to utilize Little Rock Creek more fully are described in James D. Schuyler, "Report on the Water Supply of Littlerock Creek Available for Irrigation in Antelope Valley, California," February 28, 1910, Folder #25, Schuyler Papers, WRCA. Serious plans to implement a storage reservoir on Little Rock Creek date to 1915, when J. B. Lippincott undertook a study of the watershed and surveyed two dam sites, one originally identified in 1912 by the Little Rock Power and Water Company (a company that proposed to generate electric power for use at mines in Randsburg, 60 miles north of Littlerock; these plans were never implemented), and another near the site of the "headworks" for the canal leading to Palmdale. See J. B. Lippincott, "Report on Storage Possibilities and Available Water Supply on Little Rock Creek for the Palmdale Water Company," November 29, 1915, Folder 48, Lippincott Papers, WRCA.

23. The Littlerock Creek Irrigation District was formed in 1892 under the authority of the Wright Act and held primary rights to appropriate water from the creek. The Palmdale Irrigation District (known originally as the Palmdale Water Company, and a successor to the South Antelope Valley Water Company) controlled a 7-mile canal that was built in the late 1890s to carry water from the creek to the Palmdale region. The Palmdale District's rights were secondary to those of the Littlerock Creek District. A history of the two districts is provided in Frank Adams, *Irrigation Districts in California* (Sacramento: State Printing Office, 1929). Located an an elevation of more than 3,000 feet above sea level (the "high desert"), Antelope Valley is ideally suited for pear cultivation because pear trees require annual frosts to remain healthy and productive. For more on this local industry, see the pamphlet "Among the Pear Groves of North Los Angeles County in Palmdale and Littlerock Creek Irrigation Districts," May 1, 1920, available in Folder 48, Lippincott Papers, WRCA.

24. J. W. Scott, engineer for the Littlerock Creek Irrigation District, visited the Murray, Lake Hodges, Argonaut, and Kennedy dams during 1917, and he also visited with McClure in December 1917 to discuss construction of an Eastwood dam on Little Rock Creek. See J. W. Scott to W. F. McClure, May 8, 1919, Littlerock Dam File, California Department of Water Resources [hereafter referred to as LRD, DWR]. Research into this material was undertaken by using copies of the file retained by the Palmdale Water District (successor to the Palmdale Irrigation District) and made available by Mrs. Hobart Bosworth in her capacity as president of the Littlerock Creek Irrigation District.

25. See *Antelope Valley Ledger Gazette*, November 30, 1917; and "Memorandum of Agreement between John S. Eastwood, Littlerock Creek Irrigation District and Palmdale Water Company," April 15, 1918, Littlerock Creek Irrigation District files, Littlerock, California [hereafter referred to as LCID].

26. W. F. McClure to JSE, July 17, 1918. As early as May, the irrigation districts had discerned that McClure might look with disfavor at the Eastwood design; see Jesse F. Waterman to W. F. McClure, May 1, 1918, and W. F. McClure to Jesse F. Watterman, May 6, 1918, for evidence that "it has been intimated to me that there there may be some question in your [McClure's] mind about the stability of the proposed Littlerock Dam." All in LRD, DWR.

27. See Railroad Commission to W. F. McClure, July 25, 1918, and R. W. Hawley to W. F. McClure, September 10, 1918; both in Hydraulic Division file #630.1, PUC.

28. No copies of McClure's September 30 letter to Cole exist in available archives. McClure acknowledged to Eastwood, however, that he had told Cole that a 15-inch-thick arch would be ac-

ceptable. See W. F. McClure to JSE, December 2, 1918, LRD, DWR.

29. W. F. McClure to Burt Cole, November 26, 1918, Littlerock Dam Folder (#44), JSE, WRCA. The anonymous engineer is not identified in surviving memos or correspondence; the state employee who prepared a report was E. D. Nickerson.

30. JSE to W. F. McClure, November 27, 1918, JSE 44, WRCA.

31. JSE to Burt Cole, November 27, 1918, JSE 44, WRCA.

32. W. C. Petchner to W. F. McClure, December 3, 1918, LRD, DWR.

33. See JSE to W. C. Petchner, December 7, 1918, JSE 44, WRCA.

34. See JSE to J. T. Whittlesey, January 18, 1919, Sheeps Rock Dam Folder (#10), JSE, WRCA. This quote is taken from a letter written by Eastwood to promote his "radial plan" design for a site on the Pit River in Northern California.

35. JSE to R. W. Hawley, January 17, 1919, Hydraulic Division File #F3725-6925, PUC. The plans he submitted were accompanied by a "descriptive letter relating to the stresses and to methods of making computations."

36. See "Frederic Morris Faude," *Transactions of the American Society of Civil Engineers* 100 (1935): 1762.

37. Memo from F. M. Faude to Hydraulic Engineer [R. W. Hawley], February 26, 1919, Hydraulic Division File #F3725-6925, PUC.

38. "Application No. 4319, Reporters Transcript, March 3, 1919," Hydraulic Division File # F3725-6925, PUC. The hearing was held in Los Angeles.

39. H. W. Brundige to W. F. McClure, March 28, 1919, LRD, DWR.

40. Acknowledgment of Hawley's resignation is given in H. W. Brundige to W. F. McClure, May 2, 1919, Hydraulic Division File #F3725-6925, PUC.

41. W. F. McClure to Railroad Commission, March 29, 1919. Huber's assistance is requested in W. F. McClure to W. L. Huber, April 15, 1919. No similar request to Galloway is available, suggesting that Huber may later have unofficially recommended that the state engineer bring Galloway into the controversy. McClure asked Harry Hawgood's opinion of the "radial plan" design but only elicited an equivocal response that "it is a question for personal judgement and opinion as to what is prudent." See W. F. McClure to H. Hawgood, April 15, 1919; and H. Hawgood to W. F. McClure, May 14, 1919. All in LRD, DWR.

42. Evidence that the state engineer had access to all Railroad Commission records is provided in H. W. Brundige to W. F. McClure, May 2, 1919.

Kromer prepared a report on his May 22 meeting with Huber and Galloway. See memo by C. H. Kromer, May 26, 1919. All in LRD, DWR.

43. Huber's and Galloway's official written recommendations are given in W. L. Huber to W. F. McClure, May 24, 1919; and J. D. Galloway to W. F. McClure, May 26, 1919; Hydraulic Division File # F3725-6925, PUC.

44. See "Application to No. 4319, Reporter's Transcript, May 29, 1919," Hydraulic Division File # F3725-6925, PUC. At the hearing, McClure stated that the "radial plan" dam might stand, but without the "factor of safety desired" (p. 54). Huber and Galloway participated in the hearing but said nothing more than had appeared in their written recommendations to McClure.

45. "Decision No. 6396" on "Application No. 4319" by the Railroad Commission of the State of California, June 10, 1919, Hydraulic Division File # F3725-6925, PUC. The Railroad Commission went so far as to say that "we are convinced that so far as the type of structure goes, applicant should be authorized to proceed with its construction." They still wanted "further details of design [to] be submitted for our approval," but this proviso comes across as a minor issue. If nothing else, the order provides a classic example of why it is important to read the "fine print" in legal rulings.

46. W. L. Huber to W. F. McClure, June 21, 1919; Huber's displeasure with the Railroad Commission was foreshadowed in a May 19 letter in which he complained that the upcoming "so-called legal hearing . . . appears to me to be preposterous." He opined that "one engineering authority familiar with the principals [*sic*] of engineering rather than the law should have the right of final decision after making his own investigation." Of course, McClure (acting on Huber's advice) qualified as the "one engineering authority," but Huber had no interest in ceding this same power to Hawley; see W. L. Huber to W. F. McClure, May 19, 1919; W. F. McClure to W. L. Huber, June 24, 1919, characterizes Huber's advice against approving any design details as "interesting and to the point." All in LRD, DWR.

47. W. C. Petchner to W. F. McClure, June 14, 1919, Folder #48, Lippincott Papers, WRCA; the new site was located near the headgates of the canal that carried water to Palmdale.

48. JSE to Burt Cole, July 10, 1919; JSE to W. C. Petchner, September 30, 1919; JSE 44, WRCA.

49. Memo from C. I. Rhodes to C. H. Loveland, September 17, 1919, LRD, DWR. In his capacity as hydraulic engineer, Loveland quickly accepted Rhodes's recommendation and approved the new site. See C. H. Loveland to Railroad Commission, September 17, 1919, Hydraulic Division File #D1383-85 F3439-28.

50. See W. A. Kraner to W. C. Petchner, October 2, 1919; John S. Eastwood to Bent Brothers, October 17, 1919; and John S. Eastwood to W. C. Petchner, October 25, 1919; all in JSE 44, WRCA.

51. Memo by C. H. Kromer on his conference with C. H. Loveland and M. E. Ready, November 13, 1919, and memo by C. H. Kromer regarding recommendations in connection with plans for the Littlerock Dam, January 1920; both in LRD, DWR.

52. Palmdale Water Company to Railroad Commission, May 18, 1920, JSE 44, WRCA. Despite this action, the Palmdale Water Company and the Railroad Commission continued to play a secondary role in the Littlerock Dam negotiations.

53. Memo by C. H. Kromer on conference with M. E. Ready, May 20, 1920, LRD, DWR. See Chapter 8 for more on how the "shearing stresses" referred to by Kromer were analogous to what Eastwood called the "shear ratio" and do not reflect the actual shearing stresses in the structure.

54. W. L. Huber to W. F. McClure, May 28, 1920, LRD, DWR. In this letter, Huber referred to the angle in the dam as "very undesirable" because "it will induce unnecessary stresses [and] may be the subject of serious cracks." He also recalled Eastwood's "radial plan" dam and labeled it "a freak design."

55. H. H. Wadsworth, a former engineer with the Army Corps of Engineers, had worked on Sacramento River flood control projects. His career is described in "Henry Hayes Wadsworth," *Transactions of the American Society of Civil Engineers* 88 (1925): 1449-52.

56. See H. H. Wadsworth to W. F. McClure, June 23, 1920; Burt Cole to Donald Barker, June 18, 1920; W. F. McClure to Burt Cole, June 24, 1920. All in LRD, DWR.

57. JSE to Burt Cole, July 10, 1920, JSE 44, WRCA. In this letter, Eastwood described his meeting with Wadsworth: "[I] spent nearly two hours showing him by authorities and otherwise that in each and every particular, he was not only off, but in diametrically the opposite position to the truth."

58. Donald Barker to W. F. McClure, August 2, 1920, LRD, DWR.

59. W. F. McClure to Donald Barker, August 5, 1920, LRD, DWR.

60. This competing design is described in Lars Jorgensen to W. F. McClure, October 11, 1920, LRD, DWR.

61. These protracted negotiations are documented in JSE to William Petchner, November 6, 1920; and JSE to Burt Cole, December 7, 1920; JSE to Burt Cole, December 8, 1920; JSE to Burt Cole, December 20, 1920; JSE 44 WRCA. See also C. H. Kromer to W. F. McClure, October 1, 1920; JSE to W. F. McClure, November 9, 1920; and C. H. Kromer to W. F. McClure, November 19, 1920; LRD, DWR.

62. H. H. Wadsworth to W. F. McClure, November 24, 1920, LRD, DWR.

63. W. F. McClure to W. C. Petchner, January 4, 1921, LRD, DWR.

64. JSE to Burt Cole, December 7, 1920, JSE 44, WRCA.

65. A memo by C. H. Kromer describing a conference with Burt Cole on January 11-12, 1921, does not hint that the state engineer was about to make a major decision; discussion at the meeting focused on how much money might be saved if "shearing stresses" in the dam were increased from 85 psi to 90 psi.

66. Notice of McClure's approval of the design, except for an arch thickness of less than 15 inches, is given in Paul Bailey to J. B. Lippincott, April 20, 1922, JBL 48, WRCA.

67. J. B. Lippincott to W. F. McClure, April 12, 1922, LRD, DWR.

68. J. B. Lippincott to Sheldon and Lancaster Investment Brokers, April 15, 1922, JBL 48, WRCA.

69. W. F. McClure to Littlerock and Palmdale Irrigation Districts, May 18, 1922, LCID.

70. Memo from Chief Structural Engineer to W. F. McClure, May 16, 1922, LRD, DWR.

71. "Contract between Bent Brothers and the Palmdale Water Company," June 26, 1922, JBL 48, WRCA. The contract specifically stipulated that "during all times the Engineering Department of the State of California shall have the right to examine and inspect said work in progress." Bent Brothers agreed to build the dam on a "unit cost" basis for concrete, excavations, and so on. In other words, the company received compensation in direct proportion to how much work and material were required to complete the structure. See H. Stanley Bent to Palmdale Water Company, June 24, 1922, JBL 48, WRCA.

72. Memo from A. F. McConnell to W. F. McClure, August 7, 1922, LRD, DWR.

73. Copies of design drawings for the Littlerock Dam, with W. F. McClure's signature approving them, dated November 4, 1922, are located in the files of the Littlerock Creek Irrigation District.

74. "Highest Multiple Arch Dam in the World Is Constructed Under Great Difficulties," *Southwest Builder and Contractor* 65 (August 22, 1924): 44-46. The "difficulties" related to "excavation in the creek channel, which had to be carried to an unexpected depth to bedrock."

75. Numerous snapshot photographs of the dam under construction are included in the Lippincott Papers, WRCA. Formal acceptance of the

structure is acknowledged in W. F. McClure to Littlerock Creek Irrigation District, June 5, 1924, LCID. The state's approval is also noted in the *Report of the Division of Engineering and Irrigation, November 30, 1924* (Sacramento: California State Printing Office, 1925), p. 5, where a photo of the dam appears with the caption "Highest Multiple Arch Dam in the United States, Construction Supervised by the Division of Engineering and Irrigation." The delayed filling of the reservoir is described in "Recent Floods Fill Little Rock Multiple Arch Dam near Palmdale, California," *Western Construction News* 8 (April 25, 1926): 36.

76. The State of California explicitly acknowledged this extraordinary event on page 14 of its *Final Environmental Impact Report on Revocation of the Certificate of Approval: Littlerock Dam and Reservoir;* prepared by the Department of Water Resources, the Resources Agency, State of California, November 1979.

77. J. B. Lippincott to Stevens, Page & Sperling; and to Bent Brothers, May 26, 1924, Folder 48, Lippincott Papers, WRCA. Frank Adams, *Irrigation Districts in California* (Sacramento: California State Printing Office, 1929), p. 269, reports that the complete dam cost $467,108, "divided equally between Palmdale and Littlerock Creek districts." This latter figure is believed to include some financing charges incurred during the drought of 1924–1926.

78. Bond data from Adams, *Irrigation Districts in California* (1929), pp. 268–74, 398–99. The districts could not issue any bonds unless specifically authorized to do so by the California Bond Certification Commission. See Lippincott 48, WRCA, for more on matters relating to bond approval.

79. Ibid., pp. 270, 273.

80. See, for example, JSE to W. F. McClure, August 19, 1923, JSE 4, WRCA. This letter concerns Eastwood's proposal for the Exchequer Dam on the Merced River.

81. JSE to Chester H. Rowell, September 1, 1920; and JSE to Chester H. Rowell, September 8, 1920; see also Chester H. Rowell to Hon. William Stephens, September 3, 1920; all in Chester H. Rowell Papers, Bancroft Library, Berkeley. In JSE to W. C. Petchner, October 16, 1920, JSE 44, WRCA, Eastwood also mentions the importance of getting "through to the Governor." In this context, it is worth noting that Eastwood was not particularly involved in political affairs, and his papers contain few references to politics per se. His mainstream Republican views are reflected in an addendum to a telegram in which he alluded to the 1920 presidential nominating convention with the comment: "Delighted with Harding and Coolidge." See telegram from JSE to Sespe Light and Power Company, June 13, 1920, Sespe Light and Power Company Folder (#47), JSE, WRCA.

82. No biography of Stephens's political career is available, but his experiences as a progressive politician in the 1910s and early 1920s are discussed in Mowry, *The California Progressives* (Berkeley: University of California Press, 1951), pp. 117–22, 190, 276–78, and in Jackson K. Putnam, "The Progressive Legacy in California: Fifty Years of Politics, 1917–1967," in William Deverell and Tom Sitton, eds., *California Progressivism Revisited* (Berkeley: University of California Press, 1994), pp. 250–51. Stephens first became governor in 1917, after Hiram Johnson resigned the office to become a U.S. senator; Stephens was elected on his own account in 1918, but the Republican Party did not renominate him in 1922. Putnam describes him as a "thoroughgoing pragmatist" who also "wrapped himself in the mantle of nonpartisanship."

83. William Kahrl, *Water and Power: The Conflict over Los Angeles' Water Supply in the Owens Valley* (Berkeley: University of California Press, 1982), pp. 230–317, describes the acrimonious relationship between city authorities and Owens Valley residents in the 1920s; Kahrl titles this chapter "The Politics of Exploitation."

84. In a 1922 letter, Eastwood claimed to have first developed the "curved face" design while working on a project for the San Joaquin Light and Power Corporation. See JSE to J. T. Crabbs, February 12, 1922, Anyox Dam Folder #9, JSE, WRCA. In 1933, Herman Schorer published a theoretical discourse on buttress dam design that, among other things, attempted to prove that the buttress of minimum weight should be built with a curved upstream face. See Herman Schorer, "The Buttressed Dam of Uniform Strength," *Transactions of the American Society of Civil Engineers* 96 (1932): 681–83.

85. Notice of these floods is given in "Cave Creek Flood Does Damage at Phoenix," *Engineering News-Record* 87 (September 15, 1921): 464.

86. The origins of the Cave Creek Flood Control Board are described in "Progress on Flood Prevention at Phoenix, Ariz.," *Engineering News-Record* 88 (January 26, 1922): 162. This article indicated that flooding from Cave Creek caused damage "estimated at from $50,000 to $500,000." The article also stated that "it was originally intended to build an earth-fill type of dam."

87. JSE to George L. Davenport, October 15, 1921, Cave Creek Dam Folder (#45), JSE, WRCA. This letter refers to a recent "meeting at your office" where the two engineers discussed the Cave Creek project.

88. JSE to Ed Fletcher, November 16, 1921, San Elijo Dam Folder (#6), JSE, WRCA.

89. Thomas Maddock to JSE, December 5, 1921, JSE 45, WRCA.

90. George L. Davenport to C. C. Cragin, October 18, 1921, JSE 45, WRCA.

91. See JSE to the Cave Creek Flood Control Board, December 20, 1921, JSE 45, WRCA. This letter indicates that the board wanted data on how much money could be saved by lowering the top of the dam 1 to 2 feet in elevation. Clearly, the board wished to minimize its expenditure on the structure.

92. S. M. Cotten to L. B. Hitchcock, January 6, 1922, JSE 45, WRCA. Cotten's ignorance of multiple-arch dams quickly became clear when, in attempting to discredit Eastwood's Cave Creek design, he asserted that every prior multiple arch dam had been built with strut-tie beams between the buttresses.

93. See S. M. Cotten to L. B. Hitchcock, December 30, 1921; S. M. Cotten to L. B. Hitchcock, January 6, 1922; S. M. Cotten to W. C. Foster, June 1, 1922; S. M. Cotten to Thomas Maddock; all in JSE 45, WRCA. The June 1 letter to Foster is the most revealing of Cotten's attacks on Eastwood's design. It runs thirteen single-spaced pages and includes an acknowledgment by Cotten of his "unfamiliarity with the subject of multiple arch dam design and practice." Along with referring to the "curved face" design as "this Eastwood monstrosity," he confides that "I have in mind a dam design for Cave Creek which appears feasible and which would certainly be very economical." Evidently, Cotten's attack on Eastwood's multiple arch design served an ulterior motive.

94. See S. M. Cotten's discussion accompanying Fred Noetzli, "An Improved Type of Multiple Arch Dam," *Transactions of the American Society of Civil Engineers* 87 (1924): 399-403.

95. S. M. Cotten [writing as "Enquirer"], "How Should We Figure Foundation Pressures in a Multiple-Arch Dam," *Engineering News-Record* 88 (April 13, 1922): 623-24; Cotten identifies himself as "Enquirer" in *Engineering News-Record* 89 (July 13, 1922): 78-79.

96. See letter by L. H. Nishkian and Fred Noetzli in *Engineering News-Record* 88 (June 15, 1922): 1009-10. Noetzli expressed some support for Cotten's approach, but he tempered it with a disclaimer: "however, the conditions are not quite as serious as the calculations of "Enquirer" appeared to indicate." See also letter by Gardiner S. Williams and Albert S. Greene, "Foundation Pressures in Multiple-Arch Dams," *Engineering News-Record* 89 (July 13, 1922): 79.

97. JSE to Thomas Maddock, August 9, 1922, JSE 44, 1922. In this letter, Eastwood refers to Cotten's use of R. P. McIntosh's article on designing the Lake Eleanor Dam as the source of much con-fusion and misinformation. Calling it a case of the "blind leading the blind," Eastwood complained that "it is regrettable that so much undigested matter should be published by the technical press, tending to mislead the uninformed."

98. Eastwood's ca. 1922 memo on "Limitations to Formulae," JSE 45, WRCA, is discussed in Chapter 8.

99. All data on the dam's construction are taken from W. H. Peterson, "Cave Creek Flood Control Dam Multiple Arch Structure Built Along New Lines," *Southwest Builder and Contractor* 62 (February 16, 1923): 30-33.

100. The estimate of $350,000 is given in JSE to the Cave Creek Flood Control Board, December 20, 1921, JSE 45, WRCA.

101. All quotations related to construction are taken from Peterson, "Cave Creek Flood Control Dam," pp. 30-33.

102. "The Cave Creek Dam," *Arizona Gazette* (March 8, 1923). In this issue of the newspaper, a photograph of the dam impounding water appears under the caption, "Cave Creek Dam Stops a Flood." See "Cave Creek Supervisors Accept Dam," *Arizona Gazette* (March 6, 1923), for notice of the structure's completion. This article indicates that Eastwood came to Phoenix himself for the formal acceptance of the dam by the flood control board.

103. A final accounting of expenses for the Cave Creek Dam is provided in the *Salt River Valley Water Users' Association Annual Report, 1922–1923*, pp. 105-6, Salt River Project Archives, Tempe, Arizona. This account lists the money given by various organizations to cover construction costs and identifies the total expense of the dam as $556,982.39.

104. There is a growing interest in the relation of railroads to western water development. See Richard J. Orsi, "Railroads and Water in the Arid Far West: The Southern Pacific as a Pioneer Water Developer," *California History* 70 (Spring 1991): 46-61.

105. JSE to George L. Davenport, October 15, 1921, JSE 45, WRCA, indicates that Eastwood was "planning to go to British Columbia soon." See telegram from H. S. Munroe to JSE, December 2, 1921, JSE 9, WRCA, for request to "proceed with complete designs." For more on the Anyox facility, see Charles H. Tallant, "Hydraulic Equipment of Granby Mine," *Journal of Electricity* 45 (September 5, 1920): 275-77; and "British Columbia Hydroelectric Developments," *Journal of Electricity Power and Gas* 36 (January 8, 1916): 25-27.

106. The Anyox Dam is described in H. Speight, "Multiple Arch Reinforced Concrete Dam," *Canadian Engineer* 50 (February 9, 1926): 201-4; and in Edward Wegmann and Fred Noetzli, *The Design and Construction of Dams,*

8th ed. (New York: John Wiley & Sons, 1927), pp. 500–504.

107. Telegram from J. T. Crabbs to JSE, February 9, 1922, and JSE to J. T. Crabbs, February 12, 1922, JSE 9, WRCA.

108. Notice of the meeting is given in a telegram from H. S. Munroe to JSE, February 22, 1922. Their conference was held on March 3, 1922. Telegram from H. S. Munroe to JSE, April 1, 1922, confirmed approval of design, JSE 9, WRCA.

109. Cost estimates are given in JSE to H. S. Munroe, April 20, 1922, JSE 9, WRCA.

110. In his April 20 letter to Munroe, Eastwood expressed confidence in Holyoke, saying that "his work was so satisfactory on the Lake Hodges Dam that I feel highly elated to be able to send him to you." There is no record of any contracting firm's being given responsibility for building the dam. Apparently the Granby Company undertook construction on its own, making it especially important that someone familiar with multiple arch technology be on site at all times.

111. E. A. Cleveland [Comptroller of Water Rights] to William Young, May 12, 1922; E. A. Cleveland to William Young, May 31, 1922; William Young to JSE, May 31, 1922; William Young to JSE, June 3, 1922; all in JSE 9, WRCA. The letter formally approving construction does not survive in the Eastwood Papers. However, in William Young to JSE, June 9, 1922, JSE 9, WRCA, the Vancouver-based engineer indicated that the approval process was well in hand.

112. George E. Holyoke to JSE, July 24, 1922, JSE 9, WRCA. In October, Holyoke wrote to Eastwood and expressed relief that, "[although] the new superintendent has not placed very much more yardage than the others . . . [at least] he does things without arguing the matter for five hours"; see George E. Holyoke to JSE, October 11, 1922, JSE 9, WRCA.

113. This was reminiscent of the flood weathered by the Lake Hodges Dam during its construction. Thus, on two occasions, Eastwood dams demonstrated that the absence of an arch would not trigger a total collapse of the structure.

114. Wegmann and Noetzli, *The Design and Construction of Dams,* p. 504, includes photographs of water pouring between the buttresses.

115. JSE to A. G. Wishon, May 3, 1924, JSE 62, WRCA; JSE to Ed Fletcher, April 24, 1924, JSE 62, WRCA.

116. This is confirmed in Wegmann and Noetzli, *The Design and Construction of Dams,* p. 504.

117. E. Davis and E. G. Marriott, "British Columbia Dams," *The Engineering Journal* 8 (July 1925): 305. The Granby Company's copper smelt-ing operation was closed down in the 1935 and never reopened. For an informative, yet highly personalized, history of the town written by a Vancouver journalist who spent his youth there in the 1920s and early 1930s, see Pete Loudon, *Anyox: The Town That Got Lost* (Sidney, B.C.: Gray's Publishing, 1973). Unfortunately, this account includes nothing about Eastwood's dam, but the book includes a 1971 aerial view of the structure still impounding water (p. 49).

118. See JSE to A. G. Wishon, May 3, 1924, JSE 62, WRCA.

119. In JSE to Luigi Luiggi, January 6, 1921, JSE 62, WRCA, Eastwood discusses the "triple arch" and "radial cone" designs as employing distinct structural concepts.

120. John S. Eastwood, "An Arch Dam Design for the Site of the Shoshone Dam," *Engineering News* 63 (June 9, 1910): 678–80.

121. John S. Eastwood, "The Multiple-Arched vs. the Single-Arch Dam," *Journal of Electricity* 38 (March 1, 1917): 149–53.

122. Wegmann and Noetzli, *The Design and Construction of Dams,* p. 523.

123. Eastwood's view of elastic analysis and his method of analyzing buttress stresses along horizontal sections are discussed in Chapter 8. The quotations are taken from JSE to Frank Olmsted, November 20, 1923; and JSE to Frank Olmsted, December 5, 1923; both in Balojaque Dam Folder (#29), JSE, WRCA.

124. The absence of data on the Webber Creek Dam in the Eastwood Papers is the most serious lacuna in the collection. At one time, considerable correspondence between Eastwood and Hawley about the project certainly existed. Whether this material was removed in the late 1920s when plans to raise the dam were under way or whether it was inadvertently discarded at a later date is unknown.

125. JSE to R. W. Hawley, November 1, 1919; and JSE to R. W. Hawley, December 31, 1919; both in JSE 43, WRCA.

126. R. W. Hawley to JSE, October 27, 1919; JSE to R. W. Hawley, November 1, 1919; and JSE to R. W. Hawley, December 31, 1919; all in JSE 43, WRCA.

127. The El Dorado Water Company was organized in April 1919 with R. W. Hawley as "General Manager and Chief Engineer." See "Annual Report of the El Dorado Water Company of Placerville, El Dorado County, to the Railroad Commission of California for Year Ending December 31, 1919," Hydraulic Division File #D1379-F3031, PUC. The company was subsequently reorganized as the El Dorado Water Corporation, and it later evolved into the El Dorado Irrigation District.

128. R. W. Hawley to Railroad Commission

[attention F. M. Faude], February 8, 1922, Hydraulic Division File #630-1, PUC.

129. R. W. Hawley to Railroad Commission [attention F. M. Faude], April 4, 1922, Hydraulic Division File #630-1, PUC. In the initial design, Hawley evidently stipulated use of the theoretical arc of minimum quantity at all elevations, assuming that this would provide the most economical design. Because of the site's shallow profile, however, Eastwood apparently recommended that the radial cone design be replaced with a constant-radius structure.

130. A "Report to the Hydraulic Engineer" by F. M. Faude dated September 6, 1922, indicates that Hawley had submitted "revised plans" for a "three arched dam" on August 25. Report in Hydraulic Division File #630-1, PUC.

131. In his September 6 report, Faude indicated that he had "thoroughly investigated" the dam site "on September 1, 2, and 3." By that time, "the site had been partially stripped by hydraulic methods and presented a good opportunity for detailed inspection."

132. Formal approval for construction was given in Railroad Commission to El Dorado Water Corporation, September 13, 1922, Hydraulic Division File #630-1, PUC.

133. Wegmann and Noetzli, *The Design and Construction of Dams*, p. 492.

134. Photographs of this visit can be found in Webber Creek Dam File #21, Walter L. Huber papers, WRCA. They indicate that Eastwood visited the dam on March 6, 1924.

135. Hawley's career after construction of the Webber Creek Dam is a mystery. It may be that he died shortly afterward; certainly he did not participate in plans to raise the dam in the late 1920s.

136. Correspondence and reports related to the proposed addition can be found in Walter L. Huber Papers, Folder #21, WRCA. In particular, see W. L. Huber to Edward Hyatt [state engineer], January 3, 1928.

137. See Wegmann and Noetzli, *The Design and Construction of Dams*, p. 492, for a description of Noetzli's "triple arch" Green Valley Dam in Southern California. This dam has a maximum height of 65 feet and vertical arches.

138. JSE to Ed Fletcher, June 6, 1924, Box 8, Ed Fletcher Papers, UCSD.

139. For example, in JSE to W. F. McClure, August 19, 1923, JSE 4, WRCA, Eastwood described an unsolicited "radial cone" design for the proposed Exchequer Dam in Central California. His rationale for offering this unsolicited proposal was that it would save the farmers building the dam several hundred thousand dollars.

140. In 1919–1921, after completion of Lake Hodges and before work started on Cave Creek,

Anyox, Webber Creek, and Littlerock, he experienced a "dry spell" when his only design under construction was the Fish Creek Dam in Idaho. By this time, he seems to have begun receiving some compensation for undertaking preliminary design work; and this, in combination with reports such as the one he completed for the Southern California Edison Company on the hydroelectric possibilities of the Shaver Lake properties, helped keep him financially solvent. But the big payoffs came when his designs were actually built.

141. See Balojaque Dam Folder (#29), JSE, WRCA; the origins of this project are documented in Folder #335, Schuyler Papers, WRCA.

142. In June 1923, Eastwood wrote of a "fine trip to Mexico." See JSE to George E. Holyoke, June 1, 1923, JSE 9, WRCA.

143. JSE to Frank H. Olmsted, November 20, 1923, JSE 29, WRCA.

144. The Salt River Valley Water Users' Association was one of the members of the Cave Creek Flood Control Board, which must be how it came to know of Eastwood's work. In early 1923, Eastwood proposed a two arch "radial cone" design for the Mormon Flat Dam estimated to cost approximately $400,000–$500,000. See Mormon Flat Dam Folder (#20), JSE, WRCA.

145. For more on this project, see David Introcaso, "The History of Mormon Flat Dam," HAER File AZ-14, Prints and Photographs Division, Library of Congress.

146. The Diamond Creek hydroelectric project is briefly described in "Surveying Dam Sites in the Grand Canyon," *Engineering News* 76 (August 17, 1916): 306–7. Girard's participation is noted in "Personal Notes," *Engineering News-Record* 80 (February 14, 1918): 335. A photograph of the dam site is included in the George Ward Papers, HEH.

147. See Diamond Creek Dam Folder (#28), JSE, WRCA. See also "Hunt Re-election Enlivens Colorado River Problems," *Engineering News-Record* 93 (November 13, 1924): 805.

148. See Ed Fletcher to JSE, June 23, 1923. Bluewater Dam Folder (#37), JSE, WRCA. See also Ed Fletcher to JSE, August 14, 1923; JSE to George L. Davenport, January 26, 1924; and JSE to Ed Fletcher, April 3, 1924; all in JSE 4, WRCA.

149. The advanced state of Eastwood's involvement with the Bluewater Dam project at the time of his death is documented in Ed Fletcher to Ella Eastwood, September 24, 1924; and Ella Eastwood to Ed Fletcher, September 30, 1924; both in Box 5, Ed Fletcher Papers, UCSD.

150. T. W. Mermel, ed., *Register of Dams in the United States* (New York: McGraw-Hill, 1958), p. 44.

151. The Eastwood Papers contain data on sev-

eral other single dam projects that never extended beyond the preliminary stages: Kaweah Dam Folder (#17); Chowchilla Dam Folder (#22); Clearwater River Dam Folder (#34); Alpine Dam Folder (#40); San Lorenzo Dam Folder (#42); and others; all in JSE, WRCA.

152. Correspondence and drawings related to his Sheeps Rock Dam proposal can be found in JSE 10, WRCA.

153. Eastwood served as consulting engineer/ chief engineer for this company from 1920 to 1924. He spent considerable time in Los Angeles working on the project and undertook substantial amounts of work there, including work for his other clients. For example, when Ed Fletcher wrote him on April 24, 1923 (JSE 4, WRCA), he addressed the letter to the Sespe Light and Power Company, Suite 1321, Stock Exchange Building, Los Angeles. Eastwood's involvement with the company is documented in Sespe Light and Power Company Folders (#46) and (#47), JSE, WRCA.

154. During his four years of work planning the company's hydroelectric system, the project underwent major changes as he attempted to work out the most economical locations for dams and the most economical sequence for their construction. Consequently, he developed designs for more sites than could ever have been built.

155. The efforts of this "protective association" are described in Vernon M. Freeman, *People- -Land-Water: Santa Clara Valley and Oxnard Plain, Ventura County, California* (Los Angeles: Lorrin L. Morrison, 1968), pp. 83-92; Freeman also includes (on pp. 47-49) a lengthy excerpt from a September 1921 letter from Eastwood to the SL&PC concerning the proposed system.

156. Lynn S. Atkinson and A. G. Weber, "Multiple Arch Dam Product of Pioneer Efforts of Noted California Engineer," *Southwest Builder and Contractor* 66 (January 16, 1925): 46-47. In this article the Sespe Light and Power Company is referred to as the Ventura Power Company. The Ventura Power Company's plans for a hydroelectric power system on Piru Creek are noted in "Power Permit Sought," *Engineering News-Record* 93 (September 18, 1924): 48.

157. The fate of the SP&LC is described in Freeman, *People-Land-Water*, pp. 44-49. Apparently, C. E. Grunsky (who was hired as a consultant by the Santa Clara River Protective Association) helped kill the project by recommending against its construction on grounds that it was not financially viable.

158. Material on this work is contained in San Joaquin Light & Power Corporation Folders (#48), (#49), and (#50), JSE, WRCA.

159. Evidence of Eastwood's knowledge of the hydroelectric power potential of the upper Kings

River watershed is available in JSE to M. W. Oberlin, July 24, 1914, JSE 48, WRCA.

160. See A. G. Wishon to JSE, October 15, 1919; JSE to A. G. Wishon, October 31, 1919; JSE to R. C. Starr, April 29, 1919; JSE to A. G. Wishon, June 19, 1919; A. G. Wishon to JSE, November 30, 1918; and JSE to A. G. Wishon, December 4, 1918; all in JSE 48, 49, and 50, WRCA.

161. A. G. Wishon to JSE, March 29, 1922, JSE 48, WRCA.

162. John R. Freeman to A. P. Wilson, March 20, 1925, Box 67; and John R. Freeman to A. W. Burchard, October 10, 1924, Box 66. In John R. Freeman to H. P. Wilson, May 22, 1925, he commented that "you may remember that this substitution of an earth dam [at Big Meadows] for the Eastwood dam was originally my personal invention and idea." Box 67; Freeman Papers, MIT.

163. For example, see telegram from Ed Fletcher to C. L. Cory, February 16, 1922, JSE 4, WRCA; Ed Fletcher to Thomas Maddock, June 21, 1922, JSE 31, WRCA; and Ed Fletcher to Harry Chandler, July 18, 1924, JSE 4, WRCA.

164. For example, the Henshaw Dam built at Warner Ranch in the early 1920s was an earthfill structure. In addition, Fletcher corresponded with Lars Jorgensen and an engineering firm associated with Fred Noetzli. See File Group #26, Ed Fletcher Papers, San Diego Historical Society [SDHS], San Diego, California.

165. JSE to Ed Fletcher, April 24, 1923, JSE 4, WRCA.

166. JSE to Ed Fletcher, April 25, 1924, JSE 62, WRCA.

167. Drawings, calculations, and some correspondence related to this project from 1917 through 1923 are included in JSE 6, WRCA.

168. Ed Fletcher, *The Memoirs of Ed Fletcher* (San Diego: privately printed, 1952), pp. 255-65, describes how the proposed San Elijo Dam was related to the Santa Fe Railway, the San Dieguito Mutual Water Company, and the Cardiff Irrigation District. He mentions locating a dam site on San Elijo Creek in 1916 and spending "something like $30,000 in making those surveys," using San Dieguito Mutual Water Company funds. He also claims, "I called attention a number of times to the Districts to the possibilities of this development."

169. See H. N. Savage, "Proportioning and Making Concrete on Barrett Dam," *Engineering News-Record* 87 (October 27, 1921): 695-97.

170. See Folders #1-45, Hiram N. Savage Papers, WRCA, for extensive references to his work in San Diego during the 1910s and 1920s. O'Shaughnessy had designed the rockfill Morena Dam, built in 1912, and he maintained a professional relationship with the Spreckels interests through the 1920s. His distaste for Eastwood's multiple arch dams is ex-

pressed in M. M. O'Shaughnessy to Ed Fletcher, February 6, 1922; and M. M. O'Shaughnessy to Ed Fletcher, February 28, 1922; both in File Group #26, Fletcher Papers, SDHS.

171. Savage's views on San Diego water development are presented in the *San Diego Union*, January 15, 1922, and in the *San Diego Evening Tribune*, November 27, 1922, both available in San Diego Dams Folder (#52), JSE, WRCA.

172. T. H. King to Ed Fletcher, January 23, 1922, JSE 52, WRCA. This letter provides good data on the physical dimensions of the Mission Gorge sites and their relationship to the river's recorded flow.

173. Reference to El Capitan can be found in J. W. Williams to JSE, July 7, 1924, JSE 52, WRCA. Explicit reference to the Fletcher site is made in JSE to Ed Fletcher, April 25, 1924, Box 8, Fletcher Papers, UCSD.

174. JSE to Ed Fletcher, March 18, 1921, JSE 52, WRCA.

175. JSE to Ed Fletcher, April 26, 1922, JSE 52, WRCA.

176. Photostat drawings of an Eastwood design for the Fletcher Dam dating to September 1918 are available in volume 5, Box 57, Freeman Papers, MIT. This design featured forty-nine arches with spans of 24 feet each; it was designed for an ultimate height of 160 feet. The "curved face" design for the Fletcher site and the "radial cone" design for El Capitan are noted in JSE to Ed Fletcher, April 25, 1924, JSE 62, WRCA.

177. Freeman's qualifications for this task largely stemmed from his work in planning and promoting the Hetch Hetchy water supply system for San Francisco. In this capacity, he became professionally associated with M. M. O'Shaughnessy, who had ties to San Diego. O'Shaughnessy's esteem for Freeman is evident in a letter to Fletcher in which he said, "[I] trust he [Freeman] will be able to do you some good in San Diego." See M. M. O'Shaughnessy to Ed Fletcher, August 6, 1923, File Group #26, Fletcher Papers, SDHS.

178. Ed Fletcher to JSE, February 16, 1922, JSE 4, WRCA. In this letter Fletcher noted that "over two and a half billion gallons daily [are now] passing over the spillway."

179. Ed Fletcher to Thomas Maddock, June 21, 1922, JSE 31, WRCA.

180. John R. Freeman to S. P. Eastman, September 5, 1923; Box 55, Freeman Papers, MIT.

181. John R. Freeman, "Fieldbook, 1923 San Diego Trip," August 20 entry, Box 56, Freeman Papers, MIT.

182. Ed Fletcher to JSE, August 14, 1923, JSE 4, WRCA.

183. Freeman, "Fieldbook," August 13 entry, Freeman Papers, MIT.

184. J. B. Lippincott to Charles Derleth, August 16, 1923, Folder #81, Charles Derleth Papers, WRCA.

185. See telegram from Ed Fletcher to F. M. Faude, September 10, 1923, Hydraulic Division File #D1383-85-F3440-49, PUC, for evidence that he obtained the insurance for "political reasons."

186. Wegmann and Noetzli, *The Design and Construction of Dams*, pp. 513–16. See also "Official Report on the Collapse of Gleno Dam," *Engineering News-Record* 93 (August 7, 1924): 213–15.

187. JSE to Ed Fletcher, April 3, 1924, JSE 4, WRCA.

188. John R. Freeman, "Summary of Recommendations Regarding Future Extensions of Water Supply for the City of San Diego, Cal.," May 16 and May 22, 1924 (copy on file in Water Resources Center Archives, Berkeley).

189. Ibid., pp. 81–82.

190. *San Diego Union*, May 17, 1924. (Copy in JSE 52, WRCA.)

191. "Interview: Col. Ed. Fletcher," *San Diego Union*, ca. May 20, 1924; copy of clipping in JSE 52, WRCA.

192. JSE to the *San Diego Union* (ca. May 20, 1924), JSE 52, WRCA. Much of the letter, but not the parts that were most personally critical of Freeman, was published as an article entitled "Inventor of Multiple Arch Dams Declares Freeman Is Mistaken in Hodges Criticism," *San Diego Union*, May 27, 1924.

193. Ed Fletcher to JSE, June 9, 1924, JSE 4, WRCA.

194. Hundley, *The Great Thirst*, pp. 45–58, 126–35.

195. Freeman, "Fieldbook," August 14 entry, Freeman Papers, MIT.

196. Ed Fletcher to John R. Freeman, August 23, 1923, Box 57, Freeman Papers, MIT. In this letter, Fletcher asserted that the viceroy of Mexico had made San Diego a presidio and thus had rendered moot any claim to a "pueblo right."

197. For voluminous data on the "paramount right" battle, see Savage #36, WRCA.

198. In addition, in 1943 a gravity dam was built on San Vicente Creek, essentially to replace the proposed dams at Mission Gorge.

199. Ed Fletcher to Harry Chandler, July 18, 1924, JSE 4, WRCA.

Chapter Ten

1. JSE to H. H. Garstin, August 9, 1924, JSE 62, WRCA.

2. "J. S. Eastwood Loses Life in Swimming Pool: Pioneer Engineer was Builder of Hume, Sanger Flume," *Fresno Morning Republican*, Au-

gust 11, 1924. Eastwood was buried in Fresno's Mountain View Cemetery, where his grave is marked with a simple granite slab; upon her death in 1933, Ella Eastwood was buried next to her husband. Ironically, the site of his death is now inundated by Pine Flat Reservoir, a lake impounded by a concrete gravity dam built by the Army Corps of Engineers in the 1950s.

3. Notice of his death appears in *Engineering News-Record* 93 (August 21, 1924): 319; *Journal of Electricity* 53 (August 15, 1924): 151. The one substantive obituary is Lynn S. Atkinson and A. G. Weber, "Multiple Arch Dam Product of Pioneer Efforts of Noted California Engineer," *Southwest Builder and Contractor* 66 (January 16, 1925): 46–47. His death is also noted in French Strother, "Thirteen Miles Through Granite," *World's Work* 50 (August 1925): 381–90.

4. For example, Southern California Edison Company built a large multiple arch dam at Big Creek in the mid-1920s. See "Florence Lake Multiple Arch Dam," *Western Construction News* 2 (July 25, 1927): 36–40. A relatively large multiple-arch structure was built at Lake Lure in North Carolina during the same period. See "Multiple Arch Dam Construction," *Concrete* 31 (December 1927): 43–45. The Lake Pleasant Dam is described in "Construction of Multiple Arch Dam in Arizona," *Engineering News-Record* 100 (February 2, 1928): 180–83. The Big Dalton Dam in Southern California is described in E. C. Eaton, "Design and Construction of Big Dalton Multiple Arch Dam," *Engineering News-Record* 103 (December 26, 1929): 994–97. Fred Noetzli also experimented with the design of a multiple dome structure for the Coolidge Dam in Arizona in the late 1930s. This dam used domes instead of arches for its upstream face. It is the only structure of its type ever built in the United States. For a description of its design, see C. R. Oldberg, "Features of Design, Coolidge Multiple Dome Dam," *Engineering News-Record* 101 (September 13, 1928): 396–99. See Edward Wegmann and Fred Noetzli, *The Design and Construction of Dams*, 8th ed. (New York: John Wiley & Sons, 1927), for descriptions of numerous European multiple arch dams built in the 1920s.

5. Fred Noetzli, "An Improved Type of Multiple Arch Dam," *Transactions of the American Society of Civil Engineers* 84 (1924): 342–413.

6. Walter L. Huber and Fred Dolson, "Multiple Arch Dam at Gem Lake on Rush Creek, California," *Transactions of the American Society of Civil Engineers* 89 (1926): 713–89.

7. Galloway's and Noetzli's comments are included in "Discussion" accompanying Huber and Dolson, "Multiple Arch Dam at Gem Lake," pp. 737–89.

8. The deterioration of the Gem Lake Dam's concrete is specifically noted in F. R. McMillan, "Concrete Is What We Make It," in *Symposium on Mass Concrete* (Detroit: American Concrete Institute, 1963), pp. 57–63. This article also describes deterioration in the concrete of the Florence Lake Dam but notes this structure's successful service for forty years. Successful measures taken to keep the Florence Lake Dam in constant, active use are discussed in Redinger, *The Story of Big Creek*, pp. 169–70. None of Eastwood's dams has ever suffered from major deterioration problems.

9. See Charles F. Outland, *Man-Made Disaster: The Story of the St. Francis Dam* (Glendale, Calif.: Arthur Clark, 1963).

10. Nathan A. Bowers, "St. Francis Dam Catastrophe—A Review Six Weeks After," *Engineering News-Record* 100 (May 10, 1928): 727–33.

11. Among the few articles critical of the *design*—and not just the construction—was Lars Jorgensen, "The Structural Safety Factor in the St. Francis Dam," *Engineering News-Record* 100 (June 21, 1928): 982.

12. Walter L. Huber to John R. Freeman, March 21, 1928; Freeman also received reports on the failure from other engineers, including Arthur P. Davis (Davis, March 28, 1928); and J. B. Lippincott (Lippincott, March 26, 1928). Freeman did not personally examine the St. Francis Dam site, but he soon averred that "the site plainly required many precautions that were ignored, and while I have the highest personal regard for my good old friend William Mulholland, I can but feel that he trusted too much to his own individual knowledge, particularly for a man who had no scientific education." John R. Freeman to Caleb Mills Saville, March 29, 1928; all in Box 54, Freeman Papers, MIT.

13. "The Human Factor," *Engineering News-Record* 100 (May 10, 1928): 725. After the disaster, the City of Los Angeles made a point of destroying the remaining sections of the St. Francis Dam at the site of the collapse in an effort to eliminate all reminders of the horrible event. See "Standing Section of St. Francis Dam Razed with Dynamite," *Engineering News-Record* 103 (July 11, 1929): 51. Nonetheless, large pieces of the concrete structure remain visible in the lower sections of the San Francisquito Canyon.

14. For extended justification and analysis of California's 1929 dam safety law, see A. H. Markwart and M. C. Hinderlider, "Public Supervision of Dams: A Symposium," *Transactions of the American Society of Civil Engineers* 98 (1933): 828–87. Markwart was a former business partner of John D. Galloway, Walter Huber's mentor.

15. See N. J. Schnitter, "The Evolution of the Arch Dam," *Water Power and Dam Construction*

28 (October and November 1976): 34–40, 19–21, for acknowledgment that "somewhat paradoxical caution on the part of the leading dam design office [that is, the Bureau of Reclamation] initiated the decline in the construction of true arch dams in the United States." This was exemplified by the developments in California, where the absolute number of new arch dams, as well as their number in proportion to other types, decreased sharply during the 1930s. A theoretical justification for the state engineer's view of multiple arch dams is given in George E. Goodall and Ivan M. Nelidov, "Stresses in Inclined Arches of Multiple Arch Dams," *Transactions of the American Society of Civil Engineers* 98 (1933): 1200–1239. This article provided further analysis of arch stresses based on the elastic theory and "proved" the existence of tensile stresses in arches that encompass relatively small arcs. In the article, Nelidov is identified as "Senior Engr. of Hydr. Structure Design, State Department of Public Works, Sacramento, Calif." Thus, his analysis represented the official view of the state's dam safety bureaucracy.

16. See folders #630, #631, and #632 in the Huber Papers, WRCA, for extensive correspondence, reports, and other materials concerning activities of the state engineer's Multiple Arch Dam Advisory Committee between May 1931 and the summer of 1932.

17. H. W. Dennis, G. A. Elliott, and Walter L. Huber to Edward Hyatt, State Engineer, September 15, 1932, Folder #630, Huber Papers, WRCA.

18. Harry Dennis to Walter L. Huber, August 31, 1931, Folder #632, Huber Papers, WRCA.

19. The only possible exception is the Sutherland Dam in San Diego County, which was partially built in the late 1920s and then left half-finished for more than twenty years before being completed in the early 1950s. Other than this, no multiple arch dams seem to have been erected in California since the Huber committee's report was submitted in 1932.

20. Derleth is best known to engineering historians for his involvement in the design of the Golden Gate Bridge across the mouth of San Francisco Bay. Hydraulic engineering was not his specialty; and except in a few specific instances prompted (apparently) by a personal relationship with J. B. Lippincott, he did not participate extensively in dam design and construction.

21. See "Report on Hodges Dam, San Diego County, California," in Charles Derleth to J. B. Lippincott, July 18, 1922, file #80, Charles Derleth Papers, WRCA, Berkeley.

22. See B. A. Etcheverry, F. C. Hermann, A. Kempkey, and Henry D. Dewell, "Reports of Consulting Board on Lake Hodges Dam, San Diego County, California," 1928, p. 26; in Derleth Papers, File #82, WRCA. See also "High Multiple Arch Dam Declared Safe Except from Earthquake," *Engineering News-Record* 103 (July 25, 1929): 132. Hairline temperature cracks also appeared in the Lake Pleasant Dam's buttresses during construction, prompting efforts to "strengthen" that structure in the late 1920s. For more on this, see Beardsley Project File #5, J. B. Lippincott Papers, WRCA; and David Introcaso, "History of Waddell Dam," HAER AZ-8, Library of Congress.

23. In the 1920s, seismic analysis was not a routine part of the dam engineering design process. In fact, one of the first studies dedicated to this topic appeared in 1931: H. M. Westergaard, "Water Pressures on Dams During Earthquakes," *Transactions of the American Society of Civil Engineers* 95 (1931): 418–72. This article only considered the issue in relation to gravity dams with vertical upstream faces.

24. Fred D. Pyle, "Hodges Dam Strengthened," *Engineering News-Record* 117 (November 5, 1936): 644–47.

25. "Unsafe Dam Design," *Engineering News-Record* 117 (November 5, 1936): 656.

26. Fears about the ability of multiple arch dams to resist earthquakes had been expressed since James D. Schuyler and Alfred Noble first reviewed Eastwood's plans for the Big Meadows Dam in 1911. It was a convenient way to criticize the technology because of the difficulty of "proving" the contrary assertion—that multiple arch dams *were* safe under seismic loads.

27. See, for example, "Building Hamilton Dam on Colorado River in Texas," *Engineering News-Record* 110 (January 12, 1933): 59–62; and John A. Adams, Jr., *Damming the Colorado: The Rise of the Lower Colorado River Authority, 1933–1939* (College Station, Tex.: Texas A&M University Press, 1990). "The Pensacola Project, Oklahoma," *Civil Engineering* 9 (September 1939): 529–32; and "World's Largest Multiple Arch Dam Completed," *Engineering News-Record* 125 (November 7, 1940): 597; describe the 4,282-foot-long Grand River Dam. Bartlett Dam is described in David Introcaso, "History of Bartlett Dam," HAER AZ-25, Library of Congress.

28. Efforts to expunge Eastwood's accomplishments from the records of American dam building began even before his death. In the version of an article on "Stresses in Multiple Arch Dams," which appeared in *Proceedings of the American Society of Civil Engineers* 49 (August 1923): 1093–1131, B. F. Jakobsen lauded Eastwood as "an asset to civilization" and contrasted "[Eastwood's] usefulness with the methods of another engineer who was engaged to design a gravity dam and proceeded by drawing the profile of other dams of about the same height and then determined his sections by

the simple process of making it heavier at every elevation than any other dam built." As Jakobsen expressed it, "One engineer [Eastwood] promotes civilization by the savings he makes possible, and the other retards civilization." When Jakobsen's article was later published in the *Transactions of the American Society of Engineers* 87 (1924): 276–341, praise of Eastwood was limited to acknowledging his being "a pioneer in dam design," and all mention of the gravity dam designer who merely thickened profiles disappeared. Coincidently, Freeman served as president of the ASCE in 1922–1923; he would have appreciated neither Jakobsen's praise of Eastwood nor his implicit criticism of gravity dam design.

29. See, for example, Walter L. Huber, "An Engineering Century in California," *Transactions of the American Society of Civil Engineers* CT (1953): 97–111; and Julian Hinds, "Continuous Development of Dams Since 1850," *Transactions of the American Society of Civil Engineers* CT (1953): 489–520. In the mid-1980s I was reviewing photographs of dams with a longtime engineer for the Army Corps of Engineers. When a view of Eastwood's Mountain Dell Dam appeared, the engineer expressed surprise at its design and indicated that he had never seen anything like it before; the concept of the multiple arch dam was foreign to him after almost thirty years with the Corps.

30. Clearly, Eastwood was a highly egotistical man whose promotion of multiple arch dams bordered on an obsession. At times, his enthusiasm in promoting the superiority of his designs worked against him; as McClure noted during the Littlerock controversy, "[your] extravagant claims . . . [can] cause the average engineer and layman to question either your sanity or your sincerity." But while Eastwood's arrogance gave his opponents an easy target, he was not the only important hydraulic engineer of his generation to possess a sizable ego. The supposition that Freeman, Lippincott, Huber, O'Shaughnessy, Mulholland, Savage, A. P. Davis, and other major figures in western water history were timid, self-effacing professionals is entirely unwarranted. In refusing to engage in any meaningful discussion of the technical merits of Eastwood's designs for the Mission Gorge and El Capitan sites on the San Diego River, Freeman exhibited the height of professional arrogance. And in lobbying for a municipal exemption from California's 1917 dam safety law, O'Shaughnessy did the same. Eastwood's conceit may have been considerable, but it hardly constituted a historical anomaly. Quote from W. F. McClure to JSE, June 4, 1919, Hydraulic Division File #F3725-6825, PUC.

31. See L. N. McClellan, "Economy Dictates Reclamation Design," *Transactions of the American Society of Civil Engineers* CT (1953): 428–36, for more on what later Reclamation engineers characterized as the efficiency of their designs. Although the bureau did use a multiple arch design for the Bartlett Dam, the agency's post-New Deal estrangement from the approach is exemplified by its desire to dissociate itself completely from the technology when the Buchanan (formerly Hamilton) Dam was completed in Texas in the mid-1930s; see Adams, *Damning the Colorado*, pp. 60–62. The Army Corps of Engineers' distaste for multiple arch technology was evident in their grudging acceptance of the Pensacola (Grand River) Dam in eastern Oklahoma in the late 1930s; see "Section X: Federal Power Commission," in W. R. Holway, *A History of the Grand River Authority, State of Oklahoma: 1935–1968* (Tulsa, Okla.: Tulsa County Historical Society, 1968).

32. One of the best accounts of New Deal dam building is provided in connection with the history of Lyndon Johnson's initial election to the U.S. Congress in 1937 and his relations with the contracting firm of Brown & Root; see Robert A. Caro, *The Years of Lyndon Johnson: The Path to Power* (New York: Alfred A. Knopf, 1982) pp. 369–528.

33. In the 1950s, the Bureau of Reclamation again began constructing a few large single arch designs based on the trial load method (Glen Canyon Dam being the most prominent of these); but this type of structure remains unusual in the United States. On strictly technological grounds, American engineers certainly could have concentrated on developing material-conserving designs; indeed, the structural tradition remained vibrant in the work of European engineers. See Andre Coyne, "Arch Dams: Their Philosophy," *Journal of the Power Division, Proceedings of the American Society of Civil Engineers* 82 (April 1956): 959/1-32; A. C. Xerez, "Arch Dams: Portuguese Experience with Overflow Arch Dams," *Journal of the Power Division, Proceedings of the American Society of Civil Engineers* 82 (June 1956): 990/1-27; and Carlo Semeza, "Arch Dams: Development in Italy," *Journal of the Power Division, Proceedings of the American Society of Civil Engineers* 82 (June 1956) pp. 1017/1-41. Several European structural dams are illustrated in Museum of Modern Art, *Twentieth Century Engineering* (New York: Museum of Modern Art, 1964). In addition, a large multiple arch dam was built in northern Canada in the 1960s; see William W. Jacobus and Lilli Rethi, *Manic 5: The Building of the Daniel Johnson Dam* (Garden City, N.Y.: Doubleday, 1971). And a large multiple arch dam was erected by the Chinese communist regime in the 1950s; see

Kanawhar Sain and K. L. Roa, *Report of Recent River Valley Projects in China* (New Delhi: India Central Water and Power Commission, 1955), pp. 76-91.

34. Donald Worster, "Hydraulic Society in California," *Agricultural History* 56 (July 1982), reprinted in *Under Western Skies* (New York: Oxford University Press, 1992), pp. 53-63; Donald Worster, "Hoover Dam: A Study in Domination," in *Under Western Skies*, pp. 64-78; and Donald Worster, *Rivers of Empire*.

35. Worster, *Rivers of Empire*, pp. 8, 192-93.

36. Hundley, *The Great Thirst*, pp. 407-8.

37. Billington, *The Tower and the Bridge*, p. 24.

38. Joseph Stevens, *Hoover Dam: An American Adventure*, pp. 266-67.

39. Worster, "Hoover Dam: a Study in Domination," in *Under Western Skies*, p. 73. Readers should view with skepticism any analysis of the Hoover Dam (or of any large dam for that matter) that attempts to portray it as a universal symbol of technical efficiency and/or modernity. Hoover Dam (and by the same token, any of Eastwood's dams) is not "technology" per se; rather, it is a single structure that serves the interests, desires, and objectives of the particular people who planned and financed its construction.

40. For example, Professor Emeritus Glenn L. Enke of Brigham Young University has undertaken intensive analyses of Eastwood's Mountain Dell Dam and Littlerock Dam and found them to be safe structures. See Glenn L. Enke, "Investigation of Elastic Behaviors of a Multiple Arch Dam," Ph.D. dissertation, Utah State University, 1972; and Glenn L. Enke to Ned R. Nelson [legal counsel for the Citizen's Committee to Save the Littlerock Dam, Inc.] May 21, 1977 [copy of letter in author's files]. In contrast, see "Littlerock Dam Safety Study," prepared by the Bechtel Corporation, San Francisco, January 1968, for an analysis purporting to demonstrate the structure's instability. The differing conclusions of the Enke and Bechtel reports follow ineluctably from assumptions underlying their respective analyses. For discussion of these differences, see Donald C. Jackson, "Con-troversy in Concrete: The Littlerock Dam 1918-1977," *Proceedings of the American Society of Engineering Education* (1982): 471-477. For evidence that the California Division of Safety of Dams found the Bechtel report more persuasive, see "Final Environmental Impact Report on Revocation of the Certificate of Approval, Littlerock Dam and Reservoir," Department of Water Resources, the Resources Agency, State of California, November 1979.

41. "Old Dam to be Transformed," *Engineering News-Record* 230 (February 8, 1993): 9. The history of the Littlerock Dam's treatment by the dam safety authorities since 1929—and especially since the late 1960s—is worthy of a book unto itself; readers of *Building the Ultimate Dam* would find many of the reported arguments and circumstances eerily reminiscent of those that plagued Eastwood during his attempts to obtain the state engineer's approval the first time around.

42. JSE to *San Diego Sun* (ca. May 20, 1924), JSE 52, WRCA.

43. In 1939, the Army Corps of Engineers' Fort Peck Dam in eastern Montana experienced a massive "slippage" of the hydraulic fill earth structure; eight workers died in the "Big Slide." A good description of this collapse appears in M. R. Montgomery, *Saying Goodbye: A Memoir of Two Fathers* (New York: Alfred A. Knopf, 1989), pp. 79-93, where he observes: "The well understood difficulty with hydraulic fill . . . is simply to drain the core properly. Excess water is pumped out . . . but that is only the visible water. The real danger is standing, permeating water in the core and shells." More recently, the Baldwin Hills Dam (1964) and the San Fernando Dam (1971), both owned by the City of Los Angeles, and the Teton Dam in Idaho (1976), built by the Bureau of Reclamation, have failed. Of these, only the 1915 San Fernando Dam, a hydraulic fill dam designed by William Mulholland, dates to Eastwood's lifetime. During the 1971 San Fernando earthquake a large portion of the earth structure "slipped"; however, the reservoir was not filled at the time of the earthquake so no water was released as a result of the incident.

Glossary

ACRE-FOOT   A volume of water equal to 1 acre of land covered with water 1 foot deep. An acre-foot is equal to 43,560 cubic feet or about 326,000 gallons.

AGGREGATE   Stone, gravel, and/or sand that is mixed with cement to make concrete.

ALLUVIAL SOIL   Sand, silt, clay, loose rock, and the like deposited at a site by flowing water. Alluvial soil often lies on top of bedrock and must be excavated during construction of a dam's foundation.

AMBURSEN DAM   Alternative name for a reinforced concrete, flat-slab buttress dam. The term derives from Nils F. Ambursen, who patented and built the first dam of this type, in New York in 1903.

BUTTRESS   In relation to dams, a relatively thin wall that rests on bedrock and provides support for the structure's upstream face. Buttress dams are divided into two basic types, depending on the shape of the upstream face: flat-slab and multiple arch.

CABLEWAY   A mechanism for hoisting material through the air. Wire cables strung between towers on two sides of a canyon are used to transport a platform, a concrete bucket, people, or other cargo to various parts of a construction site.

CHUTING CONCRETE   A method of transporting concrete from the mixer to the formwork. Concrete is hoisted up a central tower and then allowed to flow down to various parts of a construction site via metal chutes with a semicircular cross section; the chutes can easily be moved to deposit concrete in various locations.

COMPRESSION   The physical state that results when a weight or force presses down on (compresses) a structural member; the opposite of tension.

CONCRETE   A mixture of cement, aggregate (sand and gravel), and water that hardens into a solid mass. The addition of the aggregate makes concrete stronger and more durable than cement.

COREWALL   An impermeable barrier built within the center (or core) of an earthfill or rockfill dam. A corewall helps prevent water seepage that might otherwise cause the structure to erode and eventually collapse. Corewalls can be built out of dense earthen clay, concrete, steel sheeting, or even wooden planks.

CUBIC FOOT PER SECOND (CFS)   A measurement of flow equal to 1 cubic foot of water passing by a reference point every 1 second. For example, if 600 cubic feet of water pass by a point during a period of 1 minute, then the stream is discharging 10 cfs (since 600 cubic feet/60 seconds = 10 cfs).

CYLINDER FORMULA   A simple mathematical formula used to calculate the thickness of an arch under hydrostatic (water) pressure. It differs from the elastic theory in not considering the effect of structural deformation on the distribution of stresses. The formula is expressed $T = (P \times R)/Q$, where T = thickness, P = hydrostatic pressure, R = radius of the arch, and Q = allowable stress (for instance, 300 pounds per square inch). Eastwood used the cylinder formula to calculate the thickness of the arches in his dam designs.

DIVERSION DAM   A small dam used to divert water out of a river or stream and into a flume or canal. A diversion dam is not intended to store water in a reservoir.

DOWNSTREAM FACE   The side of a dam that faces away from the reservoir.

EARTHFILL   Loose earth or soil that can be transported to a construction site and then consolidated to form an embankment or, if desired, a dam.

ELASTIC THEORY   A method for determining stresses that takes into account that all structures deform (albeit, in some instances, only slightly) under pressure. It constitutes a mathematically sophisticated approach to structural analysis but often requires the use of highly simplified assumptions about conditions at a site or within a design.

EXPANSION JOINT   A design feature used in concrete construction that allows a structure to expand and contract in response to stresses induced by temperature changes. Expansion joints are often built to reduce the possibility that unplanned cracking will develop in a structure. In fact, expansion joints are often little more than artificially created "temperature cracks" that appear in a more regular pattern.

EXTRADOS   The outer surface of an arch. The extrados of an arch dam is the surface in contact with the water.

FERRO-INCLAVE   Corrugated metal sheathing used as formwork for concrete construc-tion. In contrast to wooden formwork, ferro-inclave sheets are left in place after the concrete is poured and become part of the permanent structure.

FLUME   A wooden (or sometime metal) channel built to carry water. In the lumber industry, flumes were designed to transport floating timber downstream.

FORMWORK   Wooden or (more rarely) metal templates used in concrete construction to provide molds for the wet concrete before it hardens. Formwork must be built to conform to the exact dimensions specified in the design.

GROUTING   A technique for injecting cement into fractured bedrock. By grouting (or filling) fissures with cement, engineers seek to reduce the amount of seepage flowing through a site, thereby strengthening the dam foundations.

HEAD (of a dam)   The upper part of a dam. For example, the "vertical head" of a multiple-arch dam is the portion of the dam that lies above the inclined upstream face.

HEAD (water pressure)   The amount of water pressure acting on a turbine or pressing against a dam. For example, if water drops 500 feet within a penstock before powering a water turbine, the power plant operates under a "500-foot head."

HEADRACE   A canal or flume used to deliver water from a river to a penstock or turbine serving a factory or hydroelectric power plant.

HYDRAULIC FILL   A type of earthfill produced by "hosing down" a hillside with water, transporting the slurry via flumes and/or pipes to a construction site, depositing the muck in a mound, and then allowing the water to drain away, leaving a (presumably) solid earthen structure. This method of building earth dams was commonly used in the early twentieth century.

HYDRAULIC INFRASTRUCTURE   Generally, all technological components that make up a regional water control system, including dams, canals, siphons, penstocks, turbines, pipelines, head gates, drainage ditches, treatment facilities, and flood channels.

HYDRAULICKING Hosing pressurized water on an earthen mound in order to create hydraulic fill. The technique was first used to help extract gold dispersed within large quantities of earth; later it was adapted to the construction of embankments and dams.

HYDROSTATIC PRESSURE The pressure exerted by a volume of water. The hydrostatic pressure exerted by a reservoir is zero at the top of a dam and increases as the water becomes deeper.

INTRADOS The inner surface of an arch. The intrados of an arch dam is the surface that is not in contact with the water.

KILOWATTS (KW) A measure of the generating capacity of a power plant. One kilowatt equals 1,000 watts and is equivalent to 1.341 horsepower. Conversely, 1 horsepower equals 746 kilowatts. In contemporary electrical engineering practice, the term kilovolt-amperes (kva) is often used in place of kilowatts to describe a plant's generating capacity.

MASONRY Stone, rock, and/or concrete.

MASSIVE DAMS Dams that resist the force of water pressure solely through their great size (or mass); the force of gravity acting vertically on the structure's mass is sufficient to hold back the hydrostatic pressure exerted by the reservoir. Massive dams include earthfill, rockfill, and masonry gravity dams.

MIDDLE THIRD A basic principle of gravity dam design stipulating that the resultant force of the water pressure and the weight of the dam must pass through the "middle third" of the foundation to ensure that the structure is only subject to compressive stresses. If the resultant falls outside the "middle third," parts of the structure will be in tension and cracking may occur.

MINER'S INCH A measure of water flow used in the nineteenth-century West that evolved from a technique early miners used for releasing water by cutting notches into wooden flumes. In most regions, a miner's inch became legally equivalent to one-forti-

eth of a cubic foot per second; that is, 40 miner's inches equaled 1 cfs. In some drier regions, however, it was considered equivalent to one-fiftieth of a cfs.

MULTIPLE ARCH DAM A type of buttress dam in which the upstream face is formed by a series of arches. Multiple arch dams constructed with stone were described in Spanish treatises dating to the seventeenth century. The first reinforced concrete design of this type was built by John S. Eastwood in 1908.

OVERBURDEN Loose rock and soil that lies on top of bedrock.

PELTON WHEEL A type of water wheel popular in the late nineteenth-century West in which a stream of water spraying out of a penstock is directed toward metal buckets attached to the rim of a wheel. The force of the water hitting the buckets causes the wheel to turn. The mechanism was first popularized by Lester Pelton to power mining equipment in the goldfields of California; later it was adapted for use in hydroelectric power plants.

PENSTOCK A pipe or closed conduit carrying water under pressure. In a hydroelectric power plant, water is delivered to the water turbines via a penstock. Some low-pressure penstocks are built out of wooden staves bound together by metal hoops, but most penstocks are made of steel.

PROFILE A dam's vertical cross section. The profile of a gravity dam reveals how thick the structure is at all elevations. The profile used for New York City's Croton Dam became widely emulated and is known as the "Croton profile."

PROFILE OF EQUAL RESISTANCE A design for masonry gravity dams developed by French engineers in the midnineteenth century that theoretically minimized the size of the profile. Its shape is intended to equalize compressive stresses at the dam's upstream face when the reservoir is empty with compressive stresses at the downstream face when the reservoir is full; hence, the phrase "equal resistance." The profile became the basis for almost all later masonry gravity designs, including New York City's famous Croton Dam.

PUEBLO WATER RIGHTS A system of water rights under which municipalities (such as Los Angeles and San Diego) lay claim to the entire flow of water in a river on the basis of rights supposedly granted to them by the king of Spain in their (centuries old) pueblo charters.

REINFORCED CONCRETE A structural material formed by imbedding steel members within concrete. Reinforced concrete conjoins the compressive strength and durability of concrete and the tensile strength of steel.

RESULTANT FORCE The magnitude and direction of forces that act as stresses on a structure. In relation to dams, the term is often used to describe the force calculated by combining the horizontal component of water pressure exerted by a reservoir with the vertical weight of the dam itself. For a gravity dam, this resultant force must pass through the "middle third" of the foundation in order to provide stability.

RIGHT-OF-WAY An easement (legally established route or passageway) across a section of land not owned by the user. For example, a canal or an electric transmission line extends along a right-of-way.

ROCKFILL Loose rock that is transported to a construction site and then consolidated or compacted to form an embankment. Rockfill dams require some kind of impervious upstream face to prevent water from seeping through the structure. This facing can be made of wooden planks, steel sheets, or concrete. Sometimes rockfill is used for the exterior of a dam, and the interior sections are composed of earthfill that is sufficiently dense to prevent seepage.

SAFETY FACTOR A numerical value (expressed as a multiple) denoting the extent to which a structure's failure point exceeds the anticipated maximum burden of stresses to which it will be subjected. For example, if concrete will not fail under a compressive stress of less than 3,000 pounds per square inch (psi) and a structure is designed for a maximum stress of 300 psi, then it has a safety factor of 10 (3,000 psi/300 psi = 10).

SLUICING Conveying water in a flume or canal. A sluiceway is a small flume or canal.

SPILLWAY The part of a dam that permits water to be released from the impoundment in case the reservoir level becomes too high and threatens to "overtop" the structure. Often, a spillway is simply a section that is built to a lower height than the rest of the dam. A siphon spillway is a more complicated structure for regulating a reservoir level by means of the suction action of large siphons.

STORAGE DAM A dam that impounds water in a reservoir for later use. Storage dams are especially important in arid environments, where much of the precipitation comes in the form of melting snow and infrequent but intense rainstorms.

STRESS The pressure acting on a structure or on one of its members, often expressed in pounds per square inch (psi). If a 100-pound force acts on a surface with an area of 25 square inches, the resulting stress is 4 psi (100 pounds/25 square inches = 4 psi). The strength of a structure is often defined as the maximum stress it can withstand before failure.

STRUCTURAL DAMS Dams that resist the force of water pressure and maintain stability because of the shape of their design, rather than because of their mass. For example, an arch design with a thin profile is a structural dam because the shape of its upstream curvature is absolutely necessary to prevent its collapse. Multiple arch and flat-slab buttress designs are other forms of structural dams.

STRUT-TIE BEAMS The bracing between the buttresses of multiple-arch dams designed by Eastwood.

TAILRACE A canal or flume used to carry water back to a river after the water has passed through a turbine in a factory or hydroelectric power plant.

TEMPERATURE STRESSES Stresses created within structures by changes in temperature. For example, concrete shrinks when it cools, and this can result in cracking; such cracks are often referred to as "temperature cracks."

TENSION   The physical state that results when a weight or force pulls up on (or stretches) a structural member; the opposite of compression.

TIMBER CRIB DAM   A simple type of gravity dam in which the structure is formed by cross-hatched timbers (known as "cribs") that are filled with loose rock. Timber crib dams are usually not very tall, but they are commonly used to divert water into canals and flumes.

TRAMWAY   A small transportation system that allows materials to be conveyed around a mine, factory, or construction site in wheeled cars.

UNIT COST   The average cost for a single unit of a product. For example, if it costs $1,300 to build a structure containing 100 cubic yards of concrete, then the unit cost of concrete for that design is $13.00 ($1,300/ 100 = $13.00). Identifying the unit costs can be a useful way of comparing the efficiency of various designs and construction processes.

UPLIFT   The physical effect of water seeping under a dam and pushing up on the foundation. Uplift can contribute significantly to downstream sliding of masonry gravity dams; it has little effect on buttress dams.

UPSTREAM FACE   The side of a dam that faces toward the reservoir. In a multiple arch dam, the extrados of the arches form the upstream face.

WATER TURBINE (or WATER WHEEL)   A device for converting the kinetic energy of falling water into mechanical energy. In a hydroelectric plant, the water turbine's rotating drive shaft is attached to the generator. Water turbines are divided into two basic types: impulse turbines and reaction turbines. In an impulse turbine (for instance, a Pelton water wheel), the force of a stream of water striking the buckets of the movable rotor causes the device to revolve. In a reaction turbine, the pressure of the water acting on the movable rotor causes rotation. The simplest form of a reaction turbine is a rotating lawn sprinkler.

Illustrations of Dams

Index

JSC Willey Library
337 College Hill
Johnson, VT 05656